National Diversity and
Global Capitalism

A volume in the series

Cornell Studies in Political Economy

EDITED BY PETER J. KATZENSTEIN

A full list of titles in the series appears at the end of the book.

National Diversity and Global Capitalism

Edited by

SUZANNE BERGER and
RONALD DORE

CORNELL UNIVERSITY PRESS

Ithaca and London

First published 1996 by Cornell University Press.

Printed in the United States of America

⊚ The paper in this book meets the minimum requirements
of the American National Standard for Information Sciences—
Permanence of Paper for Printed Library Materials, ANSI Z39.48-1984.

Library of Congress Cataloging-in-Publication Data

National diversity and global capitalism / edited by Suzanne Berger
   and Ronald Dore.
      p.   cm. — (Cornell studies in political economy)
   Includes bibliographical references and index.
      ISBN 0-8014-3234-0 (cloth : alk. paper). — ISBN 0-8014-8319-0
(pbk. : alk. paper)
      1. Competition, International.   2. International economic relations.
I. Berger, Suzanne.   II. Dore, Ronald Philip.   III. Series.
HF1414.N37   1996
337—dc20   95-48267

Contents

Preface

This volume brings together reflections and research on the future of national models of political economy in a time of growing internationalization. The contributors include economists, political scientists, and sociologists, a management theorist, a legal scholar, and a banker; we come from Europe, Japan, and the United States. The enterprise began as a long-running discussion between two of us, Ronald Dore and Suzanne Berger, colleagues in the MIT Department of Political Science and in the MIT Industrial Performance Center. It spilled over into ever-longer memos, letters to colleagues, a 1993 meeting at the Rockefeller Foundation Bellagio Center, and these essays.

Our starting question was the role of the international economy in driving the transformation of domestic structures in advanced industrial countries. We asked the authors to consider ways in which institutions of production and distribution change in response to external threats and opportunities—to competition, possibilities of imitating foreign practice, globalization of economic flows, and political pressures. None of the authors takes convergence of these institutions as a fact; none takes convergence as an unquestionable good. On these two points, the work presented here eschews the initial assumptions of much current scholarly and policy writing. Rather, the essays attempt first to canvass the evidence for convergence by analyzing changes at various levels of the economy and economic policy; then to consider the mechanisms that promote convergence and the sources of resistance to it; and finally to ask whether convergence is desirable or threatens to set off a race down to lower standards of social welfare, driving out uniquely valuable national institutions.

In time it became clear that our questioning and our differences revolved around whether international economic flows and the market would produce the convergence of national institutions. We are still divided on this issue. In this volume we have tried to lay out clearly evidence on both sides of the argument, as well as elements of the normative case for and against convergence. In contrast to most scholarly groups, which reunite old colleagues from established research communities, many of us met for the first time at Bellagio. The book reveals our groping and not always successful efforts to develop common vocabulary and criteria for evaluating these phenomena. Through it all, we have felt keenly aware of moving over territory with unsettled frontiers, on large stretches of which each of us feels far from familiar disciplinary ground.

The MIT Industrial Performance Center, the Sloan Foundation, and the Rockefeller Foundation have generously supported this project. Richard K. Lester, director of the Industrial Performance Center, provided strong moral and intellectual encouragement for the venture at every stage. We are grateful for that, as well as for his confidence in a project whose relevance to the activities of the IPC was initially difficult to define sharply. Patrizio Bianchi, Peter Hall, Michele Salvati, and Koji Watanabe joined our discussions at Bellagio and helped clarify the issues. Wade Jacoby, the rapporteur at the Bellagio meeting, wrote a remarkable analytic summary of our discussions, and that document enabled us in revising to retrace the logic of the debates and controversies that the papers stimulated, as well as to rethink the connections among the papers. This analytic summary is available as "Conference Proceedings: Domestic Institutions, Free Trade, and the Pressures for National Convergence: US, Europe, and Japan," MIT IPC Working Paper 93-002WP, June 1993. We are grateful to Joseph Bambenek at the Industrial Performance Center for research assistance, and to Helen Ray, Lois Malone in the Department of Political Science, and the staff of the Rockefeller Bellagio Center for assistance in organizing the meeting and the book. Throughout the project Betty Jo Bolivar gave generous support to us and moved the manuscript toward a book.

S. B. and R. D.

National Diversity and
Global Capitalism

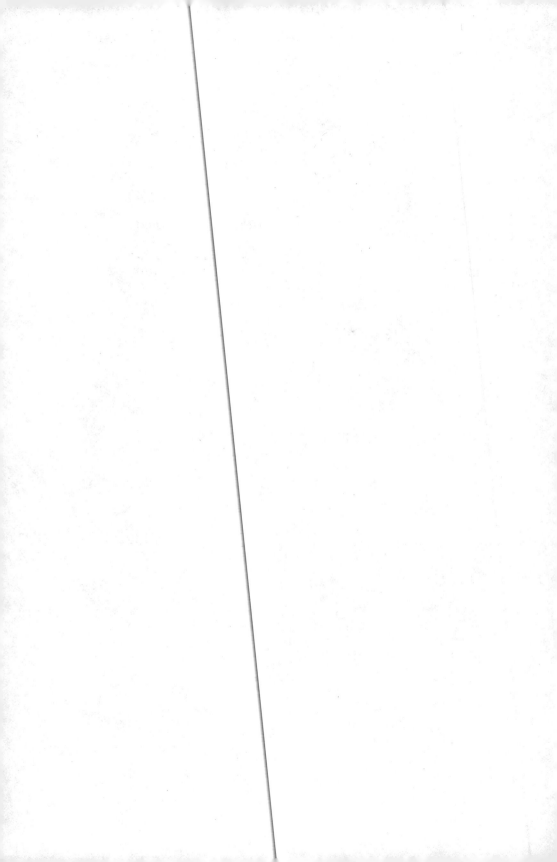

Introduction

SUZANNE BERGER

Under the clamor of demands for managed trade, level playing
fields, and new international regimes an old controversy about industrial societies is once again at work, generating conflicting theories
and policies. The point in contention is a simple and compelling set of
ideas: that all advanced industrial countries tend toward common
ways of producing and organizing economic life. Where they do not
converge, the explanation lies in distortions introduced by history and
politics.

In this view competition, imitation, diffusion of best practice, trade,
and capital mobility naturally operate to produce convergence across
nations in the structures of production and in the relations among
economy, society, and state. Variations may be found from country to
country, because of different historical legacies. But such distinctions
fade over time, giving way to common economic structures whose efficiency and universality produce superior strength in the market.
Without extramarket reinforcement—by the state, by powerful interests in society—these differences do not persist. Where differences do
remain and convergence is slow or uncertain it must be that government and/or powerful groups are using resources generated outside
of markets to sustain distinctive economic and social institutions.

This vision of the trajectory of industrial societies underpins current debates on trade policy among the advanced countries of Europe, America, and Asia. Fairness in trade among nations, the argument runs, requires common market rules and structures. Normally,
these develop over time, in parallel with the growth of market capital-

ism. But when governments intervene in order to shape markets, to build economic advantage, to shield companies from foreign competition, or to insulate national preferences against market forces, then divergent patterns become entrenched. The alternative capitalist systems that emerge in these cases may satisfy national objectives, but at the expense of others in the international economic order.

The strength of the Japanese and German economies, on this reading, depends in part at least on the possibility of exploiting a free-trading international regime in which other countries play by a more constrained and handicapping set of rules about the uses of state power. From this interpretation flows a set of demands for common institutions and regulations of government–economy relations as the basis for free economic exchange. Which—and whose—institutions and regulations these should be also follow: they must be those of the capitalist economies in which productive organizations are shaped by competition in markets. The capitalisms of Japan, Germany, and other latecomers are in this interpretation perceived as distorted by state intervention and as producing advantage in trade precisely because others play by different rules. The experiences of these more activist states cannot, therefore, provide common ground for new international rules. The case for requiring convergence or harmonization of national structures—or for extracting compensation in the form of managed trade where convergence fails—thus rests on the notion of a unique, natural, hence legitimate, set of institutions and market rules for capitalism.

Convergence and the Technological Trajectory of Industrial Societies

The new controversies over trade have in this way returned to ideas about the convergence of national models that were first systematically articulated in postwar writings about industrial societies.[1] The social sciences of the growth decades in the 1950s and 1960s located the engine of convergence in technology. The core notion was that as countries sought to increase levels of well-being for their citizenry and

[1] The nineteenth-century social philosophers Herbert Spencer (1820–1903) and Henri Saint-Simon (1760–1825) anticipated much of this in their writings on industrial society. For the postwar presentation of the case for convergence see Raymond Aron, *Dix-huit leçons sur la société industrielle* (Paris: Gallimard, 1962); Clark Kerr, John T. Dunlop, Frederick Harbison, and Charles A. Myers, *Industrialism and Industrial Man* (Cambridge: Harvard University Press, 1960); and Daniel Bell, *The Coming of Post-Industrial Society* (New York: Basic Books, 1973). For critiques of these views, see Suzanne Berger and Michael J. Piore, *Dualism and Discontinuity in Industrial Societies* (New York: Cambridge University Press, 1980), and Charles F. Sabel, *Work and Politics* (New York: Cambridge University Press, 1982).

to maintain the military requirements of survival in an anarchic world, they progressed along a common trajectory of technological possibilities. The path of innovation on which they moved was the same for all. They would advance, more or less rapidly, passing through common stages and adopting over time more and more of the same social, political, and economic structures.

Since the 1970s such theories on industrial societies have been devastated. The loss of credibility of Marxist interpretations of industrialism with the decline and collapse of state socialism has eroded the plausibility of all understandings of society that depend on technological determinism. New research has also played a role in undermining the grip of technological explanations within the social sciences. Starting in the 1970s and 1980s, a number of initially unrelated projects carried out in various countries focused on successful companies making basically the same products with the same technologies, but organizing production in fundamentally different ways. The earliest works in this vein, for example, Ronald Dore's *British Factory–Japanese Factory: The Origins of National Diversity in Industrial Relations* (1973), a comparison of two companies manufacturing electrical equipment, and the research by Maurice, Silvestre, and Sellier on matched pairs of French and German companies were at first read mainly by experts interested in the countries and the industries studied, but the findings ultimately influenced intellectual debates in far wider communities.[2] The next generation of research in this line, for example, Jaikumar's work on flexible manufacturing systems in the United States and Japan (1986) and the comparative analysis of automobile assembly plants in various countries in *The Machine That Changed the World: The Story of Lean Production* (1990), reached out to a large educated audience, now alerted to the significance of this kind of research for explaining industrial performance.[3] Even though much of the research in this vein continued to focus on limited and specific firm comparisons, the intellectual impact of the case studies was great, for they called into question a technologically based understanding of industrial societies once shared by liberals and Marxists alike. Indeed it was this understanding that had provided the basic foundations underlying most popular views on advanced industrial countries.

[2] Ronald Dore, *British Factory–Japanese Factory: The Origins of National Diversity in Industrial Relations* (Berkeley: University of California Press, 1973); Marc Maurice, François Sellier, and Jean-Jacques Silvestre, *The Social Foundations of Industrial Power* (Cambridge: MIT Press, 1986).

[3] Ramchandran Jaikumar, "Postindustrial Manufacturing," *Harvard Business Review*, November–December 1986; James P. Womack, Daniel T. Jones, and Daniel Roos, *The Machine That Changed the World: The Story of Lean Production* (New York: Macmillan, 1990).

3

These case studies stimulated new lines of speculation and research on the societal, cultural, political, and organizational factors that might explain the differential performance of firms using the same technologies in different national settings. This new research agenda appeared at the end of the 1980s at a time of an apparent weakening of the American economy and triumph of quite different economic institutions and practices in Japan and Germany. These two countries' remarkable postwar growth and prosperity seemed striking demonstration that economies work in ways quite different from those described by neoclassical economics and American practice. The notion of different forms of capitalisms—each type characterized by different institutions, practices, values, and politics—began to appear in both scholarly and popular writing. How many varieties of capitalism? With which strengths and weaknesses? Drawing on which cultural and national traditions?—answers to all these differ somewhat from account to account. But in Michel Albert's popular *Capitalism vs. Capitalism*, as in the scholarly research of David Soskice, Wolfgang Streeck, Robert Boyer, W. Carl Kester, Ronald Dore, and others, the distinctions, however labeled, between the market-based economies of the United States and England and the societally and state-coordinated economies of Germany and Japan, are characterized as coherent, resilient alternative forms of capitalism, not as detours off a common trajectory.[4] In sum, by the 1990s the idea that technology dictates a single optimal way of organizing production, thus propelling all countries toward common economic institutions and practices had largely vanished from the scene.[5] But the expectation that structures of production and of the economy at large in the most advanced industrial countries are and should be converging is still alive and well today.

CONVERGENCE AND GLOBALIZATION

The renewal and persistence of the theory of convergence draws today not on technological determinism but on conceptions of the im-

[4] Michel Albert, *Capitalism vs. Capitalism* (New York: Four Wall Eight Windows, 1993); David Soskice, "The Institutional Infrastructure for International Competitiveness: A Comparative Analysis of the UK and Germany," in A. B. Brunetta and R. Atkinson, eds., *The Economics of the New Europe* (London: Macmillan, 1991); and Wolfgang Streeck, *Social Institutions and Economic Performance* (Beverly Hills, Calif.: Sage, 1992).

[5] It would be a mistake to overstate the point, for some do see one or another of the alternative forms of production as inherently superior; thus the claims inter alia by Womack, Jones, and Roos in *The Machine That Changed the World* about the superiority of lean production, as pioneered in Japan, or in Albert about Nippo-Rhenish capitalism (*Capitalism*). But in each case what is identified as the superior practice goes well beyond a technology in the ordinary sense of the word, and the "triumph" of the superior practice is regarded as far from inevitable. In fact Albert thinks Anglo-American capitalism will win out because of it popular appeal.

pact of international competition, globalization, regional integration, and the deregulation of domestic economies on national structures. As Robert Boyer lays out in Chapter 1 in this volume, neoclassical theories of competition and trade predicted that over time the costs of production would equalize across the world. The availability and utility of technological innovation to all societies, no matter what their social infrastructure, would lead to convergent rates of productivity growth. Associated with these theories, even if not logically required by them, was the idea that common institutional configurations and ways of organizing the economy would emerge. Neoclassical conceptions of trade, competition, and growth thus sustained an expectation of convergence, understood in a general way to mean the spread across the world of the same patterns of economic life.

Even as "new trade theory," "new institutionalism," and "endogenous growth theory" began to undermine conventional views of trade and competition as leading to factor price equalization and views of technology as a universally available public good, the expectations associated with these theories received a powerful boost from another quarter.[6] In a semipopular business literature, new prophets of globalization discovered yet other forces at work in the world, smashing national borders under the rising tides of mobile technology, trade, and finance and creating a world market that national interventions were helpless to resist. In this new literature the role that economics had previously imagined being played by trade among nations is played largely by capital mobility. In much of this literature, as well as in common parlance, convergence came to be synonymous with the global mobility of the factors of production, and above all of finance.

As expressed by such writers as Kenichi Ohmae among others, globalization is the product of many forces—technology, transnational corporations, new means of communication, as well as traditional neoclassical competition—all of which are bringing into existence a global market, an economy conceived of as essentially the same in all its parts. Ohmae writes in *The Borderless World*:

> An isle is emerging that is bigger than a continent—the Interlinked Economy (ILE) of the Triad (the United States, Europe, and Japan), joined by aggressive economies such as Taiwan, Hong Kong, and Singapore. It is becoming so powerful that it has swallowed most consumers and corporations, made traditional national borders disappear, and pushed bureaucrats, politicians, and the military toward the status of de-

[6] On strategic trade, see Paul R. Krugman, ed., *Strategic Trade Policy and the New International Economics* (Cambridge: MIT Press, 1986); on endogenous growth theory and its relation to the convergence controversy, see Paul Romer, "The Origins of Endogenous Growth," *Journal of Economic Perspectives* 8, no. 1 (Winter 1994): 3–22.

clining industries. The emergence of the ILE has created much confusion, particularly for those used to dealing with economic policies based on conventional macro-economic statistics that compare one nation against another. Their theories don't work anymore. While the Keynesian economist would expect to see jobs increase as an economy picks up, the ILE economy sometimes disappoints them. Jobs might be created abroad instead. If the government tightens the money supply, loans may gush in from abroad, and make the nation's monetary policy nearly meaningless. If the central bank tries to raise the interest rate, cheaper funds flow in from elsewhere in the ILE. For all practical purposes, the ILE has made obsolete the traditional instruments of central bankers—interest rate and money supply.[7]

The claim is that since the 1970s there has been a radical change in the magnitudes of the flows of investment, services, and goods across national boundaries and in the scope of the loss, or renunciation, of control by national actors over these flows. Transnational corporations may not be newcomers on the international scene, but the expansion of the range of their activities across frontiers and the deepening of their cross-border corporate alliances may have taken on a new character. Indeed, some argue that the magnitude of these cross-border activities has become so great and inherently beyond the regulatory leverage of states that governments have effectively disappeared. Ohmae writes: "On a political map, the boundaries between countries are as clear as ever. But on a competitive map, a map showing the real flows of financial and industrial activity, those boundaries have largely disappeared" (p. 18). About the impact of foreign exchange flows on national policy autonomy, Ohmae says: "In a fundamental sense, money supply has moved well beyond the control of any single government. There are dollar- and yen-based markets everywhere. The global, interlinked, tradable FX [foreign exchange] empire allows money literally to travel around the globe in seconds. Even if, for instance, the Bank of Japan decides to tighten up the money supply at home, desired funds are instantaneously available from abroad" (pp. 161–62).

Expressed in this generic form, the case for globalization finds evidence everywhere. Rising tides of international finance flood over national boundaries, with velocities accelerated by new communication technologies. They encounter fewer and fewer national regulations. Net international bond and bank lending more than doubled from 1985 to 1990; outstanding stocks of international lending grew from 5 percent of aggregate GNP in industrialized countries in 1973 to 25

[7] Kenichi Ohmae, *The Borderless World: Power and Strategy in the Interlinked Economy* (New York: Harper Perennial, 1991), pp. x–xi.

percent of GNP in 1989, according to sources cited in Jeffry A. Frieden's study of the impact of the globalization of finance on national economic policy capabilities.[8] Trading in foreign exchange markets skyrocketed. Capital outflows in the form of portfolio investment and foreign direct investments increased. They also became more important as vectors of internationalization relative to trade. Frieden points out that capital outflows were equivalent to 15 percent of world merchandise trade at the end of the 1980s, in contrast to 7 percent at the end of the 1970s (p. 428).

MACROECONOMIC INTEGRATION?

Although statistics abound to illustrate magnitudes of capital on the move in the world today, it is considerably more difficult to determine the significance of these facts. First of all, before asking about the effects of capital mobility on national economies, we need to consider how much integration there has really been even of financial markets. Is the cost of capital the same everywhere? Is the story the same for all forms of capital? Is the degree of financial integration that has been achieved by capital mobility significantly greater than in all periods in the recent past? Or only relative to the postwar past?[9] The essays in this volume do not directly address these issues, which are hotly—and technically—debated in a rapid-growth niche in economics. The degree of controversy over them in the literature, however, suggests that even with respect to capital—the most mobile of economic factors and that over which governments have least control—integration and convergence of basic parameters are far from established.

Second, if one turns to a wider set of measures of integration and

[8] Jeffry A. Frieden, "Invested Interests: The Politics of National Economic Policies in a World of Global Finance," *International Organization* 45, no. 4 (1991): 428.

[9] The basic approaches to this question are provided by Martin Feldstein and Charles Horioka, "Domestic Savings and International Capital Flows," *Economic Journal* 90 (1980): 314–29; Jeffrey Frankel, "Quantifying International Capital Mobility in the 1980's," in D. Bernheim and J. Shoven, eds., *National Saving and Economic Performance* (Chicago: University of Chicago Press, 1991), pp. 227–60; Jeffrey Frankel, Steve Phillips, and Menzie Chinn, "Financial and Currency Integration in the European Monetary System: The Statistical Record," University of California, Center for German and European Studies, Working Paper 1.3 (March 1992), pp. 1–33. Doubts have been raised about the historical novelty of contemporary degrees of financial integration by Robert Zevin, "Are World Financial Markets More Open? If So, Why and with What Effects?," in Tariq Banuri and Juliet Schor, eds., *Financial Openness and National Autonomy* (New York: Oxford University Press, 1992). See also two special surveys in *The Economist*: "Fear of Finance," 19 September 1992 and "Who's in the Driving Seat?," 7 October 1995. On this point, see also Chapter 2 in this volume.

convergence and tries to evaluate the long-term effects of trade, competition, diffusion of innovation, and capital mobility, one finds a complex picture with no clear lines of evolution. At the level of macroeconomic phenomena, neoclassical theory and the globalization story would predict that interest rates, profit rates, wages, and incomes in general would be converging as would rates of growth and productivity. From reviewing research on industrial economies over the past century, Boyer concludes that depending on how one selects the country and the period, one may find either convergence or divergence (see Chapter 1 in this volume). When one looks at the differentials between the most advanced and the less developed countries, it is clear that there is no convergence: quite the contrary. Among the most advanced countries, however, the results are more mixed. Boyer agrees with Baumol et al. that there is some convergence, but only "among the small club of nations which have been able to invest sufficiently in productive investment, infrastructure, and education."[10] If there is a long-run tendency toward convergence of macroeconomic performance measures among these countries, it is still at a slow pace (about 2 percent per year), and even after a quarter-century, the initial productivity gap will only be reduced by half, Boyer concludes.

With respect to measures of market integration such as interest rates and exchange rate fluctuation, the evidence for worldwide convergence or even convergence among the most advanced countries is hardly conclusive. As the authors point out, real interest rates remain different from country to country; profit rates in the same sectors also vary significantly from economy to economy. Although the direction of change of macroeconomic indicators is consistent with the convergence hypothesis, it is difficult to account for the range of variation that continues to distinguish one country from another.[11] Even within the European Union, where the existence of a customs union and since 1979 of the European Monetary System should have facilitated macroeconomic convergence, the outcomes are mixed. For example, inflation rates in Germany, Britain, Ireland, and France converged, but interest rates and unemployment rates diverged.[12]

Third, if we accept that the trends, however uneven, gradual, and partially reversible, are toward convergence of macroeconomic performance, at least within the club of similar nations, if rising levels of

[10] W. J. Baumol, S. A. B. Blackman, and E. Wolff, *Productivity and American Leadership: The Long View* (Cambridge: MIT Press, 1991).

[11] See Frankel, Phillips, and Chinn, "Financial and Currency Integration."

[12] See the very useful collection of statistics and commentary in Daniel Delalande, "Les disparités économiques et sociales en Europe," *L'Europe économique, Cahiers Français*, no. 264 (January–February 1994).

trade, finance, and FDI are indeed precursors of a globalized economy, what conclusions follow about the impact of these international flows on the national economies to and from which they move? Are any particular set of domestic transformations inevitable? In fact, today do we observe these societies acquiring the characteristic patterns that have been hypothesized to emerge as a result of increased trade and the accelerated mobility of capital? Has the space for national choice been significantly narrowed? In all spheres?

ECONOMIC POLICYMAKING: AN END TO NATIONAL AUTONOMY?

To answer these questions, consider changes in national economic policies, for policymaking is a rough indicator of the discretionary realm for national differences. Here we find little support for the notion that internationalization of the economy reduces national states to passivity and impotence. The conclusions of a growing body of research on economic policymaking in advanced industrial countries, like research on economic performance, reveal no compelling evidence of an across-the-board convergence. With respect to macroeconomic policy the work of Frieden and Frankel et al. and of others underscores the considerable latitude national governments still have and exploit in macroeconomic policymaking.[13] Even as interest rate setting becomes more constrained, discretionary possibilities remain in exchange rate policy. Frieden analyzes the substantial room for sectoral policy as does Robert Wade in Chapter 2 in this volume.

Geoffrey Garrett's research distinguishes between the effects on national policy autonomy of increasing trade, on one hand, and of financial integration, on the other.[14] Growing financial integration, he argues, reduces government's possibilities of pursuing expansionary macroeconomic policies, and these constraints are reflected in the progressive convergence of interest rates. Left-wing as well as right-wing governments are compelled to tread the same narrow path. But even in this highly-constrained policy arena, domestic politics matters, if only because left-wing governments need to be more restrictive than right-wing governments in order to reassure financial markets. In the case of trade integration there is far more space for national policy and politics to vary and to make a difference. There are alternative ways of improving the competitiveness of domestic producers,

[13] Frieden, "Invested Interests"; Frankel, Phillips, and Chinn, "Financial and Currency Integration."
[14] Geoffrey Garrett, "Capital Mobility, Trade and the Domestic Politics of Economic Policy" (unpub. paper November, 1994).

9

and each may involve more or less government intervention. Thus different partisan alignments, social alliances, and national ideologies produce different programs, depending on national contexts. Garrett concludes that the effects of globalization are intermediated by domestic politics and that considerable diversity in national policies will continue.

In Chapter 3 in this volume Andrea Boltho analyzes the divergence between economic policies in France and Germany. These two countries, with economies of similar dimensions, have been operating within the European Community and the European Monetary System under constraints that even before the Maastricht Treaty obliged them to pursue largely similar monetary and fiscal policies. Despite these macroeconomic constraints, Boltho found wide contrasts in microeconomic policy as well as in the institutional configuration of the economy. Boltho discovered that although the French policymakers moved closer to German practices in monetary policy decisions, they remained as distant from each other and different as before in microeconomic management. Even as the French sought to emulate the macroeconomic stability and competitiveness of Germany, the policies of both left- and right-wing governments in France for regulating labor markets, for education and training, industrial restructuring, research and development, and so forth remained quite distant from German models.

At first, the French were uninterested in German institutions and then, when interested, were unable to create similar institutions, absent the historical resources and societal experience that underpinned the German practices.[15] Nonetheless, the macroeconomic performance of the French came close to German results. Boltho concludes that the French were able to copy German (macro) policies but not German institutions and speculates about the resilience of the outcome. If German competitiveness derives from the ways in which workplace organization promotes skills vital for high-quality production, even though the French match German macroperformance, they may be "missing an essential ingredient of the German 'model.'" To achieve German inflation rates without German microinstitutions it may take the French much higher rates of unemployment and may leave the French more vulnerable to loss of market share in important export industries. With only partial convergence toward the German pattern, French success may be fragile. As Boltho writes, "marrying of

[15] On this subject, see Jonah Levy, "Tocqueville's Revenge: The Decline of Dirigisme and the Evolution of France's Political Economy," diss., Department of Political Science, MIT, Cambridge, 1993.

German orthodoxy at the macro level and of Anglo-American laissez-faire at the micro level could generate bouts of social unrest in a world in which productivity (and hence real wage) growth is limited."

INTERNATIONALIZATION OF ECONOMIES AND NATIONAL INSTITUTIONS

How stable is a world in which countries with diverse microinstitutions are more and more constrained to match each others' macroeconomic performances? Can the disjunction between convergent macroeconomic policies and disparate national practices and institutions be anything but transitory and vulnerable? These questions arise with particular force in the West European countries analyzed in this volume by Andrea Boltho, Hervé Dumez and Alain Jeunemaître, and Stephen Woolcock, because participation in the European Monetary System and, more recently, the requirements for economic convergence laid out in the Maastricht Treaty negotiations, have obliged these nations to align their macroeconomic policies. But at root the issue is the same one faced by other advanced industrial nations. The increasing openness of national economies, the swelling volume of funds flowing across national frontiers, and the growing ease of transferring capital and production from one country to another create severe pressures to match others' macroeconomic results. The fundamental question is whether these pressures work to align diversities generated by different national traditions into an ever-more common set of institutions and practices.

The authors who have contributed to this volume generally agree in their estimates of the trends toward globalization of economic activity, even if they differ somewhat on the sharpness of the break with past patterns of international exchange. The authors are divided not so much in their interpretations of changes in the international economy as in their views on the effects of these changes on domestic practices and institutions: On what kinds of changes, if any, are inevitable; on how (that is, through which processes) trade and globalization alter national configurations; and on whether it is desirable that national life be fully opened to the blast of global winds. The fundamental cleavage cuts between one group of the authors who conclude (with varying degrees of enthusiasm or regret) that national diversities are likely to disappear; and on the other side, the authors who (with varying degrees of enthusiasm or regret) predict the long-term persistence of fundamentally different national models.

SUZANNE BERGER

The Case for Convergence

Consider first the assumptions and arguments of those who foresee the inevitable decline of national models. Why do they find convergence of the institutions of the domestic political economies of advanced countries likely today, given the long track record of the resilience of national specificities in politics, society, and economy over the whole history of industrialization? The contributors provide rather different, even contradictory, explanations. For Ronald Dore and Paul Streeten the central point is the lack of viability of institutions that privilege considerations of equality, justice, and solidarity in societies in which the public interest is now equated with market outcomes and government has withdrawn from an active role in the economy. Absent a political will to sustain institutions and values that transcend efficiency and growth, no national traditions, culture, or historical legacies by themselves can restrain market forces.

Seen from this perspective, even if the Japanese and German systems do better in the long run, they are inherently vulnerable. In a competition between the long-term calculations about the uses of labor, resources, and capital characteristic of the political economies of these two countries in the postwar period and the short-term profit maximizing of Anglo-American capitalism, economic opportunism will win out. When deregulation or open borders give national capitalists the chance to escape constraints on wages, working conditions, layoffs, financial speculation, mergers, or environmental protection, they will—no matter their previous involvement in social-democratic, neocorporatist, or Japanese-like lifetime employment systems. Given the general decline of the Left and indeed of all those political forces in Western advanced societies that might sustain collective action on behalf of values other than competition and efficiency, market forces confront little opposition. The determined voluntarism and appeal to altruism of Dore's parting salvo suggest that, absent a massive change of heart and politics, those institutions that have insulated economic security, fairness, and social solidarity against marketization are unlikely to survive. From the pessimism about politics which runs through his contribution and Streeten's, follows an expectation of the convergence of economic systems in a kind of competitive downgrading of welfare and citizenship rights that had once been protected by national consensus and legislation.

The case for convergence is made on altogether different grounds in the chapters by Carl Kester and Yutaka Kosai. Here the central idea is that economic interaction among countries in a free market leads to competition among diverse models, a kind of natural experimentation of social and economic forms. This competition may lead to convergence, not because of the overall strength of one or another model but, rather, because certain features of each system will be seen to have decisive advantages in solving certain kinds of problems. This stimulates borrowing and imitation of the desirable institutions. Kosai describes the emergence in Japan of a coexistence and overlayering of models, laissez-faire capitalism, relationship capitalism, and industrial policy, some elements of each are of national provenance and other elements, foreign imports. The interplay among models provides flexibility and the capacity of differential response to various situations and pressures. He observes that, despite internationalization, differences among national capitalisms still remain and concludes: "One may argue that this diversity is desirable, insofar as it facilitates the search for the optimal through trial and error; premature integration may deprive every country of the opportunity for social experimentation."[16]

Kester, comparing U.S. and Japanese systems of corporate governance, sees each as having certain distinctive advantages, thus each having much to gain by adopting some part at least of the institutional set developed in the other country. Kester writes:

Both the American and Japanese systems of governance are economically rational attempts to resolve universally typical problems of coordination and control among corporate stakeholders. However, each nation has evolved a system that is at once highly developed along one particular dimension of these problems while underdeveloped along another. Specifically, Japanese corporate governance emphasizes the reduction of the transaction costs associated with self-interested opportunism and investment in relationship-specific assets. This strategy fosters the building of stable, long-term commercial relationships among transacting companies, although general (i.e., noncorporate, nonlending) shareholders are often forced to bear potentially substantial agency costs. Anglo-American corporate governance, in contrast, emphasizes the reduction of agency costs associated with the separation of ownership from control, relying more heavily on formal, legalistic mechanisms to order commercial relationships among transacting parties. Thus, each national system has a comparative advantage, and, in their present configurations, neither can be easily judged to be strictly superior to the other in the long run. (Kester, Chapter 4, this volume)

[16] See Chapter 8, this volume. Starting from the same observation of the coexistence and layering of alternative models within a single country, some analysts conclude that convergence is unlikely. See Richard M. Locke, *Remaking the Italian Economy* (Ithaca: Cornell University Press, 1995).

Kester concludes with the possibility of "a constructive convergence of systems toward standards of 'best practice' that combine the best elements of both." One of the key implicit assumptions underpinning the notion of a possible convergence of the best elements of both systems is that the desired features can be detached from the societies in which they currently are located and grafted as single components on to quite different institutional configurations. The importance of this assumption can be seen if Kester's predictions are compared with those of Stephen Woolcock (Chapter 7, this volume). Woolcock analyzes outcomes of competition among various forms of corporate governance in the European Union and comes to entirely different conclusions from Kester's. Like Kester, Woolcock observes distinct strengths and weaknesses in each of the two polar types of corporate governance in Europe, the English and the German, but he sees little chance of "the different forms of corporate governance result[ing] in a synthesis constituted from the best elements of each system." Each of the components that the English, for example, might wish to modify by importing a German-inspired institution is attached to a complex of "linked policies, regulations, practices, and philosophies affecting capital markets, company structures, and industrial relations [that] are 'embedded' in national practices and institutional arrangements. Small changes or changes in one area that leave the other components of these national systems untouched do not bring about convergence," Woolcock writes.

Finally there is a case for convergence argued in this volume by Miles Kahler and Sylvia Ostry that starts not from the inherent strengths of one or another set of institutions and rules, but from rising international tensions over trade. The striking new element in these trade conflicts is their focus on domestic institutions. Kahler and Ostry lay out the ways in which national structures of finance, innovation, production, and distribution have come to be perceived as sources of advantage or as barriers for competitors from different countries.

Political Pressures for Convergence

For many observing the globalization of international economic exchanges, the issue is not whether convergence of national regulatory regimes and production structures is taking place but only whether it is proceeding rapidly enough. In the past, when convergence was understood as the product of technological imperatives, the normative idea was that economic change and modernization would pull modern liberal politics in its wake. Today, these hopes seem rather naive, as the economic growth spurts of South Korea, Taiwan, Singapore, Malaysia, and China have been launched and consolidated under an authoritarian aegis. The political agenda attached to convergence today builds not on any particular expectations of advances for democracy or rights but on a demand to legitimize the gains in trade earned by firms operating from nations with domestic structures significantly different from the Anglo-American market pattern. The absence or slowness of convergence among states at comparable levels of development suggests illegitimate gains on the part of the nonconverging partner(s). If convergence takes too long, those countries deriving advantage from the barriers their policies or domestic structures erect against the competition of goods and services from other countries are perceived as exploiting the free trade system. The advantages conferred by certain domestic structures have come to be seen as another way of "beggaring the neighbors." Thus, as Sylvia Ostry points out (Chapter 13, this volume), when market-driven convergence lags, "system frictions" are likely to escalate, as economic dislocations move trade into domestic partisan competition. Thus the domestic structures of other countries become stakes in local politics, and trade issues rise as sources of international tension.

Those who see the direction of change as inevitable but the pace too slow advocate using negotiation to accelerate a set of transformations they regard as necessary and desirable. In the Structural Impediments Initiative (SII) talks between the United States and Japan (1989–90) and in the ongoing deliberations over harmonization and mutual recognition within the European Community, political demands for convergence have forced domestic production structures and regulatory regimes on to the agenda of international negotiations. In the case of the SII, the spur was American charges that the structures of Japanese political economy as well as government policies constituted barriers to the entry of foreign goods and capital. Under the threat of American resort to special trade legislation to sanction Japanese exports ("Super 301"), the Japanese agreed to discuss changes in their domestic institutions. As Kahler comments here, the SII "represented an unprecedented effort by industrialized countries to influence structural adjustment in each other's economies and societies" (Chapter 12, this volume), and these negotiations and their outcomes receive much attention in this volume, in his contribution as in those of Ostry, Kosai, and Upham.

In the European Community, the debates, first over harmonization, then over mutual recognition of policies and institutions in member states, were driven by an understanding that without such changes there would be no single market in reality, for institutional barriers would block free flows of labor, goods, and capital as effectively as tariff barriers. The papers in this volume by Stephen Woolcock and by Hervé Dumez and Alain Jeunemaître discuss the European evolution of this issue with respect to corporate governance and competition policy, looking at fairness in trade in the one case, market integration in the other; but in both a politically driven process of convergence sought to reform domestic institutions and to shift patterns in one (or some) nation(s) toward those of another.

In the post–Uruguay Round negotiations and in the OECD there also are proposals to move beyond barriers at the borders and to examine the implications for trade and investment flows of different ways of organizing economic life within countries. Thus for the first time, starting in the 1980s, the domestic structures of political economy have become major stakes in international trade negotiations. The recent quarrels over labor practices and environmental policies in the course of the NAFTA ratification; the bitterness of the last stages of the Uruguay Round negotiations and the focus on cultural institutions by opponents of the new treaty; the emergence at the Marrakesh Conference of a strong demand to condition trade with developing countries on their acceptance of minimal labor standards—all suggest that the pressures propelling domestic institutions into central place in negotiations over the new international economic regime continue to mount.

In sum, those who see convergence on the horizon of advanced countries have very different conceptions of how this process is likely to operate. Among the contributors to the volume, three distinct notions emerge: convergence as the triumph of market forces, abetted by complicit or passive governments; convergence as the result of diffusion of best practice and competition among institutional forms; and convergence as the internationally negotiated or coerced choice of one set of rules and institutions. Indeed these three models do not exhaust the range of possibilities, as Robert Boyer argues in his chapter in this volume.

Convergence through External Pressures and Domestic Pull

Although the authors may disagree on how convergence comes about, they do have one point of strong agreement that distinguishes their arguments from much of the other literature predicting convergence. However powerful they judge external market or political forces for change, none of the contributors believes that exogenous pressures alone bring about convergence. In each of the case studies of institutional change driven by global market forces or by international political pressures or some combination of the two, the author emphasizes the significance of the domestic story, that is, of the internal constellation of political and economic forces that not only accommodates the externally pushed change but, far more actively, also pulls it in and shapes it. The account that Dumez and Jeunemaître provide of the gradual convergence of competition policy in countries of the European Union reveals how external pressures and internal incentives may work in tandem, relaying each other over a rather long time. Beginning after World War II, American pressure led to new antitrust legislation appearing on the books in a number of European countries. These laws, with only few or weak domestic allies, remained dead letters until the 1980s. At that point a new set of internal supporters (certain parts of the bureaucracy, eager to transfer high-conflict industrial issues to agencies or courts outside the reach of normal politics) and a new jolt of external pressure (European Community rules) transformed the dusty old statutes into sites of real contestation.

Several of the authors consider changes in Japanese institutions that proceeded in response both to strong U.S. pressures for convergence and changes in the international economy, on one side, and domestic transformations, on the other. Shijuro Ogata's contribution to the volume discusses the role of internal factors in Japanese politics and economy as well as of world financial markets in the liberalization of Japanese financial institutions. Frank K. Upham analyzes the success of the U.S. demand in the SII negotiations that the Japanese modify a set of practices that limited the openings and expansion of large retail distributors. This demand involved a major intrusion into the fabric of Japanese life, for it amounted to reducing the protection that small shops had enjoyed and risked alienating a large constituency of small shopkeepers. Why did the Japanese bureaucrats and politicians yield on this issue—one on which Japanese practice was in fact quite similar to that of certain European countries like France and Italy—while resisting on a number of other points, like the *keiretsu*, on which Japanese variance from the practices of other advanced countries was wider?

As Upham tells the story, the American pressures rejoined the pressures for liberalization of retail trade from a number of Japanese groups, some within the bureaucracy and some in the private sector. Moreover, the practices about which the Americans complained were not those mandated by the law but, rather, ways of implementing the law that MITI had developed in response to local pressures. The law itself suggested procedures for store approvals quite different from those effectively used, and in some sense, the result of the SII demands was to push MITI to an implementation of the law closer to its original intention. In contrast, the demand for breaking up the *keiretsu* did not seem legitimate to most of the Japanese elites, who saw these holding patterns as efficient, fair, and high-performance economic institutions, and who heard American complaints on this score as motivated by an unsavory mix of ideology and desire to weaken a successful competitor. Indeed, as the head of the Japanese SII negotiating team, Ambassador Koji Watanabe, told the Bellagio meeting members who discussed these essays, Japanese negotiators on issues such as the revision of the Large-Scale Retail Sales Law could conceive accepting the U.S demand as improving the functioning of the Japanese economy and satisfying the desires of Japanese consumers, but demands like those to break up *keiretsu* seemed unacceptable pressures to weaken their own country. When the FTC in 1992 did look into *keiretsu* practices as the Japanese had been obliged to agree in the SII final document, Upham reports, "it found no illegal behavior, and virtually none of the Americans' original demands has been effectively addressed" (Chapter 11, this volume).

Convergence toward Which or Whose Model?

Upham makes another observation about the outcome of American pressure on the Japanese to modify the retail trade law's implementation that recurs elsewhere in the papers, as in other empirical research on institutional diffusion and convergence: The results both of market pressures and of external political pressures may produce not replicas of the foreign model but new "hybrid" types. Upham writes that even though the SII obliged the Japanese to allow stores that look more like American ones, the processes by which retail establishments are authorized to open remain as different as before in the United States and in Japan, in that in Japan it remains essentially the result of a regulatory process focused on economic considerations rather than on land use decisions as in the United States. The new system may be closer to the American, but it is still quite distinct in the criteria used by the regulators, the nature of the filters through which decisions pass, and in outcomes. This result coincides with Kester's conception of a process of experimentation and institutional borrowing, from which would emerge a mixed new type of governance regime in both the United States and Japan, and not the triumph of any of the existing models.

At a certain point, of course, arguments about hybrid types blur indistinguishably into arguments about the adaptation, resilience, and reproduction of national models. But as the discussion that follows contends, between those who argue for the plausibility and likelihood of convergence, albeit on hybrid types, and those who see national models as having a long life ahead of them, there is a real distinction. The former imagine the process of institutional "hybridization" to be one in which functionality and market rationality are the drivers, even when politics is a backseat driver. If the institutions that emerge have somewhat different national or cultural colorations from place to place, it is neither surprising nor is it a major constraint. Organizations need a certain measure of fit with the "environment." As Ohmae writes after noting that his garden in Tokyo has quite different plants from those one would grow in the Arctic or in the tropics, "Why, then, when managers prepare the ground for the global organizations they hope to grow, do they often pay little attention to the quality of soil, light, temperature, and exposure? Why do they talk and plan . . . as if one special plant could grow equally well in all possible climates and situations?"[17] Ohmae's garden metaphor expresses not only the idea of a deliberate selection of institutions with a view to their adaptability and viability in given environments but also the role of the global gardener, whose purposes remain invariant from one national setting to the next. Whatever the concessions to different national climes, the objectives remain the same and are achieved both by adjusting means to ends and by manipulating the institutional array.

THE RESILIENCE OF NATIONAL MODELS

A second cluster of contributions in this volume sharply opposes the convergence perspective. The common theme here is the long-term resilience and expansion of diverse national systems and models of capitalism. The arguments against convergence laid out in these essays build on different analyses of how markets work, ideas about institutional coherence and adaptation, and alternative understandings of how politics shapes the economy.

Conceptions of the Market

As Robert Boyer's essay emphasizes, theories of convergence that predict the narrowing of productivity differentials and standards of living conceive the global economy as a single homogenous market with standard goods and the same factor prices everywhere. As Boyer summarizes, "The globalization of finance, labor, technologies, and products proceeds so that each nation comes to resemble a small- or

---

[17] Ohmae, *The Borderless World*, p. 101.

medium-size firm in an ocean of pure and perfect competition" (Chapter 1, this volume). But, he argues, there is no such real economy. The terrain of competition is far more variegated and uneven. Everywhere asymmetries of information and power, organizational factors, different social infrastructure, and the effects of scale operate to compartmentalize the market and to create "niches, far away from the abstraction of perfect competition on homogenized and standardized goods. Thus productivity levels across firms, sectors, regions, nation, and continental zones might differ, even over the long run, without any clear trend to convergence." The impact of global markets on the national production system also is attenuated by the fact that production for the domestic market continues massively to dominate that part of national product that is traded in international markets, as Wade observes (Chapter 2) and Paul Krugman argues in his provocative 1994 *Foreign Affairs* article attacking the prophets of competitiveness.[18]

Furthermore, if world markets do not have the predicted effects on national systems, the explanation may lie not only in the possibilities for success in special niches or in one's home market but also in the indeterminacy of market pressures. As Michele Salvati argued at the meeting at which these essays were discussed, the failure of market pressures to produce greater uniformity of policy and institutional configuration in individual countries reveals the fundamental ambiguity of these pressures. They may signal problems and provide general pressure for change without providing unequivocal clues about which policies or institutions need to be altered and how. If, for example, national policy is to reduce the deficit, even extreme competitive pressures might not indicate which sectors need to be privileged to reach that goal. As the example of Britain strikingly illustrates, bad models can be quite sticky. If convergence takes place at all, it may take a very long time.

Functional Equivalents in Systems of Production?

Another set of hypotheses about the indeterminant impact of changes in the international economy takes off from the question of whether there are functional equivalents in the organization of production that are equally competitive in world markets. Boyer and Wade emphasize in their contributions that different national configurations have an extraordinary capacity to refract common competitive pressures and to produce divergent national responses. If these re-

[18] Paul Krugman, "Competitiveness: A Dangerous Obsession," *Foreign Affairs* 73, no. 2 (March–April 1994).

sponses are roughly equally successful over time, then national models are reinforced and reconsolidated in their diversity. On this understanding, there are, if not an infinite number of different ways of organizing production well in the world at a given time, at least several significant alternatives. Thus even if the forces of globalization are very powerful, one would not anticipate that Germany will be forced to try to conform to the Japanese model.

The core issue is whether or not Japanese lean production, German high-skill, high-quality social market economy, Italian industrial districts, U.S. flexible mass production, and others are fundamentally different systems capable of achieving similar results in markets through quite different mechanisms. Are the systems actually different? Or are the same principles at work everywhere, decked out in national colors? In contrast to the perspective from Ohmae's garden, the authors here see real diversity. Is the production problem that diverse, although apparently all successful, national production systems actually solve the same problem? Or are German, Japanese, and American brands of capitalism in fact good at responding to rather different challenges? Some of the authors, particularly Boyer, who focuses on the contrast with Fordism, see the national systems as functional equivalents; others see the national models as specializing—the U.S. in chemicals, software, biotechnology, the Japanese in electronics, the Germans in production equipment, and so forth.

If institutional constellations and cultural legacies provide distinctive strengths and weaknesses, then each system may flourish or experience difficulties in different economic conjunctures. For example, the very features of the German model that made it poor at Fordist mass production were features that made possible the flexible, high-skilled, quality production that was so successful in the 1980s. Thus at various times one or another of the national systems may look like the model to emulate, and this can change very rapidly, as the "decline" of the Swedish model in the 1980s or the sudden resurgence of American strengths in the mid-1990s show.

Tightness of Fit in National Systems of Production

If the various systems are good at different tasks and times, it would seem desirable for each to try to incorporate those elements of the other models that would allow it to perform better. Can there be a synthesis of "best practices" along the lines that Kester discusses? Can there be piecemeal adoption of institutions? This is the issue on which the divide is widest between those who see the resilience of national models and the unlikelihood of convergence and their colleagues in this volume. The former see national production systems as rather tightly bundled packages of specific national resources, institutions, and legacies. The "tightness of fit" makes it extremely unlikely that any one practice or institution, even if dysfunctional, can be readily changed without requiring change in other pieces of the system. Thus Woolcock's essay concludes that the reason why the British have been unable to modify corporate governance arrangements is that a much more comprehensive reform would be needed, involving changes in capital markets and much else. On this wider reform, there is no consensus. Wolfgang Streeck argued at the meeting that despite great competitive pressures to reduce costs, Germans are unlikely to be able to move toward Japanese lean production, because it would require not only changes in the production model but also extensive changes in the industrial relations system.

In part, then, "tightness of fit" may have to do with the fact that institutions do not stand alone but depend for their good functioning on inputs that other parts of the system provide. These dependencies make it impossible to analyze in isolation the chances of any single institution's functional adaptation. This is in one sense obvious as, for example, when one considers the prospect of introducing a German-inspired high-quality, specialized production model into a society that lacks the institutions to educate a highly skilled work force. As several of the participants in the meeting emphasized, the market, too, depends on extramarket supports for its functioning. Relations of trust and a legal regime defining contract and property are essential to the market and created outside it. Thus institutions, taken one by one, may not be as plastic and open to opportunistic adoption and combination as conventional ideas about competition suggest.

"Tightness of fit" need not mean cultural determinism or institutional immutability. Several of the authors review in some detail the historical evolution of particular national models. In each country there are turning points of sharp discontinuity, transformation, and a break up of old patterns. Japan, Germany, the United States, each has today a form of capitalism quite different from what one might have predicted in, for example, the 1920s. Peter Gourevitch develops this argument provocatively when he describes the American economy of the past as close to a German or Japanese networked capitalism, with trusts, interlocking directorates, restrictions on competition, industrial policy, banks that financed and coordinated industrial activity, and education and training systems that turned out large numbers of skilled workers.

What happened to change the model? A variety of political pressures and alliances among the disaffected led to legislation that broke up the trusts, restricted banking, and so forth. As Gourevitch summarizes the transformation, "these policy decisions pushed the American economy down a path quite different from that of Japan and Germany. They knocked the United States off its Nippo-Rhenish trajectory and toward the current Anglo-American one—a decentralized, individualized, loosely coupled, arms-length, short-term, consumer-oriented, blind-bidding, market-driven system. . . . The American pattern has emerged out of politics and policy" (Chapter 10, this volume).

If policy and legislation are major shapers of the microinstitutions of capitalism, as Gourevitch argues, institutions will not adjust spontaneously to heightened global pressures. Rather, as Woolcock also suggested, large-scale reforms such as those of the New Deal or of the Occupation may be the precondition of adaptation. For this, in ordinary times, political will is usually lacking. It is not that the institutions and practices of the domestic political economy are immutable, but that changing them succeeds only when the process is undertaken in a comprehensive and wholesale fashion. As Michele Salvati observed during discussions of this issue, punctuated equilibria models of change may thus be more appropriate than the gradualism implicit in conventional evolutionary models, in which competitive pressures are the drivers. "Tightness of fit" in this perspective reflects the mesh between politics, policy, and economic institutions and the coherence of a system that responds only slowly and unevenly to changing markets.

The Politics of Convergence

Finally, the future of convergence is likely to be shaped by growing political opposition to changes that are perceived to be the response to external pressures. In all industrial countries processes of economic integration and globalization are generating a backwash of reaction and resistance in national politics. New political battles have broken out over whether domestic institutions and practices in one's own society or in someone else's ought to be restructured to conform to institutions and patterns elsewhere. These issues, together with new questioning about the legitimacy of economic outcomes in international exchange, are beginning to shape coherent new visions of the state's role between domestic economy and society and international markets. New political alliances are beginning to coalesce around these issues.

In Europe the astonishing reverses of popular opinion on construction of the European Union that were revealed by the Maastricht Treaty referenda show growing hostility to the prospect of giving up national practices and institutions for common European models. The debates, particularly in France, over conclusion of the Uruguay Round of the GATT negotiations similarly showed rising anxieties about the effects on national values and institutions of lowering the remaining barriers between the domestic society and economy and the outside.[19] In each case the issues that emerge are the same ones: basically, that the autonomy of national life is threatened by negotiated transfers of sovereignty to other bodies (to the European Community or to the GATT) and by a loss of national control induced by the growing internationalization of the economy. As Philippe Séguin, the French politician who organized the anti–Maastricht Treaty movement and today is president of the French National Assembly, exclaimed: "The idea of frontiers as outdated! There's a dogma to attack! Bringing back the frontiers today is the condition of any policy."[20]

Paired with the determination to defend national autonomy against external pressures is a refusal of the legitimacy of the outcomes that are seen to result from opening national borders to the outside world. This second dimension of the politics of convergence has been central in U.S. debates. It is at the core of the controversy over whether Japan's economic, political, and social institutions need to become more like American patterns if trade between the two countries is to be fair. This issue has spilled over from a quarrel among policy intellectuals and politicians into the public arena. Much of the debate in the United States over the NAFTA similarly focused on whether the competitive advantages from which Mexicans might benefit under the new arrangements would be fairly come by or would depend on exploitative labor relations and destructive environmental practices.

What is the connection between these American controversies and the kinds of issues they have propelled on to the agenda of international trade negotiations and the politics of harmonization and integration in the European Community? In both cases, political ideas and competition are crystallizing on issues involving the legitimacy of economic outcomes in exchange among nations and linking the legitimacy of these outcomes to the nature of structures of production and distribution in the trading partner's society.

A new politics is in the making. Does it matter? Can it matter in a

[19] See Suzanne Berger, "The Coming Protectionism: Trade and Identity in France," in Gregory Flynn, ed., *Remaking the Hexagon: The New France in the New Europe* (Boulder, Colo: Westview Press, 1995), pp. 195–210.

[20] Philippe Séguin, *Ce que j'ai dit* (Paris: Grasset, 1993), pp. 47–48 (my translation).

world in which globalization of economic flows may have outstripped the regulatory possibilities of governments? The conclusion that emerges from the essays in this volume is that the space for political vision and choice—and for a diversity of choices—is open and wide. The biggest question left unanswered is not whether politics can seize and use this space, but which politics and for whom?

PART I

CONVERGENCE?
MACROECONOMIC PERFORMANCE

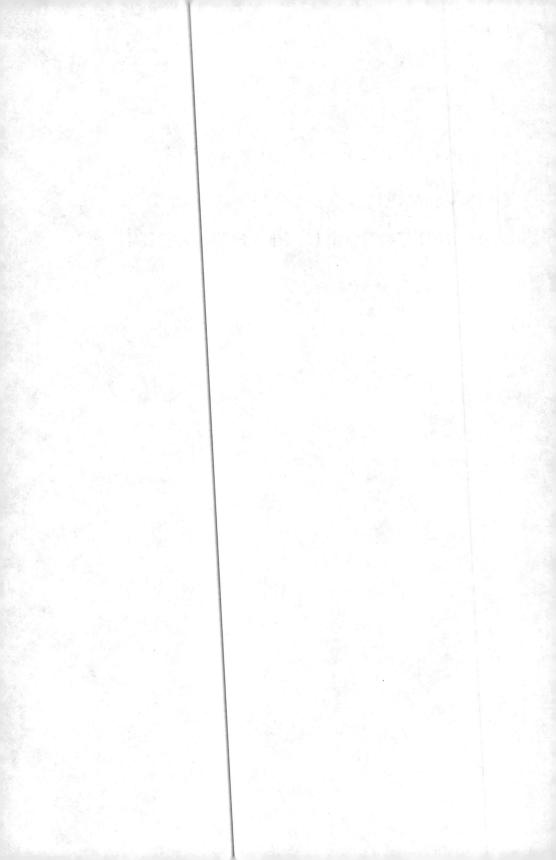

CHAPTER ONE

The Convergence Hypothesis Revisited: Globalization but Still the Century of Nations?

ROBERT BOYER

NATION-STATES IN AN ERA OF GLOBALIZATION

The current wave of globalization has revived debates about the consequences of growing economic interdependence on the ability of national societies to preserve distinctive social, political, cultural, and economic organizations. Evidence seems to suggest that firms adopt similar technologies, that life-styles are homogenizing all over the industrialized world, and that the globalization and sophistication of financial markets are aligning national economies. Many predict that the national state will soon be obsolete and that government's room for maneuver will be limited. If lean production is destined to replace old Fordist mass production of standardized goods, then most social and economic organizations have to be redesigned to conform to the most efficient firms in each sector.

Thus convergence theory is back again, with a vengeance—the more so since the collapse of the Soviet economy. At the same time the Swedish economy, once seen as a "third way" between capitalism and socialism, is drastically reforming its social democratic institutions. So, too, the painful experience of the French socialist government suggests that the statist economies are losing direction and attractive power, as they are forced to conventional economic policies and to implement financial and political organizations more congruent with an integrated Europe.

This chapter starts from these trends but argues that they need not converge toward full and complete integration. Evidence from the past and from the failure of past predictions of the end of national specificities should induce more caution. But even more important is the observation that few of the mechanisms that promote economic convergence are powerful enough to homogenize economic performances. Nor can we imagine the adoption of a single one best practice identical all over the world and applicable to any region or nation. Recent trends in the car industry underscore these general conclusions, as does investigation of the impact of Japanese transplants abroad. The threat of a Japanization of industrialized societies appears largely exaggerated. Indeed many of the mechanisms that translate external competition into the redesign of economic institutions have quite a different effect. Even when they try to copy strictly a supposed superior model, managers, workers, and governments finally produce a hybrid local management style and coordinating mechanisms. After a long period of trial and error, the end product usually differs widely from original intentions.

The argument proceeds along the following lines: First, ambiguities in the definition of convergence are spelled out by disentangling three distinct meanings: economic convergence, similarity in the style of development, and finally the characteristics of institutional settings that organize interactions between economy and polity. Second, when precise tests of the main macroeconomic variables are built, we see that no clear trend to convergence or divergence emerges. Third, even though the socialist bloc has collapsed, this has not reduced diversity. Rather it has revealed the coexistence and competition of various kinds of capitalism. The "regulation school" provides a taxonomy for the national trajectories since 1973 and even earlier, since World War II. No clear tendency to converge reappears.

CONVERGENCE: THREE DEFINITIONS

Productivity Levels and Standards of Living: Economic Convergence

According to the first definition of convergence, the globalization of finance, labor, technologies, and products proceeds so that each nation comes to resemble a small- or medium-size firm in an ocean of pure and perfect competition. Consequently, any Keynesian-style intervention is bound to fail, given that the competition is now international and foreign producers will capture the domestic market if local producers do not adjust to the costs and prices achieved by competitors. If the law of a single price for each commodity holds, then production costs would equalize all over the world. If knowledge about technology is a perfect public good, then Ricardian trade theory suggests that productivity levels should converge under a free trade regime. Note that labor mobility via migration or capital mobility by foreign investment is not necessary to arrive at such a result. Of course, in contemporary capitalism, financial liberalization and a significant flow of migrant workers would augment the convergence mechanisms associated with free trade in goods and services.

But no real economy exhibits the features required to deliver a general equilibrium under pure and perfect competition.[1] In a monetary economy with imperfect competition, asymmetry in power and information, and increasing return to scale and public goods, the possible and multiple equilibria are now closely related to the inner features of the constitutional order, the system of incentives, and finally the configuration of organizations.[2] The argument is all the more relevant for various national states and firms with unequal size and power, which may struggle for and finally find niches, far away from the abstraction of perfect competition on homogenized and standardized goods.[3] Thus productivity levels across firms, sectors, regions, nations, and continental zones might differ, even over the long run, without any clear trend to convergence.

Democracy and Markets: Convergence in Development

For many social scientists, convergence has another meaning: not pure economic performance, but the basic constitutional order, organizing interactions between polity and economy. In this tradition, modern societies are characterized by the wide diffusion of markets, which are supposed both to foster economic efficiency and to support democratic order.

Convergence in this sense is to be demonstrated by the collapse of authoritarian regimes and their replacement by more democratic constitutions. Again, the basic issue concerns the generality of such a trend and its significance. Although Chile, Brazil, Argentina, and South Africa became more democratic, other moderately democratic states became less democratic, as, for example, in the Islamic or African world. Moreover, democracy is a question of degree and not only of nature. For example, there are useful distinctions between radical developmental, legal, competitive elitist, and participatory democra-

[1] Robert Boyer, "Markets: History, Theory, and Policy," in R. Hollingsworth and Robert Boyer, eds., *Contemporary Capitalism: The Embeddedness of Institutions* (Cambridge University Press, forthcoming).

[2] D. North, *Institutions, Institutional Change, and Economic Performance* (New York: Cambridge University Press, 1990).

[3] J. Stopford, S. Strange, and J. S. Henlay, *Rival States, Rival Firms. Competition for World Market Shares* (Cambridge: Cambridge University Press, 1991).

cies.[4] A more adequate definition of convergence would consider the precise configuration and interactions between political power and economic organization. There is no single connection between the implementation of democracy and the spread of markets and economic performances. The success of some NICs such as South Korea has been obtained by authoritarian regimes, not to speak of Chile under the Pinochet regime, Brazil during the miracle, or Mexico ruled by the PRI.

Moreover, the East European case, for example, produces not one but many configurations for democracy: the Polish system is not a variant of the Russian one, nor the Czech a copy of the Hungarian system. These differences in institutional setting seem to play some role in the pattern of economic reforms, that is, the transition toward a market economy.[5] Equally important markets are economic institutions based on explicit or implicit values, norms, and legislation. Depending on the rules of the game, the market for the same product or commodity functions quite differently.[6] Indeed from a theoretical point of view, the market mechanisms can be restricted to some products or extended to all of them. Even fictitious commodities such as futures and polluting rights can be traded in a formal market.

Thus, such a sweepingly broad conception of convergence groups under the same heading many configurations with very different implications for politics and efficiency.

Institutional Forms and "Regulation" Modes: A Third View of Convergence

The interactions of political and economic interests can have multiple configurations, depending on the balance between market and democracy and the mix between public regulations, associations, private and public hierarchies, and markets.[7] The "regulation" approach suggests that five major institutional forms combine to generate a series of dynamic patterns of adjustment.[8] For example, the mix between

[4] D. Held, *Models of Democracy* (Stanford: Stanford University Press, 1987).

[5] A. Clesse and R. Tokes, *The Economic and Social Imperatives of the Future Europe* (Baden-Baden: Nomos, 1992).

[6] C. Clague and G. C. Rausser, *The Emergence of Market Economies in Eastern Europe* (Cambridge: Blackwell, 1992).

[7] A. Przeworski, *Democracy and Market* (Cambridge: Cambridge University Press, 1991); R. Hollingsworth and Robert Boyer, *Contemporary Capitalism*; P. Di Maggio and W. Powell, eds., *The New Institutionalism in Organizational Analysis* (Chicago: University of Chicago Press, 1991).

[8] Robert Boyer, *The Regulation School: A Critical Introduction* (New York: Columbia University Press, 1990).

market mechanisms, collective agreements, and state regulation may vary widely in different product, labor, and credit markets. Various national economies would then converge if and only if their basic institutional forms were similar and responded in the same way to foreign competition, unexpected disturbances, as well as internal political conflicts and economy imbalances. Strong convergence would prevail when the mutual interaction of institutional design with market competition leads to similar performances and eventually to a convergence in productivity levels and living standards.

But the same economic performances, or at least long-run viability, can emerge from quite different institutional settings. Such a model of *mixed convergence* might prevail in countries involved in a free trade agreement (NAFTA, for example), with more or less tight financial and monetary integration, but without commitments to harmonization (as in the EC). There are other cases in which institutional inertia and pressures for coping with external competitiveness produce a relative or absolute decline in economic performances, as in Britain, a case of *partial divergence*.[9]

Yet another possibility exists. Core institutional forms and performances may not conform to the dominant development model. Strong divergence can in fact be observed at both ends of the spectrum of economic performances. Many poor African countries have distinct institutional configurations and are experiencing severe economic problems. The divergence of almost an entire continent is rarely mentioned by social scientists, although econometric studies find African countries quite distinct with significant dummy variables.[10] But such factors are a poor substitute for a deeper explanation of such long-lasting differences in institutional setting. At the other extreme, Asian NICs clearly exhibit genuine business systems and more state interventions, and they experience faster growth than old industrialized countries.[11] The conventional explanation is simple: these countries are catching up. This reason may account for dynamism, but it fails to analyze institutional patterns. The genuine strains and disequilibria affecting the Asian NICs and even Japan are another *indirect* evidence for durably distinct institutional and economic configurations. Quite intuitively—and of course this hypothesis is investi-

[9] B. Elbaum and W. Lazonick, eds., *The Decline of the British Economy* (Oxford: Clarendon, 1987).

[10] R. J. Barro, "Economic Growth in a Cross-Section of Countries," *Quarterly Journal of Economics*, May 1991: 407–43; J. Bradford deLong and L. Summers, "Equipment Investment and Economic Growth," *Quarterly Journal of Economics*, May 1991: 445–502.

[11] R. D. Whitley, *Business Systems in East Asia: Firms, Markets, and Societies* (London: Sage, 1992).

gated in this chapter—the world is far from exhibiting a strong convergence, when one considers the detailed and complex interactions between political and economic institutions.

ECONOMIC CONVERGENCE IN HISTORICAL PERSPECTIVE: AN AGNOSTIC VIEW

In the conventional view of convergence competition and emulation among alternative configurations lead simultaneously to homogeneity in institutional setting and common standards of living, or at least an absence of cumulative inequalities among countries. When, for example, former socialist countries implemented more or less ambitious plans for the transition to modern society, democracy, and markets, politicians and public opinion believed this would progressively deliver ways of life and productivity standards analogous to those prevailing within the Western economies. But is it true that capitalist democratic systems tend to converge toward the same macroeconomic variables? This expectation is neither unreasonable theoretically nor without empirical support, but the process of getting there is hardly automatic.

Contemporary Growth Theories: A Challenge to Convergence Hypotheses

The convergence and stability of the capitalist growth process is an old debate in political economy. Malthus and Marx conceived of industrialization as an uneven process: the cumulative growth of the most successful industries, regions, or nations was paid for by the collapse of more archaic skills, sectors, or communities. Ricardo in contrast imagined a smooth process of growth, finally leading to a stationary state with zero growth and no institutional or technological change. Any economy was bound to converge toward such an equilibrium because of the decreasing marginal returns associated with agriculture.

Modern growth theory exhibits an equivalent controversy, this time cast in a more rigorous and elegantly formalized framework. In the 1940s neo-Keynesian authors such as Harrod and Domar regarded the dynamic equilibrium of consumption and investment decisions as delivering a quite unstable macroeconomic path. Either the economy experienced explosive growth or it was trapped in a cumulative and self-defeating depression. But after the unprecedented growth of the postwar period neoclassical economists saw a more peaceful account of the development process: if all the markets are competitive and if the same technology is available in each country, every economy would grow at the same rate—a growth imposed by technical change and corrected by demographic trends. Under these idealized conditions neoclassical theory provides a simple rationale for economic convergence in growth rates.

This framework has, however, been challenged by theorists dissatisfied with the assumption of automaticity in technical change, assumed to be independent of investment or policies to improve technological efficiency. If, for example, a country does not save and consequently underinvests, can it benefit from the same technological opportunities as a more innovative and virtuous country? Probably not, because learning by doing will be less efficient and the lack of domestic technological expertise may make it hard to capture advances in basic knowledge and technology.[12] Basically, for the new growth theorists, technological change is endogenous, that is, the equilibrium growth path depends on past efforts in research and development, education, and product differentiation.[13] Thus rates of productivity growth are likely to vary from one country to another, without unilinear global convergence.

Of course, if countries adopt similar educational and technological policies, they may end up on similar growth paths. Less wealthy countries, however, might be caught into an underdevelopment trap that prevents them from capturing the increasing returns to scale available, had they invested more in infrastructure, health, education, and research. This generalization of previous growth models exhibits the possible coexistence between fast-growth and low-growth countries, even in the long run. Thus some economies might follow the same pattern and catch up, whereas others are falling behind. Both convergence and divergence tendencies could be observed through time and space.

Convergence of Productivity among Major Industrial Countries after World War II

Empirical research on the convergence or divergence of performance indicators has been carried out by economists and economic historians[14] who constructed per capita GNP measures for the last cen-

[12] OECD, *Technology and Productivity: Challenge for Economic Policy* (Paris: OECD, 1991).
[13] For a comparison with previous theory, see P. Diamond, ed., *Growth, Productivity, Unemployment* (Cambridge: MIT Press, 1990).
[14] A. Maddison, *Dynamic Forces in Capitalist Development* (Oxford: Oxford University Press, 1991); M. Abramovitz, *Thinking about Growth* (Cambridge: Cambridge University

Figure 1-1. Widening disparities in productivity levels during the nineteenth century.

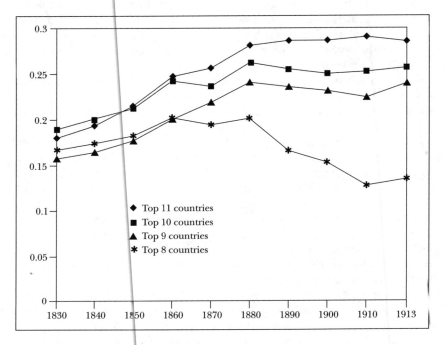

SOURCE: Data from P. Bairoch, "Europe's Gross National Product: 1800–1975," *Journal of European Economic History* 5 (1976): 286

tury. The findings are mixed: according to the period and the economy studied, sometimes they find convergence, sometimes divergence.

During the nineteenth century, productivity levels for a group of eleven advanced countries tended to diverge, especially from 1830 to 1880, which suggests the coexistence of different industrialization patterns (Figure 1-1). But when only the top eight countries are taken into account, productivity converges, particularly from 1880 to 1913. This point shows how dependent results are on the choice of countries and of periods.

After World War II economic performance indicators converged strongly, with the possible exception of the British economy (Figure

---

Press, 1989); W. J. Baumol, S. A. B. Blackman, and E. Wolff, *Productivity and American Leadership: The Long View* (Cambridge: MIT Press, 1989); P. Bairoch, "Europe's Gross National Product, 1800–1975," *Journal of European Economic History* 5 (1976): pp. 273–340.

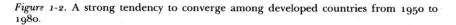

Figure 1-2. A strong tendency to converge among developed countries from 1950 to 1980.

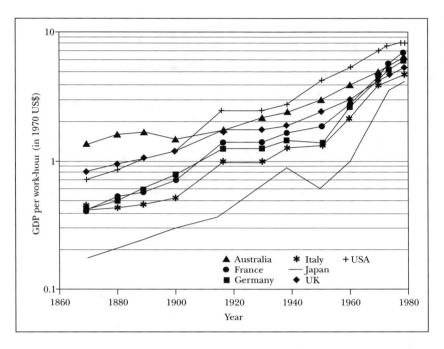

SOURCE: A. Maddison, *Phases of Capitalist Development* (Oxford: Oxford University Press, 1982), 212

1-2). In accordance with the predictions of the catch-up hypothesis,[15] more backward economies such as Japan and Italy grew faster than others between 1950 and 1980. These countries imported technologies and institutions from more advanced economies and in this way came to look more like their points of reference. The methodology of these studies has a significant bias: only currently successful industrialized countries are considered, thus convergence is partially tautological. More sophisticated analysis takes into account possible nonlinearities,[16] and the impact of innovation and educa-

---

[15] "The [catch-up] hypothesis asserts that being backward in level of productivity carries a *potential* for rapid advance. Stated more definitively the proposition is that in comparisons across countries the growth rates of productivity in any long period tend to be inversely related to the initial levels of productivity." M. Abramovitz, "Catching Up, Forging Ahead, and Falling Behind," *Journal of Economic History* 46 (1986): 386.

[16] Bart Verspagen, *Uneven Growth between Interdependent Economies* (Brookfield, Vt.: Avebury, 1993).

Figure 1-3. Other countries fall behind and thus diverge from developed and newly industrialized countries.

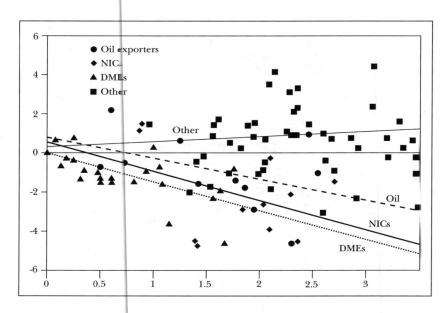

SOURCE: B. Verspagen, *Uneven Growth between Interdependent Economies* (Brookfield, Vt.: Avebury, 1993), 96–97. Reprinted with the permission of the publisher.
NOTE:

(G) is defined as the relative per capita income gap between any given country (i) and the United States. Mathematically, it is $\ln(Q_{USA}/Q_i)$ where Q_{USA} is the American per capita income and Q_i is the per capita income of country (i). Hence, negative movement in G indicates "catching up."

DMEs = Developed market economies
NICs = Newly industrialized countries
Oil exporters = Less developed oil-exporting countries
Other = Other (less developed) countries

tion[17] and examines a sample including both successful and under-developed or developing countries.[18]

The results of such efforts present quite a different picture. Overall, the initial gap in productivity level is associated with slower rates of growth, which imply that the more advanced countries have experienced better performances than the poorer countries (Figure 1-3).

[17] B. Amable, "Catch-Up and Convergence: A Model of Cumulative Growth," *International Review of Applied Economics* 7, no. 1 (1993): 1–25.

[18] Barro, "Economic Growth"; R. J. Barro and X. Sala-I-Martin, "Convergence across States and Regions," *Brookings Papers in Economic Activity* 1 (1991): 107–82; DeLong and Summers, "Equipment Investment"; D. Cohen, *Tests of the "Convergence Hypothesis": A Critical Note* (Paris: CEPREMAP, 1992); D. Cohen, *Economic Growth and the Solow Model* (Paris: CEPREMAP, 1992).

Thus, between the early-1960s and the mid-1980s there was a widening gap between the top and bottom countries of the world, that is, diverging paths. Clearly backwardness creates a potential for faster growth, but only if adequate economic strategies and probably institutions allow such a potential to be activated by an effective development process.[19] This disparity might disappear if measures of the investment effort were taken into account, both in productive capital and in education. Unless they have invested in human capital in the previous period, less advanced countries do not appear able to catch up and move further and further away from the technological frontier of the most advanced.[20]

Convergence and Divergence

A long-term review of convergence indicators (Figure 1-4) shows that the spread among countries was rather constant from 1900 to 1930 but widened drastically during the 1930s. The significant reduction of productivity differences between countries is, therefore, a recent phenomenon, dating to the period 1950–80. The mid-1970s show a possible U-turn, with dispersion indicators once again slightly increasing. Verspagen[21] has examined and categorized the economic statistics of 114 countries during two periods: 1960–73 and 1973–88. From his work, three trends among the countries that are in a position to "catch up" (are relatively backward) emerge: very poor countries that have invested so little in manufacturing and/or in education that catch-up was impossible; countries that made moderate investments in manufacturing and education, resulting in some catching up; and countries that, because of significant investments, made significant strides in catching up. In the first period, examples of the very poor countries that were "falling behind" included Egypt and Mexico. In the "catching up" category were countries such as Jamaica and Finland; and in the "strongly catching up" category were Israel and Korea. In the second period, those who were falling behind included Rwanda and Argentina. A group of "newly catching up" countries emerged, which included Costa Rica and Iran. The third set were the "established catching up" countries, such as Greece and Poland, which continued their successes of the previous period.

Finally, a rapid review of the major statistical studies of perfor-

[19] Abramovitz, *Thinking about Growth*.
[20] Barro, "Economic Growth"; D. Cohen, "Tests"; D. Cohen, "Economic Growth"; G. Mankiw, D. Romer, and D. Weil, "A Contribution to the Empires of Economic Growth," *Quarterly Journal of Economics*, May 1992: 407–38.
[21] B. Verspagen, *Uneven Growth between Interdependent Economies* (Brookfield, Vt.: Avebury, 1993).

Figure 1-4. The eighties: A possible return to divergence?

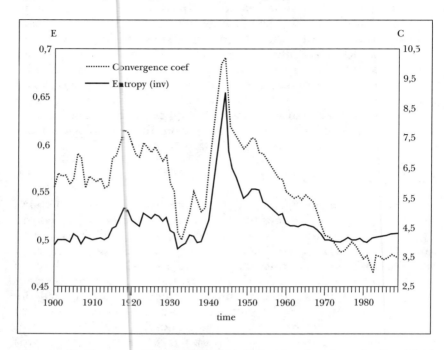

SOURCE: B. Verspagen, *Uneven Growth between Interdependent Economies* (Brookfield, Vt.: Avebury, 1993), 98–99. Reprinted with the permission of the publisher.
NOTE: The convergence coefficient (C) is the mean value across countries of the percentage deviation from the frontier (which is defined as the sample maximum of per capita GDP, which is equal to the USA value for most of the period). C is directly proportional to the degree of convergence.

The inverse of the Theil Entropy coefficient for GDP (E) indicates divergence. E is inversely proportional to the degree of divergence.

These statistics are for 16 industrialized nations.

mance across nations, summarized in Table 1-1, suggests the following conclusions, which refute both neoclassical optimism and the Marxist vision of uneven development and may reflect the character of international regimes or the features of dominant production systems.

Having the prerequisites, or *potential*, for catching up is not sufficient condition for actually growing as fast or faster than the leading country. Within the same international regime, depending on past legacies in infrastructure, health, education, and so forth, the actual strategies implemented by firms and government, a society may or may not benefit from relative backwardness.

We need to define *social capability*, for convergence is not mechanical and automatic, but results from deliberate attempts to copy and adapt technologies, organizations, and processes invented elsewhere. Consequently, some national institutions determine whether countries are among in the set of "catch-up" successes.

The convergence hypothesis can be confirmed for "the similar countries" in Baumol et al's sense.[22] When societies have the same development style and belong to the same economic area, then there is some strong probability that they will converge. The underlying speed of convergence has been estimated at around 2 percent, which means that it takes more than a quarter of century to reduce by half the initial productivity gap.[23]

But this does not mean that macroeconomic indicators are moving to complete convergence. The European Community shows the relevance of divergence, even as economies become more and more interdependent and exhibit similar productivity performances. When the Maastricht Treaty defined criteria for fiscal and monetary performance, the result was large speculative movements (Figure 1-7). Paradoxically, the objective of convergence triggered an opposite move toward divergence. The September 1992 and August 1993 financial crises ended with a quasi-collapse of the European Monetary System—one step backward in monetary integration. The convergence of industrial structures, productivity levels, and economic policy styles is a process far slower than ambitious monetary reforms. Complex interactions between economic convergence and institutional diversity and, conversely, an inadequate institutional harmonization may all induce economic divergence.

CONVERGENCE OF INSTITUTIONAL FORMS AFTER WORLD WAR II? THE PERSISTENCE OF NATIONAL SPECIFICITIES

It is possible to interpret the evidence on convergence in quite another way. For the "regulation" approaches, each epoch has a distinct institutional setting and a specific macrodynamics: long-run constancy of prices or cumulative inflation, moderate and unstable growth or stable and steadier growth.[24] Within this framework one can explain institutional convergence after 1950 as the product of the progressive

---

[22] Baumol, Blackman, and Wolff, *Productivity and American Leadership*.

[23] Mankiw et al., "A Contribution to the Empires of Economic Growth"; Barro, "Economic Growth."

[24] M. Aglietta, *Regulation and Crisis of Capitalism* (New York: Monthly Review Press, 1982); Robert Boyer, *The Search for Labour Market Flexibility* (Oxford, Clarendon, 1988); J. Mazier, M. Basle, and J. Vidal, *Quand les crises durent*, 2d ed. (Paris: Economica, 1993); A. Lipietz, *The Magic World from Value to Inflation* (London: Verso, 1985).

Table 1-1. Does productivity converge? A brief survey

Authors	Selection of countries	Periods	Convergence	Divergence	Comments
M. Abramovitz, "Catching Up, Forging Ahead, and Falling Behind," *Journal of Economic History* 46 (1986): 385–406.	16 industrialized countries	1870–1979	Coefficient of variation of productivity level has decreased	—	The potential for catching up requires social capacity to absorb more advanced technologies
W. Baumol, "Productivity Growth, Convergence, and Welfare: What the Long-Run Data Show," *American Economic Review* 76 (1986): 1072–85.	16 industrialized countries	1870–1979	The growth rate is inversely related to initial levels	—	Presumption of convergence
J. Bradford Delong, "Productivity Growth, Convergence, and Welfare: Comment," *American Economic Review* 78 (1988): 1138–54.	22 "once-rich" countries based upon their status in 1870	1870–1979	No clear tendency	No clear tendency	Convergence might be limited to a small group of countries
W. Baumol, S. Blackman and E. Wolff, *Productivity and American Leadership: The Long View* (Cambridge: MIT Press, 1989).	1. Seven industrialized countries	1870–1979	Total factor productive coefficient of variation has declined	—	Convergence among a club of select countries
	2. Top 11 industrialized countries in 1870	1830–1913		GNP per capita coefficient of variation has increased	Divergence was associated with early industrialization
	3. 124 countries—no special selection noted	1965–80	Convergence among clubs of similar countries	Divergence for LDCs	Poor countries lack education and adequate social arrangements
N. Mankiw, D. Romer, and D. Weil, "A Contribution to the Empires of Economic Growth," *Quarterly Journal of Economics*, May 1992: 407–38.	98 non-oil-exporting countries	1960–85	Within OECD countries, catching up exists	Positive correlation between productivity levels and rates	Convergence is not general even for contemporary period

D. Cohen, *Tests of the Convergence Hypothesis: A Critical Note* (Paris: CEPREMAP, 1992).	100 countries	1960–85	Slow convergence but moving target		Convergence is a partial explanatory variable
J. Bradford Delong and L. Summers, "Equipment Investment and Economic Growth," *Quarterly Journal of Economics* 106 (1991): 445–502.	61 countries—no special selection noted	1960–85	Up to investment strategy	If too low investment	Investment is a privileged means for spurring growth
B. Verspagen, "A New Empirical Approach to Catching Up or Falling Behind," *Structural Change and Economic Dynamics* 2 (1991): 359–80.	114 countries—no special selection noted	1960–85	If the technological gap is small enough	If the initial gap is too large	Convergence is not general
B. Verspagen, *Uneven Growth between Interdependent Economies* (Brookfield, Vt.: Avebury, 1993).	114 countries—no special selection noted	1960–88	Only for developed and newly industrialized countries	For most African countries	Existence of a dividing line between catching up and falling behind
B. Amable, "Catch-Up and Convergence: A Model of Cumulative Growth," *International Review of Applied Economics* 7 (1993): 1–25.	59 countries—no special selection noted	1960–85	Only if sufficient investment in education	Divergence is possible and observed	Convergence is an oversimplification of limited relevance (some strategies, some countries)

diffusion of Fordism from America to Europe and Japan.[25] When a regulation regime enters into crisis, it would, then, trigger a period of institutional flux and experimentation that might for some time at least produce the impression of divergent development.

The Fordist Era of Economic Convergence

The impressive growth after 1950 among developed countries (see Figure 1-2) reflected not only acceleration and catch-up after interwar stagnation and wartime destruction but also the workings of a genuine development pattern, the core of which lies in capital and labor institutions. Large industrial firms advanced the division of labor with wide use of specialized equipment along with a standardization of mass-produced goods. A "social pact" linked workers and managers. The former accepted managerial authority and an unprecedented division of labor; the latter agreed to increase wages based on prices and productivity. This compromise was elaborated in a dense web of interdependent institutions: welfare, collective bargaining, accommodating monetary policy, investment or intervention by the state in education, health, and transport.

The Bretton Woods system and the Marshall Plan created a facilitating international regime and an incentive for European countries and Japan to follow the American track of mass production and consumption. Contrary to the initial expectations that the reconstruction would end with stagnation and unstability, all these transformations in the relationships between states and markets sustained a genuine growth regime and development mode. Overall, most OECD countries moved along the same path. At first, the American way of producing and living served as a model. Managers, civil servants, unionists, and politicians visited the United States to observe Fordism at work. The common model, as well as the common challenge of how to launch mass production after war destruction and limited financial resources, may have induced homogenization in the political and social structures inherited from the past.

This may explain the unprecedented convergence across nations and among regions within the same national economy.[26] Considered in isolation, neither technological change and organizational innovation, nor the conceptual revolution of Keynesianism would have been sufficient to propel such a drastic shift in "regulation" mechanisms. The rather miraculous mix of pax Americana, credit, Fordist capital

---

[25] J. Mistral, "Régime international et trajectoires nationales," in Robert Boyer, ed., *Capitalismes fin de siècle* (Paris: PUF, 1986).
[26] Barro and Sala-I-Martin, "Convergence across States and Regions."

and labor compromise, oligopolistic competition, and structural and cyclical state interventions together created the Fordist growth regime.

Different countries embedded the Fordist system in different institutional constellations. The monetary regime is not the same in Germany and in France because of the role of the central state. Antitrust laws like those in the United States have no equivalent in Germany or in Japan, which has a more explicit system of oligopolistic competition. As a result, the macrodynamics of credit and interest rates, price formation, and profit and investment differ across major OECD countries. The same external shocks (oil prices, interest rates, or the uncertainties at the end of the Gulf War) do not produce the same sectoral adjustments or the same macroeconomic pattern.

Persisting national specificities in basic institutional forms are rather easy to see in the capital–labor relation. France and the United States follow a rather typical Fordist path, with strong separation between conception and production tasks, quite adversarial industrial relations, and indexation of nominal wages to past inflation and expected productivity increases. Austria and Sweden accommodate Fordist methods within a highly developed social democratic state that orchestrates labor mobility, active employment policies, and large training and retraining efforts. Industrial relations are very centralized, and consequently wage bargaining shows great sensitivity to external competitiveness and unemployment. West Germany and Japan mix the Fordist principles with a long tradition of highly skilled labor and competition via quality and differentiation, and they accompany mass production with larger product differentiation. Japan shows how an imported model of technology and industrial organization are gradually incorporated and transformed. After several decades of a continuous adjustment to local conditions, the industrial relations, and the productive system, an original "regulation" mode emerged. The imperfect Fordism of the 1950s transformed itself into a flex-Fordism in the 1970s and finally into "Toyotaism," with its distinctive capital–labor relations, job tenure, continuous learning by doing, bonus payment, and a strong segmentation of labor markets.[27] Germany, too, has distinctive patterns. Its rich institutional setting enhanced quality and skills different both from those found in U.S. Fordism and Toyotaism. The United Kingdom has followed still another trajectory. Given an early industrialization and stratification of industrial relations along skills, local bargaining, and a highly conflictual bargaining

[27] Robert Boyer, "Rapport salarial et régime d'accumulation au Japon: Émergence, originalités et prospective: Premiers jalons," *Mondes en développement* 20, no. 79/80 (1992): 1–28; and B. Coriat, *Penser à l'envers* (Paris: Bourgeois, 1991).

process, the introduction of mass production of standardized products has always been difficult.

To summarize, the mesh between political and social interests on one side and economic strategies on the other makes the capital–labor relations, and by extension most other institutional forms, very dependent on localized interactions. Such institutions change mainly by marginal adaptations of the repertoire of existing coordinating mechanisms. For instance, both France and the United States exhibit a strong Fordist inertia precisely because both societies have developed an extensive set of institutions (credit markets, education system, labor laws, and so forth) designed for mass production of standardized goods.

CONVERGENCE THEORY REVISITED

Mechanisms to Best Practice Convergence

What are the mechanisms through which convergence to "best practice" might emerge? We identify several. First, even isolated social and economic systems might converge toward the same organization if they find, by chance or necessity, the same solution to common internal problems. For example, mass production systems need particular kinds of transportation, technical training, the nature of innovation, and even state intervention. In other words, facing the same problems and opportunities, national economies could finally find the same steady state and institutional arrangements after trial-and-error experimentation, even in the absence of external competition.

Other mechanisms depend on the diffusion of science, technology, and institutional "best practices." If technological determinism prevailed, every firm would tend to adopt the same industrial organization and benefit from identical productivity levels. Managers as well as governments might try to imitate best practices in institutional and organizational innovations. International consulting firms or international bodies may diffuse the same business principles and economic policies across national borders. Scientific management, for example, spread in that way, as did the U.S. mass production after World War II, quite independently of any direct pressure from product or factor competition.

Finally, other mechanisms are initiated by transnational corporations or multinational authorities who define and enforce rules of the game within a given international regime. Such mechanisms of convergence do not rely on anonymous forms of market competition but are power relations, whether they are based on economic resources (transnational corporations) or mainly political (multinational authorities)—for instance the GATT or bilateral agreements such as the Structural Impediment Initiative (SII) between Japan and the United States. These two mechanisms are not equivalent: transnational corporations usually export their best practices and thus promote a convergence toward higher efficiency. International agreements may, on the contrary, impose an economic order favorable to the leading partner and in some cases restrict efficiency.

Evaluation of Best Practice Convergence Mechanisms

In a sense none of these mechanisms are self-implementing, and they have uncertain and varied effects according to the historical context and the precise configuration of market competition, technology innovation, the degree and nature of internationalization, or the nature of national problems and the ability to diffuse new ideas, property rights, and innovations. A brief comparison of the evolution of old industrialized countries after World War II reveals the relative frequency and intensity of the seven convergence mechanisms (see Table 1-2).

Evidence suggests that until the 1970s convergence proceeded slowly, with many reverses and with many examples of divergence. But some argue that the new constraints and opportunities provided by globalization trends are accelerating convergence. Globalization of the international economy is the first premise, the argument going that financial deregulation and innovation have destroyed the national borders for credit and that firms, at least the larger ones, have equal access to finance. Similarly, modern technologies are so complex and so capital intensive, that only transnational partnerships are able to monitor innovations. The product markets themselves, which used to be segmented according to national borders, are assumed to become more and more global. The limiting case would be of a totally transnational economy without any residual disparities across countries.

The second hypothesis builds on the first one and assumes that costs and prices˙will tend toward the same equilibrium level once transportation costs and exchange are taken into account. Firms would be literally squeezed by the pure and perfect competition operating on both product and factor markets.

The third hypothesis is that everywhere firms facing the same optimizing problems find the same solution in terms of technology, markets, and products, for there is one best way of organizing production—a single optimum among a possible multiplicity of local optima.

Table 1-2. The relative frequency and intensity of convergence mechanisms after World War II

Mechanisms	Type of mechanisms	Mode of transmission	Frequency	Intensity	Impact upon the initial gap
1. Internal common trends	Facing the same constraints and problems, each unit follows the same path	Cognitivist and immaterial	Rather high	Variable across countries	Does not imply convergence but a succession of common stages[a]
2. International competition on Products	Creative destruction	External trade	Increasing	Uneven across sectors	May imply destruction of obsolete institutional forms not necessarily their convergence
Labor	Impact on wage and technical change	Immigration	Low or moderate	Quite indirect effect	Not clear: both convergence and divergence
Finance	Impact on investment	International markets	Rising with deregulation	Possibly strong	May help to converge but from a limited range of countries
3. Globalization of technology	Organizations would follow technical change	Either public knowledge or private appropriation by firms	Significant and increasing	Varies across sectors	Convergence if public knowledge. Divergence if private appropriability

4. Imitation of best practices	Learning by copying	Personal contacts, technical literature	Rather frequent, but sometimes difficult	Growing through time	Should narrow the gap, if social capabilities exist to absorb more advanced technologies[b]
5. Power of ideas Thinkers of the past	Convincing decision makers	Cognitivist and immaterial	Significant discontinuities	Could be more important than is usually considered	Possibly important for economic policy,[c] more problematic for productive system
Experts	Paying for institutional redesign				
6. Transnational corporation	Exploitation of national disparities	Direct foreign investment, trade, and technology	Few but powerful	From enclaves to embryo for institutional redesign	Help to converge if favorable initial conditions, widen gap in others
7. Harmonization by multinational authorities	Negotiation and then coercion	Political and legal apparatus	Rather low, because of intrinsic difficulties	Potentially strong if limited scope and/or duration	Theoretically helps to institutionalize convergence at the possible cost of economic convergence

[a] W. Rostow, The Stages of Economic Growth: A Non-Communist Manifesto (Cambridge: Cambridge University Press, 1960).
[b] M. Abramovitz, "Catching Up, Forging Ahead, and Falling Behind," Journal of Economic History 46 (1986): 385–406.
[c] P. Hall, Political Power of Economic Ideas: Keynesianism across Nations (Princeton: Princeton University Press, 1989).

If this is observed for each product and sector, the best organizational forms would finally prevail whatever the localization and by aggregation, the macroeconomic evolutions would tend toward the convergence of productivity and of standard of living levels.

This syllogism that equates globalization with convergence is logically flawed, and its premises may not correspond to the current state of the world economy. Given the same stylized facts, a totally different conclusion can be reached. Internationalization and globalization are hardly complete. Even if interest rates are synchronized internationally, relative levels depend on the national styles in monetary policy and the adjustment of savings and investment. National saving rates and investment rates are still strongly correlated, which implies the importance of national boundaries. Similarly, labor mobility has not equalized wages by skills. Wage levels and hierarchies are still shaped by national institutional forms, skill formation, and social values. Thus, the choice in organization and technologies will continue to depend on national legacies.

The second hypothesis about the competition in product markets is not usually fulfilled: the same product may be sold for different prices in every national market, according to the local conditions for competition. For instance, in the car industry the same product exhibits impressive price disparities with the structural competitiveness of local producers: low and competitive prices in small countries without any national car maker, higher and oligopolistic prices if the domestic producers are lagging with respect to leading producers. Competition remains largely imperfect and firms still search out niches, thus introducing possible differentiation even if production and trade are more and more international. The second pillar of convergence theory is therefore shaky: each niche may call for specific organizational forms and deliver unequal productivity levels.

The third hypothesis can be challenged, too. Technology is not a private commodity or a pure public good, so its efficient use assumes tacit knowledge or learning effects. Thus, the one best way is not necessarily available to all producers because only the leading ones, who possess sufficient past experience, can benefit from the best practices. When imperfect competition on product markets is combined with tacit knowledge for technologies, then several productive configurations may coexist even over the long run. Some simple models in industrial analysis confirm such a possibility.[28] It may be that the actual state of the international system is closer to a series of national oligopolistic markets than to a unified world market.

[28] H. C. White, "Where Do Markets Come From?," *American Journal of Sociology* 87, no. 3 (1981): 517–47.

The same argument can be made more general by using evolutionary theory. Conventionally, competition is supposed to drive out of business the more archaic and inefficient firms, whereas the most successful innovations are imitated by a cohort of followers who finally converge toward the one best way. Empirical studies of the dynamics of industrial organization do not confirm this hypothesis, as contrasted firm organizations, technologies, and capital–labor relations usually coexist within the same precisely defined sector, even in the long run. Recent advances in the modeling of evolutionary process have delivered configurations with punctuated equilibria, such as the long-run coexistence of various species for biology: various norms and organizations for social sciences. More than one solution can be given to the same problem, a feature quite common in the history of technologies and frequently observed for economic organizations. For example, consider the alternatives to Fordism. The emerging principles, such as mass production of differentiated and high-quality goods, call for a richer skill spectrum than standardized production. But given the embeddedness of education and training in each national culture, international comparisons suggest the existence of at least three distinct national models of skill formation. (See Chapter 5 in this volume.) The German occupational model emphasizes broad skills for each employee, with overlapping technical competences. In the Japanese large firms the skills are generated by internal mobility among various tasks within the firms and are largely specific to each large company. In the United States an emerging model is building skills around teamwork, but the rotation of workers is less significant than in the Japanese model and the incentives are quite different.

In both cases the firms and sectors are clearly integrated within the international economy and, nevertheless, display very different institutional forms to cope with the same challenge of structural competitiveness. Even if the economic performances are quite similar, there is no one best way. Furthermore, evolutionary approaches remind us that the success is not warranted and that failure, such as relative decline or bankruptcy, are other possibilities for coping with competitiveness. Therefore, the convergence within the club of the surviving happy few is paid by the cost of destruction of inadequate institutional forms—in other words, a kind of diverging pattern.

International Specialization and the Persistence of National Styles in Institution Building

International trade theory usually concludes that factor incomes will converge as soon as products are freely exchanged internationally. But this does not imply that the same institutional arrange-

Figure 1-5. National institutional diversity

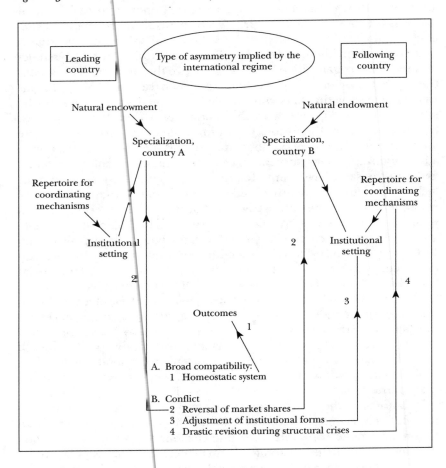

ments will be observed across countries, quite to the contrary. Imagine, for example, that a leading country is facing a follower that initially exhibits a different specialization (Figure 1-5). Basically, each country is selecting its specialization by the interaction of natural endowment, the repertoire of coordinating mechanisms, and the compatibility with the competition implied by the international regime. The architecture may display four configurations.

The first one is homeostatic equilibrium, an approximate long-run stability in specialization, industrial structures, and the nature of coordinating mechanisms. This homeostatic system does not depend on factors central to convergence. Each OECD country may, for example, specialize in sectors that are the more efficiently run by the prevailing institutional setting. The Japanese economy might specialize in consumer goods (electronics and cars); the United States in software, information, and basic science; the British in chemicals and pharmaceuticals; the German in high-quality equipment goods. In each case the countries are using at their best the coordination gains typical of their national repertoire: the large firm and its subcontractors in Japan, the excellence of university research for the United States and the United Kingdom, the richness and quality of skills for Germany. In this punctuated equilibrium convergence would be the exception, not the rule.

The second configuration, the reversal of market shares, that is, shrinking for the less efficient countries and growth for the leading ones, is another mechanism in which a series of natural endowments and constructed competitive advantages are linked to the opportunities and constraints of the prevailing institutional setting. For instance, the contemporary evolution of market shares for the car industries and consumer electronics between the United States, Japan, and Asian NICs seems to fit with this mechanism. The diversity of institutions is preserved, but the relative efficiency of national economies is continuously adjusted.

But firms, business associations, or governments may react if the current economic trends hurt the welfare of the community by reducing production, employment, and/or living standards. They may try to build new institutions, to mix the various ingredients extracted from the national repertoire of coordinating mechanisms. For instance, given the weaknesses of private entrepreneurship in France, state agencies may promote special R&D programs to promote technological innovation. The Direction Générale des Télécommunications that initiated Minitel, a home-based computer network, would thus be the functional equivalent of the American Silicon Valley start-ups. Similarly, in the 1980s the British government widely opened the car and electronics industries to Japanese transplants in order to try to build a new industrial configuration, strengthening some key features of British evolutions (the search for regional autonomy), weakening others (closed shop unionization).

A third exception to convergence theory, adjustment of institutional forms, relates to the impact of European integration. The countries that traditionally had strong regional economies and political organizations have converted this inherited advantage into a new bargaining power at Brussels via clever lobbying about the use of European structural funds. The new emerging productive model gives a new opportunity to regional economies. Old norms and social values are manufactured again into new institutional forms and sources for external competitiveness.

The fourth configuration, drastic revisions during structural crises, is quite exceptional, indeed, because it emerges when all the previous adjustment processes by market shares and the redesign of institutional forms fail. Adverse economic trends and acute social or political crises usually trigger the search for more drastic reforms in order to expand the scope and variety of coordinating mechanisms that would cope with external competitiveness and maintain a minimal social cohesiveness within the given community. "Régulation" approaches label these episodes structural crises, when the issue at stake is the redesign of institutional forms and the "regulation" modes. An example is the great depression at the end of the last century and during the interwar. The trial-and-error process, by nature quite uncertain, is very different from the smooth convergence toward a well-known growth regime. During the 1990s, the major political crisis in Italy gives a good example of a tentative complete redesign in institutional forms in order to cope with the challenge of European integration. To conclude, it is clear that the convergence hypothesis is quite challenged by these approaches.

Two Visions in Institution Building: Implications of Convergence

The issue is far more general than focused on just economic or institutional convergence and relates to alternative visions for the logic, origins, functioning, and evolution of institutions. For neoclassical theorists rational economic agents try to design optimal coordinating mechanisms (i.e., efficiency preserving or welfare enhancing). These mechanisms may result from bargaining, minimizing transaction costs, or designing by a principal of an incomplete contract to monitor a subordinate agent. Decentralized innovations prove their viability by competing efficiently on product and factor markets. If the coordinating mechanism is Pareto efficient, all other agents will have interest in adopting it; on the contrary, the agents sticking to the old mechanisms will grow slower and eventually be driven out of business. Thus, the emergence, diffusion, and maturation of institutions are the intended or unintended outcome of competition between alternative institutions.

As a consequence, the convergence toward the "best" institution is generally warranted, provided that sufficient freedom is given to economic agents and that competition prevails. Hence, according to a quite optimistic vision of how economic arrangements are reformed and transformed, a smooth process in the evolution of institutions takes place. But however intuitive and appealing, this approach is not devoid of major flaws.

First, a unique equilibrium is not warranted: the multiplicity of equilibria in an institutionally rich economy is the rule, not the exception. Every economy can be stuck into a specific local equilibrium, without any clear mechanism for convergence, unless strong institutional mimetism prevails. Second, the transition toward a superior institution can be blocked by all the sunk costs associated with the old institutions. Even in the simplest coordination game, this pathology is quite common and the problems are still worse when agents have conflicting interests. Third, neoclassical theory assumes a quasi-divisibility of microinstitutions, which can be added in order to design a complete architecture. This divisibility principle is severely challenged by recent advances in comparative analyses: a monetary regime has to be coherent with an international system, a form of competition, and eventually a capital–labor compromise. Partners in the current discussions about a European central bank modeled on the Bundesbank recognize this social coherence: without many other closely related institutions present in the German system independence is not an insurance against inflation. Moreover, efficiency is not the key objective of many social institutions: defining the respective power and role of factors, stabilizing actors' expectations, and organizing social interactions come first. Market and system competition takes place afterward—and after assessing the relative efficiency of a complete architecture of generally interdependent institutions.

All these criticisms may be the starting point of an alternative vision. First, the economic rationale of institutions cannot be isolated from political and social contexts: the rationality of *homo oeconomicus* describes only a limited, even if increasing, fraction of human behavior. Thus the analysis has to delineate the domain in which actors interact, to provide a full description of their objectives and constraints, without an a priori restriction to either pure economic factors or political ones. Note that this extension of conventional rational choice theory strengthens the specificity of each problem and makes rationality context dependent. Thus institutional convergence is less likely, because many idiosyncratic complementarities permeate the whole system.

A second difference relates to the origins of institutions. Institutions are not designed uniquely to solve an efficiency problem or fulfill social objectives, but in most cases they are the unintended consequences of the pursuit of strategic advantage by unequal agents.

Figure 1-6. Convergence or divergence of institutional forms?

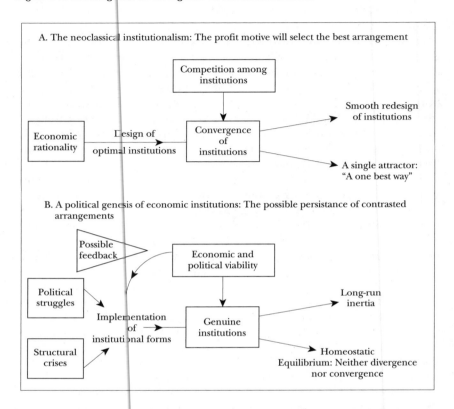

A. The neoclassical institutionalism: The profit motive will select the best arrangement

Competition among institutions

Economic rationality

Design of optimal institutions

Convergence of institutions

Smooth redesign of institutions

A single attractor: "A one best way"

B. A political genesis of economic institutions: The possible persistance of contrasted arrangements

Possible feedback

Economic and political viability

Political struggles

Implementation of institutional forms

Genuine institutions

Structural crises

Long-run inertia

Homeostatic Equilibrium: Neither divergence nor convergence

Consequently the asymmetry of power has definite consequences on the design of institutions, which only rarely enhance efficiency.[29] Thus political struggles and/or structural crises usually play a role in the invention, implementation, and the legitimation of institutional forms: this is not an accident but the very outcome of the power relations implied by any institution, in any sphere, political as well as economical (Figure 1-6).

The medium or long-run inertia of institutions is not an oddity or exception to rationality and efficiency, but it expresses the very nature of social relationships and rules of the game. Moreover, and more generally, the concept of homeostatic equilibrium describes this compatibility of an institutional architecture and the economic dynamics it generates. In such an evolutionary model, convergence or divergence

[29] J. Knight, *Institutions and Social Conflict* (Cambridge: Cambridge University Press, 1992).

are only specific cases among a large variety of other evolutions, such as partial catch-up and then collapse, autonomous evolution, catch-up and forging ahead.

Therefore convergence is not the natural "outcome" of a quite general mechanism, but the consequence of the ex post complementarity of mechanisms with unintended properties. The convergence of some components of an institutional organization may strengthen the diverging path of other institutions. For instance, financial liberalization does not necessarily lead to the convergence of more and more aspects of national regulatory regimes. In Japan during the 1980s allowing the large firms to enter into the international credit market might have produced extra profits that could then have been used to strengthen both the efficiency and the specificity of Japanese industrial organization. But, of course, in the long run this may challenge the inner stability of the large Japanese corporation. For example, because of the interlocking of corporate assets and the role of the main bank, a complete financial liberalization could destabilize the job tenure that used to prevail.[30]

PARADOXES OF CONVERGENCE THEORY: STILL THE CENTURY OF NATIONS?

Much evidence supports convergence theory: the collapse of Soviet economic regimes and the switch of their elites to markets and democracy; the erosion and structural crisis of the Swedish model; the aborted French experience of a socialist strategy out of the current crisis; the surge of Asian dragons and their impressive technological achievements; the ambition of the Maastricht Treaty to promote a fast track to real convergence via monetary integration.

But statistical evidence does not confirm any general and secular trend toward economic convergence in productivity levels and standards of living. Such convergence is restricted to the small club of nations that have been able to invest sufficiently in productive investment, infrastructure, and education. The poorest countries (for example, in Africa) have been left out of the process of economic development. Even within developed or rich countries, the long-run evolutions of Great Britain and Argentina remind us that relative or absolute decline is always a possibility and that convergence is never automatic but is associated with the choice and implementation of an

---

[30] M. Aoki, "Decentralization-Centralization in Japanese Organization: A Duality Principle," in S. Kumon and H. Rosovsky, eds., *The Political Economy of Japan*, vol. 3 (Stanford: Stanford University Press, 1992).

adequate strategy, given a changing international regime and radical changes in technological innovation.

Such conflicting views and this opposition between naive and academic representations deserve explanation. First, the idea of a single, one best way is very intuitive indeed and seems to fit with textbook neoclassical theory: if all technologies could be mastered without any cost, if institutions were totally divisible and their choice independent one from another, then economic convergence would be the rule. Note, nevertheless, that very different institutional arrangement can be imagined to solve the same economic challenge. This is precisely the strong advantage of an alternative vision. For evolutionary theory globalization is far from complete, and consequently each national economy is facing a specific system of industrial relations, money and credit, education training, and state intervention. Still more firms do not adapt passively to a given price system, but they try to discover niches more or less insulated by oligopolistic competition.

Within such a vision there may exist a multiplicity of punctuated equilibria as opposed to a single one. The simple dynamics of convergence is only one out of many other evolutions: cumulative divergence, catch-up and collapse, catch-up and then forging ahead, partial convergence and then stabilization of the productivity gap. So, the simplicity, however largely erroneous, of convergence theory is usually preferred to the complexity of evolutionary models, which nevertheless are richer and fit better with empirical evidence about long-run capitalist growth and the coexistence of contrasted national trajectories.

How to explain common belief in convergence theory? In fact, the model that is thought to be the reference point of convergence changes, either periodically or during critical episodes. In the 1990s interest in convergence theory has re-emerged precisely because the Japanese productive system and "regulation" mode are viewed as an alternative to the previous model, the American mass-production system. During such a period, because no natural law is driving convergence, the very model held up as an object of emulation and imitation is usually chosen through a political process, not only by following the evolution of the market. Which model is chosen has an important impact on the probability of convergence. If nowadays so many firms and governments want to imitate and adopt the so-called Japanese methods, this is less a proof for an invisible convergence and a Japanization of the world than an evidence of a drastic change in the model to be emulated. This triggers a process of trials and errors that may end up in a consolidation of past national trajectories.

Growth patterns after World War II may seem more favorable to the convergence thesis but do not contradict this broad interpretation. Even if internationalization is now more extended, there is no strong reason to believe that the national flavor for institution building will vanish and be replaced by the diffusion of Japanese methods. Even managers translate some of Toyota's productive methods, but who would dare to transpose all the idiosyncrasies of the Japanese society?

The 1990s and the next century, too, are likely to be still the epoch of nations. The complex set of contradictory forces that are pushing simultaneously toward convergence and divergence are far from moving toward a single best institutional design. This hypothesis has proven to be erroneous and obsolete in industrial organization. Would it not be ironic if social scientists adopted such a simplistic hypothesis at the very moment when the process of trial and error is more uncertain than ever in Europe, North America, and Japan? The shakiness of convergence theory is well evidenced by the answer to a falsely simple question: who knows toward which system Russia, Poland, or even Germany might converge over the next century?

CHAPTER TWO

Globalization and Its Limits: Reports of the Death of the National Economy are Greatly Exaggerated

ROBERT WADE

"The nation-state is just about through as an economic unit," announced Charles Kindleberger in 1969. "The world is too small. It is just too easy to get about." The agent of this dramatic transformation, he said, was the international corporation. Already by the late 1960s the international corporation was the most powerful type of economic actor, more powerful than governments. The international corporation "has no country to which it owes more loyalty than any other, nor any country where it feels completely at home."[1] Its very mobility gives it power.

Kindleberger's view recycles a much older argument. Norman Angell said much the same thing in *The Great Illusion*, published in 1911.[2] The world economy had become so highly interdependent as to make national independence an anachronism, especially in financial markets, he said. The interdependence was being driven by science, technology, and economics—the "forces of modernity"; and these forces, not governments, determined international relations. Thanks to this interdependence, war between modern nations is "an impossibility," he declared shortly before World War I.

For comments on an earlier draft my thanks to Ron Dore and to Giovanni Arrighi, Paul Streeten, Adrian Wood, Ngaire Woods, Robert Boyer, Yau-su Hu, Manfred Bienefeld, Suzanne Berger, and Tyler Cowen. The essay was written at the Institute for Advanced Study, Princeton.
[1] Charles Kindleberger, *American Business Abroad* (New Haven: Yale University Press, 1969), pp. 207, 208, 182. Harry Johnson later made the same point in *Technology and Economic Interdependence* (London: Macmillan, 1975).
[2] Norman Angell, *The Great Illusion* (New York: G. P. Putnam's Sons, 1911).

Angell himself echoed writers of the mid-nineteenth century who "looked forward to a single, more or less standardized world where all governments would acknowledge the truths of political economy and liberalism would be carried throughout the globe by impersonal missionaries more powerful than those of Christianity or Islam had ever been; a world reshaped in the image of the bourgeoisie, perhaps even one from which, eventually, national differences would disappear."[3]

Since the mid-1970s a torrent of literature along the same lines has been pouring out. "Globalization" is the buzz word. We are now in a "globalized" era characterized by an unprecedentedly high level of integration of national economies, it is said. This integration is itself a reflection of the greatly increased mobility of finance, physical capital, and even labor across the entire world.[4] Because of this mobility, "firms all over the world [now face] a common market for products and factors."[5] In these conditions government attempts to shape the national economy's evolution are about as effective as pushing on a piece of string.

I urge skepticism. The world economy is more inter-national than global. In the bigger national economies, more than 80 percent of production is for domestic consumption and more than 80 percent of investment by domestic investors. Companies are rooted in national home bases with national regulatory regimes. Populations are much less mobile across borders than are goods, finance, or ideas. These points suggest more scope for government actions to boost the productivity of firms operating within their territory than is commonly thought and than is implied in the statement that "governments today should do [à propos direct support to industry] what they find most difficult to do: nothing!"[6]

[3] E. J. Hobsbawm, *The Age of Capital* (London: Weidenfeld and Nicolson, 1977), p. 83.

[4] "The Stateless Corporation," *Business Week*, 14 May 1990. See also Robert Reich, *The Work of Nations* (New York: Knopf, 1991); Kenichi Ohmae, *The Borderless World* (New York: Harper, 1993); Paul Kennedy, "Preparing for the 21st Century: Winners and Losers," *New York Review of Books*, 11 February 1993. For arguments from a left-wing perspective that also accept the reality of full-blown globalization as the dominant process in the world economy, see Manfred Bienefeld, "Capitalism and the nation-state in the dog days of the twentieth century," *Socialist Register* 30 (1994): 94–129; and "On Transformational Growth: Edward J. Nell Interviewed by Steven Pressman," *Journal of Political Economy* 6 (1994): 107–32. David Gordon gives an alternative view from the left in "The Global Economy: New Edifice or Crumbling Foundations?," *New Left Review* 68 (1988): 24–64.

[5] Richard Nelson and Gavin Wright, "The Rise and Fall of American Technological Leadership: The Postwar Era in Historical Perspective," *Journal of Economic Literature* vol. 30, no. 4 (December 1992).

[6] Richard Brown and DeAnne Julius, "Is Manufacturing Still Special in the New World Order?," first prize 1993 Amex Bank Review awards, summarized in *The Amex Bank Review* 20, no. 9 (1993).

First I present some evidence in favor of the globalization picture and then show how the picture changes when further evidence is introduced. Indeed, I stress throughout the paper the hazards of mounting exalted generalizations about the nature of the world economy or the economic significance of nation-states, so mixed is the evidence and so disputable the meaning of any piece of it.

GLOBALIZATION OF PRODUCTION AND FINANCE: EVIDENCE IN FAVOR

If we take the textbook model of national economies as sets of immobile factors of production (capital, labor, and land) and of "uninational" firms connected across borders only through the sale and purchase of mobile goods and services, then the current world economy is obviously more interconnected than that. Or to take another standard, it is certainly more interconnected today than in 1960. At the micro level a higher proportion of firms now have operations in many more countries than before; a higher percentage of total value added is produced by firms outside their home country; and any one firm faces more foreign-based competitors, both at home and abroad. At the macro level national economies are much more integrated through trade and foreign direct investment than in 1960. National borders are consequently more permeable, what happens in one country's markets is affected more by what happens in other countries', international competition has therefore become more intense, uncertainty has increased, and the "global" dimension of national economic policymaking has become more important.

For example, interconnectedness through trade has vastly increased since 1960. Among the OECD economies (the richest 24 industrial economies), the ratio of exports to GDP roughly doubled from 1960 to 1990, rising from 9.5 percent in 1960 to 20.5 percent in 1990.[7] At the world level, trade has consistently grown faster than output, implying rising interconnectedness. From 1965 to 1990 world merchandise trade grew at an average of one and a half times the rate of growth of world GDP.[8] So an increasing proportion of production from each national economy is for foreign markets, which raises the importance of foreign markets relative to domestic markets and so makes a country's relative income more dependent on the ability of its

[7] *OECD National Accounts (Main Aggregates), 1960–1990*, vol. 1 (Paris: OECD, 1992), using 1985 exchange rates and prices.
[8] World Bank, *World Development Report, 1992* (Washington, D.C.: World Bank, 1992), World Tables, tables 2 and 14.

firms to compete against imports in domestic markets and against other producers in foreign markets.

Interconnectedness through foreign direct investment (FDI) has grown even faster than through trade over the 1980s. Measured FDI flows grew three times faster than trade flows and almost four times faster than output. Between 1983 and 1990 they averaged 27 percent a year, quadrupling over the decade.[9] In addition to FDI, joint ventures, nonequity corporate alliances, and subcontracting between firms located in different countries blossomed during the 1980s.[10] Many firms are now involved in complex international networks covering all areas of their operations (research, production, and marketing), as they were not in 1960. Even German and Japanese firms have begun to shift production out of their home bases, having been unusually concentrated at home until the 1980s.

Most large industrial and financial corporations are now multinational in the sense of holding some of their productive assets abroad, and this is a real change from 1960. In the United Kingdom, for example, 20 percent of the country's largest multinational corporations (MNCs) had foreign subsidiaries in more than 20 countries in 1963; only seven years later, in 1970, the figure had jumped to 70 percent, where it has subsequently remained.[11] On a world scale, more than a third of the employment and nearly a third of the sales of the world's sixty-eight largest manufacturing corporations in the mid-1980s was accounted for by their foreign subsidiaries. One estimate says that all MNCs now control a *third* of the world's private sector productive assets.[12] In terms of their domestic sales and income they control more than 30 percent of private GNP in Germany, France, Italy, the United Kingdom, Netherlands, Belgium, Switzerland, Canada, Australia and more than 20 percent for Japan and the United States. These figures have been rising since the mid-eighties.[13]

These trends have made for at least two basic changes in the nature

[9] Nominal flows in U.S. dollars. United Nations, *World Investment Report* (New York: United Nations, 1992), p. 1.

[10] David Levy, "International Production and Sourcing: Trends and Issues," *STI Review*, no. 13 (December 1993).

[11] Grazia Ietto-Gillies, "Transnational Companies and U.K. Competitiveness: Does Ownership Matter?," table 9.5, in Kirsty Hughes, ed., *The Future of U.K. Competitiveness and the Role of Industrial Policy* (London: Policy Studies Institute, 1993). The figure for 1990 was 72 percent. The number of firms was 44 in 1963, 46 in 1970, and 63 in 1990.

[12] *World Investment Report 1993: Transnational Corporations and Integrated International Production* (New York: United Nations Publications, 1993).

[13] The figure is calculated by adding the value added of foreign-based MNCs in the home economy to that of the foreign output of home-based MNCs. John Dunning, "The Global Economy and the National Governance of Economies: A Plea for a Fundamental Re-think," mimeo, 1992, p. 9.

63

and intensity of competition. On the one hand, competition is intensified by market interpenetration. In the United States, for example, the biggest U.S. firms typically faced two to five main competitors in 1960, almost all of them other U.S.-based firms playing by the same rules. Today, the firm may have ten or more serious competitors, half of them foreign, playing by different rules. On the other hand, competition is reduced by the growing importance of *intrafirm* trade. Intrafirm trade involving U.S.-based MNCs amounts to about 30 percent of U.S. exports and 18 percent of U.S. imports, whereas intrafirm trade of all MNCs, whether U.S.-based or not, accounts for about 40 percent of U.S. imports and 30 to 36 percent of U.S. exports.[14]

Given the increased multinationalization of firms' operations, we can agree with Robert Reich that the legal entity of a "U.S. corporation" (or British, or German) does not have the same consequences for American employment and economic growth as it did in the 1950s and 1960s.[15]

But the most dramatic multinationalization of all has come in finance. The stock of international bank lending (cross-border lending plus domestic lending denominated in foreign currency) rose in just ten years from 4 percent of OECD GDP in 1980 to 44 percent in 1990.[16] World turnover in foreign exchange, or currency trading, grew by over a third in just three and a half years between April 1989 and September 1992, at which time it was running at $900 billion each day. Yes, day. Altogether, liquid capital is ricocheting across the foreign exchanges in amounts more than thirty times greater than and quite independently of trade flows. In consequence governments have much less discretion about long-term interest rates than they did in 1960, when there were exchange controls, when lending by banks and other financial institutions was regulated, and when international borrowing and lending were tiny.

The development since the mid-1980s of markets in "financial derivative" contracts, which now in some sense implicate a large part of world finance, adds a new dimension of uncertainty and instability to world finance. Derivatives have proven very difficult to regulate, partly because little is known publicly about what the contracts look like. The IMF is on record as saying that we may only know the risk

[14] David Levy, "International Production and Sourcing: Trends and Issues," *STI Review*, December 1993: 13–59, table 4, figures for 1985 and 1988. Also see United Nations Centre on Transnational Corporations (UNCTC), *World Investment Report: The Triad in Foreign Direct Investment* (New York: United Nations, 1990). Figures are for 1985.
[15] Robert Reich, *The Work of Nations* (New York: Knopf, 1991).
[16] "Free Fall?" *The Economist*, 4–10 January 1992, p. 9.

characteristics of derivatives once an economic downturn begins.[17] In terms of the ability of governments to manage finance, derivatives make the power of private financial property still more absolute, because they are so difficult to regulate.

Technology, too, has become highly internationalized in the sense that companies are exploiting their technological innovations internationally. This is clear from figures on the extent to which firms protect their innovations by taking out patents in foreign markets, so as to reap benefits from trading the disembodied innovation or the exports that embody it. The share of the patents in advanced countries that have a foreign origin is large: 45 percent of the patents granted in 1990 in the United States came from abroad (in the sense that the inventor's address was outside the United States), and 45 percent of the patent applications at the European Patent Office came from outside Europe. (Japan is the big exception, where foreign patents account for only 12 percent.)[18] If we compare the proportion of foreign patents (45 percent) with the degree of import penetration (around 20 percent), we see that the internationalization of the exploitation of technology is substantially higher even than the internationalization of trade for the OECD economies.

These integrating developments are caused in large part—so goes the standard view, which I qualify below—by the new cluster of inventions whose effects began to transform many sectors of the OECD economies between the mid-1960s and the mid-1970s, in particular those that led to an astonishing cheapening and speeding of transport and telecommunications (inventions in microelectronics, new industrial materials, and lasers). At the same time, Western Europe regained economic momentum, Japan rose to fully competitive status, OECD trade barriers came down, and profit rates declined. The result was higher levels of competition in national markets, growing innovation intensity as a means of competition, and shifts of production to other OECD markets, or to some developing countries whose labor force could immediately master some of the operations required by the new manufacturing technologies.[19] Another result, which then became an intensifying cause, was the move to expand the scope of pri-

---

[17] IMF, "International Capital Markets: Developments and Prospects," *World Economic and Financial Surveys*, April 1989.

[18] Daniele Archibugi and Jonathan Michie, "The Globalization of Technology: Myths and Realities," *Research Papers in Management Studies No. 18* (Cambridge: Cambridge University, 1992–93). The U.S. figures refer to patents granted (because patents are only published once granted); the European patents refer to patent applications (because it is the applications that are published).

[19] Statistical series on real transport costs over time and on the distance and content of traded goods would confirm this; to my knowledge such series do not exist.

vate control of resource allocation, especially private power concentrated in MNCs.

GLOBALIZATION: THE QUALIFICATIONS

However, using two eyes rather than one we find evidence that the world economy is less internationalized, less integrated than this account suggests.

Trade

The share of trade in GDP is still quite small in all but the smallest countries. Exports account for 12 percent of GDP or less for the United States, Japan, and single-unit Europe,[20] and the Asian and Latin American averages are well below 10 percent. *This means that 90 percent or more of these economies consists of production for the domestic market and that 90 percent of consumption is produced at home.*

What is more, the current level of integration of national economies through trade is apparently not much higher than the level reached by 1913, after which trade integration plummeted, beginning to recover only after the World War II.[21]

World trade growth has been slowing over the 1980s and 1990s relative to output growth (the ratio fell from 1.65 in 1965–80 to 1.34 in 1980–90).[22] This slowdown is partly a function of the world economic slowdown of the 1970s and 1980s. (The average growth of GDP per head in the industrialized world fell from 3.6 percent a year in 1950–73 to 2 percent in 1973–89.)[23] But a long-term structural change is also involved, namely, the steep fall in manufacturing's share of OECD GDP (from 29 percent in the 1960s to 23 percent in the 1980s) and the rise in the share of less trade-intensive services. So we should not assume that trade integration will go on increasing as the world economy grows faster, because faster growth will accelerate the shift from manufacturing to services.

[20] Andrew Glyn and Bob Sutcliffe, "Global but Leaderless? The New Capitalist Order," *The Socialist Register* 28 (1992), figure 1. The earlier figure for exports to GDP was higher because it includes intra-European trade.

[21] To what extent does this finding reflect the dominance in 1913 of an island economy, Britain—with an island's high dependence on trade—and the subsequent precipitous fall in Britain's share of world GDP? To what extent does it reflect a bias in the trade and income statistics in the early period—accurate trade data, undercounted income?

[22] World Bank, *World Development Report, 1992* (Washington, D.C.: World Bank, 1992), World Tables, tables 2 and 14.

[23] World Bank, *World Development Report, 1991* (New York: Oxford University Press, 1991), p. 14.

Nor should we assume that intrafirm trade, hailed by many as a major new development, will go on increasing. Analysts have tended to exaggerate the significance of intrafirm trade in the world economy by extrapolating from the United States, which has the most (perhaps only) reliable statistics on it. But this is misleading because the United States has the highest share of intrafirm trade in total trade, insofar as we can judge. And note that the share of intrafirm trade in total U.S. trade showed no significant increase between 1977 and 1989, holding steady at around a third.[24] Overall, intrafirm trade is important but not dominant, and probably not rising as a share of total trade.[25]

Moreover, the trade figures show trends that are far from consistent with the picture of global economic integration. World trade is highly concentrated among the northern countries, and the concentration is rising; the rest of the world has a small and falling share. The North's share of world trade rose from 81 percent in 1970 to 84 percent in 1989. (*North* refers to "developed market economies" [virtually the same coverage as OECD], *South* to "developing countries and territories" plus "socialist countries of Asia" in the World Bank's World Development Report classifications. *South* includes the "newly industrialized countries" [NICs].) North–South trade has fallen as a proportion of the total. The share of northern imports coming from the non-oil-exporting South, excluding the four East Asian NICs, fell from 7.1 percent in 1970 to 6.2 percent in 1990.[26]

Trade by the United States with low-wage countries (those where wages are less than one-half the U.S. levels) equals only 3 percent of its GDP. This is not much higher than the equivalent figure in 1960, when Japan and some European countries were counted as low-wage countries by the same definition.

The "marginalization" of the South as a whole over the 1970s and 1980s is due largely to the *negative* growth of primary product exports for the world as a whole and for a sharp decline of the share of the South within that falling total. This development reflects both the fall in oil prices over the 1980s and a wider fall in the terms of trade for all primary product exports. Since 1980 average commodity prices have dropped by more than one-half in real terms.[27]

True, exports of manufactures from the South to the North have

---

[24] OECD, "Globalisation of Industrial Activities: Background Synthesis Report," *Directorate for Science, Technology, and Industry*, 26 November 1993, p. 16.
[25] See Sheila Page, *How Developing Countries Trade* (London: Routledge, 1994), chap. 6.
[26] UNCTAD, "Handbook of International Trade and Development Statistics, 1990" (New York: United Nations, 1991), table A1 3.4.
[27] World Bank, "Global Economic Prospects and the Developing Countries," summarized in "Poor Relations," *The Economist*, 16 April 1994, p. 118.

grown very fast over the 1970s, 1980s, and 1990s, at almost 15 percent a year from 1960 to 1990 (in constant 1980 U.S. dollars). The share of manufactures in the South's exports to the North rose from 16 percent to 53 percent between 1970 and 1989, with the increase concentrated in the 1980s, or from 23 percent of *non-fuel* exports to 71 percent between 1970 and 1989.[28] Fast-rising flows of southern manufactured exports to the North do represent a new, more globalized pattern in world trade. But this fast growth started from a very low base; and by 1989 manufactured exports from the South still accounted for only *16 percent* of world manufactured exports.[29] Indeed, several economists have argued that imports from the South cannot be a significant cause of unemployment in the North precisely because the share of the South in northern imports is too small.[30]

Moreover, the South experienced an adverse trend in its terms of trade even in manufactured exports: during the 1980s the prices of manufactured exports from the South rose slightly, but the prices of manufactured exports from the North rose four times faster.[31]

Future growth of manufactured exports from the South is in question because almost half of the South's manufactured exports go to just one market, the United States; yet, the United States has "only" 23 percent of world GNP. If and when the United States cures its balance-of-payments deficit, its imports will go down and its exports up. Perhaps the South's manufactured exports will be diverted elsewhere, or perhaps North–South trade integration will further decline.

[28] The figures are derived from UNCTAD's "Handbook of Trade and Development Statistics" by Adrian Wood, presented in *North–South Trade, Employment and Inequality: Changing Fortunes in a Skill-driven World* (Oxford, Clarendon, 1993), chap. 1, table 1.
[29] The statistics on which these direction of trade conclusions rest are in *current* exchange rates. This biases downward the *volume* of trade flows from the South, because less developed countries as a group have experienced a large depreciation of their exchange rates relative to the North since the 1960s (between 1960 and 1984, of 20 to 40 percent for low-income countries and up to 25 percent for middle-income oil-importing countries, with these figures probably having doubled by 1992). The depreciation is spread fairly evenly among geographic regions and low- and middle-income categories (except for the oil exporters in certain periods). Correcting for this effect is a difficult operation that has not been done for the sorts of disaggregations dealt with here. But in the judgment of Adrian Wood, who has wrestled with this issue at length, making the correction would not change the broad conclusions drawn. See Adrian Wood, "Global Trends in Real Exchange Rates, 1960–84," *World Development* 19, no. 4 (1991): 317–32.
[30] Richard Freeman, "Is Globalization Impoverishing Low Skill American Workers?," (unpublished paper), Economics Department, Harvard University, 1993.
[31] Keith Griffin and Azzur Rahman Khan, "Globalization and the Developing World: An Essay on the International Dimensions of Development in the Post–Cold War Era," *Human Development Report Occasional Papers* (United Nations Development Programme/ Human Development Report Office, 1992), p. 20.

The NICs account for a very small proportion of the North–South trade. The proportion of northern imports from the four Asian NICs increased from 2.2 percent in 1970 to 5.5 percent in 1990. But the share from the three Latin American NICs (Mexico, Brazil, Argentina) fell from 2.6 percent in 1970 to 2.1 percent in 1990. The NICs' share of world industrial output also remains small. The share of the East Asian four plus Mexico and Brazil rose from 2.7 percent in 1970 to 5.8 percent in 1989.[32] This change is small compared to shifts in earlier periods and hardly supports the idea of a globalizing transformation in world trade.

Moreover, North–South trade is strongly regionalized. Latin America trades predominantly with North America. Eastern Europe, Africa, and the Middle East trade predominantly with Western Europe. East and Southeast Asian countries have the biggest share of their trade with North America, the second biggest share with Japan.

In terms of trade policy, we see contrary movements, with trade barriers rising in the North and coming down in the South. Although northern tariffs have come down from an OECD average of 25 percent in 1950 to about 5 percent in 1990, their place has been taken by an assortment of nontariff barriers. Of the twenty-four OECD economies, only four of them on balance reduced obstacles to trade over the 1980s (the four being those that had the highest barriers to begin with: Japan, Australia, New Zealand, and Turkey). The other twenty, led by the United States, have been raising new barriers in the form of quotas, "voluntary" trade restraints, and managed trade.[33] By the mid-1980s nontariff barriers covered over a quarter of all industrialized country imports.[34] A good part of intra-OECD foreign direct investment flows is intended to hop over trade barriers to OECD markets. And a good part of foreign direct investment from OECD countries to the South is intended to capture unutilized quotas for access to OECD markets. Both flows suggest that many companies guess that trade restrictions to OECD markets will continue.

On the other hand, many southern countries over the 1980s have liberalized their trade regimes, lowering direct controls on imports and reducing the degree of overvaluation of the exchange rate. Tar-

[32] "World" includes the "socialist" economies (USSR, Hungary, etc.). Argentina is excluded because 1970 data were not available. UNCTAD "Handbook, 1991" tables 6.1, 6.3, 6.4. The four Asian NICs produced 0.74 percent of world industrial production in 1970, 2.54 percent in 1989. The European NICs (Ireland, Portugal, Spain, Greece, Yugoslavia) produced 2.72 percent in 1970, 3.15 percent in 1989.

[33] C. Fred Bergsten, "The World Economy after the Cold War," *California Management Review*, Winter 1992: 62.

[34] J. Nogues, A. Olechowski, and L. A. Winters, "The Extent of Nontariff Barriers to Industrial Countries' Imports," *World Bank Economic Review* 1 (1986): 181–99.

iffs and import controls undoubtedly remain much higher in the South than in the North, but the direction of change is sharply different.

The point to emphasize here is that in the North *national borders continue to be control points where governments can affect the quantity and price of cross-border merchandise transactions*, nowadays less through tariffs than through a whole panoply of nontariff barriers. In the South this remains true in much of Asia and Latin America (though not in most of Africa, where the state is imploding).

Overall, the trade data on both flows and policies do not support any simple idea that the world economy is operating in a new, more internationalized, or less nationally or regionally segmented, way.

Foreign Direct Investment

All statements about FDI should carry a consumer warning. The quality of the data is much worse than for trade or employment, and the data for stocks are even worse than for flows. But taking the FDI figures at face value we find that despite fast growth over the 1980s, outgoing FDI is still quite small in the major northern economies as a proportion of net domestic business investment. The typical order of magnitude is between 5 and 15 percent over the 1980s. The United Kingdom, with 65 percent, is quite exceptional. Incoming FDI is also quite small for the major northern economies relative to their net domestic business investment, between one-half of 1 percent (Japan) and 14 percent (the United States).[35] So *domestic investment by domestic capital easily dominates both direct investment overseas and foreign investment at home.*

The globalization image shows investment capital racing away from the North as companies take the whole world as their oyster. This too turns out to be largely untrue. World FDI flows are highly concentrated within the northern countries, and their share is rising (as with trade). *Two-thirds* of inward FDI flows worldwide in the 1980s have been into the United States and the EU (not including intra-EU flows). The biggest recipient by far is the United States, which alone got 46 percent of world inflows in 1985–89; the EU got just 19 percent, and Japan accepted virtually none.[36]

The South's share of the world FDI stock fell by a third between the late 1960s and the late 1980s.[37] And during the great FDI boom of the

[35] Glyn and Sutcliffe, "Global but Leaderless?," table 2.
[36] United Nations, *World Investment Report, 1992* (New York: United Nations, 1992), p. 20.
[37] Griffin and Khan, "Globalization and the Developing World," p. 23.

1980s the South's share of world inflows fell from 25 percent to 19 percent. Yet this occurred at a time when dwindling access to bank finance raised developing country dependence on FDI. Even East and Southeast Asia lost a share of FDI flows from the North; and the share is now surprisingly small. In 1989–91 only 6 percent of U.S. outgoing FDI went to Asia; 4 percent of the EU's; and 13 percent of Japan's.[38] The South's small share of world FDI stock is heavily concentrated in just six countries: the four East Asian "tigers" (South Korea, Taiwan, Hong Kong, Singapore), plus Mexico and Brazil. (So in talking about the South's integration through FDI we should disaggregate at least to two categories, these six countries on the one hand, the rest of the South on the other.) In the 1990s, however, the share of the South in world FDI flows has risen dramatically, to over a third in 1992–93. But the world total has fallen sharply since the 1980s; and most of the South's inflows have continued to be in Asia.[39]

North–South FDI patterns show the same regional clustering as for trade. That is, the dominant foreign investor in Latin America is the United States; in Eastern Europe and North Africa, Western Europe; in East and Southeast Asia, Japan followed by the United States (but there is some evidence that U.S. firms are reducing their share of foreign investment in Asia and increasing it in Latin America). With the partial exception of the United States in Asia we see rather little FDI crossover from the United States, Japan, or Europe to the low-wage region of one of the other two (e.g., EU investment in Asia or Japanese investment in Latin America). Japanese firms in northern Mexico and Hong Kong textilers in Mauritius seem to be more exceptions than harbingers. This is surprising in relation to standard FDI theories, which give little attention to spatial proximity in location decisions.

An important new development in FDI flows in the late 1980s is the emergence of the East Asian tigers as sources of outgoing FDI. In China and Southeast Asia the four are beginning to be major foreign investors, to the point where Korea and Taiwan have been the source of the biggest flows to several Southeast Asian countries in several recent years. Yet even in the case of these new FDI sources, half or more of their outgoing FDI is to North America or Europe. They fit with the bigger pattern of outgoing FDI going mostly to already rich countries.

Another parallel with the trade story (in addition to regionalization) is that countries of the South are liberalizing their FDI regimes at

[38] Ibid.
[39] Report to UNCTAD's Commission on Transnational Corporations, summarized in *Financial Times*, 4 May 1994, p. 7.

breakneck speed, led by Eastern Europe and the former Soviet re-
publics. But so also—and here the FDI story departs from the trade
story—are countries of the North. In the single year of 1991 at
least 34 countries, rich and poor alike, made a total of 82 major
changes to their FDI laws. Eighty of those changes made the rules
less restrictive.[40]

Overall, what is striking is how *few* jobs have been lost in the North
and gained in the South by MNCs seeking to exploit labor cost differentials. It is true that since the mid-1980s or so a labor force of some
1,200 million people has become accessible in developing countries, at
an average cost of less than $2 an hour, when the North employs 350
million people at an average hourly wage of $18. But an analysis of
the impact of MNCs on world employment by the United Nations
Conference on Trade and Development (UNCTAD) suggests that
MNC location decisions are driven mainly by the search for natural
resources, markets, good infrastructure, and an educated, committed
work force. Cheaper labor as such is not a major factor. Electronics
assembly turns out not to be the norm.[41]

Foreign Direct Investment: The American Case

How "transnationalized" is the U.S. economy? Taking the figures at
face value we find that today the stock of U.S. capital invested abroad
represents less than 7 percent of the U.S. GNP. That figure is, if anything, a little *less* than the figure in 1900.[42] The ratio of the stock of
FDI held by U.S. corporations over the stock of domestic investment
increased in the post–World War II years to about 1965, plateaued till
the mid-1970s, and then began to fall. Since the mid-1980s the value
of foreign to domestic assets in the United States has actually de-
creased. The same holds for employment. The ratio of foreign to domestic employees in American manufacturing firms peaked in the
mid-1970s and has declined since. In terms of sales, foreign sales as a
percentage of total sales peaked in 1980 at about 33 percent for the
United States' 100 largest corporations, declining subsequently to 25
percent.

As for foreign-owned direct investment in the United States, in
1990 the figure was about the same as the outgoing figure, or about 7

[40] "Asian Adventures," *The Economist*, 30 May–5 June 1992, p. 17. Is the direction
really so unidirectional? What about increasing use of local content requirements and
export requirements?

[41] UNCTAD, *World Investment Report* (Geneva, UNCTAD, 1994).

[42] Ethan Kapstein, "We Are Us: The Myth of the Multinational," *The National Interest*,
Winter 1991–92: 57. This article is the source of the data in this and the following
paragraph.

percent of the GNP. About the same small percentage of the American manufacturing work force is employed by foreign-owned manufacturing plants.[43] None of this suggests a huge transnationalization of the U.S. economy.

As for trade, U.S. outgoing FDI goes mostly to the North. In 1989 over 80 percent of the U.S. stock of manufacturing investment abroad was located in the North, less than 20 percent in the South (and of the latter three-quarters was located in the six countries mentioned).

These figures suggest that the U.S. economy is much less transnationalized than commonly supposed. Japan is much less transnationalized than the United States, and Germany is, if not now less transnationalized, then at least much less transcontinentalized. Overwhelmingly *world production, including manufacturing production, is nationally owned and oriented* (or in the case of Western Europe, regionally owned and oriented).[44] To the extent that investment capital has left one northern country it has been reinvested in large part in another northern country and secondarily in a southern economy within the same region.

Finance Capital

There is no doubt that the world market for standardized financial assets such as currencies, government bonds and commodity, currency and interest futures has become highly integrated over the 1980s. The governmental barriers to finance capital roaming across the OECD world have been largely eliminated. This development is fueling concern that more fully integrated financial markets may raise the risk of systemic failure, through the failure of one firm passing rapidly around the world or through fraud being easier to perpetuate on a world scale. But even in finance there are qualifications.

First, the number of financial products that are sold in highly integrated world markets—integrated enough to be called global—is quite limited: currencies, government bonds, and futures are the main ones. Stock markets are far from being fully integrated, because few companies have a sufficiently global reputation for trading in their stock to be active outside the home market. Financial regulations, tax systems, accounting practices, corporate ownership rules are all mainly national, with some increase in efforts to harmonize rules and practices between national authorities, supplemented by some re-

[43] Ibid., p. 58.
[44] For Western Europe I blur the distinction between national and (supranational) regional, treating it implicitly as an entity like the United States—in the interests of simplification and in the absence of a vocabulary for doing otherwise.

gional rules in Europe and a limited amount of global cooperation and global rules (e.g., Bank of International Settlement capital adequacy standards).[45]

Second, domestic saving and investment rates remain highly correlated among the OECD countries. This aspect has been interpreted to mean that domestic investment is strongly constrained by domestic saving, rather than being easily financed from other countries' saving; and therefore that even financial capital is not very mobile even within the OECD world. In the 1970s about 75 percent of the variance in investment share among the OECD countries was accounted for by variation in saving; in the 1980s the figure was 60 percent. By contrast, among U.S. states, which constitute as fully integrated a real-world capital market as it is possible to get, the saving–investment correlation is essentially zero. (The state-level saving rate accounted for just 2 percent of the variance in state-level investment rates in the late 1950s.)[46] So there is a huge difference between the saving–investment correlation for the U.S. states (a real-world fully integrated capital market) and that for the OECD countries. This difference can be interpreted to mean that the mobility of capital is much higher within a country than between countries; that, in other words, national borders tend to segment even financial markets. On the other hand, the fall in the OECD correlation since the mid-1970s is consistent with the idea that OECD financial markets have become somewhat more closely integrated.[47]

Third, the differences in the price of borrowed funds between different national markets remain substantial, even between the three major economies, the United States, Japan, and Germany.[48] All studies agree on this. But some find that the size of the real interest rate

[45] "Globalisation, Regional Blocs, and Local Finance," *Amex Bank Review* 20, no. 2 (1993): 2–7.

[46] Stephan Sinn, "Saving–Investment Correlations and Capital Mobility: On the Evidence from Annual Data," *Economic Journal* 102 (September 1992): 1162–70. See also George Hatsopoulos, Paul Krugman, and Lawrence Summers, "United States Competitiveness: Beyond the Trade Deficit," *Science*, 15 July 1988.

[47] The high savings–investment correlations may indicate low mobility of financial capital across borders, but it may also reflect, among other things, definitional conventions in the national accounts. In the personal sector, savings and investment are closely matched because housing, a large chunk of total investment, enters both the savings and the investment side of the accounts. In the business sector, the main source of corporate investment (in the main OECD economies) is retained earnings; but "retained profits plus depreciation" are also classed as company savings, in both corporated and unincorporated businesses. So savings and investment seem to have a large area of definitional overlap in the national accounts.

[48] See, for example, "Fear of Finance," *The Economist*, Special Survey, 19 September 1992, p. 22.

differential is declining, and others find no evidence of a decline.[49]
The differences in the price of *equity* capital in different national markets are bigger again than the differences in the price of loan capital.[50]
So the overall price of capital (loan capital and equity capital) is even
more unequal across national borders than differences in real interest
rates would suggest.

All this suggests that there is "a major mystery in the world's capital
markets. Among major countries where there was no country risk, the
predicted equalization of capital costs did not occur in the 1980s, despite the existence of what everyone took to be a world capital market,"[51] all this despite a huge increase in net capital flows, especially
from Japan.

Two qualifications are in order. First, for all the evidence that capital is not fully mobile and that the overall cost of capital is not equalized, it is equally striking that the cost of capital does not vary between
countries by anything close to the variation on many other variables.
Real interest rates differ within the North and between North and
South by no more than about five times; real wages, years of school-
ing, number of scientists in the labor force, and so on, differ by ten to
fifty times. For all the less than full mobility of financial capital across
national boundaries, labor of most types is much less mobile again.[52]

Second, the differences in real interest rates between countries today are probably not so different from the differences forty and even
100 years ago. Indeed, a recent study concludes that "every available
descriptor of financial markets in the late nineteenth and early twentieth centuries suggests that they were more fully integrated than they
were before or have been since"[53]—despite the huge improvements in
communications.

We have been considering evidence that runs counter to the notion
of the world economy as highly and unprecedentedly integrated.

[49] J. Frankel, "Measuring International Capital Mobility: A Review," *American Economic Review* 82, no. 2 (1992): 197–202, finds convergence. B. Kasman and C. Pigott,
"Interest Rate Divergences among the Major Industrial Countries," *Federal Reserve Bank
of New York Quarterly Review*, Autumn, 1988: 28–44, do not.

[50] Lester Thurow, *Head to Head: The Coming Economic Battle among Japan, Europe, and
America* (New York: Morrow, 1992), p. 43.

[51] Ibid.

[52] I am indebted to Adrian Wood for this point.

[53] Robert Zevin, "Are World Financial Markets More Open? If So, Why and With
What Effects?," in T. Banuri and J. Schor, eds., *Financial Openness and National Autonomy*
(Oxford: Oxford University Press, 1992), pp. 51–52. He uses indicators such as co-
movement between interest rates and share prices in different national financial markets; international assets and liabilities relative to domestic assets and income; and proportions of foreign securities traded on national markets.

Cross-border market exchanges are certainly much greater as a proportion of total market exchanges in 1990 than in 1960. But exports equal to 5 to 10 percent of GDP for the United States, Japan, and single-unit Europe and foreign ownership of domestic capital plus domestic ownership of foreign capital equal to 5 to 10 percent of domestic capital stock (averages for the late 1980s) hardly count as overwhelming internationalization of production. Production and investment remain very largely nationally owned and oriented (or regionally, in the case of Europe).

Crossnational "Sensitivity"

The sort of evidence just presented deals mainly with averages, and in economics it is changes *at the margin* that matter. We are interested not only in the average connectivity of national economies but also in how sensitive these economies are to each other and to cross-border flows. It could be argued that the impact of the less than 10 percent of U.S. GDP that is sold abroad is much greater than the low average share would suggest—it has a bigger effect in reducing the price differentials between domestic and foreign goods, for example, and a much bigger contribution to welfare (because it brings in entirely new goods with especially high consumer surplus).

It might also be argued that the South's 16 percent share of the North's manufactured imports has a much bigger impact on northern economies than the small average would suggest. Some new evidence suggests that the small average flow is nevertheless big enough to have a significant impact on northern labor markets and therefore on northern trade policies and northern politics. The South's manufactured exports to the North seem to have caused a fall of at least 4 percentage points in the share of manufacturing in total employment for the North as a whole between the late 1960s and the late 1980s. That is, of the total fall of 7 percentage points in the share of manufacturing in total employment in OECD countries, from 28 percent in 1969 to 21 percent in 1989, over one-half can be attributed to manufactured imports from the South.[54] The flows have a bigger impact than their value share would lead one to expect partly because value figures on trade from the South fail to convey the amount of labor locked up in the flows. Manufactured exports from the South being labor-intensive, a given value of exports has a more than proportional effect on labor demand in the North (displaces a greater amount than

[54] Wood, *North–South Trade*, chap. 5. The remainder of the fall is due mainly to faster productivity growth in manufacturing than in services. See also Adrian Wood, "How Trade Hurt Unskilled Workers," *Journal of Economic Perspectives*, Summer 1995.

would be anticipated from the value figures alone). Another reason is that northern manufacturers innovate defensively against the threat of southern imports, displacing even more labor in the North.

Similarly, it might be argued that transnationalization of world business is greater than the FDI figures suggest because more and more transnational companies are resorting to new forms of investment that do not involve a majority equity share, such as joint ventures, licensing arrangements, and franchising and subcontracting agreements. So the influence of foreign investment may be greater than is suggested by the size of the stock of foreign capital.[55] This may hold all the more for FDI in the South. Assets in poor countries are cheaper than in richer countries. For this reason the small share of the South in world FDI may understate the strategic importance of that FDI in the strategies of companies and governments.

On the other hand, transnationalization may be less than the FDI figures suggest because some of what is counted as FDI does not involve a foreign company setting up operations to compete with domestic companies for domestic sales. It represents what is really a "portfolio" investment by a holding company, as when a Japanese financial institution buys a Manhattan office block, which is not so different from the investment in foreign bonds that was a common form of foreign investment in the nineteenth century.

All we can say with confidence is that there *is* a lot of FDI being carried out by firms from countries that did not do much FDI in 1960 and in countries that did not receive much FDI in 1960; that FDI is very important in relation to total investment in some industries but not others, and in some country-to-country relationships but not others; this last statement is about equally true for the late nineteenth century, although for different industries and different countries. Beyond this we have to allow a hefty margin of error in any statement about FDI.

Similar problems arise in drawing conclusions about financial markets. The figures may show that the internationalization of financial markets is no higher today than in the early twentieth century, as indicated by the average share of foreign securities traded on national

---

[55] For example, much Taiwanese and Korean electronics investment in Southeast Asia produces products that are sold on an "original equipment manufacturer" (OEM) basis to Japanese electronics giants, who market the products under their own name. The consumer thinks they are Japanese products. The products appear in international trade statistics as, say, Thai exports of consumer electronics, and the investments appears in the FDI statistics as Taiwan or Korean investment in Thailand. Neither statistical series captures the essential Japanese role. Not only does the Taiwan or Korean company sell its output to Japanese companies, but also it generally buys the machinery from them and continues to buy the highest value-added components from them. Multiplied many times over such linkups erode the meaning of the FDI statistics.

markets or international liabilities and assets relative to domestic income and assets. But these indicators do not pick up the fact that today many more people depend for more of their income on financial markets and therefore on the state of financial markets in countries other than their own. The collapse of the BCCI bank in 1991 inflicted hardship on households of modest means in many countries, households whose counterparts in 1913 would probably have been more insulated from such a collapse because they saved less and held more of what they did save outside the banks.

We noted that the current level of integration of financial markets is fueling concern at the risk of systemic failure, through the failure of one firm knocking on failures in other firms around the world. Many financial markets may not be global, but they are certainly interconnected. The Continental Bank of Illinois collapsed in 1984 because Japanese fund managers, acting on a Japanese press report that mistranslated an American press report on Continental's troubles (the word "rumors" was mistranslated as "disclosure"), assumed incorrectly that the bank was insolvent and pulled their Eurodeposits out of the bank. Something has certainly changed in the world when Japanese fund managers acting on a mistranslation can cause the failure of the seventh largest U.S. bank.[56] Or when the U.S. government's public criticism of Germany for maintaining what the United States considered excessively high interest rates triggered the collapse of U.S. share prices in October 1987.[57]

That crossnational sensitivity is not well captured by the standard macro measures of economic integration only underlines the hazards of using those measures to support conclusions about globalization. Firm-level indicators are a necessary complement. They turn out to give fairly strong support to the proposition about the continuing economic importance of national economic units in the North.

Footloose and Stateless Corporations?

Recall Kindleberger's dictum in 1969 that "the international corporation has no country to which it owes more loyalty than any other, nor any country where it feels completely at home."[58] In the following quarter century, MNCs have become even more important actors and even more international in their operations. But contrary to what Kin-

[56] R. Taggart Murphy, "Power without Purpose: The Crisis of Japan's Global Financial Dominance," *Harvard Business Review*, March–April 1989.

[57] Felix Rohatyn, "World Capital: The Need and the Risks," *New York Review of Books*, 14 July 1994, p. 48.

[58] Kindleberger, *American Business Abroad*, p. 207.

dleberger announced, they have not become anything like stateless, footloose, and preponderant over governments.

Most MNCs hold most of their assets and employees in their home country.[59] Of the small minority that do not, almost all have the biggest single block of assets and employees located in the home country. Therefore most MNCs are quite susceptible to pressure and persuasion from the home country government, and more so from the home country government than from any other. General Motors in 1989 had about 70 percent of its employees and over 70 percent of its assets in the United States. Honda, the most internationalized of Japanese auto makers, had 63 percent of both assets and workers at home, and only 22 percent of its total manufacturing workers worldwide in the United States. Honda, Nissan, and Toyota produce 70 to 90 percent of worldwide output at home.

In most cases, a large majority of shares are held by individuals and legal entities in the home nation. (Nestlé, perhaps the most internationalized of companies with only 5 percent of assets and employees in Switzerland, limits non-Swiss voting rights to 3 percent of the total.) Shares in affiliates are not traded separately from shares in the parent company. This matters for issues of control—residents of a host country cannot influence the internal workings of an affiliate through share ownership—and it also matters for where the profits and most of the taxes accrue to, the country of the parent company.

Similarly, top management and governance rest in home country hands. In 1991 only 2 percent of the board members of big American companies were foreigners, and in Japanese companies "foreign directors are as rare as British sumo wrestlers."[60]

Multinational corporations also do the bulk of their R&D in the home nation. In the United States MNCs did well over 90 percent of their R&D inside the United States in the 1980s; Japanese MNCs do 98 percent at home (but the share is falling).[61] European MNCs do a larger share of R&D outside their home country—not surprisingly in view of the single European market and the existence of several technically advanced small countries with tiny home markets.[62] But even

[59] This section draws on Yao-su Hu, "Global Corporations Are National Firms with International Operations," *California Management Review* 34, no. 2 (1992): 107–26.
[60] "The Global Firm: R.I.P.," *The Economist*, 6 February 1993, p. 69. The 2 percent figure is for 1991.
[61] P. Patel and K. Pavitt, "Large Firms in the Production of the World's Technology: An Important Case of 'Non-globalization,'" *Journal of International Business Studies* 22, no. 1 (1991): 1–21.
[62] Christopher Freeman, "The 'National System of Innovation' in Historical Perspective," *Cambridge Journal of Economics* 19, no. 1 (1995).

Philips, with only 15 percent of its assets at home in the Netherlands, still does 40 percent of its R&D there.

So both strategic decision making and innovation are concentrated in the MNCs' home nations. These are the highest value-added parts of the firm's "value chain," and they make the biggest increment to the nation's standard of living. Indeed, *The Economist*, an enthusiastic champion of globalization, looks forward to the day when today's so-called global firms will become "relationship-enterprises," networks of alliances among big firms spanning different industries and countries. The main driver of these networks is precisely the advantages of escaping the restrictions of a home base: "To the extent that 'global' companies have a home country, governments will treat them as such, placing them at a political disadvantage. A relationship-enterprise, by contrast, is one way for firms to side-step these constraints. A multi-national alliance of independently owned firms can draw on lots of money; they can dodge antitrust barriers; and with home bases in all the main markets they have the political advantage of being a local firm almost everywhere."[63] But for the present, as *The Economist* laments, today's global firms remain tied to a particular home base and so are not fully global, which places them "at a political disadvantage." Indeed, MNCs are more accurately called, as Yao-Su Hu suggests, "national firms with international operations" (NFIOs).[64] The number that can be described as even close to global, in the sense of having no preferences for a particular country (comparative costs and returns alone determining to which country financial and management resources are allocated), is tiny. This is confirmed by the fact that stock markets remain primarily national rather than global (or regional). There are too few companies that command sufficient reputation globally for trading in their stocks to be active outside their home country.

But the point is not just that MNCs do have a home base to which they are more closely tied and generally more loyal than to other locations. It is also that, except for the most routinized assembly operations, they are much less than perfectly footloose with respect to *any* location once they have invested there. They then face a variety of sunk costs, which constitute barriers to exit. These include initial start-up costs, the costs of learning over time about a particular environment, and the costs of building reputation, gaining acceptance among government, employees, and other firms regarding their reliability as

---

[63] "The Global Firm: R.I.P.," *The Economist*, p. 69. To be fair, *The Economist* also recognizes that "such corporate monsters could act like cartels" and recommends a global antitrust watchdog.

[64] Hu, "Global Corporations."

producers, employers, and suppliers in each market. Knowledge and information are not fully codifiable or completely fungible between places; trust and reputation are even less so.

These factors are amplified by the new emphasis on "just-in-time" inventory reduction in the manufacture of some kinds of multicomponent products. This strategy raises the advantages of locating close to suppliers and of building up long-term relationships with them, which tends both to check the dispersion of production to far-flung sites and to reduce the mobility of production once an investment is made.

Recent changes in best practice production in engineering-intensive industries toward so-called flexible specialization make smaller production runs economic. This phenomenon reduces the advantages of global sourcing, insofar as those advantages rest on the economies of scale able to be reaped by suppliers of standardized parts for a "world car" or its equivalent in other products. Hence the advantages of flexible specialization constitute another brake on the spatial dispersion of production, reinforcing instead the tendency of production to be located close to final markets.[65]

These "new organization of production" tendencies towards colocation of supply chains are certainly not the only forces at work. The new communications technology enables firms to choose between concentrating and dispersing activities over a narrow or wide geography. The rising supply of skilled but still cheap labor in parts of the South—and other kinds of factor cost advantages—may offset the advantages of proximity in some sectors for some operations. This seems to be what is driving an increasing transfer of lower value-added parts manufacture by Japanese and American firms to Southeast Asia.

The continuing importance to MNCs of their home base suggests that the competitiveness of a given country's MNCs depends heavily on characteristics of the home base. It also suggests that the government of the home base has leverage over the home base MNCs. More generally the immobility of firms once an investment has been made provides scope for government policies that firms individually may not like—subject to the need for some consistency in policy over time (if firms experience an increase in government pressure once they invest, future investment inflows may be jeopardized). There is also

[65] Ford, having pioneered a "world car/global sourcing" strategy in the late 1970s, gave it up in the early 1980s and went back to more regionally based networks. Ford has been reinstituting the world car strategy since the late 1980s for one of its midsize models (the Mondeo). See "Ford Adds Mystique to Its $6bn. Global Ambitions," *Financial Times*, 29 March 1994.

intense competition within the set of big MNCs, some of it stemming from the rise of non-U.S. MNCs challenging the earlier dominance of U.S. ones. This intense competition presumably tends to check their accretion of power vis-à-vis governments.[66]

So there are several reasons why the fact that many more companies are involved in many more countries than in the past may not greatly erode the economic significance of national boundaries. Indeed, it is questionable whether, even if MNCs had remained as insignificant as they were in 1960, the structure of world trade would have been much different from what we see today.[67]

Globalization of Technology Production?

The continuing importance for MNCs of their home base is also apparent from evidence on the production of technology. The earlier evidence on technology globalization concerned its *exploitation*, the extent to which patents taken out in the United States or Europe come from firms or individuals based within those territories or based abroad. We saw that the share of foreign patents is almost one-half in both the United States and single-unit Europe. However, the picture is very different for the *production* of technology. Three points are important here.

First, OECD countries show big differences in their level and sectoral pattern of technological activities. *These differences persist over time,* if anything widening from the mid-1960s up to at least 1991. For example, a ranking of seventeen OECD countries by their industry-funded R&D spending as a share of GDP from 1967 to 1991 shows a high correlation between rank in 1967 and in 1991; and the standard deviation of the distribution increased markedly in the 1980s, suggesting technological *divergence* amongst OECD countries.[68] At a more disaggregated sectoral level, most OECD countries show marked differences in their patterns of technological specialization, and these

[66] It would be desirable to make a sharper conceptual distinction than I do here between the footlooseness of MNCs, their statelessness, and their preponderance over governments.

[67] I owe this point to Adrian Wood.

[68] In terms of patenting, the shares of total Western European patents taken out in the United States by individual Western European countries (that is, by firms home-based in those countries) show a very stable rank order from 1963 to 1990. But the United Kingdom shows a huge decline in its share between 1963 and 1968 and 1986 to 1990 from 25 percent to 15 percent; Germany shows a huge gain from 34 percent to 41 percent. Parimal Patel and Keith Pavitt, "National Innovation Systems: Why They Are Important, and How They Might Be Measured and Compared," *Economics of Information and New Technology* 3 (1994): 77–95.

Table 2-1. Britain and other OECD countries, technological performance and skills

	Rank order among 17 OECD countries				Share of U.S. patents granted to large national firms developed outside home base (1985–90)	Working population without post–high school education (%, late 1980s)
	Business-financial R&D/GDP		U.S. patents/million population			
	1967	1991	1963–86	1986–90		
United Kingdom	3	9	5	10	45	63
Germany FR	5	4	4	4	15	26
Japan	6	1	12	3	1	n.a.
France	9	8	8	9	13	53
United States	4	5	1	2	8	n.a.

SOURCES: P. Patel and K. Pavitt, "National Innovation Systems: Why They Are Important and How They Might Be Measured and Compared," mimeo, Science Policy Research Unit, University of Sussex, January 1994, tables 1, 6, and 8; and P. Patel and K. Pavitt, "Uneven (and Divergent) Technological Accumulation among Advanced Countries: Evidence and a Framework of Explanation," mimeo, Science Policy Research Unit, University of Sussex, March 1994, table 2.

differences have been stable between the 1960s and the late 1980s.[69] Indeed, some evidence suggests that the differences in the degree of technological specialization between OECD countries have been increasing at least since the mid- to late 1970s, that is, since the time when the new cluster of inventions (microelectronics, etc.) began to have a transformative effect across many sectors.[70] (See Table 2-1.)

Second, the overwhelming majority of the world's largest firms' technological activity is done in their *home* country. This is clear from the figures on the small share of R&D spending carried out abroad. It is confirmed by evidence from patenting. In the second half of the 1980s 89 percent of the U.S. patents taken out by 600 of the world's

[69] See ibid., tables 3 and 4. The analysis is based on the concept of "revealed technological advantage," defined as a country's or region's share of all U.S. patenting in a technological field or sector, divided by the same unit's share of all U.S. patenting in all fields. The periods are 1963–68 and 1985–90. Two sectoral breakdowns are used, the first with eleven sectors (fine chemicals, industrial chemicals, materials, nonelectrical machinery, motor vehicles, etc.), the second with 34 sectors.

[70] See D. Archibugi and M. Pianta, *The Technological Specialization of Advanced Countries. A Report to the EEC on International Science and Technology Activities* (Boston: Kluwer, 1992).

largest firms listed the inventor as a resident of the home base, a share almost identical with the one in the previous five-year period.[71]

This evidence on the foreign patenting activities of 600 of the world's largest firms is consistent with the evidence on their foreign R&D expenditures. It hardly suggests much of a trend to globalization of the production of technology over the 1980s. Multinationals are still doing most of their R&D in their home base. Such R&D as is undertaken abroad is mostly for adapting products for market conditions in the host country or for "listening in" on what host country researchers are doing.

Third, and most important for present purposes, the trends and sectoral patterns of large firms' technological activities are strongly correlated with those of their home countries (as indicated by the correlation between the share of U.S. patents granted to countries and those granted to their national large firms).

The close correlation between the technological activities of countries and those of their large national firms leaves open the direction of causation. Does the behavior of the national large firms determine the country results, or do country characteristics determine the behavior of their large firms? The globalization argument says that large firms plan and act on a world or regional scale, picking and choosing between country sites for different parts of the value chain, and that their decisions then determine the rate and direction of countries' technological activities. The national economy argument emphasizes the *continuing* impact of country characteristics on firms' propensities to invest in technological activities, country characteristics such as the education and training of the work force, the system of corporate management, and the way in which the financial system evaluates long-term R&D.

Persisting differences in the level and pattern of countries' technological activities since the late 1960s suggest causation from country characteristics to the technological activities of national large firms on the assumption that country characteristics themselves are relatively stable.

[71] See Patel and Pavitt, "National Innovation Systems," and Parimal Patel, "Localised Production of Technology for Global Markets," *Cambridge Journal of Economics* 19, no. 1 (1995). They find that geographical proximity matters: European firms in their sample tended to place their offshore R&D within Europe (except for the United Kingdom, whose firms undertook the largest share of offshore R&D in the United States). Canadian firms preferred the United States over Europe. Japan remains the least internationalized: only 1 percent of Japanese firms' patents taken out in the United States list an inventor with an address outside Japan, and less than half a percent of non-Japanese companies' patents list Japan as the address of the inventor. See also Parimal Patel and Keith Pavitt, "Large Firms in the Production of the World's Technology: An Important Case of Non-globalization," *Journal of International Business Studies*, First Quarter (1991): 1–21.

National Systems

The notion that a country's technological performance depends on a complex of system characteristics has given rise to the concept of "national systems of innovation," which comprise such features as those just mentioned—levels of general education, government policies toward higher education, the system of occupational selection for civil servants and researchers, the system of corporate management and the evaluation of R&D (e.g., the pressures coming from financial markets and the threat of hostile takeovers being such an important feature in the United States and United Kingdom, but not in Germany and Japan). Many of the factors frequently included in the concept determine not so much the production of technology as its commercial application. To emphasize this broader sense of innovation it might be better to talk about "national systems of technological and entrepreneurial capacity" (NASTECs).

The concept rests on the assumptions that technology continues, even after the big improvements in computer-based codification, to have a large element of tacit knowledge, that tacit knowledge is often costly, not costless, to acquire, and that it is cumulative and path dependent in its development. The importance of tacit knowledge is suggested by the fact that, "technoglobalism" predictions notwithstanding, firms involved in producing for world markets keep most of their technology production at home. Perhaps this reflects the high uncertainty around invention and innovation and the advantages of frequent and trusting personal communications in handling uncertainty.

National boundaries in this view are proxies for physical, cultural, linguistic, and educational nearness and sameness, which continue to affect the transfer of tacit knowledge from person to person and from organization to organization. National boundaries demarcate the nationally specific systems of education, finance, corporate management, and government that generate social conventions, norms, and laws and thereby pervasively influence investment in technology and entrepreneurship. There can be no assumption that the evolution of national systems is guided by a mechanism that selects more efficient arrangements. Indeed, the persistent differences in innovation and productivity performance within the OECD countries attest to the robustness of dysfunctional institutional arrangements in underperforming countries, like Britain.

The costs of moving resources about the globe to take advantage of differential access to raw materials, markets, or investment funds are now much lower than at any time prior to 1960. But the globalization literature extrapolates from this new *technological* potential, while overlooking the extent to which economic integration—or its opposite—is driven by social and political causes.

The world's international economic activity continues to concentrate in the North rather than disperse in a way that integrates the South; the pattern of industrial location shows a strong tendency toward spatial clustering; resources are relatively immobile across international boundaries; and resource use by firms is much affected by institutional characteristics of national units. (In the EU many of these national characteristics are being made more uniform, making the juridical unit of the EU the relevant agency.) In short national economic borders still define the boundaries of systems of capital accumulation. The argument rests on stylized facts such as the following:

- In the main industrial economies about 90 percent of production is for the domestic market, and about 90 percent of their consumption is produced at home.
- Domestic investment by domestic capital far exceeds direct investment overseas plus foreign investment at home and seems to be financed mostly from domestic savings.
- World stock markets are far from fully integrated, because few companies have a sufficiently global reputation for trading in their stock to be active outside their home market.
- Multinational corporations keep strategic decision making and R&D activities concentrated in their home base.
- Firms in many industries, other than those involved in simple assembly operations, are far from fully footloose with respect to any location once they have invested.
- OECD countries show persistent, not converging, differences in the rate and pattern of technological activities at least since the late 1960s, which suggests that NASTECs are robust and themselves tend to determine the technological activities of large national firms more than the other way around (which would be the globalization prediction).
- At the end of World War II or even in 1960, the time when most of the globalization literature starts the clock, national economies were *unusually* closed. By that standard what has happened since then does represent dramatic internationalization. However, in a longer perspective even some financial markets are not qualitatively more internationalized in some important respects than before World War I; and the same is broadly true for trade and FDI and even for labor.[72] The fact that economic integration within western Europe and between Europe and North

[72] See Carl Strikwerda, "The Troubled Origins of European Economic Integration: International Iron and Steel and Labor Migration in the Era of World War I," *American Historical Review* 98 (October 1993): 1106–29.

86

America declined sharply after 1913, only regaining the same level as recently as the 1970s, attests to the importance of political causes of economic trends. The great advances in transport and communications technology between 1913 and 1960 did not cause economic integration, even though integration became economically more and more feasible.

The picture that emerges from evidence of this sort shows resources as relatively immobile across national economic borders (or regional borders in the case of the EU). Ironically, some of the reasons for the continuing immobility have to do with the greater ease of mobility. The lower costs of closing great distances mean that the competitive position of nations and firms is today less determined by differential access to raw materials, markets, or investment than it has been at any time prior to, say, 1960. At least in skill- and innovation-intensive activities competitive advantage is now far more affected by factors such as physical infrastructure, a committed, flexible work force, and by the growth of unique characteristics in supplier–user and other support relationships that can—not being open to all—generate more innovation, higher productivity, and quasi-monopolistic rents. These new factors in competitive advantage raise the advantages of immobility and colocation in the production of skill- and innovation-intensive goods and services.

Governments can do a lot to enhance the advantages of immobility and proximity, through public policies for education, infrastructure, business networks, and targeted industrial support. The overwhelming bulk of a nation's resources that are not mobile, including physical capital and the high value-added functions of even the biggest of the home-based MNCs, give governments leverage to work with. The interest of firms in social and physical infrastructure and in a skilled and committed work force may check the temptation for governments to cut social and labor standards in the hope of securing extra jobs. On the other hand, the privatization drive that has swept through both North and South over the 1980s and 1990s may have facilitated just this response, as both states and labor unions lose the ability to exercise social control over resource allocation. The point is that the picture is mixed.

Even in the case of international finance, apparently the most technology-driven liberalization of all, we may be on the verge of a reassertion of international regulations and national controls. There is now a growing reaction against some of the consequences of financial liberalization for the "real" (national) economy, including instability and loss of policy autonomy and growing political support for at least mild measures to reduce international capital mobility (such as a small transactions tax on spot foreign exchange transactions). During a financial crisis proponents of greater control will gain ground in the face of the need to defend the balance of payments. Spain, Portugal, and Ireland did in fact impose or tighten capital controls during the European financial crisis of 1992. And crisis apart, U.S. and U.K. financiers, who led the drive to financial deregulation worldwide, may begin to see some collective reregulation as a way to lessen the competitive pressures from upstart financial centers.[73]

In the states of the South we may see a reassertion of the role of the state and even a deliberate step toward disintegration from the world economy for another, more distress-driven reason. The catch-up of southern economies is about moving up the ladder of skill-intensive activities. But the North has a comparative advantage in skill-intensive activities, first, because skilled people are less scarce and therefore less expensive than unskilled people compared to the South, and second, because externalities and economies of scale mean that skills are not only cheaper but also more productive, because skilled people have a greater envelope of skilled activities (people, firms, industries) to interact with. Many countries of the South that have fast-rising populations will find it difficult to raise the ratio of skilled to unskilled people as fast as the ladder itself is rising. It is at least possible that the difficulties of competing in international markets will strengthen the hand of political forces that seek to pursue more autarchic, state-led policies. This would then be another way in which, in the South as well as in the North, reports of the death of the national economy are greatly exaggerated.

[73] Eric Helleiner, "Post-globalization: Is the Financial Liberalization Trend Likely to Be Reversed?," in D. Drache and Robert Boyer, eds., *The Future of Nations and the Limits of Markets* (Montreal: McGill-Queen's University Press, forthcoming).

CHAPTER THREE

Has France Converged on Germany? Policies and Institutions since 1958

ANDREA BOLTHO

Neoclassical economic theory generates a set of long-term predictions that involve relentless moves toward greater uniformity in the world economy. Although individual countries specialize in production, in line with factor endowment, their factor prices and even their per capita incomes are expected to converge and their institutions to become more similar, as best (i.e., market conforming) practices and policies chase away their inferior (i.e., interventionist) counterparts. This may not be the "end of history," but it certainly sounds like the "end of economic change."

In fact, the very rapid growth in intra-industry trade has seriously dented the predictions of standard international trade theory. Similarly, the experience of widening income differentials between many parts of the world has thrown into doubt the optimistic conclusions of neoclassical growth theory. The hypothesis of institutional convergence, forced on countries by the pressures of increasing international trade and financial integration with the rest of the world, may, however, seem more robust. Thus, the privatizations and deregulations that have been pursued by so many industrialized countries in the 1980s could be seen as one manifestation of this trend. Indeed, recent government-driven moves may be reinforcing convergence in national practices—witness the United States–Japan Structural Impediments Initiative (SII), designed to modify specific traits of the Japa-

The author is indebted to Chris Allsopp, Wendy Carlin, Ron Dore, and Pascal Petit who made helpful comments on an earlier version of this essay (but bear no responsibility for the present one).

nese economy or the EEC's 1992 project, which promotes "institutional competition" within Europe.

The chapter's aim is to explore more closely the presence (or absence) of regime convergence between France and Germany since the late 1950s, when the two countries joined the Common Market. At the time, their economic institutions and policies were very different. Germany, largely as a reaction to its earlier history, had opted for an "ordo-liberal" economic constitution, under the influence of, for instance, Eucken and Hayek.[1] France, by contrast, had moved away from its relatively market-oriented interwar order to a much more managed economy.

Between the late 1950s and the early 1990s, as the two countries drew together (each now is the principal trading partner of the other and has been its largest export market since 1961), their policies were clearly modified—more so, it would seem, in France than in Germany. The text that follows looks at the nature of, and reasons for, some of the French changes. The first section sets up the areas for discussion, and the second and third sections consider a number of policy and institutional developments in two periods separated by the 1973 outbreak of stagflation.

CONVERGENCE IN WHAT?

To large numbers of European observers, the "superiority" of the German economy is almost self-evident. High living standards, the strength of the currency, the quality of manufacturing production, to name just a few, are all attributes that seemingly set Germany (and perhaps also Switzerland) apart from other European countries. At a macroeconomic level, many would share the judgment that (at least until the reunification shock with the Eastern *Länder*) "the German economy has been more successful than its neighbors in attaining the employment objective stressed by the Keynesians, the price-stability objective stressed by the monetarists, and the objective of international competitiveness stressed by the Scandinavians."[2]

French public opinion would seem to share such feelings. Thus, a recent analysis of the country's industrial policy highlighted as a French characteristic: "A continuing obsession with Germany, a continuing need to treat the performance and structure of the economy

[1] H. Giersch, K.-H. Paqué, and H. Schmieding, *The Fading Miracle—Four Decades of Market Economy in Germany* (Cambridge: Cambridge University Press, 1992).

[2] R. J. Flanagan, D. W. Soskice, and L. Ulman, *Unionism, Economic Stabilization, and Incomes Policies: European Experience* (Washington, D.C.: Brookings, 1983), p. 215.

across the Rhine as the benchmark for its own success."[3] Similarly, a well-known French public figure has recently put forward Germany as a model for modern-day capitalism, not just for France, but for other countries as well.[4]

Using a foreign country as a benchmark or model implies, presumably, that a multitude of aspects may require emulation. To limit the essay's scope a selection is inevitable. This is in part dictated by what appear, from a French perspective, as areas of undoubted German strength. Two, in particular, stand out. First, is Germany's international competitiveness, a competitiveness reinforced by a long tradition of relative price stability and seemingly little influenced by constant appreciations of the currency. Second, is Germany's industrial relations system, seen to be based on much greater cooperation between management and the work force than is the case in many other European countries.

For France, international competitiveness has been a continuing policy preoccupation, particularly so in the light of the perceived "fragility" of the country's foreign trade, a "fragility" that has received constant attention in the literature throughout the period.[5] Similarly, a strong currency has been a long-standing, if elusive, aim of macroeconomic policymaking that runs through modern French economic history from Poincaré to De Gaulle and from Giscard to Mitterrand.

The attraction of enterprise models of codetermination may seem less obvious. Yet, in the presence of what a comparative analysis of labor market institutions and policies described as the "antediluvian behavior of [French] employers,"[6] it is reasonable to suppose that the German setting of "responsible" unions, relative harmonious collective bargaining, and related practices and policies, might have seemed more attractive. After all, there is evidence showing that such features, often referred to as "corporatist," can have favorable effects on economic performance.[7] And in a widely known ranking of twelve West European economies according to the degree of "corporatism"

[3] W. J. Adams, *Rethinking the French Economy* (Washington D.C.: Brookings, 1989), p. 259.

[4] Michel Albert, *Capitalisme contre capitalisme* (Paris: Seuil, 1991).

[5] J. M. Jeanneney, *Forces et faiblesses de l'économie française* (Paris: Colin, 1959); L. Stoléru, *L'impératif industriel* (Paris: Seuil, 1969); A. Cotta, *La France et l'impératif mondial* (Paris: PUF, 1978); J. Mazier, M. Basle, and J.-F. Vidal, *Quand les crises durent . . .* (Paris: Economica, 1984).

[6] Flanagan, Soskice, and Ulman, *Unionism, Economic Stablization, and Incomes Policies*, p. 567.

[7] J. McCallum, "Unemployment in the OECD Countries in the 1980s," *Economic Journal* 96, no. 384 (December 1986): 942–60. E. Tarantelli, "Néo-corporatisme et régulation de l'inflation et du chomage dans les pays occidentaux," in A. Grjebine, ed., *Théorie de la crise et politiques économiques* (Paris: Seuil, 1986).

of their institutions, Germany was placed second, and France was second from last.[8]

In the following two sections I try to see how far France moved away from its late-1950s macroeconomic policies and microeconomic institutions in these two major areas of concern, be this in response to the perceived "superiority" of the German model or under the pressure of other events.

FROM THE TREATY OF ROME TO THE FIRST OIL SHOCK

France's 1958 entry into the EEC was bound to represent a major shock for the country's industry. Until the late 1950s protectionism at home and on the export markets of the Franc zone had cushioned the domestic manufacturing sector from the full force of external competition.[9] Of Europe's major economies, France was the most closed to import penetration, as well as the most reliant on virtually "captive" foreign outlets, as it had been for nearly three decades or more (Table 3-1).[10]

This state of affairs was well-known. From the mid-1950s onward, the country saw an outpouring of complaints about its trading weaknesses that concentrated on its lack of competitiveness in the machinery sector,[11] the broader "inadaptation" of its industry to international demand,[12] or its "wrong specialization" in slow-growing branches of industry.[13] Yet, surprisingly perhaps, this same literature, when drawing international comparisons and pointing to other countries' successes, seldom looked at Germany.

Thus, the mid-1950s debate on France's "modernization" made no reference to Germany's economic miracle of the time.[14] Similarly, in a late-1950s balance sheet of France's economic strengths and weak-

[8] M. Bruno and J. Sachs, *Economics of Worldwide Stagflation* (Cambridge: Harvard University Press, 1985).

[9] Thus, it was agricultural pressure groups that strongly contributed to the French parliament's adoption of the Treaty of Rome, "in contrast to the hesitations of industrial circles," P. Drouin, *L'Europe du Marché Commun* (Paris: Julliard, 1963), p. 54.

[10] The 1958 Sterling Area share in British exports, at over 40 percent, was even larger than that of the Franc Area in French exports at the time, but, arguably, the degree of foreign competition in markets such as Australia or India was much greater than that to be found in Morocco or Gabon.

[11] Stoléru, *L'impératif industriel.*

[12] P. Arnaud-Ameller, *La France à l'épreuve de la concurrence internationale, 1951–1966* (Paris: Colin, 1970).

[13] INSEE, *La mutation industrielle de la France*, Collections de l'INSEE, Série E no. 31–32 (Paris: INSEE, 1975).

[14] F. Bloch-Lainé and J. Bouvier, *La France restaurée, 1944–1954* (Paris: Fayard, 1986).

92

Table 3-1. France's foreign trade exposure (%)

	Exports		
	1932	1958	1970
Share of total exports going to			
Franc area	32	38	10
EEC	26	22	50

	Imports	
	1958	1970
Share of manufactured imports in GDP		
France	2.6	7.8
Germany	4.0	8.4
Italy	2.9	6.8
United Kingdom	3.2	7.8

SOURCES: *Annuaire statistique de la France* (various issues); OECD, *Foreign Trade Statistics—Series B* (Paris: OECD, various issues); and OECD, *National Accounts* (various issues).

nesses, international comparisons seemed confined to countries such as the United States, Britain, or even Belgium—Germany was mentioned only in a few charts. Although a decade later more attention was given to Germany, the models that were held up for imitation in the area of international competitiveness were Italy or Japan (as examples of interventionist countries) and the United States or Switzerland (as examples of free market economies), with Germany described as a mere copy of the American model.[15] Even by the mid-1970s, in an exhaustive survey of French industry, mentions of and comparisons with Germany, although now more frequent, hardly conveyed the impression that here was a model that needed detailed study, let alone emulation.[16] Not surprisingly, therefore, the policies followed to stimulate competitiveness and the "right" pattern of specialization were totally different from those pursued in Germany. Across the Rhine, the federal government refrained from medium-term projections, let alone detailed intervention in industry.[17] In France, by contrast, not only was indicative planning pursued, but it was also complemented, through the 1960s, by an ambitious industrial policy primarily de-

[15] Stoléru, *L'impératif industriel.*

[16] In a special, early-1960s number of the *Revue économique* devoted to West Germany, the only feature that was explicitly selected as worth copying by France was Germany's capacity to base its decisions on a "pragmatic and methodical knowledge of reality, helped [in turn] by an unparalleled information system." A. Piettre, "L'Economie allemande est-elle vraiment libérale?," *Revue économique* 3 (May 1962): 339–54.

[17] This, however, was not always the case of the *Länder* governments.

signed to foster large firms, or "national champions," in particular sectors. Interventionism also took the form of continuing and detailed controls on the allocation of credit and on price formation.

By the mid- to late-1960s France and Germany stood at almost opposite ends of the West European spectrum in terms of macroeconomic policy formulation, with no apparent trace of French attempts to copy German practices. Indeed, one contemporary observer of the European scene predicted the reverse outcome—the spreading of indicative planning from France to other countries, including Germany.[18] In the event, of course, only Britain and Italy (both unsuccessfully) attempted to copy France. Yet, it could be argued that the Bonn Parliament's adoption of the 1967 Stability Law showed that, at least in the area of demand management policies, Germany was tending to converge on to other countries, including France.

Lack of interest in Germany was also apparent at the more microeconomic level. It is true that the authoritarian treatment of the work force in the private sector and the near absence of collective bargaining had been matters of long-standing concern for parts of the French establishment. In such areas, it would seem, Germany could have provided a clear example of a success story. Not only were German institutions at the company level more democratic, but also they seemingly resulted in less social strife. Thus, throughout the 1960s (even excluding the exceptional year of 1968 from the French data), Germany's record of industrial peace was far superior to that of France (Table 3-2).

Yet, neither the debates nor the policies of the period were much inspired by German practices. In an influential book that launched the process of company reform, the German codetermination system was criticized as being "equivocal" and "counterproductive."[19] Indeed, some went as far as judging it almost an "illusion."[20] As for the piecemeal reforms that took place (e.g., the 1967 requirement that employees receive a share of corporate earnings, the 1968 measures that obliged companies with more than 50 workers to accept a trade union presence, or the turn of the 1960s attempts at strengthening collective bargaining), these seem to have been influenced more by the Swedish than by the German example.

The only paradigm at the time, which extolled efficiency rather

---

[18] It is true that, at the time, even the very market-oriented Kiel Institute saw some advantages in the French planning system. See A. Shonfield, *Modern Capitalism* (Oxford: Oxford University Press, 1965), and L. Müller-Ohlsen, *Wirtschaftsplanung und Wirtschaftswachstum in Frankreich*, Kieler Studien no. 80 (Tubingen: J. C. B. Mohr, 1967).

[19] F. Bloch-Lainé, *Pour une réforme de l'entreprise* (Paris: Seuil, 1963), pp. 21–22.

[20] Piettre, "L'économie allemande est-elle vraiment libérale?," p. 354.

Table 3-2. Industrial disputes (number of days lost through strikes per 1,000 employees; annual averages)

	1960–69	1970–79	1980–89
France	270[a]	220	80
Germany	20	50	30
Italy	1,400	1,350	630
United Kingdom	270	600	330

Source: *Department of Employment Gazette* (London: Her Majesty's Stationary Office, various issues).

[a]Excluding 1968.

than industrial democracy came not from German companies but from U.S. multinationals. The latter provided the technocrats, who were modernizing French industry, with the model of how production should be organized.[21] And it was the great strength and alleged domination of large American corporations that enlivened public debates on the strategy the country (and the EEC) should follow.[22]

Ignorance of what was happening across the Rhine may partly explain this fascination with the American example. The economic literature of the time, for instance, follows quite closely developments in the United States, in Britain, or in Italy, but much less so those in Germany.[23] A much more important reason, however, is to be found in France's macroeconomic performance, which, in these years of interventionism, was exceptionally good, indeed better in a number of areas than that of Germany (Table 3-3). Thus, output and productivity growth outstripped those of Germany; cyclical fluctuations were almost absent, in contrast to Germany's fairly marked business cycles (notably the sharp recession of 1967), and even if France's export performance did not match Germany's, market penetration abroad rose in the wake of two very successful devaluations of the currency.[24]

It is true that the vacuum in industrial relations could have been seen as a threat to macroeconomic success, because it periodically led to strike waves (of which 1968 was the most important but not the only example). Yet, on balance, the policymakers must have felt that, over the longer run, paternalism in the labor market was more conducive to (growth-promoting) high profits and that sudden outbursts in

[21] P. Petit, *La modernisation face aux métamorphoses de l'économie française, 1945–1985*, no. 8608 (Paris: CEPREMAP, 1985).

[22] J.-J. Servan-Schreiber, *Le défi américain* (Paris: Denoël, 1967).

[23] Paradoxically, France probably knew more about the Japanese economy, thanks to several scholarly books, than it did about Germany.

[24] J. Mistral, "Vingt ans de redéploiement du commerce extérieur," *Economie et statistique* 71 (October 1978): 23–40.

ANDREA BOLTHO

Table 3-3. Comparative macroeconomic performance, 1958–73

	France	Germany	Italy	United Kingdom
	Average annual percentage changes			
GDP	5.5	4.9	5.4	3.4
Industrial production	5.4	5.4	7.4	3.3
Manufacturing productivity[a]	6.4	4.5	6.9	3.6
Consumer prices	4.6	3.1	4.2	4.4
	Annual averages			
Current account balance[b]	0.9	0.8	1.0	−0.1
Unemployment rate[c]	2.0	0.9	5.4	2.0
Gap between actual and potential output[d]	0.9	1.8	2.4	1.8
Share of world exports of manufactures[e] 1958	8.4	18.1	4.0	17.7
1973	9.5	22.1	6.8	9.4

SOURCES: International Monetary Fund, *International Financial Statistics* (Washington, D.C.: IMF, 1984); NIESR, *Economic Review* (London: NIESR, various issues); OECD, *National Accounts, 1953–1982* (Paris: OECD, 1984); OECD, *Historical Statistics, 1960–1990* (Paris: OECD, 1992), and OECD, "The Measurement of Domestic Cyclical Fluctuations," *OECD Economic Outlook—Occasional Studies* (Paris: OECD, July 1973).
[a]Value added per employee, 1960–73.
[b]In percent of current price GDP, 1960–73.
[c]In percent of the labor force.
[d]Absolute value of gap, 1958–72.
[e]Share in the exports of the eleven major industrialized countries.

wage pressures could be successfully dealt with by changing the value of the currency.[25] No wonder, then, that an above-average rate of inflation was tolerated. If there was a "German model," it did not seem obviously more attractive, as openly admitted in 1971 by Valérie Giscard d'Estaing, then minister of finance: "West Germany has chosen to put the accent on disinflation. . . . We retained the pursuit of growth as a fundamental objective."[26]

FROM THE FIRST OIL SHOCK TO "COMPETITIVE DISINFLATION"

As elsewhere, the first oil shock had pronounced economic effects that, it was argued, revealed France's long-standing weaknesses.[27] The

[25] Flanagan, Soskice, and Ulman, *Unionism, Economic Stabilization, and Incomes Policies.*
[26] Cited in H. Dumez and A. Jeunemaître, "A Style of Economic Regulation, France, 1969–86: A Comparison between France and West Germany," *Government and Policy* 8 (1990): 141.
[27] R. Barre, *Réflexions pour demain* (Paris: Hachette, 1984).

96

policy response to the generalized feeling of *crise* that set in after 1974 was radical. Excluding the mid-1970s confused reactions to stagflation and the early-1980s attempt at "socialism in one country," one can detect a fairly steady progression away from *dirigisme* and toward market-oriented policies, away from some of the typical aspects of French interventionism toward some of the more German aspects of macroeconomic laissez-faire.

A major element in this change was the perception of how Germany had fared after the first oil shock. In virtually all industrialized countries inflation in 1974 and 1975 rose above the already high rates of 1973, but Germany (and Switzerland) managed to achieve *lower* average inflation in these two years than in 1973 (Table 3-4). Similarly, and equally surprisingly, Germany was (again with Switzerland) one of the very few oil-importing countries whose current account balance in 1974–75 *improved* relative to 1973. Nor did Germany's performance in other areas worsen dramatically. It is true that unemployment rose sharply (and would have done so even more had Germany not been able to shed a significant number of foreign workers), but it still remained below the (also rising) French rate. As for currency appreciation, this seemed to have few lasting negative effects on the country's competitiveness.

Conversely, the Franc's 12 percent loss of value vis-à-vis the Deutschmark between 1973 and 1976 appeared to have been much less effective in stimulating competitiveness than had been the 1957–58 and 1969 devaluations. Those, seen as near-permanent changes in relative prices, had generated strong supply-side effects. The main impact of depreciation, in the uncertain world of floating, seemed, instead, to be higher inflation and larger oil import bills. As a consequence, Germany now figured much more frequently in the literature as a model to be imitated. Deutschmark appreciation, for instance, was seen as

Table 3-4. Macroeconomic reactions to the first oil shock

		France	Germany	Italy	United Kingdom
Consumer prices	1973	7.3	7.0	10.8	9.1
(average % change)	1974–75	12.8	6.5	18.1	20.1
Current balance	1973	1.5	5.0	−2.5	−2.5
($ billion)	1974–75	−0.6	7.4	−4.3	−5.4
Unemployment	1973	2.7	0.8	6.2	3.0
(% of labor force)	1974–75	3.4	2.6	5.6	3.6

SOURCES: International Monetary Fund, *International Financial Statistics* (Washington, D.C.: IMF, 1990); OECD, *Economic Outlook* (Paris: OECD, various issues).

contributing to a virtuous circle of "favourable specialization, trade surpluses and improvements in competitiveness."[28]

The first major policy switch came with the September 1976 "Plan Barre." Although Germany was not quoted as an explicit model, many of the new policies were clearly inspired by practices across the Rhine. Low inflation and a stable exchange rate were to be achieved via tight fiscal and monetary policies, and higher competitiveness was to be obtained by the relaxation of price controls and greater domestic competition.[29] Conversion to German ideas was, however, only partial. For one thing, the macroeconomic policy followed was never as dogmatic.[30] For another, "behind the belligerent and often caustic economic liberal rhetoric of Barre, lurked a powerful practice of *dirigisme*."[31] Thus, credit controls were still used to steer monetary policy, despite some token gestures to money-supply targeting. Similarly, industrial policies were vigorously pursued, even if intervention moved from the promotion of national champions to that of selected activities.[32]

A further step in the abandonment of the traditional posture came in the mid-1980s when both left- and right-wing governments agreed on the necessity of what came to be called "competitive disinflation." Rather than allowing periodic, if modest, realignments of the currency within the European Monetary System (EMS), so as to maintain its real value broadly unchanged, the new policy aimed at nominal exchange rate fixity and hence, for a time at least, a real appreciation. Although the strategy was risky, considering that French exports have traditionally been more price-elastic than German ones,[33] its defense clearly echoed German views—a strong franc would not only dampen inflationary pressures but also force firms to become more competitive. However costly in terms of employment, the policy was pursued even after the EMS's collapse in mid-1993.

In addition, detailed interventionism was gradually wound down.

[28] B. Nezeys, *Les rélations économiques extérieures de la France* (Paris: Economica, 1982), p. 306. On the superiority, finally recognized, of German vocational training, see J. Silvestre, "Education et organisation industrielle: Les enseignements d'une comparaison internationale," *Revue d'économie industrielle* 23 (1983): 218–27.

[29] R. Barre, "L'économie française quatre ans après (1976–1980)," *Revue des deux mondes,* September 1980: 513–32.

[30] A. Boltho, "Why Has Europe Not Co-ordinated Its Fiscal Policies?," *International Review of Applied Economics* 4, no. 2 (1990): 166–81.

[31] H. Machin and V. Wright, "Economic Policy under the Mitterrand Presidency, 1981–1984: An Introduction," in H. Machin and V. Wright, eds., *Economic Policy and Policy-Making under the Mitterrand Presidency, 1981–1984* (London: Pinter, 1985), p. 33.

[32] Y. Morvan, "La politique française depuis la Libération: Quarante années d'interventions et d'ambiguïtés," *Revue d'économie industrielle* 23 (1983): 19–35.

[33] J. Mathis, J. Mazier, and D. Rivaud-Danset, *La compétitivité industrielle* (Paris: Dunod, 1988).

Industries were (partially) denationalized, antitrust legislation was reinforced, price controls were abolished, as were barriers to international capital mobility. In general, France accepted and implemented the very market-oriented 1992 EEC Programme. Monetary policy jettisoned the panoply of credit restrictions and opted for instruments that are very similar to those used by the Bundesbank.[34] In some areas France went even beyond what was being done in Germany (e.g., very low minimum reserve requirements for banks, or the creation of a highly successful futures market), in an attempt to transform Paris into a major financial center. Institutional change has now led to a virtually independent Banque de France.

By the early 1990s scepticism, bordering on renunciation, was also impinging on a major aspect of the country's tradition, industrial policy. One reason for this may have been the climate of opinion, be it German or Anglo-American, that sees industrial policies at best as ineffective and, more usually, as detrimental to a country's welfare. Another would seem to be a growing recognition that past intervention, despite some successes, had failed to generate the competitive *créneaux* (or *filières*) that had been targeted.[35] Even more important, however, was the realization that in today's world, a purely French industrial policy (however well conceived) had little chance of success—if there is to be a policy, it should be set in Brussels.

In the area of collective bargaining and industrial relations, on the other hand, changes in institutions and policies seem to have been very limited. Not unlike the 1960s, wages were compressed during the Barre Plan and through most of the 1980s via income policies that were virtually imposed by the government on public sector employees, with little or no union consultation.[36] This, in turn, had a demonstration effect on to the private sector, aided and abetted by a very high level of unemployment.

As for enterprise reform, and despite the recommendations of the 1975 Sudreau Commission, which, as others in the past, had argued for greater employee participation, it was admitted that, in the early 1980s, company structures were still highly traditional and paternalis-

[34] Lehman Brothers, *Monetary Policy in Europe* (London, 1992).

[35] Interestingly, it turns out that among the major European economies France is least specialized industrially (Commissariat général du Plan, "Défis à l'économie française," *Etudes et recherches* 3/4 [December 1986]); lacks "poles of competitiveness" (R. Z. Lawrence, "Trade Performance as a Constraint on European Growth," in R. Z. Lawrence and C. L. Schultze, eds., *Barriers to European Growth* [Washington, D.C.: Brookings, 1987]); and has a manufacturing structure closest not to that of Germany but to that of Britain (Adams, *Rethinking the French Economy*).

[36] D. Soskice, "Wage Determination: The Changing Role of Institutions in Advanced Industrial Countries," *Oxford Review of Economic Policy* 6, no. 4 (Winter): 36–61.

tic: "At the top of the hierarchy, the head of the firm exercises power that is still virtually total . . . the employee is not a member of the firm, he is at its service."[37] It is true that the early-1980s "Lois Auroux," inspired by the German example, were an attempt at democratizing such authoritarian practices. Yet the measures (which increased union power, extended the scope of collective bargaining, and allowed the election of workers' representatives to public sector company boards) "did little to modify in a fundamental way the traditional structure of French industrial relations."[38]

In summary, therefore, France seems to have moved toward the German model at the macroeconomic policy level: "The trends observed over the last 10 to 15 years are leading to a gradual convergence of the two economies."[39] At the micro level, on the other hand, paternalism continued and German practices of social dialogue were clearly considered as "cumbersome, paralyzing . . . far too time-consuming."[40]

This switch to German demand management policies on the surface seems paradoxical. Earlier on France had shunned such a model when its own performance seemed superior. It now embraced it even though German performance (bar the short-lived experience of 1974–75) was hardly exceptional (Table 3-5). Several reasons may explain such a conversion. First, was the fear, widespread also elsewhere, that rapid (and variable) inflation was inimical to economic growth. Second, was the feeling, again shared by other countries, that depreciations had uncertain effects on competitiveness as currencies had become more flexible and nonprice factors more important. Because instruments that had earlier been successful now seemed impotent, France had to embrace orthodoxy.

Seen in this light, the refusal to countenance any serious change in industrial relations is more understandable. "Competitive disinflation" requires an acquiescent labor force and weak unions. Germany's codetermination need not ensure either, at least in the absence of many of the other conditions that have shaped the country's industrial relations. The danger of such a dual strategy is, however, that eruptions of militancy in the wake of deflation cannot be excluded (and indeed have occurred in the early 1990s, if only in piecemeal fashion). In the

[37] Commission du Bilan, *La France en mai 1981*, vol. 3 (Paris: La Documentation française, 1981), p. 178.
[38] D. Gallie, "*Les Lois Auroux*: The Reform of French Industrial Relations?," in H. Machin and V. Wright, eds., *Economic Policy and Policy-Making under the Mitterrand Presidency, 1981–1984*.
[39] J. Mistral, "France-Allemagne: Concurrence et convergence," *Economie et statistique* 246–47 (September 1991): 5.
[40] Albert, *Capitalisme contre capitalisme*, p. 132.

Table 3-5. Comparative macroeconomic performance, 1973–90

	France	Germany	Italy	United Kingdom
	Average annual percentage changes			
GDP	2.4	2.1	2.8	1.9
Industrial production	1.5	1.4	2.0	1.0
Manufacturing productivity[a]	2.9	1.8	4.3	2.9
Consumer prices	8.2	3.5	12.5	10.3
	Annual averages			
Current account balance[b]	− 0.3	1.8	− 0.7	− 1.0
Unemployment rate[c]	7.4	5.5	8.8	7.4
Gap between actual and potential output[d]	3.6	4.7	2.5	5.0
Share of world exports of manufactures[e] 1973	9.5	22.1	6.8	9.4
1990	9.7	20.6	8.6	8.6

SOURCES: Central Statistical Office, *Monthly Review of External Trade Statistics* (Newport, Gwent: CSO, December 1992); International Monetary Fund, *International Financial Statistics* (Washington, D.C.: IMF 1992); NIESR, *Economic Review* (London: NIESR, various issues); OECD, *National Accounts, 1960–1990* (Paris: OECD, 1992); OECD, *Historical Statistics, 1960–1990* (Paris: OECD, 1992).
[a]Value added per employee.
[b]In percent of current price GDP, 1974–90.
[c]In percent of the labor force, 1974–90.
[d]Absolute value of gap; tentative author's estimates derived using data from R. Torres and J. P. Martin, "Measuring Potential Output in the Seven Major OECD Countries," *OECD Economic Studies*, no. 14 (Spring 1990), pp. 127–149.
[e]Share in the exports of the eleven major industrialized countries.

1960s such eruptions were defused by rapid productivity growth and/ or devaluations. The first option is not available in the low-growth climate of the 1990s; the second has, so far, been ruled out by policy.

CONCLUSIONS

Since the 1960s France has moved from a distinctive way of formulating macroeconomic policies to a much less differentiated set of instruments, gradually jettisoning some of its special forms of intervention. Diffuse protectionism, still popular in the 1950s, was whittled down in the process of European integration. Economic planning, erstwhile deemed to have been very successful, lost much of its appeal and influence through the 1960s. Demand management, seen to have stabilized activity and improved competitiveness thanks to two "aggressive" devaluations, was progressively abandoned (not only in

France, of course) during the stagflation of the later 1970s and early 1980s. Industrial policies, considered as a main element in a design to keep France competitive and technologically advanced, were scaled down from the mid-1980s.

In part these trends reflect the perception that policies had either failed or were no longer relevant. Protectionism was clearly not a viable long-run strategy. Planning was of diminishing use in an increasingly sophisticated and open economy. Devaluations lost some of their effectiveness in a world of erratically floating exchange rates and high inflationary expectations. Industrial policies, in the eyes of some at least, were of dubious utility. Throughout, the constraints of the Common Market, of the EMS, and, now, of the European Monetary Union (EMU) project, were essential ingredients in this retreat. European integration, more than emulation of Germany, seems to have been the driving force behind changes in policies.

These changes suggest that there may be, after all, an inverse Gresham's law by which "good" institutions and policies chase away "bad" ones. Such a judgment would imply, however, that what is best in Germany is macroeconomic management, whereas the micro institutions and practices of what has been called "Rhineland capitalism,"[41] were not clearly superior to those of France to warrant imitation. Yet, many observers would disagree with this view. Germany's growth performance, for instance, has been relatively mediocre since the mid-1970s, and an obsessively tight macroeconomic policy may bear some of the blame. By contrast, the microeconomics of German industrial relations has much to commend itself, be it in the areas of social peace, low cost-push pressures, or in the unions' traditional aversion to inflation and even to protectionism.[42]

This would suggest that convergence across countries may not only reflect the genuine superiority of one country's practices over that of another but also can be a function of other forces. It could simply reflect inertia and lags. Since the mid-1980s new policies were imported. Over the coming decade maybe institutions will change under the influence, for instance, of the EEC's Social Charter and of its many, German-inspired features of industrial democracy. Intellectual fashions may also play a role, as they did in the 1960s, when imitation contributed to the rapid extension of welfare states across Europe. Copying "corporatism" has hardly been popular in the recent past, whereas orthodox macroeconomic stances have been fashionable.

Yet, more important reasons must be sought elsewhere. A central question to ask is why institutional or policy changes occur. The

[41] Albert, *Capitalisme contre capitalisme.*
[42] Giersch, Paqué, and Schmieding, *The Fading Miracle.*

Keynesian/social democratic tradition would point to governments perceiving new constraints and acting in the public interest to overcome them. Hence, for instance, policies of "competitive disinflation" may have been seen as indispensable in the slow-growth world of the 1980s if membership in the EMS and the EEC was to be preserved. The policymakers, conscious of this necessity and of the broad consensus surrounding it, hoped that imitation of German demand management behavior would provide a solution. On the other hand, the same policymakers felt that France had little need for German-style industrial relations. Weak unions made for an atomistic labor market that could be counted on to deliver low-wage inflation.[43]

An alternative interpretation, be it neoclassical or Marxist—and the two are often quite similar—would focus on either rational, maximizing economic agents or on organized groups in society, pressing for (or against) particular institutional changes. Such an approach could also throw light on French reluctance toward moves to a more democratic system of industrial relations. The *patronat* was, understandably, opposed throughout the period to any significant loss in its powers of control. The trade union movement was, for a time, similarly opposed, if for very different reasons. In the eyes of the militants of the two main confederations, codetermination was seen as a betrayal of syndicalist solidarity,[44] as a "sell-out" by workers to the interests of capitalists. This attitude has changed, but the union movement, traditionally weak, has recently "been collapsing"[45] and hence has been unable to effectively push for more reformist aims.

Whatever truth there is in these two interpretations (and both seem plausible), the outcome has been one in which France has found it feasible to copy policies, but has either refrained from, or been unable to, copy institutions. The former is clearly much easier because all that is needed is to modify the way certain existing instruments (taxes, expenditures, discount rates, etc.) are used. In the latter case, the need is for changes not only in legal arrangements but also, and more important, in informal ways of behavior whose roots may often go back a long way in history.[46]

It could be argued that France's imitation of the German model, by

---

[43] L. Calmfors and J. Drifill, "Bargaining Structure, Corporatism, and Macroeconomic Performance," *Economic Policy* 6 (April 1988): 14–61.

[44] J. Lecerf, *La percée de l'économie française* (Paris: Arthaud, 1963).

[45] D. Soskice, "Wage Determination," p. 47.

[46] An example of how institutional changes can be hijacked was given to the author by Robert Boyer. In 1970–71, as part of the labor market reforms of the period, firms were asked to devote funds to the training of their workers. The scheme's main aim was that of improving the skills of manual labor (in line with Swedish and German practices), yet the funds used were overwhelmingly given to the training of higher paid white-collar employees (*cadres*). See R. Boyer, *How to Promote Cooperation within Conflicting and Divided Societies?* (Paris: CEPREMAP, 1992).

having been only partial, will raise issues in the future. First, there is always the danger that the marrying of German orthodoxy at the macro level and of Anglo-American laissez-faire at the micro level could generate bouts of social unrest in a world in which productivity (and hence real wage) growth is limited.

Second, insofar as Germany's longer run achievements were due not so much to its macroeconomic policies but to its microeconomic practices and institutions, such as its industrial relations system and the social partners' behavior, France may have been missing an essential ingredient of the German "model." By ensuring work force cooperation such a model is much more appropriate to an industrial structure that needs quick responses to changing demand conditions and no longer relies on large inventories as buffers against strikes. Similarly, success on world markets may require "institutions adapted to promoting non-price competitiveness in international trade . . . and capable of improving price/cost competitiveness through wage restraint."[47] Germany may come close to this ideal by having a system that ensures not only relatively low inflation but also a "virtuous circle of innovation, retraining and employment security."[48]

If this is true, copying one aspect of German practices without the other is no guarantee for success. The strong Franc policy "has been successful at eliminating the French inflation differential. It has been much less successful as a strategy to return to full employment through improved competitiveness."[49] Even the first achievements may well be fragile in the absence of the long-standing consensus on the major industrial relations issues that has been much more in evidence in Germany than it has in France.

This conclusion holds a more general lesson for the ongoing process of unification in Europe. Macroeconomic convergence in inflation or public finance (as enshrined in the Maastricht Treaty) can be achieved, at least by some countries, but such an achievement is no guarantee for a smooth passage to EMU. Shocks, whether symmetric or asymmetric, in the presence of differences in institutions and in labor market behavior, could still generate very different reactions and hence adjustment costs. A long process of institutional and not merely macroeconomic convergence may be necessary before Europe is ready for monetary union.

[47] D. Soskice, "Reinterpreting Corporatism and Explaining Unemployment: Coordinated and Non-coordinated Market Economies," in R. Brunetta and C. Dell'Aringa, eds., *Labour Relations and Economic Performance* (London: Macmillan, 1990), p. 173.

[48] Ibid., p. 196.

[49] O. J. Blanchard and P. A. Muet, "Competitiveness through Disinflation: An Assessment of the French Macroeconomic Strategy," *Economic Policy* 16 (April 1993): 43–44.

Part II

CONVERGING OR NATIONAL AND AUTONOMOUS?: INSTITUTIONS AND POLICIES

CHAPTER FOUR

American and Japanese Corporate Governance: Convergence to Best Practice?

W. CARL KESTER

National differences in corporate governance have been drawn into sharp relief in recent years by the advent of European economic union and the generally greater degree of capital and product market integration elsewhere in the world. Members of the EC continue to face the challenge of harmonizing disparate national laws that influence patterns of corporate governance within their borders (e.g., one share, one vote rules; chartered caps on voting rights; possible limits on bank ownership of equity; regulations governing tender offers and takeovers; and so forth). The privatization of state-owned enterprises in both western and eastern Europe, Latin America, and many parts of Asia have also forced government and business leaders to think anew about how privatized companies should be owned and controlled in the private sector.

More broadly, heightened international business competition and cross-border investment have pitched different systems of corporate governance against one another as never before, raising questions about the efficacy and fairness of one system versus another. Do Japanese industrial groups (*keiretsu*), for example, result in unfair competitive practices and impediments to trade, and is the U.S. Justice Department justified in its avowed policy of extraterritorial extension of U.S. antitrust laws? Should the "equal national treatment" principle being applied in the EC result in corporate takeover rules more nearly like the U.K. standard, which facilitates an active market for corporate control, or the German standard, which supports a more quiescent market? In general, do the corporate ownership and control practices found in economies organized around large industrial groups (e.g., Germany, Italy, Japan, Korea, and Sweden, among others) result in genuine economic efficiency fairly gained through efficacious corporate governance or in unfair restraint of trade that ultimately reduces global economic welfare? In either case, what is the potential for one or another system to emerge as a dominant means of governing large corporations, and what is the potential for an eventual convergence of various national systems of governance to some hybrid model constituting "best practice"?

By comparing typical Japanese and American patterns of corporate governance and by analyzing the observed practices in each country within the context of transaction–cost economics and agency theory, in this essay I advance two basic arguments. First, I argue that both the American and Japanese systems of governance are economically rational attempts to resolve universally typical problems of coordination and control among corporate stakeholders. However, each nation has evolved a system that is at once highly developed along one particular dimension of these problems while underdeveloped along another. Specifically, Japanese corporate governance emphasizes the reduction of the transaction costs associated with self-interested opportunism and investment in relationship-specific assets. This strategy fosters the building of stable, long-term commercial relationships among transacting companies, although general (i.e., noncorporate, nonlending) shareholders are often forced to bear potentially substantial agency costs. Anglo-American corporate governance, in contrast, emphasizes the reduction of agency costs associated with the separation of ownership from control, relying more heavily on formal, legalistic mechanisms to order commercial relationships among transacting parties. Thus, each national system has a comparative advantage, and, in their present configurations, neither can be easily judged to be strictly superior to the other in the long run.

However, it is also argued here that the two systems need not be mutually incompatible. In fact, best practice in corporate governance will involve some of the formal shareholder safeguards of the Anglo-American system, the informal arrangements of the Japanese system that tie companies together in enduring commercial relationships, and the high-powered market incentives associated with exposure to market discipline. That is, it will involve vigorous competition among vertically cooperative (possibly global) networks of companies characterized by extensive information sharing; public disclosure of critical data about performance; and close monitoring by major shareowning stakeholders, large financial institutions in particular, who have direct board representation. In principle, therefore, there is wide scope for constructive convergence of different national systems of corporate governance. But for convergence to take place, legislative action will likely be necessary to permit American companies to engage in more overtly cooperative financial and commercial relationships and to strengthen the monitoring capabilities of contemporary Japanese shareholders.

NATIONAL DIFFERENCES IN SYSTEMS OF GOVERNANCE

Considerable differences exist between Anglo-American and Japanese systems of corporate governance, so much so that confusion is invited by using the single term *corporate governance* to describe both systems.[1] For reasons to be given, it may be more suitable to label the ownership and control of Japanese corporations a system of "contractual" governance and that of American corporations of "corporate governance." For the time being, however, in order to economize terminology, the term *corporate governance* will be applied to both systems with the broadest possible interpretation, to imply the entire set of incentives, safeguards, and dispute-resolution processes used to order the activities of various corporate stakeholders, each seeking to improve its welfare through coordinated economic activity with others. Thus, the term implies more than simply the process by which the board of directors relates to corporate shareholders and top management. This process is part, but only part, of corporate governance as defined. A stylized summary of major differences in the two national systems is provided in Table 4-1.

Contracting

The comparison begins with the contracting milieu within which transactions among various corporate stakeholders take place. Broadly, Anglo-American contracting tends to be highly formal and explicit. It is quite discrete in that the scope of agreements among transacting parties (in capital, product, and labor markets) is carefully defined, as are the exact terms of exchange, performance specifications, specific duties under relevant future contingencies, and even, at times, formal procedures to be followed (e.g., third-party arbitration)

[1] For a more detailed comparison, including a comparison to German corporate governance, see W. C. Kester, "Governance, Contracting, and Investment Time Horizons: A Look at Germany and Japan," *Continental Bank Journal of Applied Corporate Finance* 5, no. 2 (Summer 1992): 83–98; and Robert W. Lightfoot, "Note on Corporate Governance Systems: The United States, Japan, and Germany," Harvard Business School Note no. 292-012, 1992.

Table 4-1. Comparison of Japanese and American corporate governance systems

	Governance element	Japan	United States
	Contracting	Implicit and rational	Explicit and formal
Information asymmetries	Public disclosure	Less than in the United States	Extensive
	Private information sharing	Extensive and partly institutionalized	Limited
	Managerial interaction	Routine, involving many people, all levels	Usually arm's length
Ownership structure	Cross-shareholdings	Highly extensive, long-term	Uncommon
	Lender ownership	Highly extensive, long-term	Constrained
Investor activism	Board composition	Inside boards; de facto stakeholder representation	Mixed board; institutional shareholders not well represented
	Stakeholder intervention	Common, especially by banks; direct influence	Uncommon, except by proxy; banks limited by equitable subordination

to settle disputes arising from unforeseen circumstances. At all points during the life of the agreement, whether it be in its execution, adjustment, or in the adjudication of a dispute, the point of reference is the formal contract itself.

Japanese contracting, in contrast, tends to be informal and implicit. The typical "basic agreement" between a Japanese auto assembler and one of its suppliers, for example, is little more than a legal boilerplate stipulating that the supplier and assembler will operate on a basis of mutual respect for each other's autonomy and maintain an atmosphere of mutual trust in their business dealings. Ballon and Tomita point out that Japanese contracts often do not even state definitely the transactions at stake so as not to restrict the flexibility considered necessary to modify the supply agreement over time.[2]

Whereas Anglo-American contracting generally relies on the written agreement itself as the central point of reference in its execution, adjustment, or in the adjudication of a dispute, Japanese contracting relies chiefly on the ongoing business relationship itself. The execu-

[2] Robert J. Ballon and Iwao Tomita, *The Financial Behavior of Japanese Corporations* (Tokyo: Kodansha International, 1988), p. 54.

tion and adaptation of business agreements in Japan are made primarily by reference to an internal set of norms and expectations built over a long history of transacting. Good managers in Japan are those who understand the interests and priorities of various stakeholder groups, are alert to the network of implicit contracts binding the company to these groups, and can be *trusted* to uphold these over time through changing circumstances.

Trust and forbearance from self-interestedly opportunistic behavior is essential to the conduct of business when implicit contracting is commonly relied on. These are engendered by a variety of factors in Japan. One is Japanese ethnic and cultural homogeneity. Well-defined and widely adhered-to social and religious norms regarding one's obligation to others make it easier to form reliable expectations about the behavior of counterparts in an exchange relationship. So-called *keiretsu* (groups of companies federated around a major bank, trading company, or large industrial manufacturer) may also have evolved their own subcultures within the broader Japanese culture that further enhances the formation of trust relationships within the group itself.

But widespread trust and forbearance are not exclusively, or even primarily, cultural phenomena. A considerable investment is made by Japanese companies in the building of trust relationships through the careful hiring, development, and *entrenchment* of managers. Most Japanese managers are hired directly after graduating from college; undergo years of training and development in which they are rotated among various functional areas of the corporation, thereby receiving exposure to a wide array of the company's internal and external constituencies; and are discouraged from separating by a reward system that makes it unattractive to leave the company.[3] It is also common for Japanese managers to be temporarily seconded to key customers, suppliers, or subcontractors to work on a collaborative project or to help solve performance problems.

Whatever other purpose these rotations and transfers may serve, they inevitably result in the creation of an extensive network of enduring personal relationships among individual managers inside and outside the company. These are crucial to the efficacy of implicit contracting in Japan, for the terms of such agreements are held more between individual managers interacting at the trading interface than between the companies per se. It is at this individual managerial level that mutual obligations are formed and bonds of trust are forged.

[3] See James Abegglen and George Stalk, Jr., *Kaisha: The Japanese Corporation* (New York: Basic Books, 1985), pp. 191–205; and W. C. Kester, *Japanese Takeovers: The Global Contest for Corporate Control* (Boston: Harvard Business School Press, 1991), pp. 66–67.

Once created, the Japanese practice of lifetime employment serves to preserve these personal relationships for many years. It also raises the cost to individual managers of untrustworthy, opportunistic behavior. Consider the following observation by a senior Japanese executive: "It's especially important in Japan for both sides [in a business relationship] to be forthcoming. The reason is that we have lifetime employment. If you treat someone badly either inside or outside the company by taking advantage of them to profit for the moment, it will not soon be forgotten. This is because people remain with the same company throughout their entire careers."

In short, a Japanese manager's effectiveness depends quite heavily on that manager's reputation for trustworthiness and his or her ability to contract implicitly with counterparts in other companies. This gives the individual manager a personal stake in ongoing transacting relationships. In doing so, the individual is given an incentive to act prophylactically against whatever broader organizational impulses may exist to take advantage of implicit agreements through opportunistic behavior.[4]

Information Asymmetries

One of the essential functions of any system of governance is to reduce the scope for engineering welfare transfers through hidden action or the exploitation of hidden information. With this objective in mind, the job of monitoring and controlling corporations is normally delegated to a board of directors, who are elected by shareholders to act on their behalf. However, the board's limited effectiveness as a shareholder safeguard has prompted virtually all countries to require periodic public disclosure of material information about performance to investors. The United States has been especially diligent in this regard, generally requiring as much, if not more, formal public disclosure of financial information than any other major industrialized nation. The Securities Act of 1933 and the Securities and Exchange Act of 1934 require companies with securities publicly traded in domestic markets to disclose considerable information on a periodic basis. In the United States generally accepted accounting principles are also among the more demanding in the world as far as public disclosure of information is concerned. In addition to such public disclosure, limited information about one or another aspect of performance may also be disclosed to lenders, trade creditors, rating agencies, and so forth.

Japanese securities laws and accounting standards generally require less public disclosure of financial performance information than is

[4] Kester, *Japanese Takeovers*, p. 63.

true in the United States. However, public disclosure of information in Japan is augmented by private, informal information sharing among companies engaged in long-term business relationships with each other. Though informal, some of this information sharing is virtually institutionalized through the various business interest associations, councils, committees, and clubs in which a large company's senior management will actively participate. Among the major *keiretsu* are at least six presidential councils that are composed of presidents of prominent companies within the group who meet monthly.[5] The resolutions of these councils are not binding on members, and they resist fiercely the image of being a group-level management body. But even so, their activities have extended to the level of coordinating group public relations, controlling the use of group trademarks, managing group joint ventures in research and production, and even discussing top personnel appointments in group members. In short, whatever the overt purpose of these councils, the collection and dissemination of information about members' experience among themselves or, in the case of supplier groups, with a common purchaser are inevitable byproducts of the association. The existence of hidden information is diminished, and the scope for hidden action is narrowed.

Augmenting these institutional associations as information-gathering tentacles are networks of executive "alumni" from main banks and other core group companies that have formally retired from lifelong careers at their original employers' and been placed in "second careers" as senior officers and directors of client companies. The aforementioned practice of transferring mid-career managers and engineers among manufacturing companies linked in a vertical chain of production also contributes to this ability to gather vital information in a timely manner.

Ownership Structure

Another factor underlying major differences between the Japanese and Anglo-American corporate governance systems is corporate ownership structure in each nation (see Table 4-2). Approximately half of all shares in American companies are held by individuals and the

[5] The best-known of these are the *Fuyo-kai* of the Fuyo group, the *Hakusui-kai* of the Sumitomo group, the *Kinyo-kai* of the Mitsubishi group, and the *Nimoku-kai* of the Mitsui group. Although a core company of its own group, Toyota Motor is a member of the *Wakabu-kai* of the Tokai group and has "observer" status in the Mitsui group's *Nimoku-kai*. Toyota's 175 primary suppliers are also organized into a group known as the *Kyoho-kai*. Nissan's 162 primary suppliers are organized into the *Takara-kai* and Mitsubishi Motor's, into the *Kashiwa-kai*. See *Industrial Groupings in Japan, 1990/91*, 9th ed. (Tokyo: Dodwell Marketing Consultants, 1990), and *The Structure of the Japanese Auto Parts Industry*, 4th ed. (Tokyo, Dodwell Marketing Consultants 1990).

Table 4-2. Ownership structure of listed corporations in Japan and Anglo-American nations, 1990–92

| Country | Financial sectors | | | | | Nonfinancial sectors | | | |
	Banks[a]	Insurance companies	Pension funds[b]	Investment companies and other	Total	Nonfinancial businesses	Households	Government	Foreign
United Kingdom	0.9	18.4	30.4	11.1	60.8	3.6	21.3	2.0	12.3
United States	0.3	5.2	24.8	9.5	39.8	n.a.	53.5	—	6.7
Japan	25.2	17.3	0.9	3.6	47.0	25.1	23.1	0.6	4.2

SOURCES: Tokyo Stock Exchange; ProShare; Federal Reserve Board "Flow of Funds."
[a]All types, including bank holding companies.
[b]Public and private.

Table 4-3. Selected cross-shareholdings in the Mitsubishi group, 1990 (%)

	Mitsubishi Bank	Mitsubishi Corp.	Mitsubishi Heavy Industries
Mitsubishi Bank	n.a.	5.0%	3.6%
Mitsubishi Corp.	1.7%	n.a.	1.6%
Mitsubishi Heavy Industries	3.0%	3.2%	n.a.
Total owned by Mitsubishi Group	18.1%	25.5%	17.2%

SOURCE: *Industrial Groupings in Japan, 1990–1991*, 9th ed. (Tokyo: Dodwell Marketing Consultants, 1990), pp. 284–323.

other half by financial institutions, other investment funds in particular. Although individuals own about half of all shares, they do only about 20 percent of the trading, whereas institutions do about 80 percent. Heavy institutional trading is not surprising, however, when one considers the types of institutions holding major equity positions in American companies: pension funds, investment companies (mutual funds), and endowments. Notably absent from this list are commercial banks and other lending institutions, which American law (the Glass-Steagall Act of 1933, the Bank Holding Company Act of 1956, and a panoply of state insurance and banking regulations) prohibits from owning stock outside of their trust departments, and nonfinancial corporations, which hold virtually none of one another's stock.[6]

In Japan corporate ownership patterns are quite different. Reciprocal equity ownership is a common practice used in Japan to link together companies with important business relationships. Cross-shareholdings usually involve only minority equity positions with no more than a few percent of outstanding shares being exchanged on a bilateral basis (see Table 4-3 for an example involving core companies in the Mitsubishi group). In the aggregate, however, as much as 25 percent of the stock of member companies in an industrial group is owned under cross-shareholding arrangements within the group itself (see Table 4-4). Substantial numbers of shares are also typically owned by corporations and financial institutions with important business ties to companies within a group, even if they are not themselves part of that group. Indeed, as shown in Table 4-2, 70 percent of the outstanding equity of publicly listed Japanese companies are owned by financial institutions and other corporations. Accompanying many (though not all) of these holdings by the financial and corporate sectors are implicit but widely understood and rigorously observed

[6] Lightfoot, "Note on Corporate Governance Systems," pp. 3–5.

Table 4-4. Percentage of reciprocally owned shares in Japanese industrial groups, 1987 (%)

Mitsui group	18.0
Mitsubishi group	25.3
Sumitomo group	24.5
Fuyo group	18.2
DKB group	14.6
Sanwa	10.9

Source: Industrial Bank of Japan.

agreements not to sell shares held in connection with ongoing business relationships.

Investor Activism

Perhaps the most powerful safeguard in the Japanese corporate governance system is the ability of one or more equity-owning stakeholders to intervene directly and explicitly in the affairs of another company when needed to correct a problem. This is by no means a routine or highly frequent occurrence, but it is common—indeed, expected—under certain circumstances. Their assistance can be as modest as helping a troubled company generate new sales or as dramatic as injecting new capital, restructuring assets, and replacing top management.

Typically, such intervention is led by a company's main bank, usually to remedy nonperformance in the face of impending financial distress. This "responsibility" generally falls to the troubled company's main bank because it usually is the largest single supplier of capital and typically holds both debt and equity claims against those companies for which it acts as main bank. It also has quicker access to more information and a larger network of client companies than most other equity-owning stakeholders. Sumitomo Bank, for example, aided one of the group clients, Sumitomo Metal Industries, by exploiting its lending relationship with Nissan, Mazda, and Matsushita Electric to act as go-between in arranging new sheet-metal supply contracts.[7] Whereas fear of triggering equitable subordination of their loans keeps most American lenders on the sidelines until a loan agreement is formally breached, and even then restrains the degree of intervention, Japanese main banks effectively assume such subordination from the outset and take far-reaching, early steps to limit the damage.

[7] Michael Gerlach, "Business Alliances and the Strategy of the Japanese Firms," *California Management Review*, Fall 1987: 129.

Intervention is by no means limited to banks, however. Although less common, major industrial stakeholders will sometimes take quick, decisive steps to supplant an important supplier's or customer's autonomy with temporary de facto administrative control when nonperformance becomes imminent. Mitsubishi Electric, for instance, played a leading role in the restructuring of Akai Electric, a major supplier and purchaser of electronic parts and equipment within the Mitsubishi group. In 1990 Nissan Motor also assumed effective operating control of Fuji Heavy Industries, the maker of Subaru automobiles. Although Nissan owned only 4% of Fuji Heavy Industries' stock at the time, it consistently sent executives to become directors of Fuji, relied on Fuji to produce Nissan-brand passenger cars until 1986, and collaborated with Fuji in the manufacture of aerospace and marine products. The de facto "takeover" occurred without the restructuring of any debt or a single share of stock changing hands among Fuji's major equity-owning stakeholders.

For its part, the United States has witnessed considerable experimentation with shareholder activism in the 1980s and early 1990s. Although most large institutional shareholders still refrain from interfering with management, the number of shareholder proposals sponsored by institutions rose from 28 in 1988, to 70 in 1989, and to 120 in 1990. The 1991 proxy season saw a decrease in shareholder resolutions, however: Only 101 of 153 of those submitted by institutions came to a vote.[8]

Despite this discernible pickup on shareholder activism and SEC attempts to accommodate such activism, the proxy voting mechanism remains a relatively weak and infrequently successful safeguard of shareholder interests in the United States.[9] Consequently, the United States and other economies where the Anglo-American system of governance is widely used (e.g., Australia, Canada, and the United Kingdom) have depended heavily on active markets for corporate control. Through takeover activity equity ownership of an underperforming company can be concentrated in the hands of new shareholders who may then change the target company's patterns of investment, revoke other policies having a deleterious effect on shareholder value, and perhaps change management itself.

---

[8] "Cutting Loose from Shareholder Activists," *Business Week*, 8 July 1991, p. 34.

[9] An example of successful action by shareholders was Time-Warner's 1991 withdrawal of a rights offering after shareholders, including at least three pension funds, sued the company in fourteen separate actions. The deal was not stopped by shareholder sentiment alone, however. Shareholder influence became pivotal, but only after the SEC itself raised objections to the offering. Whereas this market is relatively quiescent in countries such as Japan and Germany, it is quite active, and often hostile, in Anglo-American nations.

GOVERNING MANAGERS VERSUS STAKEHOLDER RELATIONSHIPS

These broad differences between Japanese and Anglo-American corporate governance are both striking and significant.[10] They naturally beg the questions of how such different systems evolved in these two highly industrialized nations, and whether or not one system is superior to the other. Can we eventually expect, in other words, one system to dominate another in the long run?

Answers to these questions begin with an understanding of the economic purposes ultimately being served by the Japanese and Anglo-American systems. Both are attempting to address problems of coordination and control associated with the tendency of fundamentally self-interested corporate stakeholders to undertake some actions or to exploit some information, hidden from the view of other stakeholders. However, each emphasizes different aspects of the coordination and control problems.

Broadly speaking, problems of coordination and control can be classified into two categories: those associated with the separation of ownership and control in the modern corporation, and those associated with the establishment and maintenance of contractual exchange among separate enterprises.[11] Problems of the first type were initially identified by Adolph Berle and Gardiner Means and substantially extended by Michael Jensen and William Meckling.[12] The central problem treated by these writers is that, for reasons of self-interested opportunism, agents (e.g., corporate managers) hired to do a job cannot always be counted on to act in the best interests of the principals (e.g., shareholders) who engaged them. This natural tendency induces principals to expend resources in the development of incentives and safeguards designed to reduce self-interestedly opportunistic behavior by agents. The cost of designing and running these systems and the value lost because of the remaining self-interested opportunism by agents that cannot be eradicated are the "agency costs" that rational investors must take into account when pricing the company's securities. From this perspective the primary purpose of corporate governance is to create cost-effective monitoring, bonding, and incentive systems that will reduce the amount of foregone value associated with the separation of ownership from control.

[10] See Kester, *Japanese Takeovers*, and "Industrial Groups as Systems of Contractual Governance," *Oxford Review of Economic Policy* 8, no. 3 (Fall 1992): 24–44.

[11] Kester, *Japanese Takeovers*, pp. xvi–xvii.

[12] Adolph Berle and Gardiner Means, *The Modern Corporation and Private Property* (New York: Macmillan, 1932); Michael C. Jensen and William Meckling, "Theory of the Firm: Managerial Behavior, Agency Costs, and Capital Structure," *Journal of Financial Economics* 3 (October 1976): 305–60.

The problems associated with contractual exchange were first identified in the economics literature by Ronald Coase and further analyzed by Oliver Williamson, among others.[13] The central problem addressed by these economists is the optimal means of organizing exchange. When should a company procure its needs in the market, and when should it "internalize" the market by integrating operations so as to be self-sufficient in one or more capacities? What, in other words, is the optimal boundary between the administrative hierarchy of a firm and the competitive marketplace? Reliance on arm's length transactions in markets allows for greater specialization in production activities and the realization of scale economies but also poses risks associated with self-interested opportunism. After a company invests in some expensive and highly specialized assets to support transactions with particular customer or supplier, for example, that counterpart could threaten to abandon its relationship with the company if terms of trade are not shifted in its favor. The courts might enforce the original agreement, but legal adjudication of such disputes is often too slow, costly, and cumbersome to be relied upon routinely as a means of handling opportunism of this nature. Absorbing important upstream suppliers or downstream customers provides greater control over the transaction stream and relieves some of the hazards of opportunism—but often at the expense of efficiency. The high-powered incentives provided by competitive markets can be difficult to replicate and manage inside an organization. Moreover, other conditions that Williamson labels "bureaucratic disabilities" (e.g., an overextension of managerial capabilities or the internal politicization of decision making) may emerge.

From the perspective of the contractual exchange (or "transaction cost economics") literature, the central problem is to devise methods for governing agreements or relationships among companies that optimally balance the economies and hazards of transacting in the market with those of administratively controlling the same activities within an organizational hierarchy. Henceforth, such a system will be referred to here as a "contractual" governance system. Following Gilson and Roe[14] and Kester, it should be differentiated from the more common term *corporate* governance, which here specifically implies the system used to align the priorities of managers with those of share-

---

[13] Ronald H. Coase, "The Nature of the Firm," *Economica N.S.* 4 (1937): 386–405. Oliver E. Williamson, *The Economic Institutions of Capitalism: Firms, Markets, Relational Contracting* (New York: Free Press, 1985).

[14] Ronald J. Gilson and Mark J. Roe, "Understanding the Japanese Keiretsu: Overlaps between Corporate Governance and Industrial Organization," John M. Olin Program in Law and Economics Working Paper no. 97, Stanford, Calif., August 1992.

holders. Contractual governance may span a continuum bounded at one end by the writing of explicit, detailed contracts, which may then be enforced by court order in the event of attempted breach by one of the parties. At the other end is reliance on implicit contracting founded on trust relationships and possibly reinforced by largely non-legalistic mechanisms structured to encourage voluntary compliance with informal agreements.[15]

The essential differences between the Anglo-American and Japanese systems of governance reflect the relative importance assigned by the respective nations to each of the dual problems of coordination and control—the Berle and Means/Jensen and Meckling problem (i.e., the governance of managers by owners) versus the Coase and Williamson problem (i.e., governing transactional relationships). Consider the structure of financial claims against corporations domiciled in both nations. Typically, the ownership of claims against large, publicly owned U.S. corporations exhibits a high degree of specificity in risk bearing. Fairly clear, bright lines tend to delineate one stakeholder group from another. American equity investors in particular are a distinct, separate, and largely dispersed class of claimants against the corporation.

One advantage of such risk specialization is that it tends to increase capital availability and to lower corporate capital costs by providing issuers and investors alike with a broader menu of risk–return alternatives from which to choose when executing financing and investment decisions. It also yields a clear-cut residual claimant—equity—with unambiguous incentives to monitor corporate management, for it is the residual claimant who will benefit most from efficient production and the reduction of agency costs.[16] Thus, for the contemporary Anglo-American corporation with its largely specialized stakeholders and its distinctly separate residual claimants, the problems associated with the separation of ownership from control become central to the governance issue, more so than the governing of intercorporate business relationships. The election of outside directors, the use of the proxy voting mechanism, and, as of late, the development of shareholder advisory committees have emerged as preferred techniques for solving many of these problems. And when these governance techniques fail, the market for corporate control has been depended upon to concentrate ownership in the hands of new shareholders who may then change an underperforming company's patterns of investment, revoke other policies having a deleterious effect on shareholder value, and perhaps change management itself.

---

[15] Kester, "Governance, Contracting, and Investment Time Horizons."
[16] Gilson and Roe, "Understanding the Japanese Keiretsu."

Table 4-5. Debt and equity ownership in Nissan Motor Corp.,
top ten shareholders, 1990

Shareholder	Equity ownership		Debt ownership	
	Yen (billion)	%	Yen (billion)	%
Dai-Ichi Mutual Life Insurance	150.2	5.6	n.a.	n.a.
Industrial Bank of Japan	123.3	4.6	57.3	9.9
Fuji Bank	123.3	4.6	56.5	9.8
Nippon Life Insurance	112.6	4.2	9.0	1.6
Sumitomo Bank	69.7	2.6	38.4	6.6
Yasuda Trust & Banking	69.7	2.6	25.9	4.5
Kyowa Bank	64.4	2.4	n.a.	n.a.
Sumitomo Life Insurance	59.0	2.2	5.0	0.9
Mitsubishi Trust & Banking	56.3	2.1	n.a.	0.0
Nissan Fire & Marine Insurance	53.6	2.0	192.1	n.a.
Total, top ten	882.1	32.9	579.5	33.3
Grand total	2681.5	100.0		100.0

SOURCE: *Industrial Groupings in Japan, 1990–1991*, 9th ed. (Tokyo: Dodwell Marketing Consultants, 1990), p. 496.

In Japan residual claimants are not for the most part separate and distinct from other stakeholders. Rather, a majority of stock is often owned by a mere dozen or two shareholders who quite often possess other claims against the firm. Note the distribution of debt and equity ownership among Nissan Motor's top ten shareholders, shown in Table 4-5. Of those seven whose lending positions were known at the end of fiscal year 1990, six alone account for 192.1 billion yen of Nissan's then total outstanding borrowing of 579.5 billion yen (33.1 percent); these same six held shares in Nissan worth approximately 558 billion yen (20.8 percent of total market value). These financial institutions were neither pure debt nor pure equity holders. Their overall investment in Nissan was akin to owning a strip of Nissan's capital base.

Such commingling of claims is even more pronounced in other cases. It is not uncommon, for example, for a large *sogo shosha* (Japanese trading company) sitting at the center of a major Japanese *keiretsu* simultaneously to have purchase agreements and supply agreements with a particular industrial corporation within its group, extend trade credit to it, take up a pro rata share of its publicly issued bonds (if any), and own equity in the company. Even if only one of these contracts may be dominant at any given time, it is nevertheless difficult to classify unambiguously the nature of the relationship between the trading company and the industrial corporation.

In this sort of environment the Coase and Williamson problem—achieving efficiency of exchange—is central to the governance process. The role of equity in Japan is less to vest ownership rights in residual claimants with strong incentives to monitor management than it is to bind otherwise diverse stakeholders to one another, a kind of financial "glue" that helps hold parties together in long-term trading relationships. It does so by attenuating frictions that normally arise among various stakeholders when they each hold separate and distinct claims. The incentives to breach contracts with suppliers and customers in the interests of transferring value to shareholders, or to borrow money and then take extraordinary risks that might benefit shareholders at the expense of lenders, are reduced when the injured stakeholders are also the company's principal shareholders. Helping troubled companies work out financial problems is also made easier when the principal providers of capital hold roughly comparable bundles of senior and junior, short-term and long-term claims against the company; conflicts of interest and free-rider problems are minimized.

The common assertion by Japanese managers that shareholder interests rank comparatively low on their list of priorities is partly explained by the fact that a substantial number of a large company's shareholders are its major creditors, customers, and suppliers. For most of these shareholders, their commercial trading/lending relationships with the company are as important, if not more so, than their equity investments per se. Not surprisingly, therefore, Japanese managers tend to view their proximate task as the preservation and enhancement of these complex relationships rather than an immediate, direct pursuit of any one stakeholder's interests, such as is the case with pure equity owners.

The agency problem is addressed in Japan by placing representatives of significant share-owning stakeholders on the board and by relying on main banks as delegated monitors for other major lender or owners. The production process itself may also serve as a kind of monitoring system for share-owning stakeholders in Japan. Intense product market rivalry in many industries; the organization of production into less vertically integrated enterprises; and the comparatively high levels of relationship-specific investment undertaken by factor providers, subcontractors, industrial customers and so forth, all combine to yield substantial incentives for mutual monitoring among key stakeholders. Their interdependence, combined with their risky, relationship-specific investment, and their joint exposure to fierce (in some industries) competition means that *all* suffer if their joint efforts are unsuccessful. [7]

Such monitoring by large share-owning stakeholders does not, of course, completely obviate the Berle and Means problem of the sep-

---

[17] Gilson and Roe, "Understanding the Japanese Keiretsu."

aration between ownership and control. Indeed, from the perspective of Japanese household or nongroup institutional shareholders without a voice on the board, this sort of problem may actually be *worse* in Japan than in the United States. Overinvestment in declining core industries, excess manpower, excess product proliferation, and speculative uses of excess cash, among other problems, appear to be at least as problematic in Japan as in the United States.[18]

In the final analysis, however, the overarching effect of the Japanese focus on *contractual* rather than simply *corporate* governance may have yielded better long-run corporate performance and more valuable enterprises than in the Anglo-American nations, notwithstanding the fact that Japanese companies may do no better (and may even be worse, on a relative basis) in the achievement of maximum potential shareholder value as measured by stock prices. Put differently, the system of *corporate* governance in Japan may yield only "satisficing," not maximizing, behavior with respect to shareholder value; but Japan's *contractual* governance system permits managers to "satisfice" relative to a higher production possibility frontier for a given level of inputs.

Toward a Model of Best Practice

The foregoing analysis suggests that Japanese-style corporate governance, like its Anglo-American counterpart, is fundamentally a rational attempt to control and coordinate the activities of diverse, self-interested stakeholders. What appear, from an Anglo-American perspective, to be subtleties and idiosyncracies with no rationale other than cultural artifacts or attempts to restrain trade and entrench management arguably arise from a somewhat different governance objective, that of achieving transactional efficiency rather than minimizing agency costs, the latter being the proximate objective of the contemporary Anglo-American system of governance.

These two objectives of governance are not inherently incompatible, however. Indeed, the differing relative strengths of the Japanese and Anglo-American systems of governance suggests a model of "best practice" with respect to governance. An ideal system of governance would combine the adaptive efficiencies associated with the sort of long-term, cooperative relationships found in abundance in Japan with the high-powered market incentives and safeguards against abuse that are the dominant forces in the Anglo-American system. In brief, the key characteristics of successful corporate and contractual

[18] Kester, *Japanese Takeovers*, pp. 169–235.

governance systems that in combination may yield best practice would include a high degree of implicit, relational contracting on the basis of strong trust relationships; concentrated ownership by active, knowledgeable stakeholders with long-term commercial as well as financial interests in the corporation; vigorous product and/or factor market rivalry; and for publicly owned corporations, extensive public disclosure of financial performance information.[19]

Taken individually and in various subsets, these elements may be found as characteristics of many systems of governance found around the world. But they are seldom, if ever, found together as a complete set, although it is only in complete combination that their efficacy as components of a governance system is maximized. Concentrated equity ownership among large investors is likely to be of less value if those owners have short holding periods or prefer simply to sell their interests if and when difficulties arise; the temptation to be opportunistic in order to achieve short-run gains is likely to be higher under such an ownership regime. Likewise, having long horizons will be helpful only to the extent that investors have the voice and power to involve themselves in corporate affairs (to become active investors on a selective basis) if and when performance falters. Active involvement, in turn, will be constructive only if the investors, as represented by their nominated directors on the board, have the knowledge and expertise necessary to make intelligent policy changes. Without genuine rivalry among horizontally competitive firms, long-term cooperative relationships among firms joined in a vertical stream of production and distribution might achieve little more than a cooperative shirking equilibrium.[20] Similarly, lack of adequate disclosure may lead to unwarranted private gains by managers at the expense of other stakeholders, shareholders in particular, and the compromising of the capital market's ability to price securities fairly. In short, the absence of any one of these elements of governance makes more likely the emergence of a suboptimal outcome. Corporate and contractual governance at their best require the simultaneous presence of all.

The importance of horizontal rivalry to the effectiveness of the type of corporate governance system advocated here cannot be overstated. Although not part of an agency design, horizontal rivalry creates nonetheless a context that helps to ensure that stable, long-term relationships will not be turned into self-serving shirking arrangements. Consider Japan's industrial groups. However cooperative they may be internally, major Japanese manufacturers normally compete extremely aggressively with each other. Indeed, in many cases, Japanese

---

[19] Kester, "Governance, Contracting, and Investment Time Horizons," p. 39.
[20] Ibid.

industrial activity can be described as intense *horizontal* rivalry among *vertically* cooperative groups.

The automotive industry in Japan presents a classic example of this cooperation–competition duality. Although it has a smaller domestic market for cars and trucks than do the United States, Japan nonetheless has fifteen assemblers of cars and trucks compared to only six domestically owned assemblers for the United States. Admittedly, some of these Japanese producers heavily depend on alliances with larger assemblers (e.g., Fuji Heavy Industries and Nissan Motors; Hino Motors and Toyota). But even after adjusting for these alliances, at least nine major independent auto assemblers remain.

A similar story can be told of the steel industries in Japan and in the United States: though smaller in size domestically, Japan's steel industry today contains more than fifteen major independent domestic rivals with annual sales of $1 billion or more; the number of rivals of similar size in the United States has shrunk to only eight. Although the Japanese steel industry has been well-known for engaging in horizontally cooperative cartels under government auspices during periods of overcapacity, these have been notoriously difficult to maintain. More often than not, efforts at price maintenance during the 1960s collapsed in the face of dissent of one or more of the major producers (usually the independently minded Sumitomo Metal Industries). Even when pricing discipline was maintained, producers continued to compete for future market position through investment in productive capacity, which more than quadrupled between 1960 and 1970 despite only a doubling of domestic demand.[21]

Even within groups, a healthy respect for, and preservation of, high-powered market incentives arising from horizontal product market rivalry is in evidence. Intragroup commercial relationships are never exclusive. Notice, for example, that the intragroup sales and procurement figures shown in Table 4-6 vary between 8 percent and 30 percent, indicating extensive dependence on nongroup business as well. Executives of the major Japanese auto assemblers report that they are constantly striving to strike the right balance between exerting control over and respecting the autonomy of their group suppliers. Although high degrees of control ensure more focused attention to the assemblers' specific needs, thus yielding adaptive efficiencies in responding to changing market conditions, high degrees of autonomy yield greater operating efficiencies induced by high-powered market incentives. Japanese assemblers are acutely aware of the need to signal consistently their intent to persist in long-term relationships with their suppliers, thereby encouraging invest-

---

[21] Kester, *Japanese Takeovers*, pp. 88–94.

Table 4-6. Intragroup sales and procurement in major Japanese *keiretsu*, 1981 (%)

	Six major keiretsu	Original zaibatsu groups[a]	Modern groups[b]
Average intragroup sales[c]			
Presidents council members	10.8	13.4	8.6
All group industrial companies	20.4	29.0	14.9
Average intragroup procurement[c]			
Presidents council members	11.7	14.8	9.1
All group industrial companies	12.4	18.6	8.2

SOURCE: Kigyo Shūdan no Jittai ni tsuite [Concerning the actual condition of business groups], 21 June 1983.
[a]The Mitsubishi, Mitsui, and Sumitomo groups.
[b]The Fuyo, DKB, and Sanwa groups.
[c]Statistics are exclusive of group financial institutions.

ment by suppliers in relationship-specific assets while stopping well short of granting suppliers an outright guarantee of business, which would blunt incentives to manage efficiently.

Predictably where vigorous horizontal competition among efficient-scale rivals is lacking in Japan, so too is good industry performance. McCraw and O'Brien contrast the efficiency of the Japanese distribution sector with that of the Japanese steel industry and with the distribution sectors of other nations.[22] They observe that the restoration in 1956 of the previously repealed Department Store Act (which slowed the spread of chain branches of large department stores), its 1976 extension to manufacturers' direct retailing outlets through the Special Act for the Adjustment of Retailing, and the Large-Scale Retail Store Act of 1973 have all been used in Japan to protect small shopkeepers by limiting the competitive advantage of larger chains. The result, they conclude, has been a proliferation of small-scale wholesalers and retailers and a complex, multilayered system of distribution in Japan in which superfluous middlemen add to the cost of bringing products to market without creating offsetting efficiencies.

FORCES OF CHANGE

Japan

Relative to Anglo-American practice and the standard of best practice just described, the chief shortcoming of Japanese governance is its

[22] Thomas K. McCraw and Patricia A. O'Brien, "Production and Distribution: Competition Policy and Distribution: Competition Policy and Industry Structure," in T. K. McCraw, ed., *America versus Japan* (Boston: Harvard Business School Press, 1986).

low ability to control the agency costs associated with the separation of corporate ownership from corporate control. In modern Japanese business history controlling agency costs has been of second-order importance, though perhaps for good reason. So long as attractive real growth opportunities were abundant and product and factor market rivalry was fierce, corporate managers were likely to deploy resources in a highly disciplined way. High rates of real growth, moreover, can do much to attenuate disputes among corporate stakeholders by relieving pressures to compare one group's gains to those of another from a zero-sum perspective. So long as growth could be sustained, virtually all stakeholders benefited and conflict among them could be held to a minimum.

Even though they possibly recognize deficiencies in the value-maximizing behavior of the corporations in which they invest, independent, noncontrolling Japanese shareholders may nevertheless acquiesce to such behavior so long as they perceive the advantages of sustaining long-term business relationships that support efficient, relationship-specific investment to be worth more than the foregone incremental value. They may tolerate agency costs associated with the separation of ownership from control as high or even higher than those present in Anglo-American corporations if the offsetting gains from bearing such costs are greater efficiency in production arising from higher levels of relationship-specific investment and substantially reduced transaction costs arising from a greater use of flexible, implicit contracts; the mitigation of hazards associated with relationship-specific investment; reliance on nonlegal dispute resolution techniques instead of costly legal adjudication; and so forth.[23]

However, as Japan progresses through the 1990s, it is no longer clear that its emphasis on contractual governance, evidently so well suited for a high-growth environment, will be acceptable in the future. Indeed, there is mounting evidence that for some Japanese corporate shareholders a concern for agency costs is beginning to dominate concern for transaction costs.

In Japan the 1980s saw a buildup of tremendous financial slack in Japanese corporations, a distancing of companies from traditional main bank relationships, and a deployment of cash into speculative securities investments and strategies of unrelated diversification of dubious value.[24] These trends were tolerated by the vast majority of Japanese stakeholders so long as market returns on equity investments remained high. But the bursting of the Tokyo Stock Exchange

[23] Gilson and Roe, "Understanding the Japanese Keiretsu."
[24] Kester, *Japanese Takeovers*, pp. 219–35.

bubble in 1991 removed this last mask from the underlying agency costs that arguably have always been present and, more recently, growing in Japanese business.

The mounting realization that the Achilles heel of Japanese corporate governance is its inability to control these agency costs has led to pressures for reform arising from many different quarters, including supposedly traditional stable shareholders. Reduced to their essentials the proposed reforms are calls for a greater transparency of corporate dealings and the payout of more cash to investors. Japanese insurance companies, for example, have been in the vanguard of those calling for higher cash dividend payouts—one means of reducing the agency costs associated with high free cash flow.[25] In the same vein even the Keidanren (the Federation of Economic Organizations, the leading Japanese business association representing private sector business interests) has been advocating the relaxation of prohibitions in the Japanese commercial code against a company repurchasing its own shares, which is yet another means of disgorging cash from bloated corporate balance sheets. Akio Morita, chairman of Sony Corporation, has also called on Japanese businesses to focus on profitability; provide better returns to shareholders, particularly in the form of higher cash dividend payments; and to adopt financial reporting practices that better reflect actual corporate performance.

Recently a special government advisory panel formed partly in response to U.S. demands arising from the Structural Impediments Initiative (SII) has recommended that companies be required to appoint an independent outsider as one of its statutory auditors to monitor the activities of senior management and the board of directors. So-called statutory, or standing, auditors in Japan (to be distinguished from the auditor of financial statements) are nominally responsible to shareholders, but in fact they report to the company's chairman and chief executive officer. With but few exceptions, they have traditionally been appointed to this position from the ranks of management itself, a practice that has rendered their effectiveness as a shareholder safeguard almost meaningless. In a related recommendation, the panel also recommended that shareholders be given easier access to company accounts. Presently only shareholders owning 10 percent or more of a company's stock have the legal right to demand inspection of company books.[26]

Perhaps the most overt sign of concern about corporate governance in Japan can be found in a recent article on the subject published by

[25] Ibid., pp. 215–16.
[26] Robert Thomson, "Move to Make Japanese Groups More Transparent," *Financial Times*, 11 Februrary 1993, p. 6.

the Nomura Research Institute. The authors, Shigeru Watanabe and Isao Yamamoto, link steadily declining returns on capital for Japanese industry since 1981 with inadequate corporate governance that has allowed financial slack to be expended in poor investments.[27] They go so far as to label the current Japanese recession a "corporate governance recession."

Significantly, however, what is *not* being called for in Japan is an unwinding of cross-shareholding relationships, the further diminishment of the power of the large city banks, or a general breakup of *keiretsu*. Instances of sales of crossheld shares and termination of main bank relationships have been more frequently observed in recent years. But it is premature to infer from these observations an abandonment of Japanese-style governance in favor of Anglo-American–style governance. Many sales of stably held shares are little more than efforts to book current period gains that can be used to boost sagging profits and are followed by nearly immediate repurchases of the same shares. Other sales represent only a fraction of stably held stock, not the entire amount; still others are sales to some other stable owner of the stock in question, thereby causing little substantive change in the cross-shareholding relationships.[28] As for the main bank relationships, the short-listing of clients for which banks are willing to serve as main banks is less a breakdown in the system then a process of adjustment and consolidation following a decade that saw banks overextending themselves in such tie-ups and accepting too little return for the risks incurred. In short, Japanese governance may be undergoing a period of stress and transformation that will see it adopt some of the features of Anglo-American corporate governance, but there is little evidence that it is likely to converge completely with the Anglo-American system in its current configuration.

The United States

The United States is also witnessing considerable foment in its corporate governance practices, most of it having to do with widening of scope of shareholder activism and perfecting the board of directors as the primary safeguard of shareholder interests. The most visible and widely discussed changes involving strengthening the role of outside directors (e.g., via increasing their numbers on boards, creating a "lead director," ensuring the independence of nominating commit-

[27] Shigeru Watanabe and Isao Yamamoto, "Corporate Governance in Japan: Ways to Improve Low Profitability," *NRI Quarterly* 1, no. 3 (Winter 1992): 28–45.
[28] W. C. Kester, "Banks in the Board Room: Germany, Japan, and the United States," in Samuel L. Hayes, III, ed., *Financial Services: Perspectives and Challenges* (Boston: Harvard Business School Press, 1993), p. 86.

tees, separating the roles of chairman of the board and chief executive officer, and relaxing proxy voting regulations to make it easier
for large shareholders to communicate with one another regarding
matters requiring a shareholder vote). These are important and noteworthy innovations, but they are essentially refinements of the traditional Anglo-American systems of governance.[29] That is, their focus is
chiefly on remedying problems associated with the separation of ownership from control.

Such changes will doubtlessly reduce agency costs still further, but
they will do little in and of themselves to move Anglo-American governance toward the standards of best practice set forth. Although
large financial institutional shareholders will gain a stronger voice in
the boardroom and shareholder activism will generally increase, the
aforementioned changes are likely to do little to increase expertise on
American boards, attenuate frictions among various classes of stakeholders, and foster the sort of stable, long-term relationships that
have been important sources of transactional efficiencies in other environments. Thus, to the extent that the lack of an effective contractual governance system has contributed to suboptimal investment by
some sectors of American manufacturing, incremental changes targeted at the board of directors offer little promise of closing the performance gap separating U.S. industrial corporations from their foreign rivals.[30]

Failure to observe more sweeping reforms of American corporate
governance is not entirely surprising, however, in light of the many
pieces of legislation that contribute to its present configuration. A
plethora of laws and regulations prevent many large American financial institutions from becoming major shareholders in industrial corporations and from exercising significant influence, either individually or as a group, in the governance of these corporations.[31] The
Glass-Steagall Act of 1933, for example, prohibits banks from owning
stock in other companies directly or indirectly through affiliations
with investment banks. The Bank Holding Company Act of 1956 prohibits banks from owning more than 5 percent of the voting stock in
any nonbank company or from otherwise controlling an industrial
firm. In addition, the U.S. tax code encourages diversification of
bank-managed trust holdings so that no more than 10 percent of a

[29] See Martin Lipton and Jay W. Lorsch, "A Modest Proposal for Improved Corporate Governance" (unpublished MS), Harvard Business School, Boston, August 1992.
[30] See Kester, "Governance, Contracting, and Investment Time Horizons," and Michael Porter, *Capital Choices: Changing the Way America Invests in Industry* (Boston: Harvard Business School, 1992).
[31] Lightfoot, "Note on Corporate Governance Systems."

bank's trust funds are invested in any one corporation. Finally, lenders that exert actual or effective control over a company could (under standards that remain ambiguous) be subject to "equitable subordination" of their loans in the event of a bankruptcy proceeding.[32] For their part, American insurance companies, which are regulated primarily by state laws, must abide by the most restrictive of these state laws if they wish to operate nationwide. The strictest of these prohibit insurance companies from putting more than 2 percent of their assets into a single company and from owning more than 5 percent of the voting stock of any one corporation.

Although pension funds control nearly two-thirds of institutionally owned equities, they have virtually no representation on corporate boards as a result of laws that limit their voting power and discourage their active involvement in corporate governance. If it wishes to receive favorable tax treatment as a diversified fund, a pension fund must not hold more than 10 percent of any one company's stock. Other laws discourage pension funds from becoming too involved in management issues. The Employees Retirement Income Security Act of 1974 established a prudent standard for fiduciaries: managers of pension funds must be "prudent experts" in the business they undertake. Hence, if pension fund managers were to become active on the boards of business corporations in which their funds invest, they could become liable to meet higher standards of care in their investments. Although funds might attempt to coordinate themselves by initiating shareholder resolutions and voting in blocks on issues of mutual concern, until quite recently they were required to obtain approval from the SEC if they wished to influence the voting of more than ten stockholders.

As with pension funds, mutual funds managers tend to refrain from exercising large shareholder rights in order to receive favorable tax treatment. If a mutual fund is not diversified, its income is taxed first at the corporate tax rate and then again when it is distributed to the fund's shareholders. To be considered diversified under the tax code and the Investment Company Act of 1940, a fund must have at least half its investments in companies that constitute 5 percent or less of its portfolio, and it cannot own more than 10 percent of any one company's stock. Even if a fund owned 5 percent of a company's stock, the portfolio company would become a statutory affiliate of the mutual fund and its principal underwriter. If the fund wished to exercise control with another affiliate, it would need SEC approval.

[32] Jeremy Dickens, "Equitable Subordination and Analogous Theories of Lender Liability: Toward a New Model of Control," *Texas Law Review* 65 (March, 1987): 801–58.

The Potential for a Convergence of Systems

Whether or not Japanese and Anglo-American corporate governance can converge, given their present substantial differences, centers around the questions of how and why they evolved along such different paths in the first place. It is important to recognize that in the late nineteenth and early twentieth centuries, some features of Japan's contemporary system of contractual governance could be observed in American commerce and finance.[33] Although the United States did not develop giant zaibatsu, large American banks owned equity in, as well as provided loans to and underwrote the bonds of, their major industrial clients. The fortunes of these financial institutions were intimately linked to those of their major customers, resulting in close monitoring and coordination of their borrowers' activities. Reciprocal trading agreements among companies were common, as were various forms of discriminatory pricing and subsidization among companies that had trading relationships and common suppliers of capital. Tie-ins, resale price maintenance, and territorial restrictions, for example, formed vertical contractual restrictions where outright vertical integration were absent.

As such relationships and contractual restrictions became more prevalent, the two nations evidently studied the arrangements through different lenses. Japan chose the lens of transactional efficiency, magnifying the role of these arrangements as potentially useful elements of an effective system of contractual governance. The United States, in contrast, tended to view similar arrangements through a lens of antitrust laws. Market power and restraint-of-trade effects were magnified relative to others. Where Japan saw transactional efficiency and sought to preserve it, the United States saw abuse and sought to prohibit it. American antitrust legislation, originally targeted toward monopoly power created by large horizontal mergers or trade agreements, was gradually interpreted as applying to *any* type of nonstandard contractual restraints, vertical as well as horizontal, notwithstanding the transactional efficiencies that may have been fostered by long-term relationships. By the 1960s nearly any action or agreement that restricted the actions of transaction parties in a perfectly competitive market characterized by arm's-length transactions was construed as anticompetitive per se.[34] Meanwhile the U.S. banking, securities, and tax legislation came to constrain the degree to

[33] Kester, "Governance, Contracting, and Investment Time Horizons," p. 95.
[34] For further discussion of this point, see Oliver E. Williamson, "Antitrust Enforcement: Where It Has Been; Where It Is Going," in John Craven, ed., *Industrial Organization, Antitrust, and Public Policy* (Boston: Kluwer-Nijhoff, 1982).

which banks and other large "inside" investors could involve themselves in corporate supervision.

One consequence of U.S. public policy toward ownership and control relationships among firms was that many of the building blocks of governance considered so vital in Japan for joining together the interests of diverse stakeholder groups were cast aside in the United States. In place of the ownership of commingled claims by long-term stakeholders, the United States saw the proliferation of separate and narrowly focused claimants that interacted more like holders of special interests within the corporate body. Their claims became more explicit, more sharply differentiated from one another, and less customized in ways designed to preserve the continuity of long-term trading relationships.

Dispersed and separated from management and other stakeholders, equity investors retained only weak, indirect control over the companies they owned through their election of directors. In place of selective intervention by equity-owning banks such as evolved in Japan, the United States, with its bias for market-ordered solutions to trading hazards, developed an active market for corporate control to remove the hazards of investment and to effect substantial change when shareholder interests become subject to abuse.

This American approach to ownership and governance was, in many respects, extraordinarily well adapted to its historic economic and political environment. American private enterprise stayed private, unlike the companies that were nationalized in other industrializing nations, and it was able to source sufficient efficiently priced capital to sustain its expansion. But recent experience suggests that the efficacy of the American corporate governance system was greatest when its exposure to "foreign" competition was limited primarily to companies in Great Britain and Canada—close "relatives" in terms of political and economic traditions. The tremendous success of many German and Japanese companies in global and even domestic U.S. markets since the mid-1970s and the apparent inability of so many American companies to respond with maximum effectiveness to these competitive inroads have called this efficacy into question.[35]

Specifically, two major conceptual underpinnings of Anglo-American corporate governance are now under reexamination. One is that close, cooperative, and even exclusionary relationships are inimical to economic welfare. This need not be so when the restrictive relationship is of a vertical, rather than horizontal, nature. The antitrust culture of the United States has tended to tar vertical cooperation among

[35] Kester, "Banks in the Board Room," p. 87.

businesses with the same brush used to blacken horizontal collusion, efficiency gains notwithstanding; nearly any tie-in arrangement or other form of customized, nonstandard contracting has typically been viewed as anticompetitive per se and subject to legal scrutiny. This is too narrow an interpretation of these arrangements. As practiced in Japan, close vertical relationships can give rise to efficiency in contractual exchange without necessarily engendering substantial offsetting losses, provided that there is sufficient horizontal rivalry. Anti-trust enforcement in the United States should remain steadfast in its mission to preserve vigorous horizontal competition, but be more circumspect about calling into question seemingly restrictive vertical relationships among independently owned corporations.

A second premise being challenged is that substantial equity ownership by large financial institutions holding commingled claims against a single enterprise and actively involved in its governance is necessarily prone to abuse. Again, the experiences of Japan and of several other nations suggest the opposite. In Japan, Germany, and Sweden, among others, financial institutions, banks in particular, are vital components of a *contractual* governance machinery used to support efficient production and exchange relationships. They are so by acting as delegated monitors of major borrowing clients, selective interventionists in the restructuring of client companies in advance of insolvency, and even, occasionally, as mediators of disputes among other corporate stakeholders or as agents in the promotion of new business between clients. Although there may be instances in which close relationships between industrial corporations and financial institutions have been abused, there is scant evidence to support U.S. concerns that such relationships will inevitably lead to widespread, systemic imprudence in financial dealing. The extensive commingling of claims against a given company and cross-monitoring among corporate stakeholders, including the providers of capital, mitigates this risk at relatively low cost in other major capitalist economies.

Substantial change in ownership and governance appears necessary for U.S. industrial corporations to bridge the performance gaps separating many of them from their foreign rivals. Incremental improvements in existing institutions will surely help but are unlikely to be sufficient in and of themselves. The United States must also initiate reforms that will foster the ability of companies to build and sustain long-term commercial and financial relationships.

There is evidence, although it is not yet prominent, of "grass-roots" experimentation with such reforms. Thus, we observe increasing numbers of American businesses turning to private ownership as part of a strategy for improving performance; the emergence of investment management companies specifically dedicated to serving as long-term, active corporate shareholders (e.g., Alliance Capital Management Corporation and Corporate Partners, Inc.); and efforts by industry to build and maintain stable, long-term vertical relationships using contracting techniques similar to those found among Japanese companies. Some of this has come at the hands of foreign rivals who carry with them the contractual governance practices of their home environments as they invest in the United States. Japanese-affiliated automakers in the United States, for example, have successfully entered into supply contracts with American auto-parts producers that are patterned after their relationships with suppliers at home. Typically, these involve heavier reliance on suppliers in the initial design and development of some auto parts and subassemblies, close coordination of production to take advantage of just-in-time delivery systems, rapid responses to needed product changes, and extensive monitoring and even occasional intrusion by the assembler into the operations of the supplier. Long-term relationships with a few suppliers, sometimes accompanied by minority equity stakes in them, are also used in the United States in lieu of the more common American practice of entering into one-year, bid-price contracts with many suppliers. However foreign this method of doing business may be at first, American suppliers that have successfully won the business of a Japanese-affiliated producer claim that they have been favorably affected. Higher production efficiency, better quality, and lower costs are the benefits most commonly reported. Some American suppliers are even extending the same kind of practices to their own upstream suppliers. So, too, are American automobile assemblers with respect to their direct supplier relationships.[36]

Since the early 1980s a kind of "competition" among systems of corporate governance has emerged. Despite the twentieth-century international economic hegemony of, first, the United Kingdom, followed by the United States, it is by no means certain that the Anglo-American system of governance as currently configured will win this competition. The remarkable contemporary successes of Japanese and German companies give credence to the view that there is more than one model of effective governance.

By examining the Anglo-American and Japanese systems of governance through the analytic lenses of both transactions cost economics and agency theory, I argue that both systems constitute eco-

[36] U.S. General Accounting Office, National Security and International Affairs Division, "Foreign Investment: Growing Japanese Presence in the U.S. Auto Industry," GAO/NSIS 0-88-111, Washington, D.C., March 1988, pp. 39–40.

nomically rational attempts to resolve problems of coordination and control. However, the two nations have chosen to focus on different aspects of these problems. Whereas the United States has elected to emphasize the resolution of agency problems associated with the separation of ownership from control, Japan has sought to use the governance process chiefly to reduce transaction costs, broadly construed. In this regard, both systems have strengths and weaknesses. Arguably, neither one in its present form is likely to be globally dominant.

Indeed, the fact that these two systems differ in their relative advantages suggests the possibility of a constructive convergence of systems toward standards of "best practice" that combine the best elements of both. Ideally, best practice will lead to simultaneous exploitation of high-powered market incentives associated with exposure to market discipline and development of stable, long-term commercial relationships with their attendant transactional efficiencies. Vigorous *horizontal* competition among stable, vertically cooperative networks of companies may describe the eventual outcome of such governance practices.

Faltering corporate performance in both nations have created a hothouse for change in corporate governance that may be stimulating some movement toward best practice in each case. Japan appears to be taking slow, tentative steps toward increasing shareholder safeguards against agency problems and to reduce agency costs by disgorging excess cash from corporate balance sheets. It is not, however, abandoning Japanese methods of contractual governance in favor of Anglo-American corporate governance.

For their part, U.S. investors and corporations are also experimenting with innovations aimed at improving the performance of American boards of directors. In most instances, however, these are incremental changes aimed at perfecting the role of the board of directors as the chief shareholder safeguard in the traditional Anglo-American system of governance. The changes do little to move toward best practice and might even hinder such movement if, for example, large investors became more active but lack the industrial expertise necessary for exercising sound business judgment in board deliberations.

Although many American companies are attempting to build and sustain better long-term relationships with suppliers, customers, creditors, and so forth, they are impeded from making substantial progress on this front by a host of antitrust, securities, banking, insurance, and tax rules and regulations and by countless judicial interpretations of these laws. Consequently, substantial reform and convergence toward best practice will likely come about only through a comprehensive reappraisal of the entire body of legislation impinging on corporate and contractual governance. Chief among rules that deserve reexamination are those that impede the establishment of closer ties between the industrial and financial sectors and the exercise of greater voice in corporate governance by large financial institutions. Hand in glove with this removal of barriers holding commercial and financial interests at arms length should be the relaxation of those aspects of U.S. antitrust law that discourage restrictive *vertical* relationships among independently owned and operated corporations.

CHAPTER FIVE

Lean Production in the German Automobile Industry: A Test Case for Convergence Theory

WOLFGANG STREECK

How irresistible are market-conveyed pressures for cross-national institutional convergence in a global economy? To explore this question, in this chapter I look at the impending collision between "lean production" (LP), as invented by Japanese firms and codified by American researchers,[1] and the German pattern of organizing industrial work, taking the automobile industry as the main empirical reference.

In studying the fate of lean production specifically in German manufacturing and within Germany in the automobile industry, I select a strong prima facie case for market-driven convergence to occur. Lean production is widely considered a universal best manufacturing practice, obligatory for firms that want to survive international competition. With the exception of Sweden's, no major national automobile industry in the Western world is as much exposed to competition as the German one. Not only is the German domestic market wide open to imports, but also German automobile manufacturers export about two-thirds of domestically produced cars. In such conditions any loss of international competitiveness spells disaster. One would therefore expect German producers to be among the first to adopt whatever new "best practice" may emerge.

On the other hand, the German automobile industry was quite successful in its own way during the restructuring period of the 1970s and 1980s, which should make it prone to resist rapid and wholesale

I am grateful to Ronald Dore for extremely critical and extremely helpful comments.
[1] J. P. Womack, D. T. Jones, and D. Roos, *The Machine That Changed the World: The Story of Lean Production* (New York: Harper, 1991).

adoption of foreign production methods.[2] Also, as historical and sociological research has amply documented, LP's predecessor, "Fordism," never completely penetrated German industry.[3] There were strong Fordist tendencies that culminated in the mid-1960s, but Germany retained in particular its traditional reliance on skilled labor even in mass production. Indeed it has been argued that it was above all its rich supply of trained manual workers—an excess supply of skills by Fordist-Taylorist standards—that enabled the German manufacturing sector after 1973 to move up market, into a pattern of "diversified quality production" that was to prove highly competitive in subsequent years.[4] To the extent that such competitiveness may today be in jeopardy, the German case points to the possibility of resistance of national institutional conditions to economically expedient organizational change, and it raises the question of equally competitive functional equivalents to LP that fit a non-Japanese institutional context better.

The essay opens with a brief review of the main properties of LP as described by American researchers and received in Europe. It then proceeds to report the received view that LP can easily be transplanted cross-nationally by good management, drawing attention to a number of problems recognized but not regarded as critical by management-oriented literature. Third, some of the fundamental incompatibilities between LP and broader institutional conditions in Western societies in general and Germany in particular are presented. Fourth, I show how the German way of adjusting to international competition in the 1970s and 1980s was compatible with German institutions, and I emphasize the differences from the Japanese, LP way. Fifth, and finally, the current politics of LP in German industry, the limits of LP for German industrial restructuring, and the expectation of institutional convergence under market pressure are reviewed.

Lean Production

Lean production as interpreted by Womack et al. is highly flexible, high-quality production on a large scale.[5] As such it reaps the econ-

[2] Unlike the United States and the United Kingdom whose automobile industries were much less able to withstand Japanese competitive pressure. As a consequence they would appear particularly predisposed for fundamental change.

[3] S. Tolliday and J. Zeitlin, eds., *The Automobile Industry and Its Workers: Between Fordism and Flexibility* (Oxford: Polity Press, 1987).

[4] W. Streeck, "Industrial Relations and Industrial Change: The Restructuring of the World Automobile Industry in the 1970s," *Economic and Industrial Democracy* (1987); W. Streeck, *Social Institutions and Economic Performance: Studies of Industrial Relations in Advanced Capitalist Economies* (Beverly Hills, Calif.: Sage, 1992).

[5] Womack, Jones, and Roos, *The Machine That Changed the World.*

omies (of scale) of mass production while avoiding its diseconomies, by reducing capital requirements, facilitating product turnover and product differentiation, and improving production quality. Flexibility and quality are simultaneously attained through continuous organizational learning, or "permanent improvement," involving all members of the organization, and in particular frontline production workers. Efforts at permanent improvement are stimulated by ambitious and "sacred" production targets, systematic elimination of organizational slack (or "buffers"), and decentralization of responsibility and competence. Participants in LP face an environment in which they are expected to accomplish ever more demanding tasks with ever fewer "reserves" in a process that is kept artificially fragile, saving resources and extracting responsible participation through production targets achievable only under full utilization of available experience, ingenuity, and ability to improvise.

The principles of LP extend to the entire production system, including product design, supply management, work organization, and marketing. The following discussion, however, is limited to the organization of *manual work*, especially in assembly operations. Here, "leanness," following Womack et al., refers in particular to four interlocking, mutually reinforcing features:

(1) *Decentralization of responsibility.* Production workers are urged, and given the competence and resources, to make as many decisions as possible on their own, without recourse to management or staff departments. For example, being responsible for the quality of their work, workers have the right and the duty to stop the production line if defects cannot otherwise be prevented. Generally production workers are expected to take over an ever-growing range of functions, such as "simple machine repair, quality-checking, housekeeping, and materials-ordering," resulting in flatter hierarchies, a broader span of control, and increasing autonomy of workers from direct supervision (p. 99).

(2) *Elimination of buffers and enforcement of constant work effort.* The role of management under LP is to support direct production workers in performing their tasks, ideally only at their request. In addition, however, management has to identify and eliminate "buffers." As Womack et al. point out: "One of the most important tenets of the Toyota production system is never to vary the work pace. Therefore, as efficiencies are introduced . . . or as the rate of production falls, it is vital to remove unneeded workers from the system so that the same intensity of work is maintained. . . . Excess workers must be removed completely and quickly from the production system if improvement efforts are not to falter" (p. 259).

Constant work effort is required to keep the organization searching for improvement; efficiencies resulting from organizational learning must therefore be used to increase output, not to underwrite relaxation of effort. Management must set production targets high enough for frontline workers to be forced to devise efficiency improvements, and targets must be moved forward to maintain the pressure. "Permanent improvement," in other words, requires that the organization always operate at the limits of its capacity and be driven beyond these by management continually raising production targets as new capabilities develop.

(3) *Team work.* Workers must be organized in teams to be able to perform their wide-ranging tasks without buffers and to improvise successfully under the pressures of "permanent improvement." "In the end," write Womack et al., "it is the dynamic work team that emerges as the heart of the lean factory. . . . Workers need to be taught a wide variety of skills—in fact, all the jobs in their work group so that tasks can be rotated and workers can fill in for each other" (p. 99).

Management staff, as providers of assistance to the direct work force, must see to it that all workers are endowed with broad, polyvalent skills. Work teams, in turn, are responsible for deploying such skills so that the perennially demanding, forward-moving production targets can be met. Where each worker can do everything the team may have to do, team members can be flexibly rotated in rapid response to the exigencies of the intentionally created permanent crisis that is quintessential of LP.

(4) *Motivation by "stress" and "reciprocal obligation."* Why should workers be willing to respond to management-imposed zero-buffer constraints by embarking on an unending search for ever-higher efficiencies that will never be used to alleviate work pressure? Womack et al. suggest that motivation may come from "the continuing challenge of making the work go more smoothly," from LP offering "a creative tension in which workers have many ways to address challenges" and from similarities between LP manual work and "professional 'think' work" (pp. 100–102).[6] Elsewhere the word is of "performance bonuses." Coercive peer group pressures induced by organizational stress are not mentioned, and neither is the Japanese practice of overtime on short order to make up for shortfalls in the production schedule.

---

[6] Indeed, in one place we find the remarkable observation that, "lean manufacturers [. . .] try to make employees understand that their capacity to solve increasingly difficult problems is the most meaningful type of advancement they can achieve" (p. 199) and that it should be accepted as a substitute for the promotion opportunities that are absent in LP.

There are, however, repeated references to Japanese internal labor markets and the practice of "lifetime employment": "The work pace was clearly harder at Takaoka [than at the counterpart American plant], and yet there was a sense of purposefulness, not simply of workers going through the motions with their minds elsewhere under the watchful eye of the foreman. No doubt this was in considerable part due to the fact that all of the Takaoka workers were lifetime employees at Toyota, with fully secure jobs in return for a full commitment to their work" (p. 80).

Lifetime employment is presented as part of a broader covenant between management and workers that transforms the company into a "community" (pp. 53–55) and includes seniority-based pay, access to company housing and recreational facilities, union agreement to flexible work assignments, and, not least, worker participation in permanent improvement. Company community entails identification of workers with their employer and a "sense of reciprocal obligation" between management and labor: "To make this system [LP] work . . . management must offer its full support to the factory work force and . . . ensure job security. . . . It is truly a system of reciprocal obligation" (102). "Workers respond only where there exists some sense of reciprocal obligation, a sense that management actually values skilled workers, will make sacrifices to retain them, and is willing to delegate responsibility to the team" (p. 99).

THE PROBLEM OF TRANSFERABILITY

Lean production is unambiguously described by its discoverers as universally adoptable, "applicable anywhere by anyone": a managerial best practice that good management can "transplant . . . successfully to new environments" (pp. 9, 84). As evidence for LP's transferability from Japan to other, especially Western societies the authors point to the NUMMI plant in California, and generally "the best American-owned plants in North America" (pp. 84, 88). The view is concisely summarized in a quote from an interview with a Japanese manager: "We believe that our production system, with its many nuances, can be learned by anyone" (p. 243).

The authors are, however, aware of at least two difficulties LP must overcome as it is transplanted to Western countries. One of them has to do with skill structures, the other with employment security. For the former LP and its preferred form of work organization, teamwork, require not just high skills—higher than those of the average American production worker—but also a particular kind of skills, described as broad rather than specialized,[7] and company-specific as opposed to portable between companies: "The paradox is that the better you are at teamwork, the less you may know about a specific, narrow specialty that you can take with you to another company or to start a new business" (p. 14). The authors realize that this may be problematic:

> Most workers in the West place a very high value on having a portable skill—something they can take with them if things don't work out in a particular company. This concept is tied quite tightly to Western educational systems that stress discrete competencies and certify students to prove that the skills have been attained. . . . However . . . for the lean-production system to succeed, it needs dedicated generalists willing to learn many skills and apply them in a team setting. The problem . . . is that brilliant team play qualifies workers for more and better play on the same team but makes it progressively harder to leave. (p. 251)

Under the flat functional hierarchies characteristic of LP, there are also few opportunities for promotion along job chains and career ladders. Employees expecting individual advancement may therefore "feel trapped" in LP and in response "hold back their knowledge or even actively sabotage the system" (p. 251). "Western" notions of "careers," as the authors point out several times, are hard to reconcile with "the needs of lean production." These are better served by worker identification with the company as a "community," as reinforced by the Japanese "conventions" of seniority wages and new hiring only at the bottom of a firm's internal labor market (p. 251). Womack et al. conclude, somewhat lamely, that "Western companies, if they are to become lean, will need to think far more carefully about personnel systems and career paths than we believe any have to date" (p. 251).

Concerning employment security, which is essential for a Japanese-style company community to come about, Womack et al. observe that in the United States (which they regard as identical with "the West"), automobile firms have much less steady employment and supplier relations than in Japan. According to them, this is because the markets U.S. producers face are more cyclical than Japanese markets, forcing firms to dismiss workers and terminate supplier relations on short notice. Disruptions such as these, it is pointed out, are "extremely corrosive to the vital personal relationships" at the heart of LP (p. 248). Japanese automobile manufacturers have made ingenious efforts to

[7] As is pointed out later in some detail, the concepts used here are heavily colored by the American experience and are therefore often misleading when applied to other countries.

learn how to "smooth production" to avoid sharp fluctuations in their volume of output (p. 151), and their success is primarily attributed by the authors to steady growth, due to both growing world markets and superior Japanese competitiveness, as well as to peculiarities in the behavior of Japanese customers. The authors offer no reason to believe that these can be reproduced in Western countries. They suggest instead that to facilitate conversion to LP, cyclicality of demand may be reduced by more steady macroeconomic management, and they urge "Western companies and employees" to "embrace the concept of reciprocal obligation, making a long-term commitment to the company or group," with firms providing "full citizenship to their employees and suppliers drawn from many countries and regions across the globe" (pp. 274–75).

The answers offered by Womack et al. to the problems of skill structure and employment security are not as unsatisfactory as they are by accident. Indeed, they reflect formidable social-institutional obstacles to management-engineered convergence of "Western" or, for that matter, "German" manufacturing on Japanese LP methods. These obstacles arise from the fact that skill structures, work organization, and employment practices are closely interrelated, with a range of larger institutional, political, and cultural arrangements and understandings that extend far beyond the individual firm and deep into the fabric of society. To the extent that these are inhospitable to core elements of a particular workplace regime—as in Germany, it will be claimed, they are to LP—that regime cannot simply be imported as a matter of economic expediency. Rather, regardless of whatever economic merits it may have, it will encounter resistance and cause conflict, and in the process it will either be significantly transformed or altogether rejected.

THE SOCIAL CONTEXT OF SKILLS AND WORK: GERMANY AND JAPAN COMPARED

At first glance, Germany might seem a comparatively receptive environment to LP methods. Unlike in the United States, the skill levels of manual workers are high, and employment spells are almost as long as in Japan.[8] Closer inspection reveals, however, that underneath the superficial similarities there lie fundamental differences in the *kind* of skills and the *character* of long-term employment that are re-

[8] The median tenure of all employees is 7.5 years in Germany and 8.2 years in Japan, as compared to 3 years in the United States (*OECD Employment Outlook*, July 1993).

lated to and supported by central features of the two societies' social and political organization.

To begin with, German work skills are *occupational*, whereas Japanese skills are *generalist and organization centered*. In German the concept of "occupation," or *Beruf*, signifies a body of systematically related theoretical knowledge (*Wissen*) and a set of practical skills (*Können*), as well as the social identity of the person who has acquired these. Achievement of such identity is certified by a diploma upon passing an examination and is on this basis recognized without questioning by all employers. A German occupation is in this sense not fundamentally different from what in Anglo-American culture is referred to as a "profession"; in fact, there is no special word for the latter in German, electrician and lawyer both being referred to as a *Beruf*.

An occupation is not a job. A job belongs to an employer, and an occupation belongs to an employee—or, better, employees belong to occupations, and occupations belong to the society that defines and redefines them. If electrician is an occupation, then someone can be an electrician without having a job as an electrician. Because occupations are capacities of individuals that are socially standardized and certified, occupational qualifications are by definition portable in external labor markets and are standardized and certified exactly for this purpose.

Occupational qualifications are acquired through systematic training. In Germany about two-thirds of young people learn an occupation, manual or nonmanual, by undergoing apprenticeship training of between three and three-and-a-half years. There are about 400 apprenticed occupations recognized by the national government. Recognition involves the legal stipulation of a "qualification profile" (*Berufsbild*), which specifies the knowledge and the skills one must command to be certified as a member of the occupation. The law also regulates in detail the curriculum that trainees have to go through and how their skills are to be examined before the certificate is awarded. National qualification profiles and training regimes are enforced by a wide variety of agents, including local chambers of commerce and artisans, employers associations, unions, works councils, and *Länder* governments to ensure that certificates remain universally credible and acceptable in all parts of the German labor market.[9]

Most of the training for German occupations takes place at work

[9] W. Streeck, J. Hilbert, K.-H. van Kevelaer, F. Maier, and H. Weber, *The Role of the Social Partners in Vocational Training and Further Training in the Federal Republic of Germany* (Berlin: European Centre for the Development of Vocational Training [CEDEFOP], 1987).

and is supervised by elite skilled workers, *not* by professional teachers. Apprentices do go to school, but usually only one day a week; otherwise their place of learning is the workplace. *This does not, however, make the skills they acquire workplace-specific.* The entire governance structure of the German vocational training system, from local chambers of industry to the national government, is designed to make employers teach apprentices standardized, that is, portable skills. Employers who are found to deviate from the national curriculum may lose their license to train. Although the German training system utilizes the work environment as a cognitive and motivational resource to support learning, it enlists it, as it were, for a public purpose distinct from the private interests of individual employers.

Employers who might want to defect from the training regime would find this hard to do. Although formally qualification profiles and training curricula are decreed by the federal government, decrees are issued only after they have been agreed on between the industrial union and the employers' association of the respective economic sector. No profile or training regime is passed into law or changed without explicit union assent. De facto training regimes are more like industrial agreements than government decrees. It is only after unions and employers associations have fully agreed on a new training regime that the government, having ascertained its compatibility with the respective regimes for other sectors or occupations, signs it into law.

German-style occupational skills correspond to a particular organization of work and mode of coordination of work roles. As widely emphasized in the literature, there is comparatively little exercise of formal hierarchical authority in German workplaces.[10] Spans of control are broad and hierarchies flat. Discourse at the workplace between workers and supervisors is in terms of technical problems and competence, avoiding reference to formal authority that elsewhere often gives rise to disruptive conflict. The German foreman, or *Meister*, is a highly trained technician, not, or not exclusively, a disciplinarian wielding delegated management authority. *Meister* are not necessarily loved by their subordinates, but they are respected for their advanced technical qualifications, added during a lengthy second period of

[10] See C. Lane, *Management and Labor in Europe* (London: Edward Elgar, 1989), esp. chaps. 6, "Job Design and Work Organization," and 7, "New Technologies and Changes in Work Organization," pp. 137–95; P. A. Lawrence, *Managers and Management in West Germany* (New York: St. Martin's Press, 1980); M. Maurice, F. Sellier, and J. J. Silvestre, "Rules, Contexts, and Actors: Observations Based on a Comparison between France and West Germany," *British Journal of Industrial Relations* 11 (1984); A. Sorge and M. Warner, *Comparative Factory Organization: An Anglo-German Comparison of Manufacturing, Management, and Manpower* (Aldershot, Eng.: Gower, 1986); and others.

training to their occupational knowledge as skilled workers and shared with the workers under their supervision.

In a system of occupational skills, workers claim, and are granted, considerable discretion over their work performance. Work satisfaction in such a system is derived from recognition by others of a worker's technical competence; the most important form such recognition takes is organizational arrangements that leave workers space for independent judgment. Indeed, where occupational skills prevail, the very motivation to work, and to work efficiently and at a high level of quality, depends on workers' perceiving themselves as being trusted for their technical competence and occupational work ethos. Coordination problems are addressed by further training producing overlaps in skills that enable workers to cooperate more competently with workers in neighboring occupations. Emerging new tasks that cannot be integrated in existing occupations ultimately give rise to the creation of new skilled occupations, defined so that their areas of competence, again, overlap with those of workers performing adjacent tasks.

The German, occupational-professional model of skill and work organization differs from the Japanese, generalist-organizational model (Table 5-1). Japanese skills are *not* occupational, in that there are no socially defined "bundles" of intrinsically related work capacities, the acquisition of which provides a basis of social identification. Rather than belonging to an occupation, workers in the core of Japanese industry belong to a company; they are not electricians but "Toyota men." (Note that in Japanese, employees are referred to as "members" of the firm.) Nor are there certificates of occupational attainment, at least not nearly to the extent that they exist and are accepted in Germany, and work skills are not regarded as transportable from one employer to another in an external labor market.

Japanese skills are generated in the firm, by the firm, and for the firm.[11] In contrast to what happens in Germany, what the firm teaches its workers is not regulated by outside institutions, such as unions, employers associations, or the government. Workplace training is not complemented by training in public vocational schools, and curricula are designed exclusively to match the needs of the employer who does the training and who, given the lifelong attachment of core workers to

---

[11] On training in Japan see R. Dore and M. Sako, *How the Japanese Learn to Work* (London: Routledge, 1989); T. Ishikawa, *Vocational Training*, Japanese Industrial Relations Series no. 7 (Tokyo: Japan Institute of Labor, 1991); M. Sako, *Enterprise Training in a Comparative Perspective: West Germany, Japan, and Britain*, Report Prepared for the World Bank (London: London School of Economics, Industrial Relations Department, 1990).

Table 5-1. Skills, work organization, and employment practices in context: Germany and Japan

	Germany	Japan
Skill type	Occupational-professional	Generalist-organizational
Social identification	Certified *Wissen und Können*; "Electrician"	Organization "membership"; "Toyota man"
Training	Apprenticeship based on nationally standardized qualification profiles	Rotation through company-specific jobs and work teams
Work organization, mode of coordination of task performance	Quasi-professional self-regulation: overlapping competence, expert knowledge of supervisor (*Meister*); "professionalism"	Group self-regulation: mutual dependence of polyvalent workers in fragile, "lean" production process; "Toyotism"
Labor market structure	Occupational labor markets; access of employers to external labor market limited by union and political intervention	Internal labor markets; worker entry in employment above lowest level limited by concerted behavior of employers
Sources of long-term employment	Joint regulation, institutionalized "voice"; societal bargaining	"Reciprocal obligation"; company community
Industrial relations	Political-industrial unionism, pluralism	Company unionism, monism
Social integration: individuals in firms	Negotiated involvement, codetermination	Organizational totalitarianism: traditionalism, personalism, informal obligation
Social integration: firms in society	Public regulation, societal corporatism, tripartism	"Enterprise feudalism"

one and the same "enterprise community," can expect with certainty to internalize all its benefits.[12]

Japanese workers learn mostly by doing, in groups with other workers at the workplace. A central, if implicit, element of their curriculum is how different productive activities relate to each other at the workplace in which the work is performed. To learn this, as well as to add to their more specific abilities, workers are *rotated* from one job to another, in the process accumulating a growing stock of human capital. That stock, however, is not, as in an occupational system, kept together by intrinsic or systematic affinities; instead, the principles organizing a worker's configuration of skills are the organizational

[12] Japanese firms give their workers training in general skills only to the extent that it serves their specific needs, and the reason why they can afford to invest in general skills is that they can be certain that their workers will stay in their present place of employment.

structure and culture of the firm and the worker's movement through it over his or her lifetime. This is the deeper reason why an individual in such a system properly comes to be called a "Toyota man": the makeup of a worker's capacities reflects not a socially established concept of a "well-rounded" occupation but the person's career experience in a given firm.

In addition to work skills proper, rotation also teaches Japanese workers what might be called "organizational empathy": an ability to "feel themselves" into new situations, "understand" how specific work activities fit in the organizational context, and learn from more experienced fellow-workers. Work groups serve both as teachers and as foci of social identification; they substitute for public vocational schools, recognized skill profiles, curriculum enforcement agencies, examinations, and in part internalized work motivation. Both skill formation and coordination of work performances require that workers identify with the work group, and through it with the company at large and accept being guided by it rather than by occupational rules of competent practice or by a specific occupational ethos.

The different kinds of skill and modes of work organization in the two countries correspond closely to different labor market structures and employment practices (see Table 5-1). Employment is long-term in both Japan and Germany, but for very different reasons. Japanese workers, as Womack et al. have pointed out, stay in their place of employment because their skills are firm specific, their pay is seniority based, and employers collude with each other by refusing to hire workers from other firms above entry level. Workers stay, that is, because they are caught in their firms' internal labor markets. Employers, on their part, are willing to make efforts to keep their workers regardless of market fluctuations, in order to retain their experiential skills—including the critical ability to function under "lean" conditions—and cultivate their organizational and group loyalty.

German employers, too, have an interest in keeping their highly skilled work forces in steady employment, to save recruitment costs and not lose firm-specific skills. Unlike Japan, however, the skills of German workers are certified and portable in external, occupational labor markets, and German employers have never been able to agree among themselves not to hire workers from one another or pay their workers by seniority. This leaves workers the option to exit from their present employment if it no longer suits them. German employers must therefore give their workers reasons *not* to leave. Industrywide collective bargaining, which requires less cooperation among employers than refusal to hire from each other and, unlike the latter, is welcomed and supported for their own reasons by industrial unions, is used to mitigate wage competition for workers. The price for this, however, is that it lays the employment relationship and firms' labor policies open to external intervention and joint regulation. Firms also offer workers informal lifetime employment commitments as an inducement to stay and opportunities for "voice" as an alternative to exit in the case of grievances. With strong industrial unions, portability of high and costly skills thus contributes to employer acceptance of joint regulation and generally of pluralist industrial democracy, facilitating the transformation of the firm from a network of spot-market contracts into a bargained social institution as stable as, yet quite different from, the unitary "company community" of Japan.

Further adding to the picture are the limitations labor legislation and collective bargaining impose in Germany on employer access to the external labor market, through various forms of employment protection. Social regulation of this sort, while preserving for workers the option of leaving for better employment, makes it costly for employers to fire workers. The resulting combination of opportunities for worker-initiated job mobility with constraints on employer-initiated job mobility gives power to unions and workers of a kind that has no equivalent in Japan. Japanese workers find it hard to leave and depend on their employer for keeping them; German workers stay because employers find it hard to fire them even if they want and also must offer them conditions that are attractive enough for them not to leave.[13] In Japan lifetime employment results from workers not being fired; in Germany it results from employers not being deserted.

Transplanting LP, as interpreted by Womack et al., to a German setting would ultimately require workers to give up their occupational skills and identities and to reorganize their human capital into non-portable, firm-specific skills; accept coordination at work through peer group pressure rather than professional judgment, either their own or that of superiors; and depend for employment security on their uncertain indispensability to an employer that would be certain to become indispensable to them—knowing, on top of all this, that the new production system would result in numerous job losses.[14] There is

[13] Which they might not be willing to do if workers fail to deliver on their part of the "reciprocal obligations" involved in "lifetime employment." See M. Aoki, *Information, Incentives, and Bargaining in the Japanese Economy* (Cambridge: Cambridge University Press, 1988).

[14] Note that the problem in Germany is different from in the United States in that change would not be from low to high skills, but from one type of high skills to another; not from hierarchical, foreman-type supervision to delegated competence and recognition of the importance of frontline workers, but from skilled occupational work to "team work"; and not from "employment at will" to employment security, but from

no reason to believe that workers will easily submit to this, even in difficult economic conditions. Moreover, LP would have to be introduced and maintained against the grain of a range of social and institutional arrangements that support the existing skill and employment patterns: the system of industrial relations; the way in which individuals are integrated in the firm as an organization; and the integration of the firm in the wider society (Table 5-1).

Industrial Relations

In Germany transportable occupational skills give rise to social identities and identifications that are not linked to a particular firm. The collective interests attached to such identities require representation by unions organized outside and above individual companies, at the level of industries or the country as a whole. While these could be craft unions, it so happens that in the German case they are political-industrial unions each of which organizes and represents not just one occupation but a large number of them. Although German unions as a consequence do undertake to organize all workers in a given plant or firm, they have little in common with Japanese company unions that represent workers tied to their employer in a company "community of fate," reflecting the nontransferability of their skills and the closure imposed by employers on worker access to the external labor market.

German unions reflect a *pluralism* of interests inside the firm as well as inside society that does not in this form seem to exist in Japan. Japanese unions are part of a unitary, *monistic* company structure designed to support the shared interests of management and of a "committed," "dedicated" work force in the firm's economic success. Union officials and career managers are therefore typically hard to distinguish. German unions, by comparison, are independent agents of the company. They represent, and in the process help employers to accommodate, the separate interests of a potentially mobile work force, not the least of which relate to the formation and deployment at the workplace of portable work skills.

Political-industrial unions of the German kind exercise influence on firms by bringing to bear on them power mobilized in the public sphere, outside the private sphere of the firm. Through industrywide collective bargaining they subject the firm's internal operation and organization to publicly accountable, formally negotiated societal governance. Among other things, they thereby help maintain the occupationally structured qualification system and the kind of employment

---

secure employment with a possibility of exit, and the power potentially derived from it, to secure employment without that possibility.

security that support the very pluralism of interests on which their own existence as political-industrial unions is premised.

The Social Integration of Workers in the Firm

Pluralist industrial relations reflect a pluralism of life spheres, in particular of work and private life, the boundaries of which they help to define and maintain. In a society such as Germany, where workers do not primarily identify with their place of employment, involvement of individuals in secondary organizations of work must be *negotiated*, protecting workers' "privacy" from being consumed by requirements of organizational efficiency. Reliable and enforceable demarcation of rights and responsibilities, in particular of managerial power, is felt to be indispensable as a brake on what in a pluralist environment is perceived as a totalitarian tendency of organizations under competitive pressures to absorb their members. Demands by German unions for reduction of working hours, clear distinction between work and nonwork, strict legal and contractual limitations on data collection by management regarding behavior and performance of individual workers, minimal hierarchical supervision and a maximum of occupational autonomy at work; and institutional guarantees against the use of informal group pressures for supervision—all those not only express a desire for economic advantage, they are also indicative of deeply rooted "cultural" preferences for limited and negotiated, as opposed to unconditional and organizational, involvement.

Formal rights of participation at the workplace—the German system of codetermination—are instituted and highly valued not least to enable workers to police the boundaries of their involvement and to keep predictable what management may expect from them. German managers, especially those of large firms, have to contend with a massive institutional reality of legally enshrined participation rights, externally given and nonnegotiable for the individual firm, that Turner stenographically summarizes as follows:

> Works councils legally independent of both union and management, democratically elected by the entire work force, empowered by law, precedent, and plant- and firm-level agreements to consult with management before the implementation of decisions affecting personnel . . . and in many cases to participate actively in managerial decision-making processes (with veto rights), especially in matters of personnel policy (such as hiring, firing, training and retraining, and reassignment in the event of work organization and technological change).[15]

[15] L. Turner, *Democracy at Work: Changing World Markets and the Future of Labor* (Ithaca: Cornell University Press, 1992), p. 97; see also K. Thelen, *Union of Parts; Labor Politics in*

Codetermination law removes the presence, the organization, and the basic rights of works councils and, through them, workplace unions from management's strategic calculations. Under codetermination managers know that there will always be a works council; that the council will cooperate with the union; that attempts to rid the firm of codetermination and the works council will be a waste of time because they cannot succeed; and that the present works council leaders are likely to be in their positions for many years to come. Quite appropriately, the law that creates works councils is called in German the *Betriebsverfassungsgesetz*, or Works Constitution Act, indicating that its main function is to *constitute* the workplace as a negotiating arena with designated interlocutors who have rights and obligations that, even though they are beyond the reach of the parties' contractual relations, enable the latter to be conducted in an orderly and predictable way.

Integration of individuals in the firm by negotiated involvement stands in stark contrast to the Japanese pattern. Japanese "company communities" benefit from a rich supply of social and cultural *traditionalism*, as reflected in easy acceptance of authority and hierarchy, low differentiation between work and personal life, lack of resistance by individuals to integration in dense informal groups utilized by a powerful formal organization for its purposes, and generally an astounding capacity of firms to enlist the support of informal structures and community values for organizational control—see, for example, the willingness of families and individuals to bear the brunt of a "meritocratic" public school system that generates the high general skills firms can take for granted in building their LP work groups.[16] Whereas German companies are integrated almost like public institutions, through what resembles a formal constitution, Japanese companies are integrated like informal groups, through diffuse personal obligations pervasive enough potentially to embrace the personalities of their members in their totality.

The way firms are socially integrated is crucial for the kind of reserves they can draw on in their daily operation. Japanese LP is described as "zero-buffer," but in fact it depends on worker's making themselves freely available to the organization in a way that cannot be expected in a pluralist social structure. For example, in order not to

Postwar Germany (Ithaca: Cornell University Press, 1992); and W. Streeck, *Industrial Relations in West Germany: The Case of the Car Industry* (New York: St. Martin's Press, 1984); and Streeck, *Social Institutions and Economic Performance*.

[16] Other examples are the foreman visiting the homes of applicants for lifetime employment to check out their family situation or the detailed behavioral data collected and stored by personnel departments. All of these would be anathema to German workers, works councils, and unions and indeed would often be outright illegal in Germany.

make the work situation of fellow team members even more precarious than it already is under management-imposed "leanness," Japanese workers usually do not take their vacation, and they come to work even when they are ill. Also, to enforce the sacredness of production targets, Japanese firms seem to be able to call overtime on very short order, often on the same day in which production shortfalls have occurred. The ensuing disruptions of workers' lives outside the workplace would be unacceptable in a pluralist social structure.

Lean production as described by Womack et al., if introduced in a context of negotiated involvement, would blur the boundaries between job, occupation, and private life that protect individual autonomy in Western societies from total organizational control. Lean production would replace management accountable under collective bargaining, codetermination, and the threat of worker exit, with unaccountable informal pressures by both management and work teams operating and improvising under constant shortage and crisis. Central elements of work organization under LP thus run counter to the prevailing pattern of organizational integration in Western societies, and would for their viability require a radically different pattern that could come about only after a fundamental break with existing institutions.

The Social Integration of Firms in Society

German and Japanese firms are embedded in and dependent on the societies in which they operate. Again, however, the character of this relationship differs profoundly. German society treats the internal life of an enterprise as a matter of public interest and subjects it to public intervention and regulation. Firms in Germany are in this way part of a politically constructed and legitimated public order consisting of a wide array of formally institutionalized and accountable mechanisms of governance, foremost among them an "enabling" democratic state, centralized industrial unions and employers associations, chambers of industry with obligatory membership for firms, and works councils.

External, public regulation of social relations within the firm, including the way workers are trained, paid, deployed, and hired and fired, is a core element of social citizenship, which in turn constitutes the basis of the *Sozialstaat*, the German version of the welfare state. Adding to and superseding market and property relations, social citizenship generates formally guaranteed rights and obligations that modify market outcomes and constrain the exercise of private power, trying to make a capitalist economy compatible with demands for basic equality. In this way citizenship rebuilds in a nontraditional society the social cohesion any economy, including a capitalist market economy, requires for its functioning. Germany differs from other Western countries in the extent to which it relies for economic governance on corporatist bargaining and tripartite negotiation, but in common with many of them its political order makes a social environment supportive of private exchange and organization conditional on compliance with fundamental principles of citizenship.

In Japan, by comparison, the internal affairs of large firms are not considered a matter of public concern. In fact it seems questionable whether the distinction between the public and the private, which is so central for the social organization of Western societies, can be applied at all to Japan. Just as the Japanese state, Japanese large firms seem to be able to rely for their operation on communitylike social integration that is supported by the surrounding society *as a matter of course*. Rather than their internal order being publicly regulated, large firms in Japan look like self-contained and self-sufficient entities linked to the society at large by informal, implicit, and self-understood codes of loyalty. For want of a better term, this pattern may be referred to as "enterprise feudalism." In a country like Germany the supports society provides to the formal organization of the enterprise require political definition, negotiation, regulation and legitimation, and generally formal institution building, whereas in Japan they seem to come forward spontaneously, as a matter of traditionalist obligation, freely supplying the firm with the skills, motivation, and group cohesion essential for, among other things, lean production.[17]

Just as Japanese "enterprise feudalism" corresponds to nonportable skills, "permanent improvement"-type teamwork and "lifetime employment," the public institutions that regulate the status of markets and private enterprise in Germany support and reinforce occupational skill structures and exit opportunities for workers in occupational labor markets, *and also depend on them*. In the German context a change at the workplace to a firm-specific skill structure, with the subsequent changes it implies in authority structures, employment security, industrial relations, worker involvement in the firm, and the status of firms in society is bound to conflict with a large number of politically highly legitimate social institutions. Transplanted to Germany LP would cut firms loose from public mechanisms of social regulation that are central to the relationship between state and society and between the public and the private. Far from being merely a mat-

[17] The Japanese pattern is one in which distinctions between feudal and modern institutions, paternalism and managerialism, culture and power, voluntary subordination and political suppression of labor are particularly difficult to make.

ter of an economically expedient managerial reorganization of the shop floor, as Womack et al. seem to believe, LP would be bound up with what in Germany, and indeed any Western country, would be patterns of authority and social integration that seem incompatible with pluralist democracy and social citizenship.

SKILL ADJUSTMENT AND WORK REORGANIZATION IN GERMANY

Qualification structures and work organization in Germany are far from static. But their past evolution in response to changing circumstances was conditioned both by their previous state and the larger societal institutions in which they are embedded. The direction in which this has moved them, especially and precisely in the period of growing international competition in the 1970s and 1980s, was quite different from the "lean production" model of recent management writing and in fact further reinforced the occupational model of skill formation and work organization, as well as the negotiated character of the firm as a social institution.

The path dependency of the development of German work organization has been noted before. As Maurice et al. have shown, even in the heyday of Fordism occupational skills supported relatively high autonomy of manual workers in German factories, a strong presence of skilled workers even in mass assembly operations, a broad managerial span of control, low managerial hierarchies and small managerial overheads, and low wage differentials between blue- and white-collar workers—together making for major deviations from the Fordist-Taylorist basic model. In addition, through the "societal effect" that it exercised on organizational structures, the German training system limited the capacity of firms to customize their work organization in line with local managerial taste or to employ firm-specific, as distinct from transportable, qualifications, thus making for a narrower range of managerial "strategic choice" than in the United States or the United Kingdom.[18]

Developments in the 1970s and 1980s confirm this picture. In response to technological change and pressures for increased flexibility, the union and the employers association of the metalworking sector agreed in 1984 on a fundamental reform of the sectoral training regime.[19] Traditionally there had been 48 apprenticed occupations in metalworking. The reform reduced these to six, all with an extended

[18] Marc Maurice, François Sellier, Jean-Jacques Silvestre, "Rules, Contexts, and Actors: Observations Based on a Comparison between France and West Germany," *British Journal of Industrial Relations* 22 (1984): 346–63.

[19] Streeck et al., *The Role of the Social Partners*. Similar reforms have taken place in other sectors.

apprenticeship period of three-and-a-half years. For all of the new occupations, training begins with an identical first year of basic instruction; specialization starts in earnest only after two years. "De-specialization" of occupational profiles and the introduction of common basic training are to increase the versatility of labor and thus the "flexibility" of the shop floor. Overlaps in occupational qualifications, as deliberately created by the reform, are viewed not as a waste of training effort but as the most suitable way in a system of occupationally defined skills to facilitate cooperation between workers, reducing the need for managerial intervention and allowing for continuous, decentralized adjustment to changing tasks.

As part of the training reform, the blurring between direct and indirect, unskilled and skilled, and production and maintenance work that was a universal effect of the introduction of microelectronic process technology led in Germany to the creation of a new "hybrid" occupation, the *Anlagenführer* ("equipment monitor"), nationally standardized and with the usual apprenticeship training period of three-and-a-half years.[20] The role of the *Anlagenführer* is to ensure the continuous operation of large pieces of automated equipment by monitoring the throughflow of material and performing minor repairs and routine maintenance. The new occupation combines what traditionally were production and maintenance tasks in a single work role that assigns the coordination between direct and indirect functions not to interpersonal relations within a group of equally skilled "generalists" but to a skilled worker's occupational *Wissen und Können*. Moreover, the new combination of direct and indirect production work is codified in a qualification profile and training curriculum that make it certifiable and portable in external labor markets.

The impact of the German system of vocational training on the organization of work in German industry is mediated and, indeed, reinforced by the industrial relations system. German industrial unions play an important part in the governance of *both* the national training system and the workplace, being able to use their position in one as a resource in the other. Industrywide, legally binding agreements with strong employers associations, on wages as well as on working conditions in the widest sense, give external unions considerable influence on workplaces, in particular enabling them to contain variation in work organization between firms. In addition, codetermination, at both the plant and the enterprise level, affords unions, directly as well as through union-dominated works councils, a firmly established role in work organization and reorganization.

[20] The details have been extensively reported by H. Kern and M. Schumann, *Das Ende der Arbeitsteilung? Rationalisierung in der industriellen Produktion* (Munich: C. H. Beck, 1994), and others.

In the latter respect it is important to note that flexibility in German workplaces does not flow from unlimited managerial discretion. "Although," writes Turner,

> technically management has much broader rights regarding allocation of manpower in West German industry than in the United States . . . in fact all reassignments are subject both to complex wage security provisions . . . and to works council approval. . . . For all longer-term reassignments, including those resulting from work reorganization, the works council can effectively block management moves so that consensus is sought before the use of West German industry's famous shop-floor flexibility.

> Flexibility in Germany is bargained, and exists only to the extent that it is . . . the daily process of negotiation between management and a powerful union-dominated works council that ensures smooth adjustment. When management and works council, after lengthy discussion, finally agree on both the framework and the specific details of work reorganization, implementation is smooth because most of the interests in the plant have been considered and the agreed-upon changes can be explained to the rank and file by their elected representatives—and further negotiations can be made around the margins in this system of permanent bargaining.[21]

Reinforcing the German pattern of joint regulation at the workplace, codetermination legislation was strengthened in 1972 and 1976, at the beginning of the restructuring period and preceding the break with Taylorism in the 1980s. In fact, by reassuring German industrial unions of their status in the workplace, codetermination encouraged them to follow their tendency to respond to technological change not by trying to protect existing work practices, but by demanding a general upgrading of skills for all workers, with a perspective toward an overall narrowing of skill and, eventually, wage differentials. Having no craft tradition and operating in an environment in which the centralization of the right to manage had been easy to establish for employers at the beginning of industrialization, German unions were never in a position to exercise "job control." Partly for this reason, they have always refused to make their peace with Taylorism by grafting on it detailed job demarcations and seniority rights, thereby avoiding becoming organizationally dependent on it. In fact, as German unions organize all workers in an industry—skilled, unskilled, and white-collar—preserving skill and wage differentials by defending existing job demarcations could only be divisive for them. Facing in par-

[21] Turner, *Democracy at Work*, pp. 94, 95.

ticular a need to reduce wage differentials, in order to make it easier for themselves to maintain their organizational cohesion, German unions from early on found it congenial to pursue general skill up-grading and reduction of skill differentials by turning more and more of their members into skilled workers.

In Germany union responses to Taylorism in the 1970s and 1980s thus took the form of demands, backed by extended codetermination rights, for a reorganization of work that would make it possible for growing numbers of workers to acquire and use high occupational qualifications. In fact, as Turner documents, German unions already began to press for de-Taylorization of industrial work at a time when management was still widely committed to the Fordist-Taylor-ist orthodoxy. Moreover, because as industrial unions they were or-ganizationally not dependent on the integrity of any specific occu-pation, the unions were more than willing to accept changes in occupational demarcations, as long as these helped to promote the general principle of most or all workers doing qualified occupa-tional work.[22]

As in other countries, since the mid-1970s the center of gravity of German industrial relations has been moving to the individual firm. But in Germany workplace industrial relations became embedded in the institutional framework of codetermination, and their main sub-ject became work reform and training.[23] In the 1970s and 1980s col-lective agreements at the industry level lengthened the minimum work cycle and thereby forced managements to enrich the content of jobs. In addition, to fight unemployment among young people, unions and works councils made firms take in more apprentices, cre-ating a surplus of skilled occupational labor that placed further pres-sure on the traditional organization of work. In addition, the reform of the training regime did not just broaden workers' competence, but it also laid the ground for advanced further training; later such train-ing became formally mandated in industrial agreements and in agree-ments between works councils and management in individual firms.

[22] Thus occupational skills should not be equated, as Womack et al. (*The Machine That Changed the World*) do, with craft skills, or "narrow craft skills." German occupations are defined in such a way that they can easily be redefined, among other things by merging occupations into one another and thereby broadening them. Moreover, German certifi-cates indicate to an employer what a job applicant has learned, but they do not entitle their owners to a particular kind of work. In fact reducing the overall number of occu-pational specializations and making occupational skills more broadly based and overlap-ping were other important ways for German unions of smoothing over divisions among their membership and of increasing the latter's homogeneity. The reform of the metal-working training scheme, while increasing the flexibility of the productive apparatus, also satisfied important organizational imperatives of the union.
[23] Thelen, *Union of Parts.*

In the process a German response to the new technical and economic conditions, referred to in the literature as *facharbeitergestutzte Rationalisierung*,[24] developed that may best be characterized as *reorganization of work based on and supported by expanded occupational qualifications*.[24]

It was in this context that German unions and works councils first began to call for "group work," at a time when most employers still rejected this as utopian.[25] In part, union demands for group work originated in the context of policies of *Humanisierung der Arbeit* ("humanization of work") that were at the time promoted by the Social-Liberal government. But as Turner shows, union concepts of group work involved not just better working conditions but also "the integration of skilled workers into direct production teams without sacrificing the integrity of skilled work; considerable group autonomy; an emphasis on the training of production workers for new tasks and skills to bring them up to the level of skilled workers" or, according to IG Metall itself, "the far-reaching elimination of hierarchy, control and the division of labor."[26] In fact, seen in the context of the union's simultaneous training policies and its demands for a "qualification offensive" to combat unemployment, its early support for "group work" can only be understood as part of a broader strategy of trying to *extend skilled occupational work* ideally to all workers, inserting occupational competence and autonomy in mass production and thereby transforming the latter into what has been called "diversified quality production."[27]

Conflicts with management began as soon as firms introduced their own group work projects, to the extent that these were incompatible with occupational upskilling and increased occupational autonomy at work. In the 1980s managerial concepts of teamwork were mostly inspired by the example of NUMMI and similar, "lean production" plants in the United States. As Turner shows, there were fundamental differences between the NUMMI model and IG Metall policy. The most important of which included that under the union concept, work groups had to be composed of both skilled and unskilled workers, so that group work could be used to remedy skill polarization; group tasks were to be broad and variable and cycle

[24] U. Jürgens, T. Malsch, and K. Dohse, *Breaking from Taylorism: Changing Forms of Work in the Automobile Industry* (Cambridge: Cambridge University Press, 1993).
[25] For the union position on *Gruppenarbeit*, see S. Roth and H. Kohl, eds., *Perspektive: Gruppenarbeit* (Cologne: Bund Verlag, 1988).
[26] Turner, *Democracy at Work*, pp. 131, 142.
[27] Streeck, *Social Institutions and Economic Performance*.

times much longer than the typical one-minute cycle at NUMMI; groups had to have autonomy over work-related decisions, as opposed to just having "input" in managerial decisions; disabled and socially disadvantaged group members were to receive special training; workers had to be offered opportunities for personal and *occupational* (italics mine) development; group interests were to be represented through the existing system of interest representation at the workplace (i.e., the works council); and there were to be joint steering committees of management and works council to oversee group activities. Turner concludes his discussion with the observation that "the typical group work pilot project [in Germany] includes a mix of craft and production workers, cross-training for the skilled and upgrading for the semi-skilled, longer cycle times than in the U.S. case and a greater variety of tasks, more responsibility and autonomy for the group to plan, control and execute work, and full works council participation in establishing and administering the group."[28]

By the late 1980s qualification structures and work organization in Germany were moving away from Taylorism fast in a direction prefigured by the earlier German deviations from the Taylorist basic model: increased reliance on skilled work, especially through upgrading of direct production tasks; reinforcement of the occupational character of work skills; achievement of flexibility through skill overlaps and horizontal and vertical integration of skill profiles; reintegration of conception and execution above all by expanding the content of occupations, and only on this basis by introducing "group work"; and reduction of managerial supervision and organizational pressure by assignment of broader responsibilities to more broadly trained workers. The 1980s also saw both extended rights to comanagement for work force representatives on training and work organization and a reassertion of central regulation of, and external intervention in, labor relations at the workplace, especially with respect to training, with a strong role for industrial unions.

---

[28] Turner, *Democracy at Work*, p. 163. Other researchers who have compared teamwork in the United States and Germany have found similar differences. For example, Demes and Jurgens report, "a greater emphasis (in Germany) on upgrading skills for both production and skilled workers (and many production workers have prior skills training as apprentices); union group work proposals intend to build on the skills reservoir and the notion of a 'qualification offensive' to raise skill levels across the board." H. Demes and U. Jurgens, "The Changing Status of the Skilled Trades in Mass Producing Industry: A Comparison of Recent Trends in Japan, the Federal Republic of Germany, and the USA," in T. Blumenthal, ed., *Employer and Employee in Japan and Europe* (Beer-Sheva, Israel: Humphrey Institute for Social Ecology, 1989).

THE POLITICS OF LEAN PRODUCTION IN GERMANY

Despite numerous flaws,[29] *The Machine That Changed the World* became an instant success in Germany, even though one of its most obvious deficits is the way it lumps "Western Europe" together in one category, treats it as an incomplete and somewhat deficient derivative of the United States, and explains the continued existence of European, including German, automobile manufacturing as a result of protective trade barriers.

The reasons for its success in Germany are likely to be found in the country's economic situation at the time. The export-oriented and manufacturing-centered high-wage, high-skill, and high-price economy of Germany boasts a long and impressive history of success. Still, Germans worry that they may no longer be able to continue their economic tightrope walk: to come up with ever-new superior, price-inelastic products in sufficient volume to underwrite the high prosperity to which their country has become accustomed.

In the early 1990s a great number of factors came together that made such fears seem more realistic than ever. With the postunification boom running out and the illusions about a rapid recovery in the former East Germany gone, almost all major industries found themselves with overcapacity. In the short term, the problems were exacerbated by a European-wide depression that had in large part been caused by restrictive German monetary policy, which in turn was a response to the rapid increase in German public debt caused by the high costs of unification and by the refusal of the Kohl government to pay for them by raising taxes. Moreover, in the long term the competitive position of the German economy, which can be strong only against the odds of its high costs, seemed threatened by three developments that together appeared increasingly invincible: aggressive moves by the Japanese, as exemplified by the appearance of the Lexus car line, into high-end market segments that had until then remained a German domain; the fast growth of highly productive new economies in the Pacific area; and the sudden emergence of a practically unlimited supply of low-wage but high-skill labor in the formerly Communist countries of Eastern Europe. Faced with this cumulation of adverse circumstances, even usually sanguine observers

[29] For an excellent summary of the critical literature, see P. Unterweger, "Lean Production: Myth and Reality," in W. Sengenberger and D. Campbell, eds., *Lean Production and Beyond: Labour Aspects of a New Production Concept* (Geneva: International Labour Organization, 1993).

began to entertain the idea that the "German model" might have seen its day.[30]

The message of Womack et al., that European and, by implication German, manufacturing had to change profoundly or was soon to be wiped out, thus met the mood of the time, and employers and unions were willing to take it extremely seriously. Its content and consequences, however, they read quite differently.[31] For the employers LP meant primarily lean employment and "doing more with less."[32] Engaged in protracted struggles over labor shedding, employers would point to Womack et al. to justify demands for further work force reductions and intensification of work for those remaining in employment. To achieve both, employers among other things called for introduction of "teamwork," trying to regain the initiative on the subject from IG Metall. In this respect, the book helped to give definition to a more aggressive employer strategy on work reorganization, most clearly at Ford and Opel, the subsidiaries of the two large American automobile manufacturers that had already in the 1980s begun to "learn from Japan."

The unions, in turn, tried to find in the book their own demands for a "human-centered" reorganization of work, welcoming in particular the book's emphasis on the importance for competitive production of human agency and skills; its call for less hierarchical supervision and decentralization of responsibility and discretion; and generally the attention it urges managers to pay to the social aspects of the production process.[33] Whereas employers by and large understood LP to require workers to work harder and blamed the unions for interfering with management making them do so, the unions were willing to go along with LP to the extent that it called for employers to let workers work smarter. Moreover, IG Metall in particular tried to blame whatever lack of "leanness" was found on management failure, such as insufficient attention to manufacturability of parts, or on managerial self-interest, for example in maintaining unnecessary and expensive layers of middle management.[34]

[30] See W. Streeck, "A German Capitalism: Does It Exist? Can It Survive?," in C. Crouch and W. Streeck, eds., *Modern Capitalism or Modern Capitalisms?* (London: Frances Pinter, 1995).

[31] See G. Schienstock and B. Steffensen, "Lean Production: The German Debate" (unpublished MS), Akademie für Technikfolgenabschatzung, Stuttgart, n.d.

[32] For the likely employment consequences of LP, see P. Auer, "Lean Production: The Micro-Macro Dimension, Employment and the Welfare State," Discussion Paper FS I 94-201, Wissenschaftszentrum Berlin für Sozialforschung, 1994.

[33] S. Roth, "Japanization—Or Going Our Own Way? Internationalization and Interest Representation," *Graue Reihe Neue Folge* 48 (1992): 35.

[34] For a largely positive union assessment of LP, see H. Neumann, "Lean Production

There is no a priori reason to believe that the positions of German employers and unions on LP are incompatible; on past experience, some kind of negotiated compromise would seem likely.[35] But this already implies that unilateral managerial application of an allegedly universal pattern of "best practice," on which German work organization would subsequently "converge," is very likely not what will happen. Today work reorganization is broadly under way in the German automobile industry, in part explicitly under the LP label, most visibly on some of the de facto greenfield sites in the former GDR. In the process "lean production" as a concept may well go out of fashion, but pressures to review skill structures, the division of labor, the assignment of responsibility, and the coordination of tasks in manufacturing will remain.

What exactly is happening in German workplaces today is too early to say. Several empirical research projects are presently being carried out, but their preliminary results do not yet allow generalization.[36] What seems clear, however, is that insofar as work reorgnization means introducing certain key elements of what Womack et al. have codified as "lean production," it will have to contend with a set of *restrictive conditions* that strongly militate against unmodified transfer. Rather than trying to summarize still ongoing research, I list some of these conditions:

(1) *Institutionalized defenses of a portable, occupational skill structure.* Firm-specific skills may increase in importance, and the vocational training system may undergo as yet unpredictable changes. However, there will always be a high proportion of workers in Germany with occupational qualifications. Especially in firms that must attract the best workers, work and work teams will have to be so organized that they leave space for "specialization in areas of skilled work."[37] This presumably includes pressures to reserve a place for the *Meister*, the kind of competence and

---

Needs 'Beefing Up,'" in W. Sengenberger and D. Campbell, eds., *Lean Production and Beyond: Labour Aspects of a New Production Concept* (Geneva: International Labour Organization 1993).

[35] See Roth, "Japanization," p. 31.

[36] See Auer, "Lean Production"; Turner, *Democracy at Work*; and U. Jürgens, *Lean Production and Co-Determination: The German Experience* (Labor Studies Center, Wayne State University, 1993). For research results, see Jurgens, and P. Cooke, "The Experiences of German Engineering Firms in Applying Lean Production Methods," in W. Sengenberger and D. Campbell, eds., *Lean Production and Beyond: Labour Aspects of a New Production Concept* (Geneva: International Labour Organization, 1993).

[37] The "German model," according to Roth ("Japanization," pp. 12, 25), "is centered on the special understanding of skilled work as a profession." Japanese teamwork, "would mean a renunciation of essential principles of qualification found in the German production mode. . . . The unique system of occupational training and education in Germany must remain a useful component of any future production concept."

technical authority they represent, the career opportunity their position offers to skilled workers willing to expand their occupational qualifications, and the liaison function they perform between the technical staff departments and the shop floor.[38]

(2) *Expectations of growing discretion at work.* Widespread opposition to hierarchical supervision in German workplaces aims at increased rights for workers to make autonomous decisions based on competent deliberation. Job satisfaction for workers with a "professional orientation" is not attained by substituting peer group pressure for managerial supervision or by workers' being given the freedom, and indeed the obligation, to make spontaneous improvements in struggling with artificially created organizational stress. Work reform in Germany, whatever direction it will ultimately take, has to contend with settled expectations of a decoupling of work performance from the assembly line[39] or at the very least of a significant increase in the length of work cycles—which is exactly the opposite of the short cycles and line-paced task execution that would come with LP.

(3) *Limited attachment of workers to their employer.* There will always be an external labor market in Germany, if only because firms' internal labor markets are not large enough to allow for the large-scale internal redeployment possible in a Japanese *keiretsu*. As a result identification of workers with their employer will be less than complete.[40] New forms of work organization can therefore function only if they can do so without complete identification of workers with the employing organization and with workers who have the option of leaving or not joining.

(4) *Limited and negotiated involvement of workers in the firm.* As workers have identities and interests competing with those defined by their present employer—referred to by the management literature as "individualism"—the commitment and motivational reserves that firms can tap for their purposes are finite. Any organization of work that assumes the open-ended willingness of workers to make good for deliberately undersupplied resources would therefore rapidly move from artificial to real crisis. Under limited and negotiated involvement overtime is not as a matter of course available to compensate for resource gaps;[41] reserves

---

[38] Union demands for "skilled teamwork" (*qualifizierte Gruppenarbeit* [Roth, "Japanization," pp. 40ff.]), as distinguished from teamwork pure and simple, express the tension between German skill structures and the system of "teams of highly skilled generalists" described by Womack et al. (*The Machine That Changed the World*). Although, as noted by Roth (p. 39), German unions agree on the need to improve workers' "social qualifications," such as cooperation and communication skills, this is seen as inseparably linked to technical upskilling.

[39] Jürgens, Malsh, and Dohse, *Breaking from Taylorism*, p. 364.

[40] Also because seniority pay increases will remain tiny compared to those found in Japan. Moreover, company pensions are infrequent and only marginally significant, because of the high benefits offered by the public pension system. Company pension entitlements must also be fully portable by law.

[41] The complicated "flexible" working time regimes that have been negotiated in Germany in recent years can be seen as functionally equivalent solutions that help firms

in workers are unlocked, not by the constraints of "leanness," but by opportunities to exercise professional judgment; unions and the law will restrict the kind of testing firms can employ in recruiting and evaluating workers, the information they can store in personnel records, and the performance measures they can use; recruitment and promotion will be on the basis not just of social characteristics such as "cooperativeness" or obedience but also of certifiable skills; training will be claimed as a right; and payment, if not determined by performance, will reward knowledge rather than length of service.

Where involvement is limited and negotiated, utilization by management of informal social integration for managerial purposes is possible only within narrow bounds.[42] A German, and indeed Western, enterprise can only partly be conceived as a community or family because a pluralist social structure is one in which workers honor a large number of competing commitments. In Germany limited involvement is reinforced by continuing reductions in working time, responding to increasingly significant nonwork relations of workers, as well as to a collective commitment to spread equitably the negative employment effects of productivity growth and a low permissible wage spectrum. To this extent, solidarity with family and other workers overrides loyalty to the employing organization. One consequence of this is that occupational and team skills must be taught to a large number of workers, each of which works fewer hours than a Japanese worker—which raises the costs of training in general and of the transition to "lean production" in particular.

(5) *Limits to the use of peer group pressure for motivational purposes.* The influence of peer group pressure in Germany is limited. German workers prefer to be governed by a combination of quasi-professional individual autonomy with technically competent managers whom, unlike their fellowworkers, they can hold formally accountable and with whom they can negotiate collectively. Moreover, even though peer groups may well come to play a more important role in coordinating work performance, they will continue to serve purposes that are *not* those of the firm, not least in the representation of workers vis-à-vis management. Union pressures for work groups to be given representative in addition to productive functions, in particular for group leaders to be elected by the group rather than appointed by management, are in line with the logic of a social organization of work in which commitment and involvement are limited and negotiated.

(6) *Limits to managerial discretion.* Worker participation in German workplaces takes the form not of teamwork but of *codetermination,* involving

---

attain LP efficiency without having to resort to short-notice overtime. I owe this observation to Ronald Dore. Note the important role that is granted by such regimes to codetermination and collective bargaining.

[42] "Enterprise culture" is conceived as developing "through discussion among all those involved" and through "an open, pluralistic and democratic communications process" (Roth, "Japanization," p. 45).

negotiation rather than identification with management, and responding not to the constraints of artificial resource shortages but to expectations in a pluralist society not subject to discretionary rule.[43] Codetermination, its essence being that it limits the discretion of management, is incompatible with "management by stress," as the latter would require workers to accept managerial decisions on their required work effort as unchangeable. "Leanness" may be used in Germany to save inventory costs, but as a device to set work norms it would have to be negotiated. And regardless of how "teamwork" will be organized in German workplaces, it has to remain compatible with codetermination, that is, open to oversight by the works council and not obstructive of collective representation.[44]

(7) *Limits to the appropriability by the firm of efficiency gains.* In a German environment work organization cannot rely on the *invisible buffers*, the open-ended commitment of workers to their employer, that in Japan create the appearance of "zero-buffer" production.[45] In fact, codetermination and collective bargaining amount to *negotiated replacement of latent with manifest buffers*, such as excess labor, excess skills, worker "professionalism," and ultimately industrial citizenship under workplace democracy. For example, works councils have asked that half of the savings resulting from group work be allocated to training during working hours, longer breaks, shorter working time, or a pool of relief workers. To the extent that such demands have to be conceded, efficiency gains from work reorganization can be appropriated only partly by the firm in the form of higher output or lower input, and for the other part must be allocated to maintaining "excess capacities," in violation of one of the core principles of LP.

(8) *Limits to the discretion of individual firms over their organization of work.* As German firms are subject to extensive social regulation by law and industrial agreement, they have less freedom than firms in other countries, notably Britain or the United States, to experiment with their work organization. The hold of external regulation on workplace conditions has recently weakened because of economic difficulties and technological change, but a wide range of subjects, from skill profiles to payment systems, to a significant part are not decided by the parties at the workplace alone and will not in the foreseeable future.[46] More than elsewhere, work reorganization in the individual firm must therefore be preceded by agreement at a level above the firm, which slows down change, limits diversity between firms, and protects the existing general pattern.[47]

---

[43] As a quid pro quo for the efficiencies of LP, Roth lists "regulated and accountable production conditions (organization of tasks, assignment of personnel, etc.) as well as greater participation (codetermination at the workplace)" ("Japanization," p. 37).

[44] Neumann, "Lean Production Needs 'Beefing Up,'" p. 74.

[45] Roth, "Japanization," p. 33.

[46] Thelen, *Union of Parts.*

[47] There are other constraints as well that, although not affecting work organization

For many reasons, contrary to economic-functionalist belief, convergence of institutional arrangements on international "best practice" is unlikely.[48] Local institutional conditions may be incompatible with the new practice, making it impossible or excessively costly to import it; local actors may develop functional alternatives more compatible with their traditional ways of doing things; what exactly best practice is is often uncertain and itself subject to endogenous change, at the very same time that followers try to emulate it; and because of market or technological change, shifting performance requirements may make best practice a moving target of uncertain location, with progress toward convergence continually undone by changes in its required direction.

In this essay I have emphasized the conditioning effect of institutional context at the neglect of other forces that may also stand in the way of crossnational convergence. Individual firms and management teams can always try to insert new practices in old settings, sometimes by copying what they perceive to be international "best practice." Different institutional environments are differently hospitable to experimentation and variation among firms, as well as to the specific practices a firm might want to import. In principle, however, even the most powerful firm and the most skillful management cannot entirely cut themselves off from the social context in which they operate, even from the loosest one, as much as they may want to and try. At the point where new foreign practices, however "best," must be fitted in a domestic context, some compromises must be made, and rather than convergence, the result will be a social-institutional hybrid more or less different from the model it was intended to emulate.

Unlike the U.S. model, the German institutional context limits the space for managerial voluntarism and enterprise individualism. This is why German institutions tend to be perceived as "rigid" by Anglo-American managers and firms, regardless of the high productive flexibility that is accomplished within them. Central tenets of manage-

---

in a narrow sense, limit the applicability of LP in Germany. For example, subcontracting to smaller firms under "just-in-time" production must contend with the fact that because of industrywide collective bargaining, the wage spread in Germany between small and large firms is much narrower than in Japan or, for that matter, Britain and the United States. As a consequence externally sourced supplies can either be cheap if purchased abroad, or "just in time" if purchased nearby in Germany, *but not both simultaneously*, as in Japan. This neutralizes an important cost advantage of LP and makes deep vertical disintegration of German manufacturing less likely.

[48] J. R. Hollingsworth and W. Streeck, "Countries and Sectors: Concluding Remarks on Performance, Convergence, and Competitiveness," in J. R. Hollingsworth, P. C. Schmitter, and W. Streeck, eds., *Governing Capitalist Economies: Performance and Control of Economic Sectors* (New York: Oxford University Press, 1994).

rially reconstructed "lean production" happen to be particularly hard to combine with central tenets of German institutional arrangements and are likely to create friction and rejection. This phenomenon does not preclude temporary successes for aggressive managerial experimentation, especially in times of economic stress and of a shifting industrial power balance away from unions and workers. Such successes will likely remain temporary, and deviant workplace practices in a tightly defined institutional setting will sooner or later come under the pressure of strong centripetal tendencies trying to reign them in through overt conflict or the subtle pull of dysfunction caused by lack of fit.

Of course national institutional contexts are far from fixed, and their elements are not necessarily always in harmony with each other. Indeed national "systems" often appear as such only in hindsight, to the extent that they are somehow perceived to have "worked." There is therefore no reason why firms that wish to import international "best practice" to a given country could not try to adapt that country's institutions to the new practice, rather than the other way around. But in this they will always be just one party among many others struggling over the direction of a process of institutional evolution that is both ongoing and open-ended. In the limiting case, and in certain periods and places, firms and management teams may be able to control that process unilaterally. Normally, however, and depending on the character of the institutional context itself that is at stake, influence over change is exercised by more than one party, with even the most powerful contestants having to make their peace with equally powerful institutional constraints.

Institutional analysis is not deterministic. Change in social institutions is not only continuous but typically uneven, and new stability is established, if at all, only with the next transformation already under way. Since unification major pillars of the West German socioeconomic order, in spite or because of its wholesale transfer to the *Neue Länder,* have come under pressure from industrial unions, the collective bargaining and vocational training systems, and codetermination. But then all of these have continuously changed in the past as a result of functional tensions as well as political conflict. At the same time, evolutionary outcomes were always recognizably influenced by previous states. As in the past, future change, in workplace practices and elsewhere, is unlikely to be determined by any one design, interest, actor, institutional need, or functional imperative alone. Change in work organization will continue, perhaps at an even more rapid pace, and today indeed in large part in response to Japanese competition. But it will also remain embedded in and constrained by a broader context in which many other changes will take place simultaneously and for their own reasons. The new arrangements that will result at the workplace may or may not be similar to those that presently exist, but they will certainly be more than the faithful execution of an imported managerial design.

CHAPTER SIX

Financial Markets in Japan

SHIJURO OGATA

This essay analyzes recent major changes in financial markets in Japan to identify the sources of pressure for reform and the nature of resistance to these forces. I consider (1) the traditional features of the postwar financial markets in Japan; (2) forces making for change; (3) opposition to change; (4) the role of national governmental control; and, finally, (5) the possible impact of the current recession.

TRADITIONAL FEATURES OF THE POSTWAR FINANCIAL MARKETS IN JAPAN

Before discussing recent changes in financial markets, it is important to define the major features of Japanese financial structure and practice during the first three decades after World War II.

First, *indirect finance* was a key to the system. The financial requirements of economic activities were met mostly by bank credits and not so much by securities issued by corporations. The reasons for this lay in the underdevelopment of capital markets (i.e., equity shares and bonds), even though the banking system was relatively well established, the financial crisis of the 1920s and 1930s having eliminated the weaker banks. Banks, together with post offices, were major depositories of personal savings.

Next, *compartmentalization* was important, for banks and securities houses were separate. Banks themselves were classified into different groups such as ordinary banks (city banks and regional banks), funded with short-term deposits, and specialized banks, such as long-term credit banks, a specialized foreign exchange bank, and trust banks, which were authorized to issue medium-term bonds. Despite such a difference in funding operations, the lending activities of both groups gradually became more alike, with both extending short-term as well as medium- and long-term loans.

Interest rates were regulated. To promote exports and investment, low interest rates were preferred, but in order to have a stable credit system, the profitability of banks had to be secured. For these reasons, maximum interest rates on deposits were regulated by laws and minimum lending rates were regulated by gentlemen's agreements, thereby keeping borrowing costs for corporations relatively low while securing some profit margins for banks.

Governmental financial institutions played an important part, via an enormous banking entity, the "Fiscal Investment and Loan Program" (FILP). The FILP's funding sources were personal savings deposited with post offices and governmental pension and insurance schemes, which were pooled into the "Trust Fund" administered by the Ministry of Finance. Its lending arms were governmental financial institutions, most of which were wholly government owned and nearly totally financed by the Trust Fund. These loans were financial tools of the government's industrial policies. To give some idea of the sums involved, postal savings amounted to 40 percent of total deposits in 1992; in 1993 the total new lending under the FILP was equivalent to 60 percent of the General Account Budget (the General Account Budget at 72 trillion Yen in 1993 excludes the thirty-eight Special Accounts of which the Fiscal Investment and Loan Program at 47 trillion Yen was one), and at a rough guess, to about 10 percent of total private capital investment.

Exchange controls on capital movements kept financial markets largely closed. Capital outflows were strictly regulated as long as the foreign exchange shortage persisted. The inflow of capital was permitted mainly in the form of short-term trade credits for Japanese banks and medium-term bank credits for Japanese industries. The preference for bank credits to direct investment reflected not only the predominance of indirect finance but also nationalistic sentiment against foreign control of Japanese industries.

Finally, *corporate structure* contributed in special ways to the financial system. Most major corporations in Japan are mutually owned by other corporations—often those in the same group ("cross-shareholding") and managed by a "self-perpetuating" corporate bureaucracy, consisting of those recruited directly from colleges and expected to serve their corporations for life, first as employees and trade union members and later, if successful, as managers and even executives. There is little intervention from shareholders and other stakeholders, except in certain cases from their "main banks" or leading figures in the same group.

FACTORS OF CHANGE

From the mid-1960s a number of changes began to transform the Japanese financial scene. The most important were:

- *The growth of capital markets*, particularly the markets of equity shares and government bonds. For example, the proportion of new outside funds obtained by corporations via capital markets, rather than from bank loans, increased from 20 percent in 1970–74 to 60 percent in 1984.
- *The diversification of the forms of saving, investment, and funding*; beginning with the securities companies' inauguration of interest-bearing fund accounts (Chukoku funds) in 1980 and the permission granted to banks to sell their holdings of government bonds to the public in 1982. Together, these had the following results:
- *The gradual erosion of compartmentalization* between banks and securities houses.
- *The phased deregulation of interest rates*, starting with the gradual introduction of *gensaki* transactions in the 1970s, and taking off with the introduction of transferrable certificates of deposit in 1979.
- *The internationalization and the globalization of financial transactions*, with the relaxation of exchange controls as Japan moved into current account surplus and their final removal in the late 1980s.

These changes are closely interrelated, but they seem to have been brought forth by both internal and external factors. Some of these factors are primarily domestic in origin. In the first place, from around the mid-1960s, the growth of the Japanese economy began to slow, because of the appearance of physical limits to growth in the mid-1960s and of the oil price rise and yen revaluation in the 1970s. The government had to abandon its balanced budget policy and to spend more than its tax revenue by issuing a large amount of government bonds. The increase in the outstanding balance of government bonds led to the emergence of a secondary market in government bonds, which had previously not existed because it had not been allowed to exist. As bond prices came to be freely quoted, the government was gradually forced to issue new bonds with market-based yields. In the meantime short-term financial transactions, *gensaki* (sale of government bonds with a promise of repurchase at a certain date at a certain [higher] price—virtually a form of short-term financing with government bonds as collateral), started to develop. Both freely priced government bonds and unregulated short-term financial facilities became very competitive, compared with still highly regulated instruments such as bank and postal deposits, which were gradually compelled to be deregulated. Paradoxically, then, the government's deficit spending contributed significantly to the liberalization of financial markets, hence to a certain loss of control.

Second, slower economic growth resulted in a more moderate rise of wages and other incomes. Such a trend, together with the aging of the population, made individuals more sensitive to earnings on their financial assets. They increasingly diversified their financial investment from bank and postal deposits (which fell from about 70 to just over 60 percent between 1974 and 1988–91) to other instruments, which were introduced by securities houses and other financial institutions.

Third, corporate demand for bank credits slowed down, for various reasons. The relative importance of capital-intensive heavy industries fell with the slower economic growth, rising concerns about the environment, and with the greater technological sophistication of industrial activities. The further growth of capital markets enabled the diversification of funding operations of industrial corporations, which began to rely not only on banks but also on capital markets, not only on bank credits but also on securitized instruments. The improved liquidity position of corporations increased sensitivity to rates of return on financial investment and induced financial institutions to innovate in providing more attractive investment instruments for clients.

Of the exogenous pressures for change, some were the direct result of foreign pressure, but most were mediated by the need for reciprocity if Japanese financial operators were to have opportunities abroad to use their new-found strength. Four strands may be singled out.

First, the improvement of Japan's balance of payments made it possible and even necessary to remove exchange controls on current transactions and also on capital movements, including banking transactions as well as portfolio and direct investment in both directions. Japanese and foreign financial institutions were allowed to conduct financial business not only in their respective home countries but also in other countries. The Japanese and foreign currencies could be used not only in their own countries but also in and between other countries.

Second, at the same time, the slowdown in domestic corporate demand for traditional bank credits and the growing overseas activities of their Japanese corporate clients encouraged Japanese banks to expand international activities. This trend stimulated the international operations of securities houses and of other financial institutions. These Japanese banks, securities houses, and other financial institutions quickly adopted the financial practices of international markets.

Third, the growth of unregulated Euro-currency markets and the reduction of restrictions in many countries, together with the technological improvement of means of communication, promoted the globalization of financial transactions. When there remained some differences in the degree of liberalization between Japanese and foreign markets, financial transactions tended to shift from less liberalized and more taxed markets at home to more liberalized and less taxed markets abroad—particularly in London, Zurich, and Hong Kong (e.g., "regulatory arbitrage," "regime competition") and created pressures for further liberalization of less liberalized markets in Japan.

Finally, there was direct government-to-government pressure from foreign governments, who were pushed by private financial institutions to promote further liberalization of Japanese financial markets through bilateral and multilateral consultations and negotiations.

OPPOSITION TO CHANGE

Who resists these changes? Mainly those who would lose their powers or privileges. Despite the interests at stake, there is no politically organized opposition to changes in financial markets, although there is always some lobbying of politicians and bureaucrats by different financial sectors. Smaller financial institutions are generally against deregulation of interest rates, because they fear profit squeeze due to higher funding costs and competitive lending charges. Securities houses are against liberalized commissions, again because of profit squeeze and concern about intensified competition if banks enter the securities business. The postal saving service, which does not worry much about profitability because it is run by the state, opposes market determination of interest rates on deposits because of their fear of losing their competitive advantage over banks. Finally, the Ministry of Finance, who had to accept the market-related yields when issuing new bonds, is still opposed to the market-led determination of the costs of its short-term borrowing from the central bank.

THE ROLE OF NATIONAL GOVERNMENTAL CONTROL

With the liberalization and internationalization of financial transactions, it is generally recognized in Japan that the gradual reduction of national govermental control is inevitable. But government officials seem to be trying to retain their control as much as and as long as possible, fortified by their belief that markets do not always produce the socially optimal result—which may be true—and their belief that they are able to manage market trends—which may less often be true. After the recent disclosure of scandals in securities markets, some strongly argued for an independent regulatory agency for securities markets on the ground that too much governmental control would result in too much protection, too little self-discipline of market participants, and too little transparency of market practices. But the ministry succeeded in setting up such a regulatory agency under its own jurisdiction.

The globalization of financial transactions and the general trends toward "regulatory arbitrage," or "regime competition," rule out the effective supervision of financial activities without close coordination with other countries in accordance with the international standards of conduct and accounting. Similarly, enhancing "national competitiveness" through national protection becomes more and more difficult. Harmonizing financial practices to bring them closer to those of more advanced countries becomes necessary, even if not desirable.

One serious problem here is the global spread of overly complex, sophisticated, and risky financial devices, including a variety of derivatives—transactions not accompanied by cash delivery or entry into balance sheets and carrying the danger that, within the pyramids of claims of many parties mostly unknown to one another, the failure of one party may lead to unexpected adverse chain reactions. No single agency, governmental or independent, in any country, can effectively deal with this issue. Nor will the introduction of detailed rules and regulations be a solution. The only possible answer would be in greater international coordination of regulators and market participants at various levels to strengthen risk management.

The question arises of whether recent financial excesses, such as too easy bank lending and too speculative financial transactions of other forms in Japan and elsewhere, may not be due to too much harmonization with Anglo-Saxon financial practices, or rather, should be attributed to inadequate policies and practices in individual countries. In my view the harmonization of financial practices itself is not the major cause of the excesses. The chief cause, in Japan as elsewhere, lies in the easy monetary conditions created by inadequate macroeconomic policies. They lead market participants to ignore the inevitability of cyclical changes in the real economy and in asset markets. Those policies also weakened the will of market participants to discipline themselves to the new deregulated regime. The squeeze on profits from greater competition should have forced them to concentrate on the profitability and quality of their loans, rather than on volume and market share, which had traditionally been their major preoccupation.

POSSIBLE IMPACT OF THE CURRENT RECESSION

The current recession in Japan seems to be influencing Japanese financial practices. First, because of the deterioration of their loan assets and the weakening of their capital position, banks and other financial institutions have become extremely cautious in new lending. The continued stagnation of equity markets is reinvigorating so-called relationship banking, which in Japan has historically meant corporate reliance on "main banks." This may change when equity markets recover.

Second, in view of (1) foreign institutional investors' growing interest in the management of Japanese companies' share issues and (2) the newly emerging self-criticism among Japanese executives about their traditional management practices, some Japanese companies have begun to reconsider seriously their pattern of corporate governance for instance, by appointing independent individuals as nonexecutive directors in addition to the now legally required independent auditors. However, it is not certain what will happen to cross-shareholding. The fall of stock prices—bringing the Nikkei index below 20,000, half its previous level—may have been at least partly caused by some unloading of cross-shareholding, leading to a fall in price and further unloading with spiral effect. However, the stabilization of stock prices and their occasional return to the 20,000 index level suggest that such unloading is not a continuing tendency. The future of cross-shareholding would seem to be affected by stock market conditions and the state of the economy, even though many companies value them, both as means of cementing relationships between companies and as protection against hostile takeovers.

Third, the disclosure of financial and political scandals has strengthened the belief in the need for further deregulation and the need for transparent and voluntary rules of conduct by market participants, rather than arbitrary governmental guidance. At the same time, however, current financial difficulties require some official support, in order to avoid the failure of financial institutions and to obtain generous tax treatment for bad loans. Such a trend seems to invite more governmental intervention. The difficulties of smaller securities houses are already delaying the pace of reform in the separation between banks and securities houses. Altogether, the current recession seems to be slowing the speed of financial liberalization for a while, and the increased political instability after July 1993 is most likely to delay any important policy decision.

Financial markets in Japan have been undergoing a number of changes over two decades since the 1970s in three major directions: (1) diversification; (2) liberalization; and (3) internationalization. These changes are not only due to external factors such as the globalization of financial transactions but also to internal factors such as the increase in the outstanding balance of government bonds, which has resulted in the development of liberalized financial transactions.

All these developments, some contradictory, some convergent, make it difficult to predict the direction of change in Japanese traditional financial practices such as cross-shareholding. The current recession may reinforce some traditional practices such as corporate reliance on "main banks" and may preserve relatively strong governmental intervention, at least temporarily. Nevertheless, because of the increasingly global nature of financial transactions, financial markets in Japan may become inevitably more exposed to international developments than some other sectors of Japanese economy such as distribution, transportation, and agriculture.

CHAPTER SEVEN

Competition among Forms of Corporate Governance in the European Community: The Case of Britain

STEPHEN WOOLCOCK

In this essay I consider the competition between different forms of corporate governance within the European Union (EU). For some time there has been a renewed interest in differences that exist between the various forms of market economy.[1] This interest has been intensified by the demise of Soviet communism. Without the contrast to communism differences among the market economies became more apparent.[2] Increased trade and investment liberalization and deregulation have also removed (or are removing) many of the nontariff measures that previously constituted differences between the national models of market regulation. For example, the level of direct state intervention in the economy through nationalization, subsidies, and other such instruments of industrial policy has declined. This change has resulted in the focus shifting onto other differences between the market economies, among them, corporate governance.

Increased awareness of differences has also resulted from increased economic interdependence and the globalization of competition. The most obvious differences have been between the United States and Japan. These were reflected in the U.S. criticism of the *keiretsu* as part

This chapter draws on research into competition among rules in the EU funded by the Economic and Social Research Council of the United Kingdom carried out by the author while he was Senior Research Fellow with the European Programme of the Royal Institute of International Affairs.
[1] J. R. Hollingsworth, P. C. Schmitter, and W. Streeck, eds., *Governing Capitalist Economies: Performance and Control of Economic Sectors* (New York: Oxford University Press, 1994).
[2] Michel Albert, *Capitalism vs. Capitalism* (New York: Four Wall Eight Windows, 1993).

of the Structural Impediments Initiative (SII). But differences in corporate governance may also lie behind other trade tensions. For example, the ability of companies in countries such as Japan to sell at cost price or below cost price for an extended period derives from the expectations of the owners of capital. With the Anglo-Saxon form of corporate governance the owners of capital expect a rapid return on capital. In short import competition from Japan is seen as "unfair" competition, and remedies in the form of anti-dumping duty actions are taken.[3]

Corporate governance also influences market access in the shape of inward investment. In many sectors of the economy, especially in services, effective market access requires a market presence. One way of gaining quick and effective market access is therefore to acquire a local operation already accustomed to local market conditions. In Britain and the United States takeovers and acquisitions are day-to-day occurrences and a normal way of bringing about corporate restructuring. This is not the case in Japan or Germany where takeovers are uncommon. Gaining market access through acquisitions is arguably harder in such countries. If access is related to the levels of foreign direct investment (FDI), a number of differences between German (FDI roughly 1 percent of manufacturing GDP) and Japan (less than 1 percent) on the one hand and the Anglo-Saxon economies, such as the United States (4 percent of manufacturing GDP) may be important.[4]

In the EU the process of integration has resulted in high levels of economic interdependence. The internal market program initiated in the mid-1980s is removing all nontariff barriers and regulatory barriers. If the program is effectively enforced there will, indeed, be a single market for goods, services, and most important, capital within the EC. But differences in corporate governance will remain. The most pronounced difference is between the British version of Anglo-Saxon corporate governance and the Rhineland (or Alpine) form of corporate governance found in Germany and with variations in the Netherlands, Austria, and Switzerland. France falls between these two forms of capitalism, as does Italy. The EU therefore provides an opportunity of assessing what happens when different forms of corporate governance compete within the same market. Developments in Europe may therefore illuminate the effects of intense competition on different forms of corporate governance.

In this paper I focus on the impact of competition on Britain, al-

[3] It is no accident that dumping duties are then based on profit margins, which would be acceptable under an Anglo-Saxon system of corporate governance.
[4] See Stephen Thomsen and Stephen Woolcock, *Foreign Direct Investment in Europe: Competition between Firms and Governments* (London: Pinter, 1993).

though there are references to developments in other EU member states. The definition of corporate governance used here is broad and includes the nature, size, and regulation of the capital markets; the structure of ownership of companies; the relationship between management and the various stakeholders in a company; the structure of companies themselves (i.e., unitary or two-tier boards); and the method of bringing about corporate restructuring.

THE ISSUES

First, are there indeed substantial differences between different forms of corporate governance? What forms do they take? Second, what impact will the efforts at European harmonization have on the differences? Will there be common rules for financial markets, company law, and takeover activity that will create a common European corporate governance? I argue that the degree of harmonization that has taken place is not enough to bring about a common system of corporate governance within the EC. I show that differences in policy, practice, and philosophy have in fact frustrated efforts to agree on a number of measures affecting corporate governance. Indeed, the area of company law is one of the few in which the legislative proposals set out in the Cockfield White Paper of 1985, which provided the legislative agenda for the creation of a single European market, have not been adopted.

This leaves the question of whether a common European approach to corporate governance will emerge as a result of competition among the different forms that will result in a convergence toward a common approach. If so will it be more like the Anglo-Saxon or the Rhineland model, the other distinct model that exists within Europe?

The issue for Britain is why, despite consistently poor industrial performance and repeated calls for changes to be made in the British model, there has been no substantial change. Will the intensification of competition among rules in the single market bring about change in Britain or other countries? Indeed, will the different forms of corporate governance result in a synthesis constituted from the best elements of each system? Or will the different national systems of corporate governance continue to exist side by side? I argue that there is pressure for convergence as a result of "competition among rules," largely as a result of the internationalization of capital markets.[5] This has led France and to a lesser extent Germany to shift to accept ele-

---

[5] For a detailed discussion of the issue of competition among rules, see Stephen Woolcock, *Regulation in the Single European Market: Centralization or Competition among National Policies?* (London: Royal Institute of International Affairs, 1994).

ments of the Anglo-Saxon model. Thus larger companies are, for example, raising funds on the London capital market, without, however, changing their whole system of corporate governance. The effects of competition among the different national systems of corporate governance are dampened, because each is made up of a set of linked policies, regulations, practices, and philosophies affecting capital markets, company structures, and industrial relations. They are "embedded" in national practices and institutional arrangements. Small changes or changes in one area that leave the other components of these national systems untouched do not bring about convergence. Change in Britain requires comprehensive reform, which in turn requires a consensus on the need and content of the reform. This consensus does not exist.

Is convergence is a good thing? In Chapter 4 Kester has argued that each system of corporate governance contains some of the "good" elements needed for efficiency but that none incorporates all of them. The argument appears to be that one should aim to achieve a synthesis that incorporates best practice from each country. Others have argued that diversity is good because it allows for national preferences to be expressed in different regulatory approaches and for a dynamic, continuous process of experimentation.[6] If this is correct, the objective of European integration should not be to bring about convergence but to retain diversity. In the short to medium term it is possible to reconcile these two positions, because convergence can come about as a result of competition. But views on whether there is a "best" form of corporate governance in Europe will influence policymaking. In this essay I argue that, on the basis of the case study of Britain, there will be no Euro-norm for corporate control and no single model for European capitalism. Europe is more likely to be characterized by competing systems of corporate control from the Anglo-Saxon to the Rhineland systems.

The Different Systems of Corporate Control

The Different Models

There are a range of different forms of corporate governance in the EU.[7] But two of the countries offer clear and distinctly different

[6] Horst Siebert and Michael Koop, "Institutional Competition or Centralisation," *Kiel Working Papers* 548 (January 1993).
[7] T. Jenkinson and C. Mayer, "The Assessment: Corporate Governance and Corporate Control," *Oxford Review of Economic Policy* 8, no. 3 (Autumn 1992).

forms: Britain with its version of the Anglo-Saxon form of corporate governance, and Germany with its Rhine capitalism.

Broadly speaking the Anglo-Saxon model is based on a system that places the emphasis on equity finance for business. Capital markets therefore tend to be large and regulated in a manner favorable to trading in equities. As banks provide a relatively small share of business finance, the links between banks and companies are not strong. Ownership of shares is largely in the hands of institutional fund managers, whose focus is on relatively short-term return on capital, rather than longer term market share issues. There are no extensive cross-shareholdings. Insider trading or bankruptcy regulation also discourages institutional shareholders from playing an active role in companies. Links between the stakeholders in the company and management also tend to be weak. As a result corporate restructuring occurs through takeovers as shareholders are tempted to accept bid premia and sell or "exit" rather than become actively involved in the rescue by "voicing" concern about the performance of management. Company law is based on existing directors and a unitary board system that is seen as most efficient. Studies or investigations into "poor" corporate governance tend to focus on how to improve the operation of these unitary boards, rather than on the overall system of regulation and practice. Finally, the emphasis is on individual merit rather than the building of a consensus among all those involved in the company. This aspect is reflected in large differentials in pay and training.

The Rhineland form of corporate governance relies more on debt finance by banks, which have retained relatively close links with companies through their role as shareholders in their own right, through their role as proxies for smaller shareholders, through participation in supervisory boards, or by fulfilling the role of lender of last resort in crises. Capital markets tend to be smaller and have fewer public companies. The relationship between the company and all the stakeholders—investors, employees, and local communities dependent on the company for prosperity—tends to be closer than with Anglo-Saxon corporate governance. When problems arise, the normal practice is for these stakeholders to voice concern and for changes in management to take place, rather than stakeholder "exit" and a change in ownership. This characteristic enables implicit contractual relationships to develop between management and the stakeholders and means that takeovers or change in ownership are not the norm for corporate restructuring.[8] Finally, consensus has a higher priority than

[8] Julian Franks and Colin Mayer, "Capital Markets and Corporate Control: A Study of France, Germany, and the UK," *Economic Policy*, no. 10 (April 1990): 189, 231.

in the Anglo-Saxon system, both within society and the company. Within the economy as a whole it is supported by the social market economy; within the company it is supported by solidarity in the shape of moderate wage and skill differentials and institutions such as works councils.

The French model of corporate governance falls between the German and British models. Paris has a larger capital market than any of the German capital markets, but smaller than London. It has more links between financial and industrial concerns than Britain, but less than Germany. Takeovers play a greater role than in Germany, but not as great as in Britain. The state has played a more important role in France than in either Britain or Germany, and this is reflected in the remaining state holdings. There are also cross-shareholdings in France, but not as many as in Italy, where the leading industrial concerns have an extensive network of cross-shareholdings.

Capital Markets and Regulation

Perhaps the most clear-cut distinction between the Anglo-Saxon system of corporate governance in Britain and the rest of the EU is the size of the London capital market, for historical reasons relating to the growth of London as a center for international finance in the nineteenth century. The capitalization of the London market has remained at between 90 and 100 percent of GDP in recent years, a large figure compared to those of the much smaller capital markets in Germany and France, where capitalization is some 20 percent of GDP, and Italy, where it is 16 percent of GDP. Only the Netherlands (50 percent) and Belgium (33 percent) come anywhere near the level of Britain.[9] The Netherlands has a similar history of financial/trading interests to that of Britain, but it is a less open as a market for corporate control as many of the shares traded on the Amsterdam stock exchange are nonvoting shares. In recent years there have been suggestions from journalists and market participants that Paris and Frankfurt liberalize their capital markets in order to compete with London. There may well be some convergence, but London still accounts for no less than 95 percent of cross-border share issues in the EU, and such business accounts for some 44 percent of turnover in

[9] See Department of Trade and Industry, in *Barriers to Takeovers in the European Community*, Vol. 1 (London: HMSO, 1989). The other exception is Luxembourg where market capitalization is greater than 100% because of the small size of the Luxembourg economy and the use of Luxembourg as a low-tax treatment location for certain transactions.

London. This role provides a powerful incentive for London to regulate its market in such a fashion as to keep this business.[10]

Related to the size of capital markets is the number of publicly listed companies. In Britain there are some 2,500 companies trading their shares in the London market. This figure is higher than any other EC member state. In Germany, for example, there were around 600 quoted companies in 1991, an increase on the number listed in the early to mid-1980s. Indeed, after a period during the 1970s when there were some 600 listed companies in Germany, there was a decline to about 450 by 1984. During the latter half of the 1980s securities firms and banks were able to sell the attractions of going public, which has resulted in some recovery in the number. But this recent increase does little more than bring the number of companies up to the earlier level. In France and Spain there are in the order of 300 to 400 listed companies, and in Italy there are only about 200. The existence of cross-shareholdings and state holdings in France means that in practice very few of these companies are targets for potential takeovers.

The Structure of Ownership

The Anglo-Saxon form of corporate control in Britain is also distinctive in its structure of ownership. Table 7-1 shows institutional shareholders to be far more important in Britain than in other European countries. The low incidence of cross-shareholdings between companies is reflected in the low figure for shares held by other companies compared to other countries.

These structural features of the British capital market are unlikely to change very quickly, even if there were concerted efforts to do so

Table 7-1. The structure of ownership of shares in selected countries

	France	Germany	Britain
Households	40	16	28
Companies	22	40	5
Financial institutions	20	15	58
Overseas	16	31	4
Other	2	8	5

SOURCE: Davis, "Taking an Interest versus Charging Interest: Corporate Banking Relations in the UK," mimeo, London, Bank of England, 1992.

[10] Amsterdam has lost a considerable amount of business in share trading to London, and about a third of German shares are traded in London.

on the part of regulators and participants. There are some signs of change in other parts of the EU that might bring about some convergence toward the British structures, but again at the current pace of change, it will take many years to bring structures about equivalent to those in Britain. One can speculate about the impact of a single currency in Europe on capital markets. The U.S. example would suggest that there would be one major capital. But the desire to retain regional capital markets is likely to be strong in Europe, with the result that one might well have one major capital market used by international companies and smaller regional markets serving the smaller and medium-size national firms. This could combine the benefits of low costs of capital from a large open market with the advantages of smaller regional and more accessible capital markets. But such long-term developments remain speculative.

The Relationship between Stakeholders and Management

The Anglo-Saxon form of corporate governance is also characterized by arms-length relationships between all stakeholders and the management of companies. Neither investors nor employees nor the local communities within which firms invest have any close links with companies. The British form of corporate governance makes no attempt to incorporate all stakeholders. Investors are given pride of place and in more ways than one. The checks and balances in British corporate governance are geared almost exclusively to the relationship between management and investors or rather shareholders. Company law, stock market regulations and takeover rules are all oriented to the defense of shareholder interests. Recent efforts to strengthen corporate governance, such as the Cadbury Committee's report on the financial aspects of corporate governance in Britain, seem if anything geared to strengthening the rights of shareholders. This contrasts with the still-close relationships between all stakeholders in the Rhineland form of corporate governance.

Although the relationship between investor and company can be seen as a deep-seated "cultural" feature of the system of corporate governance, it originates and is supported by regulatory policies that are shaped by interest groups. This can be illustrated by looking at Britain. As has been shown by a number of studies,[11] the role of banks in industrial finance is limited in Britain. There is no relationship banking as in Germany where banks have important shareholdings and have participated directly in the supervision of company performance through their professional representative on the supervisory

[11] See, for example, Franks and Mayer, "Corporate Ownership and Corporate Control."

boards of companies and through their role as proxy for many smaller shareholders.

There are some signs of a weakening of the role of banks elsewhere in continental European members of the EU. For example, concern in Germany about the excessive influence of banks has led to some discussion of placing controls on their participation in industrial and service sector companies.[12] Increases in retained earnings and securitization (i.e., increased use of share issues to raise capital) have also reduced what was in any case an overstated importance of German house banks. Moreover, EC legislation, in the shape of the Second Banking Coordination Directive, which came into force on January 1, 1993, also limits bank holdings in all EC countries. A single bank holding in a nonbanking company may not exceed 15 percent of the bank's equity, and total bank holdings must be less than 60 percent of the bank's equity. International capital adequacy rules agreed under the auspices of the Bank for International Settlement (BIS) and largely incorporated into the EC through the EC's Capital Adequacy Directive, also increase the costs of bank equity holdings. If the value of shareholdings exceeds a set percentage of a bank's own capital, the value of the shares must be deducted from the bank's capital when calculating capital adequacy holdings. This measure is designed to account for the risk involved in holding share capital and represents a limitation of the potential role of banks in large companies through major shareholdings.

These moves toward a smaller role for banks in "Europe" have been taking place at the same time that the Anglo-Saxon system has moved further away from relationship banking. Deregulation has resulted in increased competition among banks as well as between banks and other financial institutions. This has tended to undermine any remaining relationship banking that existed. Faced with strong competition, banks have tried to "poach" new customers, and companies have found an advantage in maintaining links with competing institutions in order to get the best conditions. As a result close relationships, based on trust, between companies and banks have become harder rather than easier to maintain.

As in the United States bankruptcy laws in Britain also militate against relationship banking in that any bank that intervenes in order to assist a customer in difficulties is likely to have its seniority as a debtor reduced. These laws are based on the principle that creditors of any bankrupt company should be treated equally, but its effect is to provide a fairly powerful disincentive to active intervention.

[12] Ellen Scheider-Lenne, "Corporate Control in Germany," *Oxford Review of Economic Policy* 8, no. 3 (1992).

National regulation also militates against close relationships between large shareholders and companies. For example, under British takeover rules it is necessary to make a full bid for a company once 30 percent of the shares have been acquired. In most other EC member states the threshold is when a single shareholder has 50 percent. Under the British takeover code it is then necessary to provide all shareholders with a "right to exit" by making a bid for 100 percent of shares, even when considerably less would be sufficient to gain control of the company. This is again primarily geared at ensuring equal rights for all shareholders, such as small shareholders. Similar legislation that increases the transparency requirements for the transfer of major shareholdings has been adopted in the EU. But the more important adoption of common takeover regulation has been blocked by the opposition of a number of member states, including Germany.

The passive nature of shareholders and the tendency to focus on short-term quarterly financial statements has led to criticism of the "short termism" of the City of London. Despite repeated investigations into the topic, such as the City-Industry set up by the Confederation of British Industry (CBI) in 1986, there remains no consensus on the fact that there is even a problem, let alone the need for change or what change might be required.[13] All that has emerged from these studies have been recommendations on how to improve shareholder–management relations. The competitive pressure on British companies has, however, kept the issue on the agenda. A 1990 survey of more than 200 of the largest British companies, found that more than 90 percent thought the City was "short-term" and too much oriented to short-term earnings per share criteria.[14] Recommendations continue to be made on the need to have more active institutional shareholders, but even if they had the motivation to become more active, institutional shareholders, unlike the German banks, have neither the resources nor the expertise to follow all their investments, which are generally widely spread, in order to reduce risk.

Insider trading legislation militates against active institutional shareholders, because if they obtain price-sensitive information as a result of involvement in a company they cannot trade without infringing insider trading legislation. The fund manager concerned will therefore be at a disadvantage, rather than at an advantage, compared to other fund managers. Attempts to develop more active shareholders runs into general skepticism or outright opposition from the institutions. For example, in one notable case in 1992 concerning the manu-

[13] Confederation of British Industry.
[14] House of Commons, *Takeovers and Mergers*, First Report of the House of Commons Trade and Industry Committee, Session 1991–92, November 1991.

facturer of environmental equipment, a leading institutional share-holder with a 5 percent share of the company exercised "voice" and sought to bring about a corporate restructuring by changing the management, which it considered was not performing well. The institution, which had backing from the Bank of England and media, which saw this as a model for more active shareholders, sought in vain for support from the other institutions with shares in the company. The predominant view was that this was not consistent with the objectives and duties of fund managers who should look to the interests of their clients. After a protracted and open dispute, the company was taken over.[15] Rather than providing an example of active institutional share-holders, the case therefore illustrated that corporate restructuring in Britain is still more easily brought about by a change of ownership.

The case in Germany could not be more different. When companies begin to run into difficulties it is the major shareholders, usually the banks, that step in to coordinate a rescue. Rather than sell up to a predatory holding company, which would probably realize the value of assets "locked up" in its structure, the German approach is to seek to preserve as much as possible. This is the case for even large companies such as A.E.G. The structure of regulation and practice tends to favor such longer term commitment to companies. For example, insider trading rules have been introduced only recently in Germany, in part as a result of EU provisions.

Another example of where German national regulation has consolidated the German approach can be found in the limited requirements on disclosure of information about companies.[16] This contrasts with Britain, in which extensive obligations to provide information on company accounts to protect the individual shareholder has promoted the growth of a highly professional and important accountancy profession in Britain. This in turn has led to ever-better provision of financial information and contributed to the bias in favor of financial results and the domination of accountancy over engineering and science in the professions of directors of companies. This relative lack of information in Germany has been seen as one of the reasons for the lack of a level playing field for acquisitions within the EU, because foreign acquirers of British firms have better information about their potential targets than British firms have of continental targets. There has been some harmonization of disclosure requirements in European company law directives, but this has not been enough to bring about much convergence. For example, in a recent legal case, *Caparo*, the

---

[15] See *Financial Times*, 6 April 1992.
[16] "Proposed Fifth Company Law Directive," *Official Journal of the European Communities*, C 131, December 13, 1972.

British House of Lords (highest national court) confirmed that accountants are responsible only to the directors of a company, as representatives of the shareholders, and the shareholders themselves, but not to any other stakeholder in the company, such as representatives of employees.

Company Law and the Structure of the Company

In company law there is a clear example of how efforts to harmonize at a European level have been frustrated by a determination, led by the British, to retain different national traditions. The British system of company law is based on a unitary board rather than the two-tier structure that prevails in continental Europe. The rationale for the unitary board is that it avoids fragmentation of responsibility and is more efficient. Proponents of the two-tier system argue that the supervisory board provides for more effective independent monitoring of management performance. This difference has precluded progress on a number of European company law directives. The representative bodies of British business as well as the British governments since the mid-1970s have been insisting on the ability to continue with a unitary board structure in the face of EC proposals based on continental practice and law. As a result the original 1972 EC proposals on board structure, which were contained in the draft Fifth Company Law directive,[17] had to be modified to accommodate the Anglo-Saxon system. This was done in revised proposals produced in 1983. But the captains of British industry opposed these because the alternative proposed was the greater use of nonexecutive directors with employees having a role in the election of half of the nonexecutive directors. A further revision of the Fifth Company Law Directive sought to separate out the question of employee representation by providing for alternative means of ensuring employee representation. This included the possibility of using the "voluntarist," that is, nonstatutory, approach favored by British business and the British government, but the opposition continues.

The latest test of British opinion on the structure of companies can be found in the report of the Cadbury committee on the financial aspects of corporate governance, and the responses to it. The Cadbury report did not consider the merits or demerits of a two-tier board system but pushed the idea of a greater use of nonexecutive directors by means of a voluntary code.[18] The pressures that led to the

[17] See Proposed Fifth Company Law Directive of 13 December 1972.
[18] See Cadbury Committee, *The Financial Aspects of Corporate Governance* (London: HMSO, 1992).

Cadbury report were primarily endogenous, in the sense that they flowed from the concern about managerial failures during the 1980s. It was argued that weaknesses in the system of corporate governance had been disguised by the boom of the 1980s and became all too obvious during the recession. There were also a number of cases of blatant malpractice, such as those involving Polly Peck and Maxwell. This concern about the declining standards of corporate governance led the London Stock Exchange and the Financial Reporting Council, with the backing of the Bank of England, to initiate the investigation by the Cadbury Committee.

The Cadbury report was not the first time proposals had been made for more use of nonexecutive directors. In 1991 the House of Commons, Select Committee on Trade and Industry, recommended strengthening links between institutional shareholders and the boards of companies through nonexecutive directors.[19] As on these previous occasions, there was concerted opposition from business interests such as the Institute of Directors and the CBI to even the slightest suggestion that there would be a requirement. The business lobbies were concerned that any requirement under British law would open the way to European legal requirements for nonexecutive directors and be the first step down a slippery slope to a two-tier board. To get support the Cadbury Committee was therefore obliged to limit itself to a recommendation in favor of a voluntary code rather than legislation. The report argued that it is "essential that there is a strong and independent element on the board with a recognized senior member." It also included provisions on subcommittees, financial reporting, and directors' responsibilities. The recommendation was that all listed (public) companies should comply with a voluntary code and that company annual reports should include a declaration of compliance with the code or, if a company decided not to comply, the reasons for not doing so. Public censure was seen as the means of ensuring compliance. Thus the Stock Exchange will require all listed companies to declare compliance with the code. Institutional shareholders will bring moral pressure to bear on companies to comply.

The establishment of the Cadbury Committee suggests that there is still concern about British corporate governance, but the outcome consolidates the Anglo-Saxon approach by trying to improve financial reporting and control. The current debate is therefore about improving best practice in terms of the current system of corporate governance, not changing the whole approach to corporate governance.

[19] House of Commons, Select Committee on Trade and Industry, *Takeovers and Mergers*, Session 1991–92 (London: HMSO, 1991).

Consensus and the Issue of Employee Representation

Another clear distinction between the British and continental European forms of corporate governance is on the issue of statutory employee representation. In contrast to most of the rest of continental Europe, especially Germany, which has laws requiring parity codecision making in supervisory boards and works councils, British governments and business have in the past and continue to oppose any statutory requirements on participation. Again this opposition is as long as Britain's membership in the Community, going back to the initial draft Fifth Company Law Directive.

Underlying the opposition to any form of employee participation is a legacy of confrontational attitudes to industrial relations, especially during the 1970s, compared to the more consensual approach in Germany. More fundamentally, however, there is a deep-seated difference between the (neo) liberal, free market philosophy in Britain and different forms of "social market economy" in continental Europe. The predominant view in British industry and government circles is that increased social provision or efforts to seek consensus are costs that undermine competitiveness and thus general economic prosperity. For many continental Europeans, or at least for northern continental Europeans, social provision and consensus are seen as prerequisites of stable (long term) economic growth. The conviction that cooperative forms of industrial relations is not possible in Britain continues to shape the employers' approach. In contrast, a decade of Thatcherism has resulted in British trade unions moving to a position in which they appear to have embraced the German-style consensual/social market economy approach that is reflected in EC proposals.

The strength of feeling on the issue is illustrated by the willingness of the British government to seek an optout of the extension of qualified majority voting on issues concerning working conditions in the Maastricht Treaty because this would have resulted in the adoption of an EC directive on consultation and information or European works councils. British industry argues that it has effective, voluntary employee representation. European statutes are seen as introducing undesirable rigidity into the system and increasing costs for British companies. The representatives of British industry argue further that social Europe will also be detrimental for European competitiveness and thus the prosperity of the Community as a whole. One consequence of this dogmatic position is that one of the few areas in which the Cockfield 1992 objectives for the single market were not achieved was company law.[20]

---

[20] Commission of the European Communities, *Completing the Internal Market. White Paper from the Commission to the Council* ("Cockfield White Paper") (Luxembourg: Office for Official Publications of the EC, June 1985).

Corporate Restructuring

Takeovers are used far more as a means of bringing about corporate restructuring in Britain than in any other European country. Britain accounts for the bulk of mergers and acquisitions with the EC. The number of takeovers in Britain in 1988–90 when the latest takeover wave was at its peak far exceeded those in other countries. The French shift toward the Anglo-Saxon system can be seen in the relatively high figure for takeovers in France, but in Germany and Italy takeovers are still the exception rather than the rule. Since 1990 there has been a significant reduction in takeover activity because of the recession. The use of takeovers in corporate restructuring is due to the size and regulation of the London capital market, which is in effect also an open market for corporate control.

As on other aspects of corporate governance there is no broad consensus on the benefits of takeovers as a means of corporate restructuring. Some companies, such as the aggressive corporate raiders, argue that the threat of takeover is a spur to more efficient management and does keep management on its toes. The examples of B.A.T. and ICI are sometimes quoted as examples of companies that initiated major restructuring measures in part in response to the threat of takeovers. Others argue that the threat of takeover means that management focuses on short-term objectives and share prices rather than long-term investment. It is also argued that premium payments on shares, which have been a good deal higher in Britain than other countries in recent years, means that funds go to keep shareholders happy and stop them selling up, rather than going into investment in research and development.

Takeover activity is also affected by regulatory practice and by the bodies involved in regulating takeovers. Because of the importance of takeovers in Britain a sophisticated system of control has been built up. In 1968 the City Takeover Panel was set up by City institutions to administer the City Code on Takeovers and Mergers that had been agreed in 1967. This body is nonstatutory, although there are sanctions against noncompliance in the sense that statutory established bodies such as the Securities Investment Board or the Self Regulatory Organisations, as well as the Stock Exchange, may withdraw authorization to do business if the code is breached. There has also been judicial review of the Panel's decision in the case of Datafin. But, as the Takeover Panel is at pains to point out, the precedent set in that case only means that the decisions of the (British) courts can influence the interpretation of the Code in future cases. There is no direct review of individual decisions of the Panel and no question of a decision of the Panel being overturned or modified by the court.

The objectives of the Panel and Code are to ensure (1) the equality of treatment and opportunities of all shareholders during a takeover bid; (2) that shareholders have adequate information; (3) that existing boards do not seek to frustrate a bid without first gaining the approval of the shareholders; and (4) that markets are fair and orderly. This regulation of takeovers has been criticized on the grounds that it is essentially carried out by the City institutions that have a vested interest in the level of takeovers being maintained. Of the seventeen Panel members eleven are from "the City" (i.e., merchant bankers, securities firms, and corporate lawyers). Until recently there was only one member, from the CBI, who could be said to have represented industrial firms. In 1991 the Panel responded to criticism and appointed two further independent members from industry. The Panel argues that the difficulty with representatives from industry is that they are likely to have a direct interest in some takeovers. But it must also be recognized that self-regulation by institutions that profit from takeovers is a form of regulatory capture on a grand scale. This critical view recently found some support from the House of Commons Select Committee on Trade and Industry, which argued in favor of placing the Panel under a statutory umbrella.[21]

With considerable experience of takeovers and a code developed over more than twenty years it was not surprising that the British Takeover Code was used as the basis of the EC's Thirteenth Company Law Directive on the harmonization of takeover regulation across the EC.[22] With increasing cross-border takeovers in the EC the Commission wished to establish common rules. Apart from Britain no member state had a sophisticated takeover provision, and some had no general rules at all. The basic objectives and structure of the Thirteenth Directive were therefore based on the British Takeover Code. For example, it proposed that all shareholders should be treated equally, that there would be an obligation to launch a full bid once a single shareholder had acquired 33.3 percent of the shares, that any bid must be for 100 percent of shares, thus ensuring that minority shareholders are not denied the right to sell once a bidder has gained enough shares to control the company. In a 1990 revised proposal additional provisions were added, prohibiting defensive devices by existing managements, such as issuing nonvoting shares, unless specifically approved in advance by shareholders.

[21] See House of Commons, *Takeovers and Mergers*. The Select Committee made this proposal despite the weight of evidence against such a move coming from the institutions, including the CBI, and the government.
[22] See Proposal for a Thirteenth Council Directive on Company Law concerning takeover and other general bids (COM[88] 823, final 16 February 1988), Office of the Official Publications of the European Communities.

Insofar as it helped to create a level playing field for takeovers the Directive was in Britain's interest. But it still ran into determined opposition from the City, government, and most bodies representing industry. The British objection was that an EC directive would establish a statutory basis for the hitherto voluntary (i.e., nonstatutory) Takeover Code and Panel and that this would introduce rigidities into the system and offer an opportunity for companies defending against hostile takeover bids to initiate legal proceedings as a means of frustrating a bid.[23] This view was strongly held by the City and the institutions involved in the Panel, despite efforts by the Commission to find a compromise by providing scope, within the Directive, for national governments to designate nonstatutory bodies as the supervisory bodies. The fact that review by European institutions would undermine the regulatory capture of takeovers by the City institutions may have also played a role in the Panel's opposition to review of its decisions.

Germany and the other countries that view high levels of takeover activity with concern were happy to keep their own procedures. Germany was hostile to the idea of more effective regulation of takeovers and measures to remove barriers to takeover, because it could prove to be the first step down a slippery slope leading to the extension of the Anglo-Saxon open model for corporate control system to the continent. Without active support from the member state that stood to gain most from it the Directive slipped off the agenda and has not been discussed within the Council of Ministers for some two years. It therefore seems likely to join the other proposed directives on company law gathering dust on the shelves.

Europe provides an interesting example of intense competition among different forms of corporate governance. The two strongest models of corporate governance, the Anglo-Saxon model and the Rhineland model are in direct competition. Countries such as France fall between the two and have adopted elements of each.

The impact of this competition on Britain and the British application of the Anglo-Saxon model of corporate governance have produced few signs of change in Britain. The system of corporate governance is made up of a complex set of established practices and regulatory policies. Policy in any given area, whether it is in capital market regulation, company law, accountancy, or stakeholder management relations therefore tends to be "embedded" in a system made

---

[23] For an extensive discussion on this issue and evidence on the views of the various parties, see House of Commons, *Takeovers and Mergers*.

up of all the other policies and practices. Change in one area, for example, as a result of EC harmonization or competition from other countries, will not therefore change the whole system. In such circumstances modifications of the existing approach to corporate governance that accommodate the new circumstances is more likely. This embedding of policies and practices has the effect of dampening competition among rules in any given area. Real change would require root and branch change, and as there is not even a consensus on the need for change, let alone a consensus on what that change should be, root and branch change in Britain has not and is unlikely to occur.

At the same time, however, increased internationalization of business and especially greater integration within Europe, have meant that concerns have persisted about the ability of the British form of corporate governance to deliver in terms of ensuring the long-term competitiveness of British companies. There is, in particular, an awareness that the creation of an internal market for goods and services is bringing British companies into direct competition on the same market with companies that operate under very different forms of corporate governance.

In this essay I have focused on the impact of pressures for change on Britain. Convergence could, of course, be brought about by changes in the rest of Europe. Indeed, those who favor the Anglo-Saxon model of corporate governance or industrial finance have a tendency to argue that liberalization of international capital markets will inevitably force countries such as Germany to move toward the British approach. Such a change seems far from inevitable as each of the other national forms of corporate governance is embedded in established practices and regulatory policies. On the other hand, countries such France and possibly Italy, after the changes in the established structure of links between political power structures and industry, seem to be more flexible. For the Anglo-Saxon model to prevail in Germany a convincing case would have to be made in terms of its performance. To date the performance of British manufacturing has not convinced German management or stakeholders of the arguments. But additional case studies would be needed to explore the impact of pressures for change, especially those emanating from the internationalization of capital markets.

For the foreseeable future, Europe will continue to be characterized by competition between different forms of corporate governance, rather than converge toward a single model of Euro-capitalism. There will be a spectrum of approaches, from the British Anglo-Saxon to the Rhineland approach, so that Europe as a whole will tend to span the divide between the United States and Japan.

CHAPTER EIGHT

Competition and Competition Policy in Japan: Foreign Pressures and Domestic Institutions

YUTAKA KOSAI

There are fundamentally different views on competition in Japan. Some think of Japan as a society controlled by government. Others regard it not as a market economy, but as an exclusive network of inside traders. Still others see it as a country of excessive competition. Moreover, the state of competition in Japan has been deeply affected by foreign pressures. Japan imported capitalist institutions after the forced opening of the country in the mid-nineteenth century. As a result of the economic reform under the Occupation after World War II Japan came to have an Anti-Monopoly Act that, although more lenient in several respects than U.S. antitrust laws, is a good deal closer to the American pattern than the antimonopoly laws of other countries. Despite this, there are frequent tensions over the aggressive export behavior of Japanese firms and the slow progress of Japanese liberalization policies. In the latest phase the pivotal issue seems to be a choice between an American-impelled managed trade and/or a Japanese reform of domestic institutions.

In this chapter I consider the state of competition in Japanese markets, paying particular attention to the effects of foreign pressures as well as of domestic inertia. Three factors form the basis of the Japanese market economy: (1) laissez-faire capitalism, which was introduced into Japan after the Meiji Restoration in the mid-nineteenth century and again reintroduced under the Occupation after World War II nearly a century later in the form of the enforced adoption of American-style antimonopoly measures, subsequently strengthened through trade and capital liberalization during the high-growth period; (2) the more or less innate characteristics of industrial organization in Japan (relationship capitalism), which feature excessive competition on the one hand, and on the other hand the zaibatsu, cartels, and guildlike trade associations of the prewar period, and the relational transaction networks of *keiretsu* in the postwar, high-growth era; and (3) state control of industry during the war and industrial policy afterward. In this essay I consider how these three factors interact under foreign as well as domestic pressures.

First, the evolution of Japanese industrial organization in the period up to World War II is discussed. Then, the conflict and compromise between the antimonopoly policy initiated by the Occupation Army on one hand and, on the other, an industrial policy steeped in the legacy of wartime controls is traced. The next section focuses on excessive competition and relational transactions, situating them in the general characteristics of the Japanese market system. Then come reviews of the recent Japan–U.S. trade frictions, the "third wave" of foreign pressure following the Meiji Restoration and the Occupation. The final section concludes with remarks on international convergence and the harmonization of national institutions.

HISTORICAL BACKGROUND: TWO VIEWS OF JAPANESE ECONOMIC DEVELOPMENT

Interpretations of the driving force of Japanese economic growth from Meiji to the 1930s differ. Some economic historians emphasize the laissez-faire aspects of Japanese industrial organization.[1] By contrast, the view that prevailed in the mid-1980s and that still figures in high school social studies textbooks, claims that Japanese industries were developed under government protection and were dominated by the zaibatsu combines. The new revisionist view goes as follows. It is true that the government tried to modernize Japan's industries. There is no denying its success in providing infrastructure for modernization—education, the legal system, public utilities. In contrast with such "indirect" support, the "direct" measures to transplant modern industries in Japan were of doubtful success. The Meiji government, as a result of the concessions made by the previous Edo government during the opening of Japan, had from the start been deprived of the right to impose tariffs on imports, the most important weapon

[1] Ryosin Minami, *The Economic Development of Japan* (London: Macmillan, 1986), pp. 154–55; for an extreme view on this, see Yutaka Kosai and Yutaka Harada, "Economic Development of Japan: A Reconsideration," in R. Scalapino, S. Sato, and J. Wanandi, eds., *Asian Economic Development—Present and Future* (Berkeley: Institute of East Asian Studies, 1985).

for protection of infant domestic industries in the nineteenth century, intensively resorted to by other contemporary latecomer capitalist nations such as the United States and Germany. There were indeed efforts on the part of government to build industries through direct action in the 1870s. But very quickly the factories built by the government were privatized, mainly in order to stop losses. Similar efforts later were sporadic. The establishment of Yawata Steel, which began operation in 1901, is the most notable example. But all this did could not transform Japan into a heavy industry nation with a pen stroke.

Instead, the most important industry of prewar Japan was cotton textiles. Japan remained a nation of "light" industry until the beginning of the 1930s, sixty years after the Meiji Restoration. Changes in industrial structure took place only very gradually. The textile industry was relatively independent from government interventions, and its relation with the zaibatsu also remained rather indirect. The textile producers dealt with the sogo shosha (general trading companies), which were zaibatsu related, but also with the senmon shosha (specialized trading companies), which were not.[2] Some textile producers were regarded as zaibatsu related, but they were zaibatsu related only in the same loose sense in which Toyota today is Mitsui affiliated. They competed with each other as fiercely as with foreign producers (British and Indian in particular). They formed cartels that were broken as often as they were formed—another indicator of severe competition among producers. Osaka, where many head offices of textile producers were located, was called the "Manchester of Japan," and it was in fact the center of a genuine free-trade, "small-government," movement.

Modern industrial capitalism in Japan had to coexist with traditional economic institutions that survived and adapted to the new conditions of the Meiji era. Among them were the zaibatsu and trade associations. Some of the zaibatsu families came from the great merchant houses of the feudal ages and some from the parvenus of the Meiji Restoration. They enjoyed privileged relations with the government. They dominated banking, foreign trade, coal mining, and some other industries, while competing fiercely with one another. As mentioned, they were not dominant in the textile industry, or in many

---

[2] Sogo shosha deal with many kinds of commodities and senmon shosha specialize in specific commodities such as textiles, iron and steel, or paper products. In the prewar period, sogo shosha were zaibatsu related and represented by Mitsui Bussan and Mitsubishi Shoji. Most of the senmon shosha were not related to the zaibatsu, with the exception of Sumitomo Shoji (specialized in metal products), and most specialized in textiles (in which the sogo shosha also traded). After the war, even though bussan and shoji were dissolved by order of the Occupation Army, some of senmon shosha (Itochu, Marubeni, Sumitomo Shoji, etc.) developed into sogo shosha.

other important branches, and they remained rather hesitant about investing in the heavy and chemical industries, although there existed remarkable exceptions such as Mitsubishi Heavy Industries. It was the new zaibatsu[3] that emerged in the 1930s that took the initiative in aggressive investment in heavy industries.

Smaller firms in the traditional sectors, although still dominant in the prewar period, faced intensified competition from modern capital-intensive firms from the 1920s onward. Some of them formed trade associations (dogyo kumiai[4]), traditional guildlike organizations modeled on those of the Edo period, some of which were reorganized as compulsory cartels for the purpose of wartime economic control. They reemerged after the war, partly as small and medium firm cooperatives, partly as subcontractors' cooperation associations. They are the archetypal example of an intermediate organization (intermediate between enterprise and state), spontaneously developed from tradition, later used as a building block of the modern network system of face-to-face transactions.

Legacies of Wartime Economic Control

The war was to create yet another legacy in economic regulation. From the late 1930s to the early 1940s Japan experienced a command economy under imperative planning. Still, the prescriptions of the 1938 Total Mobilization Law notwithstanding, private ownership and management remained largely intact. Government did not choose to nationalize many sectors of the economy. Instead, it established a system of price controls and supply quotas for major commodities. Compulsory cartels were formed and industrial associations were utilized to ensure effective control over prices and quotas. Furthermore, private corporations were put under the obligation of reporting to, as well as submitting to the guidance and supervision of, government officials. For more efficient control, the government instituted a system of designated banks and designated "supporting factories" (providers of parts to other factories).

One school of economic historians stresses the continuities from the

---

[3] Old zaibatsu refers to Mitsui, Mitsubishi, Sumitomo, and Yasuda. New zaibatsu refers to Kuhara (Nissan), Kodaira (Hitachi), Mori (Showa Denko), and Noguchi (Nichitsu).

[4] For *Dogyo Kumiai*, see Hiromi Arisawa, *Nihon kogyo toseiron* (Control of industry in Japan) (Tokyo: Yuhikaku, 1937). For smaller firms in the prewar period in general, see Miyohei Shinohara, "A Survey of the Japanese Literature on Small Industry," in Bert F. Hoselitz, ed., *The Role of Small Industry in the Process of Economic Growth* (The Hague: Mouton, 1968).

wartime to the postwar economic system.[5] According to them, the "main bank" is heir of the designated bank, the subcontracting system grew from the system of designated supporting factories, and administrative guidance from intimate relationships during war time between government and business. To summarize, when Japan was defeated in World War II she had an industrial organization in which wartime control was imposed on a basically laissez-faire capitalist regime.

POSTWAR REFORM AND INDUSTRIAL POLICY

The previous section compared the three models of the prewar Japanese economy, one of basically laissez-faire capitalism, one dominated by zaibatsu and cartels, and an economy under state control imposed during wartime.

Postwar reforms initiated by the U.S. Occupation Army aimed to destroy the second pattern.[6] The Occupation Army ordered the dissolution of the zaibatsu and other major corporations (the Exclusion of Excessive Concentration of Economic Power Law). The Anti-Monopoly Act, much influenced by American antitrust law, was subsequently enacted. These measures sought to strengthen competitive capitalism. On the other hand, industrial policy remained an important force as the Ministry of International Trade and Industry (MITI) tried to continue and further develop the state control of industry established in wartime Japan, but modified to meet postwar conditions.

The aims shifted from the mobilization of resources for total war to economic reconstruction in the late 1940s, later to economic growth and strengthening of competitiveness of Japanese industry in world markets in the 1950s and 1960s. In the late 1940s MITI relied heavily on (1) supply quotas; (2) price controls; (3) subsidies; and (4) financial support from government-affiliated institutions (the Reconstruction Bank, for example). The last was important for the Priority Production System of 1947–48 (Keisha Seisan Hoshiki), in which priority was given to an increase in domestic output of coal and steel. By 1950 price controls, subsidies, and quotas on domestically produced goods were largely abolished. The new set of tools of industrial policy com-

[5] See Takafusa Nakamura, ed., "Keikaku-ka to minshu-ka" ("Planning and Democratization"), *Nihon keizaishi* (Economic history of Japan), Vol. 7 (Tokyo: Iwanami Shoten, 1989), and Tetsuji Okazaki and Masahiro Okuno, *Nihon keizai sisutemu no genryu* (Origin of Japanese economic system) (Tokyo: Nihon Keizai Shimbunsha, 1993).

[6] For postwar reforms, see Yutaka Kosai, *The Era of High Speed Growth* (Tokyo: University of Tokyo Press, 1986), and Juro Teranishi and Yutaka Kosai, eds., *The Japanese Experience of Economic Reforms* (London: Macmillan, 1993).

prised (1) quotas on imports of raw materials and capital goods; (2) a permit system for acquiring technological licenses from foreign producers; (3) special tax treatment for accelerated depreciation allowances for designated types of machines (as well as special tariff reductions for their import); and (4) financial support from government-affiliated institutions (the Japan Development Bank, for example). As trade and capital liberalization progressed in the 1960s and 1970s, industrial policy relied more and more heavily on (5) subtle methods of administrative guidance and (6) special legislation for promoting growth industries (e.g., the Promotion of Specified Machine Industries Law) as well as for smooth adjustment in troubled industries (e.g., the Adjustment of Designated Depressed Industries Law). These laws typically included provisions for collective industry rationalization plans, cartels to manage rationalization and capacity reduction, government advice and financial support for rationalization projects, and so on.

The conflicts and compromises between the Anti-Monopoly Act and industrial policy in the high-growth era of Japan (1955–70) can be illustrated by the following episodes. In 1953, immediately after Japan recovered its independence, the Anti-Monopoly Act was amended. Most important, the formation of recession cartels and rationalization cartels[7] was legalized provided approval was given by the FTC. This amendment was criticized as a counterreform measure against the Occupation policy. Recession cartels, however, have been subject to increasingly severe reviews by the FTC, and they have been limited to shorter and shorter durations, as seen in Table 8-1. During the recession of 1990–93 no recession cartel has been formed. Progress in trade liberalization also diminished the effectiveness of recession cartels.

In the early 1960s MITI drafted the Promotion of Designated Industries Law. It aimed at the reorganization of strategic industries such as automobiles and petrochemicals in order to strengthen their international competitiveness and ensure their survival as capital transactions were liberalized. Fewer, bigger, and stronger firms were

---

[7] Cartels are generally illegal under the Anti-Monopoly Act of Japan, with five major exceptions. A recession cartel is an agreement of firms to restrict the quantity of production or to maintain the level of selling price of a commodity for a limited time and may be formed in an industry that suffers from recession. (See Anti-Monopoly Act, Article 24-3.) A rationalization cartel is an agreement of firms to cooperate for rationalization by means of standardization of parts and so on. (Anti-Monopoly Act, Article 24-4). Depression cartels are agreements of firms to scrap excess capacity. Under some conditions depression cartels can be compulsory. There are also small firm cartels and export cartels. All require sponsorship by the responsible ministry (usually MITI) and the consent of the FTC. Depression cartels additionally require special legislation, such as the Designated Depressed Industries Law of 1978.

Table 8-1. Number of recession cartels and average duration

Period	Number	Average duration (months)
1955–59	5	26
1960–64	4	12
1965–69	17	10
1970–74	15	9
1975–77	4	7

SOURCE: Kosei Torihiki Iinkai (FTC), *Nenji Hokoku [Annual Report]* (1977), pp. 770–73.

to be created through mergers supported by government and financial institutions. Investment plans in major industries were also to be coordinated through consultation among firms, government, and the financial institutions, in a way similar to French planning.[8] The proposed law was regarded as a challenge to the Anti-Monopoly Act. It had too many opponents, and MITI was forced to drop it.

In 1973 the Large Scale Retail Store Law was enacted. At that time the Liberal Democratic Party (LDP) and all opposition parties promoted the law to protect the interests of existing retailers, mostly small and family-owned, from competition with new large-scale entrants by means of a licensing system. MITI opposed the original draft as too authoritarian, and the final compromise required registration of plans to open department stores and supermarkets and consultation with the local Commercial Activities Coordination Committee of the regions involved. If no agreement between the newcomer and local interests emerged from this Committee, the government could advise changes in the plans. This procedure was presented as less restrictive, but it turned out to be more intrusive. The practice of informal negotiations before submissions to the Commercial Activities Coordination Committee became routine, and government officials began to refuse applications unless agreement had been achieved in this "precoordination" process. The law was distorted, and all MITI could do was to try to shorten the precoordination process. This case was exceptional because of the strength of political influences. MITI, accustomed to thinking of industrial policy as a means of picking the winners for tomorrow's world markets, was forced into the business of protecting weak market competitors instead.

Another salient incident was the FTC's indictment of the oil com-

---

[8] The law was inspired by French planning as that experience was transmitted through Yoshihiko Morozumi, who, after having served as the commercial attaché in the Japanese Embassy in Paris, drafted the first version of the law.

panies for illegal cartel formation during the first oil crisis in 1973. The companies defended themselves on the grounds that they had followed MITI's administrative guidance. The Tokyo High Court declared the defendants guilty. The Supreme Court later confirmed the High Court's decision. It admitted the need for administrative guidance (even intervention in the formation of market prices) in an emergency. But it made it clear that administrative guidance should not violate the anti-monopoly law in any substantive sense. The decision was generally accepted as a victory of anti-monopoly law over industrial policy. In 1977 the Anti-Monopoly Act was revised, the first post-Occupation amendment that actually *strengthened* the law. The oil crisis intensified public criticism of profiteering and there was more public support for the amendment than ever before. The 1977 amendment included fines on illegal cartels, the monitoring of synchronized price revisions, and of market shares to detect monopoly power. In the late 1970s the Adjustment of Designated Depressed Industries Law was enacted to cope with the restructuring problems brought on by the oil crisis and, later, the appreciation of the yen. Fortunately, cuts in production capacity went rather rapidly and smoothly, so that the temporary solution of depression cartels to restrict output did not have to be prolonged.

These episodes show that the history of confrontation between anti-monopoly law and industrial policy can be divided into two phases. In the first, a strong rejection reaction to the foreign graft (anti-monopoly law) was triggered. In the second, a sort of equilibrium was reached between the two. Recession cartels are now less frequently in use, and the precautionary monitoring of monopoly power has been strengthened. Sanctions on illegal cartels have been intensified, and deregulation is becoming a tool of industrial policy, particularly in low-productivity sectors.

The spirit and logic of anti-monopoly policy and that of industrial policy are in sharp conflict. How can both policies coexist? Industrial policy is comprised of three types: promotion, adjustment, and coordination.[9] "Infant industry" promotion must be temporary and transitory. Once industries mature, industrial policy should give way to anti-monopoly policy. Such promotion policies should work themselves out of a job: hence there is no *permanent* contradiction between industrial policy and anti-monopoly policy.

Much of the industrial policy of the high-growth era was of this kind, concerned with preparing the Japanese industries for the com-

[9] These three types of industrial policy correspond to Parts IV–VI of Ryutaro Komiya, Masahiro Okuno, and Kotaro Suzumura, eds., *Industrial Policy of Japan* (Tokyo: Academic Press Japan, 1988).

ing liberalization of trade and capital transaction. Perhaps MITI tried to delay the timing of liberalization unduly in some cases. But indefinite delay means policy failure, because the aim is to raise the "competitiveness" of the industry concerned and because industrial policy in one country, if successful, may contribute to more effective competition on a global scale.[10] Anti-monopoly (competition) policy need not contradict industrial (competitiveness) policy.

Whether such infant industry promotion can be really effective remains a question. According to the neoclassical view, competition policy is the sole or the best competitiveness policy. Moreover, there are questions of fairness as well as efficiency. Suppose that Industry A of a country gains competitiveness owing to industrial policy. This may bring about the appreciation of the exchange rate, thus damaging the competitiveness of Industry B in the same country (though there may be externalities between the industries that cancel out this effect).

As far as industrial policy aims at the improvement of market efficiency by rectifying "market failures,"[11] conforming to neoclassical precepts is a logical possibility. However, the extent of market failures can always be disputed. If there exists a well-developed capital market, government intervention for promoting infant industries may not be justified, because the well-developed capital market with its appropriate foresight can take care of decreasing cost within some range. As a matter of fact, such an efficient capital market did not exist for reasons that are difficult to establish. Probably the market mechanism fails to operate in capital markets, because of uncertainties, of asymmetric information, and so forth. Or perhaps it is because the capital market was under strict government control and financial intermediaries were linked with respective borrowers through long-term customer relations based on the bureaucrats' and bankers' mistaken judgment that markets would fail if left without state intervention. The

[10] *Competitiveness* (*Kyosoryoku* in Japanese) is here used to mean "the ability of nation A's industry X to compete with other nations' firms in that industry" (or in some cases, the ability to win in the competition), not to mean "the state of lively competition." The policy to strengthen competitiveness of an infant industry in this sense may include such policies as protecting the industry from foreign competition, contradicting the second sense of the term. Competitiveness in the context of industrial coordination policy appears to mean preserving the ability of weak market competitors to survive.

[11] Sueo Sekiguchi and Toshiharu Horiuchi, "Trade Adjustment Assistance," in Komiya, Okuno and Suzumura, eds., *Industrial Policy of Japan*; Sueo Sekiguchi, "An Overview of Adjustment Assistance Policies in Japan," and Sueo Sekiguchi, "Industrial Adjustment and Cartel Actions in Japan," both in H. W. Tan and H. Shimada, *Troubled Industries in the U.S. and Japan* (New York: St. Martin's Press, 1994). For a positive evaluation of policies toward troubled industries, see James C. Abbeglen and George Stark, Jr., *Kaisha, The Japanese Corporation* (New York: Basic Books, 1985), p. 33. For a detailed study of the textile industry, see Ronald Dore, *Flexible Rigidities: Industrial Policy and Structural Adjustment in the Japanese Economy, 1970–80* (London: Athlone Press, 1986).

author's tentative conclusion is that a mix of freer capital markets and of a lesser reliance on industrial policy was a real possibility.

As for the second category, adjustment policies for troubled industries, industrial policy is always in danger of degenerating into sheer protection. Government sometimes succeeds in setting time limits on adjustment assistance, but not always in enforcing them. The political influence of vested interests remains strong, and attempts to deregulate are often thwarted.

EXCESSIVE COMPETITION AND RELATIONAL TRANSACTIONS

While anti-monopoly measures and industrial policy struggled for a stable balance throughout the era of high-speed growth (approximately 1955–70), a characteristic pattern of competition among the Japanese firms gradually emerged. It partly reflects the conflicts and compromises of anti-monopoly and industrial policy. But the strategies adopted by firms to adapt to the new environment of rapid growth seem to be the most important source. The process can be seen as a metamorphosis of traditional Japanese industrial organization, responding to technological and institutional innovations.

The view that excessive competition characterized Japanese industrial organization is widely shared among business people in Japan.[12] Many appear to believe rather naively that it is inevitable in a country with a small land area and large population. Although the author knows of no detailed study of prewar competition strategies, competition seems to have been fierce, as suggested by the fact that Japan was often accused of "social dumping." Zaibatsu combines competed, and cartels often broke down. In the postwar period, as Yoshikazu Miyazaki observed, business groups were driven by a zeal for expansion.[13] Their "one set" aim to have a major firm in every industry gave rise to excessive competition in the high-speed growth era. Certainly, the belief that the level of competitiveness was excessive occupied a central

[12] Excessive competition is used as the translation of *kato kyoso* in Japanese, following the usage in Komiya, Okuno, and Suzumura, *Industrial Policy in Japan*. Motoshige Itoh, Kazuhiro Kiyono, Masahiro Okuno, and Kotaro Suzumura, "Industrial Policy as a Corrective to Market Failures," in Komiya, Okuno, and Suzumura, *Industrial Policy in Japan*, p. 255, pointed to the difference between *kato kyoso* and excessive competition as defined by J. S. Bain in his *Industrial Organization* (New York: John Wiley, 1968), but their preference for Bain's definition is not shared by the authors of other chapters of the volume.

[13] Miyazaki observed that there existed a tendency for each business group to have "one set" of industries within the group and that the tendency resulted in excessive competition. Yoshikazu Miyazki, "Katokyoso no ronri to genjitsu; Keiretsu sihai kiko no kaimei" (Logic and reality of excess competition: An exposition of keiretsu domination), *Ekonomisuto*, 10 October 1962.

position in policy debates of that time. Recession cartels, depression cartels, and the Promotion of Designated Industries Law were all originally intended to cope with the situation.

The views of economists have changed over time. In the 1950s they generally agreed that excessive competition was a problem. A change in mood took place around 1965, when Ryutaro Komiya and others began to assert that the state of competition in Japan should be regarded as normal and that the market performances in the postwar period had been generally good.[14] Komiya and others criticized many of MITI's policies that assumed the existence of or were conceived to prevent or to cope with excess competition.

Komiya's view was so influential that the words "excessive competition" went out of fashion among academic economists. When ordinary businesspeople grumbled that competition was still excessive, Kenichi Imai replied that if it was so, it was because of government intervention.[15] For example, if quotas for the import of raw materials are allotted according to the volume of sales, firms will expand their sales aggressively. Or they invest overaggressively when they expect that the government will allow them to form recession cartels when productive capacities exceed demand and prices fall. It is implied that the competition should be considered normal when there is no distortion caused by government intervention.

Around 1970 there was a revival of the concept of excessive competition among economists. Yasusuke Murakami argued that Japanese firms were faced with decreasing costs.[16] Hence expansion of market share as early as possible was an obvious strategy leading to intense competition as every firm adopted it. In order to avoid or mitigate cut-throat competition, the government had to intervene. Government limits on entry might compartmentalize competition, but it could still be very intense within compartments.

Foreigners are apt to grin at the idea that the Japanese economy is

[14] Komiya expressed his view on several occasions, mainly as passing comments. For a more or less coherent statement, see Ryutaro Komiya, *Gendai Nihon keizai kenkyu* (Studies on contemporary Japanese economy) (Tokyo: University of Tokyo Press, 1975), pp. 214–15.

[15] Ibid., chap. 10. Imai argued the case with respect to iron and steel and petroleum refining, among others. Kenichi Imai, *Gendai sangyo soshiki* (Contemporary industrial organization) (Tokyo: Iwanami Shoten, 1976). Some of his claims were criticized by Yoshiro Miwa, "Coordination within Industry: Output, Price, and Investment," in Komiyo, Okuno, and Suzumura, *Industrial Policy of Japan*.

[16] Yasusuke Murakami, "The Japanese Model of Political Economy," in Kozo Yamamura and Yasukichi Yasuba, eds., *The Political Economy of Japan*, Vol. 1, *The Domestic Transformation* (Stanford, Calif.: Stanford University Press, 1987), pp. 45–55. Murakami's view appeared first in Japanese in Yasusuke Murakami, "Sengo Nihon no keizai sisutemu" (The economic system of postwar Japan), *Economisuto*, 14 June 1982.

competitive, believing, instead, that markets are rigged in Japan by the *keiretsu* or the state. In recent years, however, some foreign economists have acknowledged that it is the severity of competition in the Japanese market that makes Japanese firms so extraordinarily aggressive in invading markets abroad and simultaneously makes it difficult for foreign firms to penetrate into the Japanese domestic market.[17]

Can the "excessive competition" hypothesis be justified by facts? An answer to that question requires first some criterion of the degree of intensity of competition that would be considered excessive and in need of correction and second, some measure of intensity. Some relevant facts regarding intensity may be quickly reviewed. First, the number of firms in Japan is large. The number of corporate entities reported to the tax authority is about two million, although half of them are in deficit and some are dormant. Concentration ratios in the manufacturing industry are not low compared with other countries, and there is no tendency for concentration ratios to rise, in contrast with the cases of some industrialized nations.

According to *Fortune*, among the world's largest 500 corporations Japan has 119 companies listed, whereas the United States has 159 and Germany 43.[18] Japan has a larger number of large corporations per billion dollars of GDP. However, total sales of Japanese companies included in the list are $1.1 trillion compared to $1.8 trillion for the U.S. companies, figures more proportional to the magnitude of the total economy. This implies that Japanese "large" firms are large in number but relatively small in size.

In fact, as shown in Table 8-2, the third and fifth largest corporations are larger relative to the top one in the same industry in Japan than in the United States, where the top one is by far larger than the next ranked. This structural characteristic of industrial organization may make competition fiercer in Japan.

On the level of "conduit," in Bain's terms, Japanese firms are known for their market-share orientation and for aggressive pricing policy. Kagano et al. found in a survey that the priority goal of Japanese management is enlargement of market share rather than raising the rate of return on investment.[19] The Japanese firms' pricing policy has been constantly attacked as aggressive. Companies are said to reduce the prices of their export goods so swiftly that foreign firms that

[17] John O. Haley, "Weak Law, Strong Competition, and Trade Barriers: Competitiveness as Disincentives to Foreign Entry into Japanese Markets," in Kozo Yamamura, ed., *Japan's Economic Structure: Should It Change?* (Seattle: Society for Japanese Studies, 1990).

[18] *Fortune*, 27 July 1992.

[19] Tadao Kagano, Ikujiro Nonaka, Kiyonori Sakakibara, and Akihiro Okuno, *Nichibei kigyo no keiei hikaku* (Japanese and U.S. management in comparative perspective) (Tokyo: Nihon Keizai Shimbunsha, 1983), table 2-5, p. 25.

Table 8-2. Relative sizes of firms ranked 1st, 3rd, and 5th

Rank	Chemical		Electronics		Food		Industrial equipment		Metals		Motors	
	Japan	U.S.	Japan	U.S.	Japan	U.S.	Japan	U.S.	Japan	U.S.	Japan	U.S.
1	100	100	100	100	100	100	100	100	100	100	100	100
2	96	24	48	20	67	26	39	50	56	58	39	24
3	87	18	43	16	53	15	35	33	41	37	25	4

SOURCE: *Fortune*, 27 July 1992.
Note: Relative size of the firm ranked: ith = Sales of the firm ranked as ith/(sales of the firm ranked as 1st × 100).

cannot follow their price reductions are pushed out of the market and eventually annihilated. This "forward pricing" is not exactly to be identified with predatory pricing in that firms may not raise prices when they expel their rivals.[20] As they enlarge their size of operation, costs are lowered. They only sacrifice profits in the transition phase by rapidly lowering prices and quickly expanding the market.

Such a mix of structure and behavior may lead to the following pattern of performance: bold investment, rapid expansion of output and sales, prompt reduction of cost and price, and small margins of profit for the firms. These stylized facts have not necessarily been established by careful studies as yet. But it is widely believed that the rate of return on investment in Japanese corporations remains low. Difficulties of measurement, however, may arise if, for example, profits take the form of capital gains and if conservative bookkeeping practices are maintained. Odagiri gives partial support to the contention that the Japanese corporate rate of profit has been a little lower than that of the United States.[21]

Let us accept that Japanese firms are more likely than those elsewhere to adopt the strategy of expanding sales, even on small margins. Other Japan-specific characteristics, such as main banks, recession cartels, and government intervention would seem to encourage this tendency. So also does the pattern of corporate relations characterized by Imai as long-term network relationships.[22] These characteristics accompany or lead to a high intensity of competition, although whether the connection is necessary or coincidental remains to be demonstrated.

Low returns on investment mean in the final analysis low rates of reward for saving. Why Japanese savers save so much and content themselves with such low returns, remains a central question of the Japanese economy, even if one discounts the extraordinarily low cost of capital during the late 1980s bubble period as a temporary phenomenon.

JAPAN–U.S. TRADE FRICTIONS AND DEREGULATION

In the late 1980s and early 1990s friction developed between Japan and the United States over trade and other issues, thus triggering another wave of foreign pressures for change larger than any since

[20] Tyson mentions that Texas Instruments followed the practice in the 1960s and 1970s. Laura D'Andrea Tyson, *Who's Bashing Whom? Trade Conflict in High-Technology Industries* (Washington: Institute for International Economics, 1992).

[21] Hiroyuki Odagiri, "Riekisei to kyososei" (Profitability and competitiveness), in Kenichi Imai and Ryutaro Komiya, eds., *Nihon no kigyo* (The Japanese firms) (Tokyo: University of Tokyo Press, 1989), translated as *The Business Enterprise in Japan* (Cambridge: MIT Press, 1994).

[22] Kenichi Imai, "The Corporate Network in Japan," *Japanese Economic Studies* 16, no. 2 (Winter 1987–88).

the end of the Occupation. At the same time the demand for dereg-ulation and administrative reforms gained momentum on the domes-tic scene. During the 1960s and 1970s trade friction between the United States and Japan revolved around such commodities as ap-parel, iron and steel, motorbikes, and machine tools. Japan repeatedly faced pressures to accelerate the liberalization of trade and capital transactions.

In the 1980s and 1990s friction and pressure took new forms. Com-plaints about Japanese exports continued, with more emphasis on im-port barriers in Japan and on trade practices and differences in do-mestic institutions regarded as having exclusionary effects. Services, investment, and intellectual property were increasingly important foci of friction. Along with sector-specific issues, overall economic policy and structure (i.e., the pattern of saving and investment, macro-economic policy, the high price of land, and *keiretsu*), became subjects of debate and negotiation, aimed at the reform of structures and insti-tutions, amendment of the Anti-Monopoly Act, and the deregulation of the financial, retail, and trucking businesses. Other measures pro-posed to change the exclusionary effects of the conduct of firms and government by, for example, new disclosure requirements for *keiretsu* ties. Still others aimed to increase the share of imports in the domestic market. Finally, negotiations proceeded under the threat, sometimes implemented, of sanctions (Super-301, for example).

The Structural Impediments Initiative (SII) talks, begun in 1989 as a way to avoid the invocation of Super-301 against Japan, was a turn-ing point. The talks were comprehensive, covering macroeconomic issues such as savings and investment patterns, together with micro issues such as land policy and the distribution system. They were structure oriented in that they proposed amendment of the Anti-Mo-nopoly Act, the Large-scale Retail Store Law, and the laws governing the trucking business. They were behavior oriented in dealing with the removal of exclusionary business practices and the reforms to make the *keiretsu* relationships more open and transparent.

The sector-specific and result-oriented approach is exemplified by the Japan–U.S. Semiconductor Trade Agreement of 1986, renewed in 1991, as well as by the Voluntary Import Expansion of automobiles and auto parts pledged in 1991. In the process of negotiating the renewed Semicon-ductor Agreement in 1991, the sanctions so far imposed were suspended, and the 20 percent target for market access by the end of 1992 was explic-itly mentioned in the agreement, although it was noted that the target ought not to be interpreted as a guarantee of market share.[23]

---

[23] An example of the sector-specific but change-of-rule–oriented approach is the MOSS (market-oriented sector-specific) talk.

These approaches differ in several aspects. One implies that a set of rules for institutions and behavior should be applied over the world, Japan being no exception. The latter assumes that Japan has and should be allowed to have rules different from other countries, as long as an appropriate degree of access to its markets is ensured. The former denies the uniqueness of Japan, and the latter regards Japan as a country that cannot change (at least in the short term). The former is universalistic, evangelical, and interventionist, and the latter particularistic, practical, and intrusionist. Import targets end up keeping the Japanese bureaucratically controlled cartels intact or rather strengthening them as an apparatus for securing a certain percentage of the market to foreigners.

There are clear indications that the Clinton Administration is increasingly emphasizing the results-oriented approach in trade negotiations, which the Japanese government is generally resisting. The Japan–U.S. summit meeting in February 1994 could not reach any agreement on Trade Framework talk that began in the summer of 1993, as Japan said no to commercial target setting on the opening of the Japanese markets. Neither the nagging fault finding of the structure/behavior-oriented approach nor the naked pursuit of commercial interest of the results-oriented approach is welcomed by the Japanese, although which they dislike more remains to be seen. On the domestic scene deregulation became a new focus, driven in part by international pressures for opening the economy. Other forces included the need for fiscal reform. To what extent the movement reflects wider support for laissez-faire capitalism in Japan is an interesting question, closely bound up with the reaction of the Japanese to the negotiating demands of foreign governments. The Japanese public was much concerned about the wide price differentials between domestic and overseas markets, and narrowing them became a popular public demand. The SII negotiations appeared to be warmly received by the Japanese public opinion, at least in the initial stage, as they put the narrowing of domestic/external price differentials in their agenda.

Privatization of Nihon Telephone and Telegraph (NTT), of the National Railway broken up into several Japan Railway companies, and the transformation of the Monopoly Tobacco Corporation into Japan Tobacco, proceeded successfully. An end to monopolization of telephone service with the entry of new competitors and suppliers of value-added services, long-distance calls reduced charges. The labor productivity of NTT improved sharply as the number of employees was rapidly reduced. The Japan Railways have been freed from accumulated debt and recovered profitability. Labor relations have also been much improved, as has the quality of service. Deregulation has proceeded in retail trade, the trucking, air transport, and finance, as well as other industries. As a result fees for services have fallen, new types of service have appeared, and new opportunities for investment have opened, but counterproductive side effects are not as yet visible. Successes in privatization and deregulation might, in turn, strengthen support for laissez-faire capitalism in Japan. If so, the reaction of the Japanese to foreign pressure may become more friendly and flexible.

There also have been signs of change in corporate philosophy. Faced with foreign pressure as well as mounting public discontent in response to the bubble economy of the late 1980s, business executives and policymakers have begun a soul-searching quest for new concepts and ideals for Japanese society as a whole and for industrial corporations in particular. Akio Morita published an influential paper, criticizing management based on low margins, low wages, and large-scale output, and proposing that business firms seek a high rate of return on investment, which in turn might support high wages and reduce the degree of excessive competition. Gaishi Hiraiwa also emphasized the need for "symbiotic coexistence" among firms at home as well as abroad and between firms and citizens.[24]

Morita's mention of relative shares raises an interesting question. The relative share of labor is low and that of capital high in Japan compared to other advanced nations. This is interpreted as reflecting the strength of capital and the weakness of labor. The situation is actually a little bit more complex. As mentioned, the aggressive competition strategy of the Japanese firms is attributable to the low cost of capital. Consequently, if the cost of capital were raised, firms might become less aggressive in competition, in expansion of market share, and in investment. Denoting the rate of profit (cost of capital) by r and capital stock by K, stylized facts in Japan so far are low r and large K. The larger K is, the lower r will be, as long as the marginal productivity of capital declines as the economics textbooks postulate. Assuming an adequate elasticity of substitution, a large K may overwhelm a low r. The capital income rK and relative share of capital income rK/wL can be large in spite of the fact that r is small, as is the case in Japan. Conversely, in the United States wages are low and the number of employees is large, so that the relative share of labor income is high. The Japanese economy has been characterized by high investment combined with low profit, as well as by high wages combined with low employment. Does the mentioned change (if any) in the philosophy of business leaders signify the direction of change in the Ja-

[24] Akio Morita, "Kiki ni tatsu nihon keiei" (The Japanese management in crisis), *Bungei Shunjyu*, February 1992; Gaishi Hiraiwa, "Symbiosis: Mission for Corporate Japan," *Yomiuri Daily*, 10 February 1992.

panese economy toward an economy of low investment combined with high profit and of low wages combined with high employment? Any answer to this question would be premature, but it is obvious that the relative competitiveness of Japan would be affected by such changes.

This essay considers the Japanese economy as consisting of three contrasting models: laissez-faire capitalism, relationship capitalism, and industrial policy. Foreign pressures used to strengthen the first through anti-monopoly policy, trade and capital transaction liberalization, and other structural reforms. Recently foreign pressures are taking a new approach, which is results oriented and more receptive to managed trade

The Japanese picture is a part of the worldwide process of increasingly deeper and more complex contact and interaction between different systems of national economies. There certainly exists a tendency toward convergence and integration in the world economy. Still, differences in the working of capitalism in the respective national economies seem to be wide and persistent. One may argue that this diversity is desirable insofar as it facilitates the search for the optimal model through trial and error and that premature integration may deprive every country of the opportunity for social experimentation. At the same time, the dissolution of the world economy into closed and antagonistic blocs should somehow be avoided.

Perhaps two things are needed. First, a certain degree of harmonization should be attained among major countries: they should have common basic market structure and principles. But they should be allowed to do business in their domestic markets in their own way as long as they do not violate market economy principles. What is needed, then, are common procedural rules for solving the possible frictions among different systems of capitalism. Still, one must confess that finding the optimal balance between convergence and coexistence and delimiting their appropriate spheres remain difficult and especially serious for Japan. Some procedures for harmonization could be followed:

(1) International rules regarding business practices should be clearly defined.[25]

---

[25] John Jackson, *The World Trading System* (Cambridge: MIT Press, 1992). He cites OECD guidelines for multinational enterprises and UNCTAD set of Multinationally Agreed Equitable Principles and Rules for the Control of Restrictive Business Practices as examples of international rules. See p. 212.

(2) National anti-monopolistic law should be strictly applied in each country.
(3) Disputes, if any, on competitive policies and practices should be solved through consultation.
(4) Buffering measures might be introduced when differences in competitive practices cause material damage, but sanctions should be imposed only when others violate established international law, as in the case of anti-dumping as defined by GATT rules.
(5) Information on business practices should be made readily available internationally.

So far Japan has mostly been concerned with frictions with the United States. But now the Japanese realize that Japan is a global economic power. The rise of the Asian economies as trade and investment partners is also having its effect. Pressed by foreign as well as domestic pressures, Japan is in a soul-searching process. It may follow the universal ideal of free trade when others appear to abandon it, seek for a multinational framework that transcends bilateral negotiations, and really try to liberalize domestic institutions. Or it may emphasize national characteristics, strengthening ties with Asian economies. Prediction is beyond the scope of this essay, but each scenario needs to be placed in a broad perspective.

CHAPTER NINE

The Convergence of Competition Policies in Europe. Internal Dynamics and External Imposition

HERVÉ DUMEZ AND ALAIN JEUNEMAÎTRE

Since World War II the convergence of European countries toward a liberal model of government–market relationships has appeared virtually inevitable. Competition policies in general and European competition policies in particular have flourished, while government intervention in markets has declined.[1] Governments have gradually discarded interventionist tools, allowing independent agencies to enact and enforce market regulations.

The situation in 1945 was very different, however. The Great Depression had undermined liberal thinking and legitimized the idea that the economy in general and markets in particular should be "planned." In the mid-1930s, with the active support or benign neutrality of governments, strong cartels emerged in Germany, France, and the United Kingdom. The wartime economy accelerated this process, with national governments exercising increased control over production through cartels and trusts.

At the conclusion of the war, however, the three countries embarked on separate paths. Cartels in the United Kingdom were dismantled, although the Board of Trade retained considerable powers

[1] As Rosenthal rightly notes, referring to competition policy, "the meaning of the term *competition policy* is unsettled. There are two polar notions. One is that competition policy is coincident with the antitrust laws and their enforcement. The other is that competition policy embraces any law or regulation that promotes or inhibits the free operation of the market mechanism. The first definition is too narrow. . . . The second concept of competition policy is too broad." D. E. Rosenthal, "Competition Policy," in G. C. Hufbauer, ed., *Europe 1992: An American Perspective* (Washington, D.C.: Brookings, 1990.)

of intervention. Germany chose to support a social market economy (*Soziale Marktwirtschaft*), but refrained almost completely from breaking up the huge industrial empires that had emerged, first, as a result of the financial crisis at the end of the 1920s, and subsequently through the formation of cartels. France freed its economy somewhat but at the same time launched a planned economy based on an array of interventionist tools, including public ownership of a significant portion of industry, price controls, subsidies, industrial policy, and so forth.

Against this background, how did convergence toward a single liberal model come about? Where did competition policies come from, and what made them start to converge? First, in response to external pressure, European nations began by implementing competition policies more for the sake of appearances than in reality. Second, as the unforeseen consequence of political and institutional dynamics within these countries, appearances gradually became reality, with individual countries adopting convergent attitudes toward market processes. Third, a dynamic of convergence imposed by European authorities was superimposed (the Commission of the European Communities and the European Court of Justice).

A CONVERGENCE MORE APPARENT THAN REAL: THE BEGINNING OF EUROPEAN COMPETITION POLICY

Between the late 1940s and mid-1950s all major European nations passed antitrust legislation: the United Kingdom in 1948; France in 1953; Germany in 1957. This convergence can be described as more apparent than real, for these measures were taken in response to external pressure (from the United States) and to complex local political and administrative conditions.

External Pressure

Following the Great Depression, European economies experienced a double shift: a trend toward the formation of cartels, and a trend toward autarchy. Cartels organized domestic production noncompetitively by fixing prices and dividing market share) and controlled exports and imports. France and the United Kingdom also established a degree of autarchy over their colonies.

During the postwar period the United States (which was providing financial support to the United Kingdom and whose own industry had recovered from the Great Depression) began to advocate free world trade, in effect an end to the European cartels that were obstacles to free trade. The American position was set forth in the Havana Charter (April 1948), an attempt to foster free trade that included a section providing for the enactment of antitrust legislation in all signatory countries. In addition to these multilateral negotiations, the United States also exerted bilateral pressure. In the occupation zone under its control in Germany, the United States on 28 January 1947 enacted Law 56 outlawing cartels. The British and French occupation forces enacted similar legislation shortly thereafter. Thus the process that was eventually to result in the creation of the Federal Republic of Germany was from the start accompanied by competition legislation.

American pressure on the United Kingdom began with the 1941 Lend Lease Agreement.[2] In 1944–45 the Board of Trade listed 125 international cartels involving British firms and 53 domestic cartels. These cartels controlled imports and exports (the United Kingdom's wartime problem was a large balance-of-trade deficit) through trade associations.

The situation in France was similar. Production had been disorganized because of the war. American financial aid was crucial to reconstruction. Economic planning was intended to modernize French industrial capacity so that France could eventually confront foreign competition and enter a free trade system. The United States was willing to concede that the French economy was too weak to deal immediately with the realities of free world trade, but it wanted a commitment for the future (see the Blum–Byrnes negotiations in the spring of 1946).[3]

In other words, the United States exerted strong pressure in favor of antitrust legislation that would prevent cartels from distorting world markets and free trade. At the same time, however, the United States recognized that the situation in Europe immediately following the war called for a period of transition. Thus, external pressure for the imposition of convergence was accompanied by a recognition that a temporary margin of divergence was unavoidable. Convergence became a goal for

[2] Article VII of the Lend Lease Agreement specifies: "The terms and conditions upon which the United Kingdom receives defense aid from the United States of America and the benefits to be received by the United States of America in return therefor, as finally determined, shall be such as not to burden commerce between the two countries but to promote mutually advantageous economic relations; they shall provide against discrimination in either the United States of America or the United Kingdom against the importation of any produce originating in the other country; and they shall provide for the formulation of measures for the achievement of these ends." The word "discrimination" is aimed at import controls by "trade associations" connected with British cartels.

[3] Philippe Mioche, *Le Plan Monnet: Génèse et élaboration (1941–1947)* (Paris: Publications de la Sorbonne, 1987).

the future, as European countries took full advantage of the duration and scope of the divergence margin they had been allowed.

Internal Politics

This margin of divergence was conditioned by the internal politics of the respective countries. First, the pressure exerted by the United States coincided with a certain change in European attitudes, although the extent of these changes varied from country to country.

In Germany the idea of a centrally controlled economy had been discredited by the Nazi experience, and the new political elite drew on the "ordo-liberal" traditions of the Freiburg group as they developed a "social market economy." Market competition was perceived as a guarantee of political democracy.

Attitudes were also changing in Great Britain. The main focus since the early 1940s had been to achieve full employment after the war. Cartels were regarded as "Malthusian" stumbling-blocks to full employment and also as inflationary. A study conducted during the first half of 1943 by two economists, who at that time were working for the Board of Trade, H. Gaitskell and G. C. Allen, entitled *The Control of Monopoly*, was seminal in shifting economic attitudes in British politics and government. The authors advocated the creation of a Statutory Commission on Restrictive Practices.[4]

In France acceptance of the competitive market concept was considerably less pronounced.[5] But a conviction that it would eventually be necessary to expose French industry to international competition did exist, notably in the thinking of Jean Monnet, instigator of the postwar "French Plan" and subsequently a major force behind the creation of the Common Market.[6] Pressure from the United States thus combined with internal politics to support the formulation of competition policy in various European countries. But the postwar economic situation was a difficult and precarious one, and the passage of legislation was, as ever, the result of complex interactions between politics, government, and industry.

In Germany, for example, there was the "battle of the cartels" (*Kartellschlacht*), a battle so intense it lasted for nine years, from 1948 to 1957. German industrialists were radically opposed to any policy

[4] J. D. Gribbin, *The Post-War Revival of Competition as Industrial Policy*, Government Economic Service working paper no. 19 (London: Price Commission, 1978).

[5] R. Kuisel, *Le capitalisme et l'état en France: Modernisation et dirigisme au XXᵉ siècle* (Paris: Gallimard, 1984).

[6] M. Kipping, "Concurrence et compétitivité—Les origines de la législation anti-trust française après 1945," *Etudes et documents* VI (1994).

aimed at dismantling the cartels. Although the cartels ultimately did escape largely unscathed, a law was passed in 1957 that would eventually prove an effective tool for fighting against them.[7] An independent body was created, the *Bundeskartellamt* (Federal Cartel Office), or BKA. The BKA was based in West Berlin, officially, in order to demonstrate that the Federal Republic of Germany was committed to reunification and considered West Berlin an integral part of its territory, but unofficially, because Berlin's relationship with the rest of West Germany was still problematical and distancing the BKA in this way was a cushion to the Ruhr cartels. The minister retained the right to approve cartels deemed to be in the public interest but exercised it only rarely, because a political consensus was beginning to emerge in favor of active market competition.

In the United Kingdom the process was more complex. The Board of Trade consulted with industry on how to proceed with postwar reconstruction. In April 1942 the Federation of British Industries approved an interim report. In May 1942 the National Union of Manufacturers and the Association of British Chambers of Commerce also published their reports. There was broad agreement. In the words of the National Union of Manufacturers, "Trade will be more organised, more consciously directed and more regulated after the war than before." At the same time, however, a campaign in the press to discredit the cartels was being mounted.[8] Debate was stormy. One proposal was to declare all cartels illegal, unless they could prove their benefit to the economy, with the Board of Trade responsible for making the final decision; but this proposal was not accepted. Approval was finally given to a proposal specifying that cartels should be registered; should not a priori be considered as suspect; but that if the Board of Trade suspected them of having a negative effect on the economy, it should lodge a complaint with the Monopolies Commission, a body with only limited investigative powers that could act only on formal request from the government (the Board of Trade). A study was to be made of the cartels' effect on the economy, based on a fairly loose concept of "public interest." The first priority was reconstruction, to be supervised by the government and carried out by industrial cartels; second, however, the government would have at its disposal antitrust legislation to be used as a threat against cartels deemed to be exceeding acceptable bounds in controlling production (prices set too high,

[7] U. E. Koch, *L'Office Fédéral des Ententes (Bundeskartellamt): La règlementation de la concurrence en RFA* (Paris: Association pour la Connaissance de l'Allemagne d'Aujourd'hui [ACAA], 1982).
[8] *The Economist*, May 1942.

for example). Competition was not seen as inherently good, and the antitrust policy was an appendix to the industrial policies conducted jointly by the government and the trade associations. This legislation was passed in 1948. Service business and publicly owned corporations were exempt from the Monopolies Commission's jurisdiction, but in order to conform with the Havana Charter, trade associations formed to stimulate exports were subject to this law.[9]

The process was no simpler in France. The first attempt to pass antitrust legislation dates from the early 1950s, immediately following the Havana Charter. This initiative came from the left wing of a political party, the MRP (Mouvement Républicain Populaire), and was relatively populist in spirit. The proposal ultimately gained the support of a minister in the Laniel government, and the first French antitrust law was passed as a rider to a group of other laws and decrees on 9 August 1953. The head of the government approved it, on condition that "no one would ever hear about it,"[10] a political maneuver designed to pacify one of the parties in the governing coalition.[11] The proposed legislation had been drawn up by the Ministry of Economy's Price Control Department, and the Antitrust Commission, which was to be responsible for enforcing it, was housed in that department's offices. French antitrust legislation thus remained under the control of the powerful old-guard Ministry of Economy and Finance bureaucracy. The sole measure provided for by the legislation that was considered of substantial importance was the one prohibiting fixed retail prices since this was the only one designed to support the goal with which all French governments of the time were obsessed: keeping consumer prices down.[12] In their study of 1953 French antitrust legislation, two economists have termed these measures "an exercise in futility."[13]

Overall, European competition policies were a response to pressure from the United States, combined with support from selected domes-

---

[9] Gribbin, *The Post-War Revival of Competition.*

[10] H. Dumez and A. Jeunemaître, "Quand le contrôle des prix était une politique 'artiste,'" *Gérer et comprendre* 7 (June 1987): 42.

[11] In 1923 in Germany the ordinance against the abuse of economic power (Verordnung gegen Missbrauch wirtschaftlicher Machtstellungen) was promulgated in a similar political context. German Chancellor Streseman led a coalition government, and anticartel legislation was a gesture to the social democratic party, the left wing of the coalition. Implementation of this ordinance was not particularly disturbing to the German cartels.

[12] L. Franck, *Ministres: Souvenirs d'un directeur général des prix (1947–1962)* (Paris: Comité pour l'Histoire Economique et Financière de la France, 1989).

[13] F. Jenny and A. P. Weber, "French Antitrust Legislation: An Exercise in Futility?," in *The Antitrust Bulletin* 20 (Autumn 1975).

tic political parties. The enactment of antitrust legislation throughout Europe occurred within a complex political process during the reconstruction period that tended to safeguard the ability of traditional bureaucracies and industrialists to drain it of substance and rob it of any potential for real effectiveness. In Germany an emerging political consensus supporting a competitive economy impelled competition policy beyond its modest beginnings until it rapidly became reality. In France and the United Kingdom, however, this type of policy had little real impact, being stymied by the joint efforts of old-guard bureaucrats and industrial trusts.

European antitrust policy has thus from its inception harbored real divergence under an appearance of convergence. How did this "appearance" work in practice?

"Apparent" Convergence: How Did It Work?

As noted, Germany, France, and Great Britain passed antitrust legislation during the postwar years and also created ad hoc agencies to enforce it.[14] These countries therefore appeared to be converging toward the American-inspired liberal model—but "appeared" was the operative word.

The passage of antitrust policy in these countries involved choices reflecting the respective local context and history. Germany is an interesting case in point. Because postwar German antitrust legislation was the result of direct pressure from the United States and of American decisions in their occupation zone, there has been a mistaken tendency to see German competition policy as the child of American antitrust policy. Actually, the measures adopted in Germany at the end of the 1950s had deep roots in the nation's own history. The principle underlying the creation of an antitrust agency (*Kartellamt*) was initially passed by the Reichstag in 1908. From the end of the nineteenth century until the rise of the Nazis, German legal experts had been trying to reconcile what was seen as the public benefits of cartels, with limitations of potential abuses. A 1923 ordinance defined these abuses and created an Antitrust Court.

One of the reasons why appearances did not always reflect reality is thus historical. The second is that individual governments were careful to retain control over the planned economy levers. Initially, at any rate, the watchdogs were kept chained and their teeth filed. They

[14] H. Dumez and A. Jeunemaître, *Political Intervention versus "L'Etat de Droit Economique": The Issue of Convergence of Competition Policies in Europe*, Essays in Regulation no. 5 (Oxford: Regulatory Policy Institute, 1994).

were tightly controlled by politicians who "stacked the deck against them."[15] Control was maintained by imposing various "cumbersome procedures" on the new agencies.[16]

The first method for keeping the watchdogs on their chains was to allow only ministers or civil servants to lodge antitrust complaints. This was the method used in both France and the United Kingdom. The Monopolies Commission could consider complaints lodged only by the Board of Trade, and the Antitrust Commission only those lodged by the minister of the economy. Under the circumstances, it is hardly surprising that the first case considered by the Antitrust Commission did not target major industries but involved collusion among manufacturers of wooden ladders.[17] This system of antitrust control ensured that competition policy would not make inroads into any areas the government wished to keep free of it.

The second method for keeping the watchdogs under control was to place specified areas or fields outside the province of competition legislation. We have seen, for example, how public services and publicly owned corporations in the United Kingdom were exempted from Monopolies Commission control.

The third method was to place general limitations on the ability of these agencies to operate, particularly on their right to conduct investigations. In contrast to the Bundeskartellamt, the British agencies were not authorized, for example, to conduct searches on business premises or to seize documents.

The fourth method was to restrict agencies to an advisory role and to deprive them of independent decision-making power. The 1948 legislation specifies that the Monopolies Commission receives complaints from the Board of Trade, studies them, and then returns an opinion to the Board. The Board is then free to act or not. The same was true of the Antitrust Commission in France. The minister made the final decision and was free to rule in favor of a sector receiving a critical report from the Commission (although not to increase the severity of penalties recommended by the Commission). Extensive legislative measures thus enabled European nations to give the impression they were converging toward a liberal model of market regulation, but actually they were continuing their interventionist practices.

[15] McNollGast (Mathew D. McCubbins, Roger G. Noll, and Barry R. Weingast), "Positive and Normative Models of Procedural Rights: An Integrative Approach to Administrative Procedures," *Journal of Law, Economics, and Organizations* 6, special issue (1990).
[16] Antonio Scalia, "Vermont Yankee: The APA, the DC Circuit, and the Supreme Court," in Philip B. Kurland and Gerhard Casper, eds., *Supreme Court Review* (1978): 345–409; H. Dumez and A. Jeunemaître, *La concurrence en Europe* (Paris: Seuil, 1991).
[17] D. Brault, *L'Etat et l'esprit de concurrence en France* (Paris: Economica, 1987).

This state of affairs persisted until recent times, although in attenuated form. Even today antitrust measures in Europe are subject to political considerations. In Germany, for example, the minister retains the right to intervene in especially important cases. This explains why the merger of Daimler Benz and Messerschmitt-Bölkow-Blohm was eventually approved, even though it had been held up on competitive grounds by the Bundeskartellamt (when such a situation happens, the minister is required to lodge a complaint with the Monopolkommission, which then publishes an opinion that is not, however, binding on the minister).[18]

France is occasionally tempted to continue its old "national champions" policy.[19] For example, on 26 January 1990, the French government announced a merger of its three major national airlines, Air France, Air Inter, and UTA. The new group controlled 97 percent of air routes originating in France. The Competition Commission was not even asked for an opinion (the minister is not required to seek one in the case of a merger).[20]

The United Kingdom continues to employ the ambiguous term *public interest*. In 1981, for example, the takeover of the Royal Bank of Scotland by the Hong Kong and Shanghai Corporation was not approved, although no problem of competition was involved. Here, the goal was to protect interests in Scotland.

A scrutiny of competition policies in Europe thus shows that governments sought the appearance rather than the reality of convergence. But, paradoxically, the dynamic they set in place gave impetus to a shift toward real convergence.

FROM APPEARANCES TOWARD REAL CONVERGENCE

The strategy of various European states was to enact fairly similar antitrust legislation and to create agencies to enforce it, while, as noted, working behind the scenes to limit those agencies' enforcement power. In democratic countries with parliamentary and political opposition parties, this course is fundamentally unstable. The very existence of "independent" agencies encourages the executive to entrust

[18] Monopolkommission *Zusammenschlussvorhaben der Daimler Benz AG mit Messerschmitt-Bolkow-Blohm GmbH. Sondergutachten 18* (Baden-Baden: Nomos Verlagsgesellschaft, 1989).
[19] S. Berger, "Lame Ducks and National Champions: Industrial Policy in the Fifth Republic," in W. G. Andrews and S. Hoffmann, eds., *The Fifth Republic at Twenty* (New York: State University of New York Press, 1981).
[20] This decision was made by the French government at a time when regulations for overseeing monopolies in Europe had already been passed but were not yet being implemented.

them with those especially difficult cases in which the executive and the old-guard bureaucrats find themselves in conflict, cannot decide on the proper course, or face contradictory pressure from powerful private interests. Independent agencies, which have little power, cannot help. Sooner or later, conflict erupts between the executive, the legislature, the civil service, and the "independent" agencies. Opposition parties then have an opportunity to underscore the actual dependence of supposedly "independent" agencies and to advocate reforms aimed at establishing real independence and increased powers. Successive reforms have gradually broadened the scope of European agencies dealing with competition policy and endowed them with genuine independence. There thus exists a political trend toward reinforcing the power and real independence of "independent" agencies, to the detriment of the traditional civil service.[21] This independence involves three components: (1) autonomous decision making; (2) a larger jurisdiction; and (3) the development of an international network.

The decision-making process, formerly the almost exclusive province of government ministers, is now increasingly controlled by the judiciary, a trend approaching the American model. As noted, the first French agency, the Antitrust Commission, was actually set up within a Ministry of Economy department, the Price Control Office. It was then virtually an integral part of the traditional civil service, as the British Monopolies Commission was of the Board of Trade. It was symbolically important that its successor, the Competition Commission, was allowed to move into its own headquarters, separate from those of the Ministry of Economy. Although only the minister had been able to lodge complaints with the earlier agency, the new Competition Commission was given authority to hear complaints from industry groups or to investigate problems on its own. This major reform, the work of Prime Minister Raymond Barre, a former professor of economics, substantially reduced the Commission's dependence on the minister. The Competition Commission, however, was still unable to do more than give an opinion; final decisions were made by the minister. Following the 1987 reform, implemented when price controls were definitively abandoned as an instrument of economic regulation, the Competition Council (which succeeded the Competition Commission) began to make its own antitrust and antimonopoly decisions, which could then be taken before a court of appeals.[22] Decision

[21] See G. de Margerie, "Un nouveau type d'autorité," *Le Débat* 52 (November/December 1988), for an analysis of this impetus in France.

[22] H. Dumez and A. Jeunemaître, *Diriger l'économie: L'Etat et les prix en France (1936–1986)* (Paris: L'Harmattan, 1989).

making was thus transformed from a political/bureaucratic process to a quasi-judicial one. This shift reflected the increase in power and independence enjoyed by the antitrust agency. The minister retained full decision-making power only in the area of mergers.[23]

Similarly, in Germany decisions of the Bundeskartellamt can be appealed before the Berlin-Tiergarten Court of Appeals and, if necessary, before the Karlsruhe Federal Court (Bundesgerichtshof). This shift of decision-making power from the world of politics and government to the world of jurisprudence changed the nature of the decisions themselves. They must now be supported by economic and legal analysis, and they must conform to the principles of jurisprudence—something that was not the case with classic interventionism. Consequently, independent agencies for enforcing competition policy have tended to converge, because the economic analyses they apply to the cases are the same (relevant market, barriers to market entry, etc.).

As the decision-making process in the field of market competition regulation began to win autonomy from the classical political decision-making process the watchdogs' field of activity began to broaden, leading to broader powers of jurisdiction.

The regulatory agencies' jurisdiction broadened progressively, on various levels, and this broadening became an important factor in convergence. One of the most sensitive points of monitoring competition was antitrust regulation, which in the United Kingdom was enacted in 1965.[24] It was then that the Monopolies Commission became the Monopolies and Mergers Commission and was authorized to recommend that the secretary of state withhold approval from any merger that would create or strengthen a monopoly on the British market as a whole or on a substantial portion of it. By 1973 the Bundeskartellamt was also empowered to prohibit mergers, a power embodied in the 1973 reform that created the Monopolkommission, a new and independent agency responsible for, among other things, publishing a report every two years on changes in German industrial concentration. In France regulation of monopolies came in with the 1977 reform. There, however, the broadened scope for the antitrust agency remained apparent rather than real: Notification by corporations of an intent to merge was not compulsory, and the minister could seek the Competition Commission's opinion or not; if he or she

[23] French competition policy thus shifted gradually from an "exercise in futility" to reality; F. Jenny became vice-president of the Competition Council.
[24] A. Jacquemin, ed., *Merger and Competition Policy in the European Community* (Oxford: Blackwell, 1990).

chose to seek it, he or she was in no way obligated to follow it. This system might be described, once again, as one designed not to work as intended.[25]

Concurrently, however, the European watchdogs' field of intervention was, indeed, broadening. When the German government was faced with the prospect of concentration in the media, which seemed threatening to democracy, it decided to adopt special antitrust legislation applicable to the press and to empower the Bundeskartellamt to enforce it, thus extending the jurisdiction of the latter. Mrs. Thatcher's government, hostile in principle to publicly owned corporations and monopolies, also placed publicly owned corporations under the regulatory authority of independent agencies, under the 1980 Competition Act.

In addition, as regulatory agencies won independence from government bureaucracies, they also joined together in an international network. Contacts increased and were institutionalized. At the OECD there is a Competition Legislation and Policy Committee; a 1980 Franco-German agreement formalized cooperation between agencies in the two countries (the agreement provides primarily for the exchange of bureaucrats between the French and German agencies). In December 1982 the Bundeskartellamt invited antitrust agencies from the other major European countries to celebrate its twenty-fifth anniversary. Participants included what BKA president Dr. Wolfgang Kartte called "the extended international family of competition law."[26] This meeting was an opportunity to discuss various approaches to merger regulation. W. F. Baxter, for example, presented his European colleagues with the U.S. Department of Justice's new merger guidelines. The success of this meeting encouraged the Bundeskartellamt to organize a symposium for antitrust agencies to be held every two years. Now problems encountered by antitrust policy in the developed countries in general and in European countries in particular have a forum for discussion and debate. All these exchanges have facilitated convergence.

Overall, internal developments have thus led to increased antitrust policy autonomy from the control of European governments and to preliminary steps toward genuine convergence. Increasingly political intervention in market regulation (industrial policy), a potential source of divergence, has been met with opposition as decision-mak-

[25] C. Momege, "Les concentrations," *Cahiers de droit de l'entreprise* 12, no. 1, supp. (12 March 1987).

[26] Knud Hansen, ed., *International Conference on Competition* (Berlin: Bundeskartellamt, 1982).

ing has gradually fallen under judicial authority. This trend, in turn, has transformed the very nature of the decisions made.[27]

CONVERGENCE IMPOSED FROM WITHOUT

As the agencies regulating competition on national markets in individual European nations moved toward greater independence and established exchanges among themselves, an external process imposed from without by the EC authorities reinforced convergence.

When the effort to establish a European Defense Community failed, thus making it clear that political union for Europe was not yet a possibility, the governments involved decided to create an economic union instead. A start was made with coal and steel, two sectors rife with cartels. There was a major attempt to push the two sectors toward freer, more integrated trade. This effort was formalized by the European Coal and Steel Community Treaty. Later the Treaty of Rome reiterated the provisions of its predecessor, aiming to create a common market in which goods and services would circulate freely from one country to another.[28] To achieve this objective, competition regulations in the respective countries had to converge. W. J. Adams rightly notes that the signatory countries were aiming not so much at a purely economic objective (competition between their own national industries and those of the other countries) when they approved the treaty as a political one.[29] What they, particularly France, wanted was to create an interdependency with Germany that would rule out new conflicts resulting from rivalry between autarchic countries. The primary objective was wholy political, although the means employed to achieve it were economic. This situation explains why countries with attitudes to competition policy as diverse as those of Germany, France, and Italy all signed the treaty.

It was thus that a European competition policy was instituted, its objective to harmonize competition by eliminating barriers to free trade among member nations. As noted, European competition policy had a dual thrust: first, as antitrust policy in the American sense (merger supervision, action against trusts, monopolies, and abuses of dominant market position); and, second, as regulation. The distinctiveness of the European approach resides in the fact that the Commission of the European Communities was given ultimate control

[27] McCubbins, Noll, and Weingast, "Positive and Normative Models of Procedural Rights."

[28] D. G. Goyder, *EEC Competition Law* (Oxford: Clarendon, 1988).

[29] W. J. Adams, *Restructuring the French Economy: Government and the Rise of Market Competition since World War II* (Washington, D.C.: Brookings, 1989), chap. 4.

over both. This competition policy, enforced centrally (from Brussels) and implemented in the individual member nations, led to vertical convergence, voluntarily accepted and enforced under law. This convergence moves from the center to the periphery (Commission decisions imposed on member nations) and from the periphery to the center (national problems referred to Brussels for decision).

From the Center to the Periphery

Although there is still no real centralized power in Europe, decisions made by agencies in Brussels are nevertheless imposed on member nations. These decisions are framed, essentially, as either directives or individual decisions.

The construction of Europe is distinctive in that regulations are formulated by the Commission (the center), negotiated politically with the individual nations, and then integrated into the statutes of those individual nations (the periphery). The goal of much of this legislation is to strengthen the competitiveness inherent in the construction of a single market. Passage in 1985 of the Single-Market Act, which provided for the creation of a supranational market starting on 1 January 1993, introduced a major procedural change: henceforth, certain types of directives would not have to win a unanimous vote in the Council of Ministers but could be passed by simple majority. This legal innovation led to the accelerated passage of almost all the 282 measures and directives listed in the 1985 white paper on harmonization of standards and procedures for Europe. By June 1990 174 out of 282 had been passed. The stated goal was to foster the convergence of standards in order to guarantee an "equal playing field" for all European competitors on all European markets. This process of convergence had a profound effect on both macro- and microeconomics in Europe, as shown in the two following examples.

In Europe, as in the United States, public procurement was an instrument of industrial policy. Between 1984 and 1988 the Bundespost purchased 99.5 percent of its supplies from German firms, and the figure was 100 percent for the telecommunications industry in France, England, and the Netherlands. In the mid-1980s as a rule, nondomestic firms controlled less than 2 percent of the European public procurement market share by volume.[30] The Commission enacted a series of directives dealing with public procurement and establishing rules for transparency and competition in European public procurement markets. These rules covered public supply contracts (directive 77/62, dated 21 December 1976; directive 88/295, dated 20

[30] Hufbauer, ed., *Europe 1992*.

May 1988); public works contracts (directive 71/305, dated 26 July 1971; directive 89/440, dated 21 July 1989); and also, later, utilities (water, energy, transport services, telecoms), which had not previously been covered by directives on public works and public contracts (directive 90/531, dated 29 October 1990). The Commission forced national public agencies and firms to give sufficient advance notice of tenders for bids, and these were opened to firms throughout the Community. The Commission also monitored the bidding process: public agencies had to submit a written report on the bidding and to justify their final choices. The Commission can request that these reports be submitted to it (directive 89/440, article 5). When construction of the Olympic village in Barcelona was planned, for example, the Commission noted that the tender had not been made public. On further investigation, it was found that the Consorci de la Vila Olimpica had not been given the status of a "contracting authority" in the sense stated by the 1971 directive. Spain recognized its violation of European law and changed the legal status of the association, which was then subject to European legislation governing public procurement, upon which the Commission dropped the case.[31]

The Commission has received support from the European Court of Justice for the regulation and supervision of public procurement in Europe. The latter has limited member nations' margin of maneuver and forced them to converge toward a free-competition model. For example, in order to maintain their margin of maneuver and their ability to award contracts to domestic firms, the member states exploited an ambiguity inherent in the word *state*. However, in *Gebroeders Beentjes B.V. v. Netherlands* (1990), the Court decreed that "the 'state' must be interpreted in functional terms. A local land consolidation committee, which was not part of the State administration in formal terms, was held to fall within the concept of 'the State' because it had no legal personality of its own, its functions and composition were governed by legislation, its members were appointed by the regional government and it was obliged to apply rules laid down by a central committee appointed by the Crown."[32]

The Commission has also been involved in regulating details of everyday European life in order to foster convergence. In the mid-1980s, for example, beer experienced a growth in sales volume. Specifically, European consumers were attracted by a new product, nonalcoholic beer. In some countries this beverage is genuinely nonalcoholic (0% alcohol), whereas in others a small amount of alcohol

---

[31] Commission Press Release 1P(91) 384 dated 3 May 1991.
[32] *EEC Rules on Public Procurement* (London: Allen & Overy, 1991).

(0.5%, 1%, 1.5%) is allowed. Some countries define beer restrictively. This is true of France, where beer made from rice could not at the time be sold under the name *beer*. These differences in standards acted as a brake on competition and free trade among the European Community nations. The Commission therefore decided to harmonize the technical standards for beer and to establish broad categories marketable throughout the Community. These regulations were subsequently incorporated into member state legislation (in France, through a decree dated 1 April 1992, which allowed beer made from rice to be marketed in France from that date as *beer*).

Operating in the name of competition policy, the Commission has thus embarked on an intense process of regulation, reaching into even minor details of European citizens' lives, and imposing convergence from above.

The Commission also makes decisions prohibiting certain types of operations, decisions binding on individual member states or firms. It can prohibit mergers or a state from awarding subsidies to public corporations if such aid would imperil competition and sentence a cartel to the payment of heavy fines. In this decision-making process the most salient feature is the progressive expansion of the Commission's powers to the detriment of the member states' ability to intervene—and thus to diverge. Two examples are instructive.

The Treaty of Rome is officially neutral concerning firm ownership, and it authorizes awarding monopoly rights to firms providing a public service. This reflects the fact that the Treaty's prime movers (notably Konrad Adenauer and Alcide de Gasperi) were Christian-Democrats who feared criticism of a "Vatican Europe." They were careful to ensure that the Treaty could accommodate social-democratic or socialist policies. At the same time, in an effort to prevent obstacles to trade between member states, the Treaty banned state subsidies to industry, because such subsidies distort competition. Objectively, the Treaty of Rome thus allowed for diverse choices with respect to public enterprises. Each country was free to nationalize or privatize its industries at will. In fact, however, convergence toward the liberal model is currently being imposed on the member states by virtue of increasingly restrictive European attention to government subsidies.

In its *Intermills* decision (14 November 1984) the Court of Justice approved a Commission decision stating that acquisition by a government or a public agency of capital share in a given industry could be considered a subsidy. In its *Meurat* decision (1986) the Court declared that, in order to determine whether acquisition of capital share in a corporation by the government constitutes a subsidy distorting free competition, the relevant consideration is whether or not a private investor in the same position as the public investor would have made the same decision. If not, the subsidy must be considered as contrary to the Treaty of Rome.

The Commission of the European Communities, with the support of the European Court of Justice, went even further. It declared that any share taken by a government in a corporation belonging to a sector experiencing economic difficulties must be presumed to be a subsidy, even if, under the same circumstances, a private investor might have made the same decision.[33] "One cannot deny that this attitude gives rise to a degree of discrimination against public investors," comments M. Waelbroeck.[34] The Commission's aggressive attitude, supported by the Court, was one of the factors leading to the privatization of public firms in Europe and to policy convergence among the various member states.[35] In 1994, in an attempt to bring to a nonconfrontational conclusion investigations initiated in 1993 by the Commission into subsidies to Bull, a publicly owned French information systems firm, the French government was forced to announce the privatization of the firm. Thus ended a long history of French government intervention in the computer industry, a history going back to the Plan Calcul of the 1960s.[36]

The second point concerns the regulation of monopolies. Because European corporations were—and still are—smaller in size than their American (and Japanese) counterparts, the problem of mergers was considered in Europe to be political. European governments frequently encouraged mergers, even when their effect would clearly have been to hinder competition. However, in response to a wave of mergers in the late 1960s and at the request of the Commission, European governments at the 1972 Paris summit meeting entered into an agreement supporting the creation of an agency to monitor monopolies in Europe. On 20 July 1973, the Commission then submitted draft regulations on the question to the Council. In February 1974 the Commission received the support of the European Parliament and the Economic and Social Committee. Nevertheless, because the member states were determined to retain their margin of maneuver, discussions on the proposed regulations broke down. Having failed to win formal approval for monopoly monitoring, the Commission then

[33] *EC Bulletin* 3.5.1 (September 1984).

[34] M. Waelbroeck, *Is the Common Market a Free Market?*, Essays in regulation no. 1 (Oxford: Regulatory Policy Institute, 1992), p. 9.

[35] H. Dumez and A. Jeunemaître, "Privatizations in France (1983–1993)," in V. Wright, ed., *Privatizations in Europe* (London: Frances Pinter, 1994).

[36] J. Zysman, *Political Strategies for Industrial Order* (Berkeley: University of California Press, 1977).

in a way simply usurped this power. In 1972 the Commission determined that any firm already occupying a dominant position on a given market that then attempted to purchase a competing firm would be abusing its dominant position (violation of the Treaty of Rome, article 86). On this legal basis, the Commission prohibited Continental Can from purchasing Europemballage (decision 72/21). The case was then argued before the Court of Justice (*Europemballage Corporation and Continental Can v. Commission*, 1973). The Commission went even farther several years later. In a 1966 memorandum, the Court itself had argued the thesis that article 85 of the Treaty of Rome, designed to suppress monopolies and cartels, did not apply to mergers. In 1982, however, in a statement of objections addressed to two firms that had entered into a share-swapping deal, the Commission determined that this type of undertaking, which amounted to a de facto monopoly, was contrary to articles 85 and 86 of the Treaty of Rome. In the 1987 *Philip Morris/Rothmans* case decision, the Court of Justice again supported the Commission, confirming the latter's opinion that article 85 applied to two firms entering into a share-swapping agreement.

This opinion had considerable impact: under the terms of article 85, firms entering into an agreement that could limit competition must submit the agreement to the Commission for an opinion. De facto, following the Court's decision, notification of certain joint ventures had to be submitted to the Commission, which thus gained considerable regulatory power previously denied it by the Council.[37] Governments of the member states thus found themselves subjected to intense pressure: if they did not (finally) pass legislation to regulate monopolies, the Commission would use articles 85 and 86 of the Treaty of Rome.[38] Finally, in December 1989 the Council passed a regulation empowering the Commission to prohibit mergers on a European scale that might have the effect of hindering competition. The Commission has used this power only once, to prohibit a Franco-Italian firm from acquiring Canadian aircraft maker De Havilland.[39] But on several occasions, it has forced divestitures on to firms wishing to merge.

[37] On the Continental Can and Philip Morris/Rothmans cases, see Advokaterne Bredgade, ed., *Merger Control in the EEC* (Deventer: Kluwer, 1988).
[38] In a speech to the Association of European Corporate Legal Experts on 18 April 1985, European Competition–Policy Commissioner Peter Sutherland expressed the dilemma: "As I have already indicated on other occasions, if the proposal for merger control which has been pending now before the Council for twelve years is not enacted, the Commission will be forced to examine the direct applicability of articles 85, 86 and 90 to mergers. In that event, I could propose to the Commission to adopt appropriate guidelines before applying this policy in individual cases."
[39] H. Dumez and A. Jeunemaître, "La France, l'Europe et la concurrence: Les enseignements de l'affaire ATR/De Havilland," *Commentaire* 57 (Spring 1992).

The decision-making powers of the European authorities have thus gradually been extended, imposing common regulations and shared modes of operation on member states from above.

From the Periphery to the Center

Member states have gradually been forced to incorporate European law into their respective national laws. But at the same time the scope of national legislation has narrowed, because the Treaty of Rome is directly applicable to member states. If a person thinks that national legislation has negative effects on inter-European trade, he or she can decide to violate it. If brought before a national court of law, he or she can plead a contradiction between national law and the Treaty of Rome. The Court will then submit the case to the European Court of Justice in Luxembourg for an opinion. If the European Court decides that the national legislation is, in fact, contrary to the Treaty of Rome, the member state will be forced to amend its national law to conform with the Treaty.

The decisive turning point was the European Court of Justice famous *Cassis de Dijon* decision in 1979. This decision established that member states must recognize each other's regulations. If a product is considered in conformity with safety standards according to French law, for example, it cannot be rejected by Germany on the pretext that it does not conform precisely to legal German standards. It is thus no longer possible for member states to protect their own markets by establishing their own technical standards. Although this decision did not directly force member states to harmonize their legislation—or to converge—it did limit the protectionist impact of national regulations and the individual states' margin of maneuver.

But this convergence through mutual recognition of regulations gave way in the early 1980s to more aggressive action on the part of European Community agencies, as the Commission and the Court of Justice forced member states to rescind regulations conflicting with the Treaty of Rome. For example, in 1982 France had passed a regulation limiting discounts on the price of gasoline at the pump. The aim was to help small rural service stations. A French supermarket chain, Leclerc, decided to violate the regulation, and to offer deeper discounts than those authorized. Legal action was immediately taken against Leclerc. A lower court ruled in Leclerc's favor, stating that the Treaty of Rome has precedence over national regulations. The Paris Court of Appeals submitted the case to the Court of Justice at Luxembourg for an opinion and enjoined the Leclerc chain to obey the French regulation until the Court delivered an opinion. But even before the decision came down from the Court (on 22 January 1985), and because it was obvious what that decision would be, the French government rescinded the regulation. Economic actors can thus exert pressure on domestic legislative and regulatory processes, forcing their governments and their parliaments to converge with European competition law. The European system does not, however, include the "treble damage" clause of American law. Although it is thus free of the perverse effects this clause can have, it also lacks its advantages in terms of antitrust law enforcement.[40]

Convergence by Jurisprudence: A Long, Obscure, and Ongoing Process

In the field of European competition policy, the decision-making process culminates at the Court of Justice in Luxembourg. This explains why convergence follows a vertical path, from the center to the periphery.

Decisions made by the Commission of the European Communities, which may be appealed to the Court of Justice for final decision, are passed "down" to the member state periphery. As noted, competition problems at member state level may also wend their way "up" to the Court.

The convergence process in Europe, involving industrial and market regulation (a fundamental aspect, as Europe has until now been conceived of essentially as a huge market), is thus ultimately underwritten by the Court of Justice, not by traditional political institutions (governments, parliaments). The Court's role was crucial, for example, in implementing the act creating the Single European Market.[41]

The process is notable for three characteristics; it is slow, lacking in transparence, and ongoing. The Commission makes its decisions in an almost judicial way. An institution with relatively modest means, it takes considerable time studying each case. Time is also required to accommodate the formalities of the decision-making process. Because both sides must be given a fair hearing and facts must be fully disclosed, complaints registered against governments or corporations must be couched in the form of a strong legal case; responses to the complaint must be given a full hearing; and, in fact, every point of view must also be given a hearing. The Lower Court and the European Court of Justice both operate in the same way. Their concern

[40] L. J. White, *Private Antitrust Regulation: New Evidence, New Learning* (Cambridge: MIT Press, 1988).
[41] M. Waelbroeck, "Le rôle de la Cour de Justice dans la mise en œuvre de l'Acte Unique Européen," *Cahiers de droit européen* (1989).

for procedural rules slows the decision-making process.[42] Decisions are also technical in nature and difficult to understand and interpret. In contrast to traditional political decisions, they do not lend themselves to dramatization and projection by the media, and their ultimate impact, with few exceptions, is not always clearly understood from the start.

Last, decisions handed down by a court of final appeal are binding, nonnegotiable, and without further recourse. They differ by nature from political decisions, which are reversible in as much as they are inevitably the fruit of a temporary coalition, vulnerable to defeat or replacement. The fact that the decision-making process in market regulation (until very recently the core of the construction of Europe) culminates before a court of justice has therefore affected the way in which European economies tend to converge, which is slowly, cautiously, relatively invisibly, and continuously.

MAASTRICHT: CONTINUITY OR TURNING POINT?

The creation of a common market in 1957 was not an end in itself, but an interim objective. Once the market had started operating effectively, once European economic integration was well on its way, the political construction of Europe became the next entry on the agenda. The early 1990s marked this turning point.

The dual convergence process analyzed may be considered to have succeeded. Member states have implemented competition policies that are credible because they rest on an internal process of increased independence for the agencies that enforce them within the traditional political context (executive, legislative). Community institutions have also imposed convergence by building up a common judiciary. This convergence process is now coming to an end, precisely because it has achieved its objective. As the Single European Market became a reality on 1 January 1993, the Treaty of Maastricht, designed to transform the EEC into the EU, became a factor in the debate. Has Europe, with Maastricht, gone on to another model of convergence?

The answer appears to be yes. The Treaty attempts to redistribute institutional power by allocating new powers to the European Parliament and by substantially strengthening the concept of subsidiarity. It also sets new guidelines for the construction of Europe and for industrial and monetary policy that seem to mark a return to classic bu-

[42] In the Wood Pulp case the Commission's investigation began in 1977. The statement of objections was submitted in November 1981, and the Commission's decision was handed down in December 1984. The Court subsequently annulled the decision in March 1993, twelve and one-half years after the statement of objections had first been submitted.

reaucratic politics. When the situation is studied more closely, however, this first impression must be modified.

First, the convergence process under the control of the European Court of Justice has not been completed. We have seen the degree to which public procurement and government subsidies remain the focus of major initiatives by both the Commission and the Court. Community institutions are now also applying pressure to one of the last bastions of member state economic intervention: public services and monopolies. Through the application of competition law to these areas and of legislation on state subsidies, Brussels and Luxembourg are forcing member states to converge toward the British model: privatization of public monopolies and the creation of independent regulatory agencies responsible for overseeing the operations of privatized monopolies and for introducing the maximum amount of competition possible into traditionally monopolistic markets.[43] All major networking operations (rail and air transport, telecoms, utilities, etc.) are today prime targets for European competition policy. The process of convergence thus continues.

Some provisions of the Maastricht Treaty suggest that convergence will continue to be one of the most powerful engines for the construction of Europe, although perhaps in a slightly modified form. We might point out three important examples. The first is industrial policy. One of the articles of the Treaty explicitly refers to European industrial policy. This could imply policies similar to those followed in France from the 1960s to the 1980s, including measures running counter to European competition policy (approval for agreements that would have the effect of creating protected markets, the creation of European "national champions," etc.). But this article of the Treaty also specifies that "European industrial policy" cannot run counter to competition policy. Moreover, industrial policy measures must be approved unanimously by all member states, and it is unlikely that Germany or the United Kingdom would ever vote in favor of industrial policy measures similar to those sometimes adopted in France.

The second example is the so-called subsidiarity principle. Article 3b of the Treaty states that in the future Community institutions will not intervene in areas that can be adequately handled by member states themselves. Here again, the application of this provision will not be uniform, and European competition policy is a good example of this.[44] In a sense European competition policy has always respected the principle of subsidiarity. A good example is monopoly controls:

---

[43] C. Velijanovski, *The Future of Industry Regulation in the UK: A Report of an Independent Inquiry* (London: European Policy Forum, 1993).

[44] C. Jones, *Recent Trends and Developments in European Competition Policy*, Essays in regulation no. 4 (Oxford: Regulatory Policy Institute, 1993).

there is a threshold of 5 billion ecu, above which concentration becomes the exclusive province of the Commission, except when the firms involved earn two-thirds of their revenues in a single country of the Community. In all other cases, authority devolves on the authorities of the member states. But this subsidiarity is exercised under the vigilant supervision of the Commission, which controls how it is enforced. It is the Commission that selects the cases that appear important to it (*Automec* decision, 1993); and it is the Commission that allows member state agencies to deal with cases if it deems these agencies to be sufficiently credible. In other words, the concept of subsidiarity exerts pressure on member states to create competition policy agencies that are independent and effective. When the internal institutionalized convergence process is strong and effective, less emphasis needs to be placed on convergence imposed from above.

The third and last point has to do with monetary policy. Monetary policy convergence includes an institutional component. Maastricht provides for the creation of an independent European monetary institute whose decisions will be binding (imposed convergence). Further, member states' central banks will have to sever the umbilical cord linking them to their governments. With this in mind, in January 1994 the Banque de France gave up its status as the French executive's secular arm for monetary affairs and received a new statute guaranteeing its independence, one similar to that of the Bundesbank (institutional processes governed internally by member states). This convergence dynamic thus combines convergence imposed by a sovereign European institution independent of member states' governments with a network of national central banks that are themselves independent of their governments and able to adopt common regulations. In this way the type of convergence that emerged in the field of competition policy continues to be operative, becoming at the same time a model for aspects of the process of construction of Europe.

CHAPTER TEN

The Macropolitics of Microinstitutional Differences in the Analysis of Comparative Capitalism

PETER A. GOUREVITCH

Once upon a time the United States had trusts, combines, main banks, interlocking directorates, weak unions, fair trade laws, and restricted retail competition. Its economy flourished, overtaking England, the first industrializer, and Germany, the rival late developer.[1] Its education system pioneered mass education, sending the world's highest percentage of people to high school and college, while apprentice systems flourished in various skill areas. Government worked with industry to promote railroads, harbors, canals, and other kinds of infrastructure, to develop agriculture, and to fund research and product development. Specific industries were subsidized and sheltered. Large banks provided both finance and managerial coordination among companies and industries. American companies innovated with new products and new production systems, such as the assembly line and the use of standardized parts. In some rough way, the United States resembled what Michel Albert refers to as the Rhenish-Alpine-Japanese mode of production: a densely networked, alliance capitalism.[2]

As that mode of production flourished in the United States, it also

---

*Thanks for comments on an earlier draft to editors of the volume and conference participants.
[1] See the well-known discussion of Alexander Gerschenkron, "Economic Backwardness in Historical Perspective," in *Economic Backwardness in Historical Perspective* (Cambridge: Harvard University Press, 1962).
[2] Michel Albert, *Capitalisme contre capitalisme* (Paris: Le Seuil, 1991). For a typology that cuts across countries, see John F. Krafcik, "The Triumph of the Lean Production System," *MIT Sloan Management Review*, Fall 1988: 41–52; and James Womack, D. T. Jones, and D. Roos, *The Machine That Changed the World* (New York: Harper, 1991).

provoked antagonism from groups who felt disadvantaged by it. Farmers, urban consumers, exporters, workers, shippers, environmentalists, and other elements of society fought the trusts and combines. The Interstate Commerce Act, the Sherman Anti-Trust Act, the McClarren Act, the Glass-Steagall Act, the Wagner Act, the Agricultural Adjustment Act, the Securities and Exchange Act, along with many other pieces of legislation broke up several aspects of the American version of the Rhenish system.[3] Trusts like Standard Oil were ordered to separate into competing firms, banks were prohibited from interstate consolidation, investment and commercial banking were separated, independent trade unions were given rights at collective bargaining and organization, stock selling was regulated to prohibit insider trading and churning, retailing was opened to competition, and labor unions were given collective bargaining rights.

These policy decisions pushed the American economy down a path quite different from that of Japan and Germany. They knocked the United States off its Nippo-Rhenish trajectory and toward the current Anglo-American one—a decentralized, individualized, loosely coupled, arms-length, short-term, consumer-oriented, blind-bidding, market-driven system. The American economy is (relatively) open, permeable, fluid. Regulations favor stockholders and external investors, restrict interlocking directorates, allow management great latitude in dismissing employees, and facilitate the selling, consolidation, and dismemberment of companies.

The American pattern has emerged out of politics and policy. On repeated occasions for over a century the American polity has fought, at times bitterly, over the micro-institutions of American capitalism. These policy battles have led to the writing of rules that give the American system its distinctive character. Policy and politics are not the exclusive determinants of the micro-institutions of American capitalism, but they have played a very substantial role in bringing it about.[4]

A similar stylized story emphasizing politics can be told about the development of capitalism in other countries. In Japan, from the Meiji Restoration onward, conservative institutions excluded popular pressures that had voice in the United States. Japan adapted models drawn from Germany and the European continent to its own institutions in a framework of restricted, elitist politics. Defeat in World War

[3] Other elements of that system persisted and even grew: extensive systems of regulation developed for agriculture, airlines, oil, defense procurement, land and resource management, and so on.

[4] Wartime production and postwar economic dominance played a very specific role in institutionalizing buffered production methods in the United States and in insulating American manufacturers from new trends. See Michael Piore and Charles Sabel, *The Second Industrial Divide* (New York: Basic Books, 1984).

II altered Japan's trajectory. The American occupation created land reform, protected unions, and ordered the breakup of the zaibatsu. Overtime, political processes helped the zaibatsu to return as *keiretsu*, helped management to create company unions, and integrated the small farm-holders into the conservative ruling party. Today Japanese politics protect a wide range of rules and regulations that preserve the distinctive forms of Japanese capitalism. A similar role for politics can be found in the various European countries.

These stylized stories about the evolution of the American and Japanese economies have a moral: politics shapes the policies that shape the micro-institutions of capitalism.[5] The features that differentiate the internal firm and industry organization of German, Japanese, American, French, British, Italian, Swedish, Austrian, Korean, Taiwanese, and other market economies are institutionalized in the regulatory systems constructed in all nations by their political systems. The regulatory system sustains the micro-institutional patterns of the economy. The regulatory systems are sustained, or changed, by choices made in a political process by policymakers. Changes in the internal organization of firms and industries require in part modifications in public policies concerning regulatory structures. An analysis of comparative microcapitalism requires therefore that we find a linkage between political processes and the regulatory policies that influence micro-institutions. This essay makes the following assumptions: (1) The microstructure of industries and firms has a substantial effect on the efficiency of economies and is thus an important object of study in comparative capitalism; (2) these microstructures are shaped by regulatory policies within countries that structure incentives to use one organizational form or another; (3) changes in policy that modify those incentives can alter the institutional structures that influence efficiency; (4) the policies themselves arise from political processes in each country; and (5) changes in structure within countries in response to international competitive pressures do not happen automatically. They require changes in policy that depend on shifts in politics to produce new rules and regulations. Differences in micro-institutions among countries reflects differences in the politics of regulatory policy.[6]

If we are to understand the micro-institutions that influence national economic behavior, we must therefore seek to understand the

[5] The American debate over the right capitalist road goes back at least to Hamilton, advocate of the Rhenish approach, and his disagreements with Jefferson, advocate of the Anglo-American approach.

[6] Herbert Kitschelt, "Industrial Governance Structures," *International Organization*, Autumn 1991: 453–94. Kitschelt does an excellent job relating firm organization, product type, and national patterns of firm organization. He notes the factors that inhibit or encourage change in organizational patterns.

political processes that make these policies, sustain them, produce change, and deter change.

POLICIES

What policies shape the micro-institutional forms of market economies? Many laws and regulations do so.[7] My concern is primarily with the internal structure of firms and industries as they have bearing on efficiency in production and development of goods and services. The Nippo-Rhenish model stresses networks: it is a form of vertical and horizontal integration that favors interconnected ownership, command, relationships, while integrating elements of market competition within the network (in that regard it is different from total vertical integration within the firm). The Anglo-American model stresses arms-length contractual relations. What policies have a bearing on which form is adopted, which form rejected?

To narrow the focus, it may be useful to emphasize one end of a continuum. Policies that have an impact on firm structure can be said to have primary, second-order, and third-order effects. *Primary* effects refer to policies that deal explicitly with firms or industries: utility monopolies, telecommunications systems, banking, and, the most general of these, antitrust policy. *Second-order* programs refer to broader micropolicies that may not be aimed explicitly at firm structure but may have significant impact on it: labor relations systems, social service charges, research, education, and human resources development. *Third-order* policies are very general, such as macroeconomic policy, but may nonetheless have some effect on firm and industry structure: demand management influences predictability and levels of economic activity. Some firms and industries may be more vulnerable to instability, those with large fixed investments, for example, so that economic volatility may discourage network systems.

The emphasis here is on the first two effects. In the advanced industrial economies a substantial body of legislation, administrative regulation, and judicial interpretation shapes firm and industry structure. Several of these are examined in the following. The list is not exhaustive and deals with those areas that conceptually seem important and that have drawn the most attention in the comparative policy debate.[8]

---

[7] Indeed, the foundations of any specific market economy rest on laws and rules that accumulate over many years. Russia and Eastern Europe are discovering this with considerable pain.

[8] Roger Noll points out that volatility of policy substantially influences firm behavior (oral communication, 5 June 1993).

Corporate Governance versus Contractual Governance

Whom and what are managers responsive to? In this volume and elsewhere Kester contrasts two different modes of structuring authority in the firm and industry. "Corporate governance" focuses on the relationship between owners and managers by stressing the "reduction of agency costs . . . relying on formal, legalistic mechanisms to order commercial relationships among contracting parties."[9] "Contractual governance" seeks the "reduction of transaction costs associated with self-interested opportunism and investment in stable relationships."[10] The building of long-term relationships among all participants in a productive system is emphasized at the risk of agency costs to shareholders, the very element that the "corporate governance" approach seeks to protect. Corporate governance is the Anglo-American model. Contractual governance is the Nippo-Rhenish one.

The differences in these systems can be seen in a variety of regulations, laws, and institutions that formalize and protect the practices in each. These include:

- Takeover codes. The Anglo-American system experiences far higher takeover rates than does the Nippo-Rhenish model. In the United Kingdom those who control 30 percent of the shares must make a full bid for the company, whereas in most of the other EC member states the threshold is 50 percent; in the United Kingdom the takeover bidders must provide an exit option to all shareholders by offering to purchase 100 percent of the shares, a provision absent in other countries.[11] In the United Kingdom, the City Code on Takeovers and Mergers is administered by a nonstatutory body, the City Takeover Panel, whose members are overwhelmingly drawn from financial institutions for whom mergers and acquisitions are an important source of income. In the United States, the rules are more formalized, but their substance is similar.
- Institutional investors and insider information. Institutional investors are inhibited from overseeing of managers in the United States and United Kingdom by insider information rules. This keeps at arms length those investors most likely to have the incentive to get and use information. At the same time these rules provide external investors with information valuable for buying and selling and for mergers and acquisitions.

[9] W. Carl Kester, "American and Japanese Corporate Governance: Converging to Best Practice," draft for the Conference on Domestic Institutions, Trade, and the Pressures for National Convergence, Bellagio, 1993, p. 3; and W. Carl Kester, "Industrial Groups as Systems of Contractual Governance," *Oxford Review of Economic Policy* 83 (1992): 24–44.

[10] Kester, "American and Japanese Corporate Governance," p. 2/3.

[11] Stephen Woolcock, "Corporate Governance in the Single European Market," Royal Institute of International Affairs discussion paper no. 32 1990; see also chapter 7 in this volume; Colin Mayer, "Corporate Ownership and Corporate Control: A Study of France, Germany, and the United Kingdom," *Economic Policy* 10 (1990): 191–231.

- Accounting rules and administration. The accounting professions in the United States and the United Kingdom are highly developed, with rules stressing obligations to shareholders and their agents, the directors, but not to any other stakeholders.
- Stakeholders. German law gives voice to nonstockholder members of the company community through *Mitbestimmung*, which provides labor representation on company boards. Businessmen in the United States and the United Kingdom have resisted provisions of this kind. In Japan lifetime employment norms (though not legislation) makes the labor voice quite important, even if union representation is not formalized.
- Financial institutions. The relationship to capital and directors is an important element of governance, as well as a system of its own (see next section).

Finance

Financial systems shape firm structure through incentives for managers, employees, and other elements of the production system. Regulatory policy determines the relationship among financial institutions, between finance and the firms who borrow, and between each of these and government regulators.[12]

One set of rules deals with finance as a sector: The McClarren Act, for example, constrains interstate banking in the United States. This makes U.S. banks smaller than their counterparts, and to some extent it makes the banking industry inefficient. Another set of rules governs the relationship between lenders and borrowers. The Glass-Steagall Act separates commercial banks from investment banks. The Securities and Exchange Act and the Federal Reserve Act define permissible behavior among directors, shareholders, and lenders.

This ensemble of rules and oversight structures in finance makes the American production system quite different from the European and Japanese practice.[13] The U.S. system favors the short-term appreciation goals of shareholders, undervalues intangibles such as training and research, encourages investment in high-tech or emerging industries with rapid growth, but undervalues other kinds of companies and activities with long-range growth potential. Laura Tyson writes: "the structure of American capital markets and the nature of relations between suppliers and customers, investors and managers, and executives and workers, are more powerful determinants of the availability

[12] The argument between industry and finance is an old one. Should finance be evaluated for its internal efficiency as a sector or for its effects on other industries and sectors? Peter Gourevitch, *Politics in Hard Times* (Ithaca: Cornell University Press, 1986).
[13] Note the title of Michael Porter's article, "Capital Disadvantage: America's Failing Capital Investment System," *Harvard Business Review*, September/October 1992: 65–82; Michael Dertouzos et al., *Made in America* (Cambridge: MIT Press, 1989).

and price of long-term capital than are the federal deficit and long-term interest rates. Reforms in the system of allocating capital within and across companies are needed to provide a competitive capital market environment for American companies."[14]

Extensive reforms have been proposed, involving wide-ranging change in regulatory policy. Many of these changes would have the effect of "allowing" American practice to resemble the European and Japanese models. For example, the U.S. Council on Competitiveness recommends that the American government remove restrictions and tax barriers on share ownership to encourage long-term ownership by banks, employees, and private owners; change accounting rules to provide better evaluation of intangible assets, rather than expensing them from current income; change insider trading rules to favor long-term holders, provided they do not share it with third parties; loosen restrictions on institutional board members and encourage membership by significant customers, suppliers, employees, and community representatives.

These are interesting recommendations coming from a business group. The actions suggested all involve public policy. If enacted, they would amount to a drastic change in the structure of U.S. capitalism, altering the incentives under which firms operate and the relationship of firms to their investors, managers, employees. They would change what is valued inside the firm and they would change the distribution of power within the firm.[15]

Although these reforms would make the U.S. system look more like the Japanese and German ones, the systems in those countries have also been the subject of criticism and proposed reform. Among the critiques of the Japanese system are lack of transparency, which makes it difficult for outsiders to know the rules; favoring of large, established clients at the expense of small shareholders; exclusion of foreigners and newcomers; preference to producers over consumers; favoring of large companies over small savers and investors.

The instruments that produce these results derive from the extensive powers of the Ministry of Finance, which has the ability to determine interest rates, credit volume, and asset prices. Formal laws in Japan provide for considerable centralization of regulatory power in the ministry, with a broad charter of authority that makes external oversight and input difficult.[16] In contrast, the European rules vary

[14] Laura Tyson, *Who's Bashing Whom?* (Washington: Institute of International Economics, 1992).
[15] Porter, "America's Capital Disadvantage," pp. 77–82.
[16] Frances Rosenbluth, *Financial Politics in Contemporary Japan* (Ithaca: Cornell University Press, 1989). See also Stephen Vogel, "Changing the Rules: The Politics of Regula-

considerably across countries. Among the major issues in the 1992 single market process was the search for uniform rules for the Community. This has proven difficult to do; national politics protect national rules.

Antitrust Policy

The area of antitrust policy deals explicitly with industry structure: it defines the degree of concentration allowed in an industry. It can also have an impact on structure within the firm by determining the permissible degree of vertical integration. Vigorous antitrust policy can inhibit the kind of network alliances associated with Japanese and German patterns, and it can influence the organization of research, standard setting, product development, pricing, and a variety of other areas of company policy.

American policy on antitrust shows quite strongly the way disagreements are given influence by American institutions. A broad alliance of farmers, manufacturers, and small-town shopkeepers brought about the Interstate Commerce Act, which regulated the railroads, followed by the Sherman Anti-Trust Act of 1890. Enforcement has at times been vigorous, following political trends. Standard Oil executives seem to have been stunned when the Supreme Court actually upheld the case against the company.[17] At other times enforcement has been lax, as in the 1980s.

Other countries have either weaker laws or weaker enforcement. What is seen as restraint of trade in the United States is taken as normal business practice in Japan and Germany. This allows the formation of the densely networked systems so characteristic of those two countries. Networked systems provide ways of linking the profits from one product to the development of new ones, encouraging long-term investment, the stability of the company, the loyalty of its members—in short the various virtues of the Nippo-Rhenish model.

Suppliers/Distributors

A variety of rules influence the linkage between manufacturing companies, their upstream suppliers, and their downstream distributors. Retailing laws vary widely across countries. In the United States, regulations encourage vigorous competition among retailing units, separating them from manufacturers' control, thus inhibiting tight in-

---

tory Reform in the Advanced Industrial Countries," diss. Department of Political Science, University of California, Berkeley, 1993.

[17] Daniel Yergin, The Prize (New York: Simon & Schuster, 1991).

tegration of distribution into the manufacturing system. Competitive retailing, independent of manufacturers, rewards consumption, drives down profit margins, aids manufacturers who need costly inputs, and may discourage long-term product development. In Japan the rules allow much tighter integration of manufacturing and retailing, erecting barriers to entry and ensuring high retail prices. Some analysts argue that this method allows manufacturers to stabilize revenue, guaranteeing profit flows that aid investment and product development.

The European continent varies considerably in practice and policy, not only between countries but also within them. Large-scale supermarkets and retailers, discount pricing, and price competition of various kinds are restricted in many countries. These restrictions often express the influence of shopkeepers, small retailers, local communities, and the desire of manufacturers for stability.[18]

At the other end of the production chain are rules that influence the linkage between firms and their suppliers. That relationship is seen by many analysts as a critical component of the Japanese "lean production" system. Taxation, employee insurance, health and safety inspection, employment protection, and a host of other regulations often differentiate between large and small firms. Large firms have more rules, costs, and restrictions; smaller firms are excused from rules or benefit from various subsidies. The effect is to make small firms more viable and to encourage large firms to cut costs by subcontracting to smaller ones.[19] This may be a major reason why Toyota and other Japanese firms add about 25 percent to the value of a car, where American firms add 50 percent.[20] Many researchers have argued that small firms innovate more and create more jobs than large ones, so this is an area of some importance. The role of small firms in lead production may be an unintended effect of rules that express the political influence of small enterprises, which are able to press for protective regulation.[21]

Labor Relations

Labor market laws have a substantial effect on how firms use labor. As noted, laws on hiring and firing can raise the costs of labor,

---

[18] Frank Upham, "Privatizing Regulation: Implementation of the Large-Scale Retail Stores Law," in Gary Allinson and Yasunori Sone, eds., *Political Dynamics in Contemporary Japan* (Ithaca: Cornell University Press, 1993), pp 254–94.

[19] John F. Krafcik, "The Triumph of the Lean Production System," *MIT Sloan Management Review* 30, no. 1 (Fall 1988): 41–52.

[20] Womack, Jones, and Roos, *The Machine That Changed the World.*

[21] Suzanne Berger and Michael Piore, *Dualism and Discontinuity in Industrial Societies* (New York: Cambridge University Press, 1980).

thereby encouraging a dualistic industry structure. Lifetime employment practices encourage investment in worker training, although it may also encourage additional subcontracting to firms that do not have it. Laws, as well as negotiated contracts with unions, may influence the use of labor in the organization of production. In the United States, unions and firms evolved very specific job categories, on which pay scales were graded; this has interfered with more flexible and experimental uses of work. A different kind of labor contract, involving lifetime employment or participatory management relationships, may facilitate more flexibility in job assignments. As is true of the rules for small firms, some labor systems may encourage subcontracting as a way of escaping regulations and costs.

Research

The research system has interesting implications for firm structure. In the United States, public funding in open universities makes research a public good. This increases the availability of research finds but also lowers the incentive of firms to fund basic research. It also makes research accessible to firms from countries whose taxpayers are not paying the bill. Conversely, Japanese research appears to take place within the firm, is thus more proprietary, possibly more applied, and less publicly available. National rules on university systems, research funding, tax write-offs, and so on all have an impact on this system. Other issues of research are important for some industries but are less clearly related to firm structure: research tax credits, levels of funding, strategic funding of critical, "spin-on," "leading industries of the future."[22]

Human Resources Training

The funding and control of different levels of training affects firm behavior and organization. The German apprentice system links firms to employee training in a very direct way, making that system an extension of the firm. The Japanese system of strong employee claims on their jobs encourages substantial firm investment in training at all levels, at least of those with lifetime relationships at the core of the process, less so to the tertiary subcontractors where employment is

[22] Tyson in *Who's Bashing Whom?* sets out a number of reforms of relevance to competitive issues, though not focused specifically on firm structure. One relevant to research has to do with the creation of an agency that could analyze manufacturing capacity and technology. In the United States, information is supplied by the private sector; in Europe and Japan separate agencies do this as well. This would be a form of "indicative planning" pioneered in France by Jean Monnet.

much less stable. The American system delinks the firm from education, concentrates firm funds on the top management, and seems to
favor public investment in universities over grade school. An interesting indicator of the difference in the systems is the power structure
within the firm: in Japan the personnel director is an important position, but in the United States human resources managers rarely become CEOs; in the United States, the chief financial officer is the de
facto second person, an heir apparent, whereas in Japan no such particular presumption exists.

THE MACROPOLITICS OF MICROREFORM

In a variety of ways, public policy influences the internal organization of firms and industries. In each country a wide range of laws,
rules, and administrative procedures creates incentives that reward or
punish various institutional forms in the economy. These policies
range from the very general (macroeconomic policy) to the specific
(public utility monopolies). If these structures are to change, the policies must change.

If the American polity concludes that efficient production requires
new forms of vertical and horizontal integration, then changes need
to take place in the regulatory system that influences the structure of
firms and industries. If Japan seeks to better trade relations by reducing barriers against foreigners or to have greater productivity from
currently inefficient sectors, then there needs to be changes in the
rules that protect the inefficient and exclude new entrants, be they
foreign or domestic. If European countries seek efficiencies from
more flexible firm organization and hiring practices, then the labor
and structural regulatory system must change.

For those changes in policy to occur, political processes must produce them. We must link political processes in each country to the
regulatory system that shapes micro-institutions—the politics of mi-
croregulation. What are the "macro politics of micro-reform?"[23]

In each country a number of forces are at work: culture, values,
preferences, ideology, interests, international pressures and opportunities, ambition, institutions, procedures, leadership, accidents—in
short the gamut of variables that influence politics. All of these forces
influence policy by their effect on policymakers. We may focus the
discussion here by exploring the possible sources of change. In each

[23] Some of these ideas are discussed in my paper "The Macro-politics of Micro-pol-
icy," in G. Ross, J. Vichniac, and T. Skocpol, eds., "Lessons from History: Festschrift for
Barrington Moore," unpublished.

country with a constitutional form of government,[24] we may observe several different sources of external pressure on the political system to change its regulatory regime: from other countries, consumer interests, domestic producers, the bureaucracy, and political parties.[25] The relationship among these variables can be illustrated by tracing out several scenarios of change. The examples here are drawn from Japanese and American cases, but could be applied to other countries and regions.

Scenario One
The Internalization of External Pressures

One source of pressure for change comes from the politics of the international trading system. Japan finds itself under increasing pressure from the governments of other countries to change its rules and regulations—the Structural Impediments Initiative (SII) between Japan and the United States is perhaps the most conspicuous example of "gaiatsu." So long as the Japanese trade surplus is large, this pressure is not likely to go away.

How will Japan respond? External pressure of this kind can only effect change within a country when a powerful bloc of domestic actors are convinced that change must occur. Within Japan the impact of foreign pressure hits actors differently. Some would be very hurt by changes in Japan's trade position: rice growers and other farm interests; small shopkeepers worried about competition in the distribution system; manufacturers and workers in industries that are shielded by exclusionary practices; bureaucrats in the ministries that handle these groups; politicians from the districts where these groups have a lot of weight.

Conversely, other interests in Japanese society would be hurt by foreign retaliation against Japanese policy or by contraction in the world trading system: exporters reliant on the large U.S. market; manufacturers dependent on a large world market share to fund their product development; bureaucrats in the relevant ministries; politicians responsive to these interests and goals.

[24] Some authoritarian regimes have successful market economies, but an exploration of that theme is beyond the scope of this paper. See Peter Gourevitch, "Democracy and Economic Policy: Elective Affinities and Circumstantial Conjectures," *World Development* 21, no. 8 (1993): 1271–80.

[25] Robert Wade, *Governing the Market* (Princeton: Princeton University Press, 1992); Stephan Haggard, *Pathways from the Periphery* (Ithaca: Cornell University Press, 1990); Fred Deyo, *The Political Economy of the New Asian Industrialism* (Ithaca: Cornell University Press, 1987). Tun-jen Cheng and Stephan Haggard, *Newly Industrializing Asia in Transition* (Berkeley: Institute of International Studies, 1987). Chalmers Johnson, *MITI and the Japanese Miracle* (Stanford: Stanford University Press, 1982).

For change in Japanese rules to come about, foreigners who desire that change must find internal allies—those seeking gains from good relations with the United States, or from open world trade, and those worried about the costs of negative responses from other countries. The SII worked in this way: for those items on the U.S. agenda that had internal support within Japan (reforms in the distribution system, increasing public spending, and to a lesser degree land policy), some progress was made. For those items that had little internal support (e.g., those dealing with *keiretsu* and exclusionary business practices) little or no progress was made.[26]

The same cluster of pressures can be seen at work in the US-Canadian-Mexican debates over NAFTA, European arguments over the Single Act and Monetary Union, GATT negotiations, and trade conflicts around the world.

Foreign pressure is always important in trade policy debates: the threat of retaliation, loss of markets, international contraction, or other noneconomic issues are all quite real and may be of great concern. In any country the effect of that pressure works through the domestic actors who are most concerned about the loss of markets in foreign countries. The advocates of liberalized trade must always fight off those who fear losses from it.[27]

Scenario Two
Internally Generated Pressure

Another agent of change could be domestic actors interested less in changing a nation's role in the world than in changing the conditions of life at home. Domestic consumers are a notable example. The phrase "rich Japan, poor Japanese" conveys a grievance felt in at least some elements of Japanese society—that rising national wealth in aggregate terms has not translated into better individual living stan-

---

[26] Leonard J. Schoppa, "Two-Level Games and Bargaining Outcomes: Why *Gaiatsu* Succeeds in Japan in Some Cases but Not Others," *International Organization* 47, no. 3 (Summer 1993): 353–86.

[27] Peter A. Gourevitch, "The Second Image Reversed: The International Sources of Domestic Politics," *International Organization* 32 (Autumn 1978): 881–912; Robert Putnam, "Diplomacy and Domestic Politics: The Logic of Two-Level Games," *International Organization* 42, no. 3 (Summer 1988): 427–60. Strong debates exist on the explanation of trade policy. See among others James E. Alt and Michael Gilligan, "The Political Economy of Trading States: Factor Specificity, Collective Action Problems, and Domestic Political Institutions," (Harvard University, unpub. paper, 1993); Ronald Rogowski, *Commerce and Coalitions* (Princeton: Princeton University Press, 1989); Daniel Verdier, *Democracy and International Trade: Britain, France, and the United States, 1860–1990* (Princeton: Princeton University Press, 1994); Patrick Magee, William A. Brock, and Leslie Young, *Black Hole Tariffs and Endogeneous Policy Theory* (Cambridge: Cambridge University Press, 1989).

dards. Housing is small and expensive, commuting times long, consumer prices high, working hours long, recreation facilities limited, leisure time constricted.

Consumers constitute a pressure for change everywhere. And it is an axiom of collective action analysis that consumers are politically weaker than producers; this is true everywhere, not just in Japan. Consumer satisfaction is a typical public good; the benefits are distributed to everyone, even those who exert no energy in getting them. Consumer movements thus have trouble organizing people to work for common goals. Producers, conversely, have the easier task of mobilizing particularistic interests, the defense of jobs and investments.

In Japan the problems faced by consumer interests have been compounded by several factors. The Japanese electoral law has divided the vote within multimember districts. This weakens consumers by rewarding particularistic political organizations who provide electoral and financial support in exchange for favors and policies. This disadvantages consumers as well as other dissidents seeking more public goods over particularistic ones.[28]

Another institution, the Japanese economic structure, its "alliance capitalism," favors the maintenance of existing networks of companies and distribution, raising barriers against dissidents and new entrants. In the United States, by contrast, private-sector firms and industries often fight one another quite vigorously on a wide range of issues. This provides consumers with opportunities to find allies in the service sector, the distribution system, and among producers that use as inputs the manufacture of other products. Retail distribution chains in the United States help to drive down prices and often are able to draw manufacturers into competitive price cutting. In Japan many retailers are integrated into the production system through *keiretsu* linkages, where price cutting is contained. Many regulations protect small "mom-and-pop" stores. Thus Japanese consumers have fewer producer and distribution allies than may exist in other countries.

A third aspect of Japanese decision-making systems that has inhibited consumer interests is the bureaucracy. From the earliest years of the Meiji modernization process the bureaucracy has focused its energies on producer-led economic growth. Key agencies, such as MITI and the Finance Ministry, have developed extensive links with major producer groups in Japanese society. Their goals are to help these producer groups, not champion the more diffuse goals of consumers.

In the Japanese political system, then, consumer interest faces a for-

[28] Gary Cox and Frances Rosenbluth, "The Electoral Fortunes of Legislative Factions in Japan," *American Political Science Review* 87, no. 3 (1993).

midable set of obstacles, as does any group seeking change. Agents of substantial change would have to break the Japanese "iron triangle" (a phrase borrowed from U.S. politics): interest groups, bureaucracy, party. This would surely be difficult. The breakup of the Liberal Democratic Party (LDP) in June 1993 may be a step in that direction, but it may also be a complex maneuver in a political struggle leading to its own form of blockage. (See the discussion regarding political parties.)

Even though all political systems pose obstacles to consumers, some of them appear to provide some greater opportunities for entry. The multiple veto points of the American system, created by federalism, checks and balances, and the separation of powers combine to produce weak parties and highly fragmented policy processes. This factor favors highly particularistic producer groups but also provides points of access for populist protest and those consumer groups that are able to focus on quite specific goals. In European countries competitive party politics offers some possibilities for integrating consumer goals into generalized coalitions.

Scenario Three: Producer-Led Reform

Change may come from producers instead of from consumers or foreigners. Several examples have already been noted. Producers care about the price they are charged for inputs to their own products. In the United States, for example, the computer industry often lobbies to oppose tariffs on Japanese-made screens or chips when these are part of their own finished product, even though they seek aid in fighting Japanese competition in other respects. In Japan high prices for telecommunications equipment may deter the adoption of that technology in the manufacturing process of other companies.[29] As conditions in markets and technology change, companies become interested in regulatory "reform," revising the rules to fit new competitive circumstances.[30] In Japan banking and finance rules were altered as the industry worried about its domestic and international position.

Another concern of producers may be trade retaliation by foreign countries or the general erosion of the international trading system. Producers also have a general concern with overall economic efficiency as this affects the consuming capacity of the general popula-

[29] Roger B. Noll and Frances M. Rosenbluth, "Telecommunications Policy: Structure, Process, Outcomes," in P. Cowhey and M. McCubbins, eds., *Structure and Policy in Japan and the United States* (New York: Cambridge University Press, 1995).

[30] The "capture" theory sees the regulator responsive to the regulated. This does not mean necessarily the status quo—it may mean change, when the regulated find it appropriate.

tion: funds drained into inefficient distribution are funds not spent on consumer products.

Industry may thus be an important source of pressure for change in many features of the regulatory system of microproduction. Those changes pass through politics and are both aided and hindered by the political processes of each country. In Japan regulatory change desired by industry is facilitated by the close relationship with policymakers in the governing party and the bureaucracy. Policy is thus more likely to be worked out in a comprehensive plan than in the United States. In the United States, greater conflict exists in political processes. Businesses are much less confident that policies that emerge from American processes will contain what they may like. They are thus less likely to work out comprehensive plans involving collaboration between business and government.

Scenario Four: The Bureaucracy

A fourth source of change may lie in the bureaucracy. Bureaucrats are specialists. They exist to do things their clients lack the time to do. They, the agents, usually have better knowledge than their clients, the principals. To do their job, they have substantial discretion, the authority delegated to them. Thus bureaucrats are often the source of ideas, reforms, innovation, and change. They can also be the source of obstruction and resistance. Countries vary considerably on the role bureaucracies play and how they play it. These differences do not correlate perfectly with the typology of microsystems, although there is some overlap: France, Japan, and Germany have highly formalized elite civil service systems with substantial powers. The United Kingdom has an elite tradition, but much fewer formalized modes of intervention in micro aspects of economic life. The United States lacks both the elite tradition and the modes of intervention, but it does have highly formalized systems in areas where the United Kingdom does not (securities regulation for example).

These differences among systems have implications for change in microeconomic institutions. In some areas change from one system or another in the private sector would require parallel changes in the public bureaucracy as well. Criticism is made of the absence of transparency in Japanese regulatory processes: few formal rules and a high degree of administrative discretion. The effect is to provide another barrier against new entrants into Japanese markets, be they foreign or domestic. Increasing competition would require more formalized, transparent rules and that means having different new regulatory processes. In the United States, changing the structure of microsystems of markets, be these in finance, health, telecommunications, or agriculture, would involve massive change in regulatory systems for each policy or market arena.

The ability of bureaucracies to be the source of change or opposition and the nature of regulatory change in bureaucratic authority are both affected by the bureaucracy's relations to the party system, to the formalized system of authority, and to interest groups and electors. To be autonomous, to exercise discretion to block or support change, bureaucracies need a political "cover." Bureaucracies need protection from political forces that may seek to push them down an alternative policy path. In prewar Japan that cover came from authoritarian political institutions and politics. In postwar Japan it has come from the LDP and its alliance with producer groups in Japanese society.

In the United States, conversely, conflictual party politics in legislatures and the executive branch exposes the bureaucracy more visibly to political influences, pushing it one way or another. In Europe the lines of bureaucratic behavior are influenced by electoral competition, alternation in power among parties, and the various pressures from interest groups that political competition allows.[31]

Scenario Five: Political Parties

A fifth source of change may come from political parties. In a formal sense policy in constitutional systems is made by elected representatives, legislators and executives. Elections are managed by political parties, who thus play a role in policy formation. That role varies across parties and countries. It may be that of arbiter, not a source of initiative, but the resolver of disputes among factions, ministries, and interest groups. Parties may be brokers, finding and implementing strategies of integration and reconciliation. Parties may be leaders, the source of ideas and initiative. Party competition provides incentives to take up or reject the policy goals of other social actors.

In Europe, the United States, and Japan parties face formidable challenges in developing strategies able to link voters, interest groups, policies, and bureaucracies. In Japan four decades of one-party dominance make the role of parties in policymaking the hardest to evaluate; alternation in office would make it clearer. The LDP managed a complex coalition of strong and weak economic actors, leading exporters and highly vulnerable farmers, producers and consumers. The fracturing of the LDP, its defeat in the elections of June 1993, and the formation of a new, very heterogeneous, thus unstable, coalition government are all too new to allow any conclusive observations.

[31] Upham, "Privatizing Regulation."

Nonetheless, the recent maneuvering between parties and within factions creates one mechanism whereby change might occur: different electoral rules, now that they have been implemented, may change the party system. That could in turn alter the balance of forces in Japanese society, giving greater voice to urban interests, to consumers, to export and trade-oriented industries at the expense of farmers, inefficient members of the distribution system, the construction trades, and other beneficiaries of the current system. Alternatively, the stalemate among these diverse interests could also lead to preservation of the status quo; in other countries, weak coalitions have often failed to achieve significant change.

In the United States shifts in partisan control of the White House and Congress have brought discernible shifts in policy and conflict over policy, although it is too soon to measure results. The Clinton Administration first threw its energies into recreating a business–government–researcher alliance around high-technology industries. This synergy can be seen as a type of producer coalition, aimed at using government aid to promote a set of industries in world trade, in which the Clinton Democrats seek to find a modern version of the New Deal's producer coalition of agriculture, export industry, oil and gas, aviation, mass-production industry, and labor. Even though the federal deficit constrains sharply the size of any help, the first budget written by the Clinton Administration tried to help technology through greater research funding, intellectual property protection, and institutional reorganization among federal agencies dealing with science and technology. In trade policy the Administration used political capital to secure the passage of NAFTA and worked to obtain signatures for the Uruguay Round of the GATT. With Japan it rejected face-saving agreement compromises of the past, but it is too soon to tell where this attitude will lead. Also unclear still today are explorations into reforming the U.S. financial system; so far these discussions have focused largely on the efficiency of the financial sector per se, not on the questions of corporate governance to which financial issues are linked.

The Clinton Administration is trying in some sense to recover and modernize an older dimension of American capitalism, the Hamiltonian tradition: the state partner, through research and subsidies to key industries such as airplanes, telecommunications, and electronics. The politics that underlie this effort lie in re-creating the labor/business/agriculture alliances that underlay previous efforts at Hamiltonianism. In business the Clinton Administration looks to the high-technology firms symbolized by Silicon Valley and Boston's Route 128. With labor it supports reform of health care and more vigorous dealing with U.S. trade rivals. In agriculture it continues price supports and export promotion.

So far the Clinton Administration's efforts have focused on research funding, trade management, and government structures. They have not yet gone more deeply into issues of the regulatory factors that influence the micro-institutional structures of American capitalism. The United States has contradictory internal and external politics and goals: externally it wants other countries to become more Anglo-American in corporate organization—more aggressively antitrust legislation, more open markets for corporate control, more distance between finance and management, looser links among manufacturers and suppliers, more transparency of regulation. Internally, it wants to recast its own industrial structure to be more skillful at the game of managed international trade. To some degree this means allowing American firms to adopt Japanese and European modes of micro-organization, but nothing very clear has emerged in proposals on this front. The Administration is politically weak and lacks the consensus to go very far. It would take a far stronger sense of international challenge to mobilize the coalition for extensive microchanges of the kind recommended in the various reports on competitiveness. The Republican victory in the congressional elections of 1994 has shown the power of quite different ideas about national industry strategy: the new majority seeks to cut funding for public investment in new technologies and opposes, at least rhetorically, industrial policy.

European political parties have similar problems and challenges. There are too many situations and cases to support much in the way of generalization, but high unemployment and competition from Japan, the United States, and the NICs have clearly been challenging microfeatures of the postwar European "historical compromise." German industry and unions confront the highest tensions in many decades. This situation threatens the organization of labor markets, the role of unions in the firm, the relation between banks and companies, producers and suppliers—the entire network of high-wage/high-investment/stable employment that lies at the core of European policies in the strongest economies. One result could be the uncoupling of the micro-institutional linkages, making Europe look more like the United States. The contrary result could be to rework these linkages in new directions. Faced with these challenges, the political parties of Europe show great signs of stress.

A major element of comparison among capitalist democracies lies in their microeconomic institutions: the ways in which firms and industries are organized and the incentive systems that influence the behavior of all actors in the system of production. This element of comparison deserves more attention than the focus on macroeconomic policy in comparative political economy has given it. Microeconomic institutions are shaped in substantial measure by laws, rules, and policies formulated by the political system. An understanding of micro-institutions requires therefore an understanding of the political processes that produce them.

Other factors are certainly at play in shaping the political economy of these countries. Cultural traditions are powerful: countries have different traditions in networking, personal relationships, conception of authority, models of organizations and individuals. Macroeconomic policy is surely important. International rivalry and competition matter a great deal. The argument here is that to have a decisive impact, these factors must influence the regulatory system that shapes microeconomic structures.

Many of the advanced industrial democracies have had elections in recent years. The Japanese result is the most striking because it terminated four decades of rule by one party. These elections are one of the variables that will influence the regulatory structure of microeconomic variation among capitalist systems in the world economy. Change is most likely to occur when many forces support it: producer groups, consumers, parties, bureaucracies. All of the advanced capitalist countries are experiencing considerable pressure for change. Trade disputes and pressures have caused some discussion of altering the rules. The SII and the NAFTA discussions between the United States, Mexico, and Canada involve some adjustments in micro-institutions. But in both cases, the debates have been marginal. Most policy arguments on the economy continue to focus on macroeconomic issues and tariff levels.

In Europe the discussion of microstructures has been more extensive because of the EC agreement that requires harmonization of practices according to some common rules. On many areas there has been agreement to disagree. The conflicts over the single currency and the banking system show clearly the role of politics in maintaining differences.

The role of politics in shaping these microeconomic institutions has a substantial bearing on the convergence debate. Political factors are likely to preserve divergent regulatory systems. Constituencies, parties, and bureaucracies all have substantial investment in certain patterns. When they experience pressure to change, they may resist. Or they may change, but refract those pressures through existing arrangements. The results will therefore mostly likely be path dependent—altered by previous choices. The common pressures to which all advanced economies are subject will likely lead thereby to different versions of modernity and modernization.

Even with weaker political barriers to convergence, it is likely that differences in organizational form would continue. The notion of political barriers suggests that the differences are artificial, preserved only by rent-seeking political regimes. Yet the micro-organizational differences could be seen, rather, as rational, adaptive, and useful alternatives solutions to highly complex problems, allowing various equilibrium responses and favoring different mixes of values. Variation is likely to be a virtue. National differences in regulatory policy help to sustain diversity of organizational forms. Such variety provides benefits analogous to those of genetic diversity in nature—sustaining the bases for adaptation and change. Economic tasks vary fantastically. There is no reason to suppose that the organizational forms of rice farming, software writing, VCR manufacturing, rocket launching, filmmaking, restaurant serving, and steelmaking will all be the same. It has never been thus, and there is no reason to think it will become so. Countries have always varied the ways in which they do similar things. Diversity is thus a resource. Countries will retain some freedom to do what they want—or, more exactly, to do what political processes in each of them creates.

No matter how open and vigorous international economic pressure becomes, complete convergence in organizational form is thus most unlikely. The cues, the signals, from the market in relation to national regulatory policy are never likely to be perfectly clear. Actors are likely to have divergent understandings of the results of change. Practice and policies are thus likely to produce divergent regimes and systems. The particular mix in each country will turn on political entrepreneurship framed by the interaction among interests, institutions, and ideology in each system.

PART III

NEGOTIATED CONVERGENCE

Retail Convergence: The Structural Impediments Initiative and the Regulation of the Japanese Retail Industry

FRANK K. UPHAM

In virtually every democracy in the world small retailers have persuaded governments, at least from the early part of this century, to protect them from new forms of competition. Until recently this protection has not been an issue in the international trade debate. Services in general developed into a trade issue later than did goods, and within services attention has focused on the financial, insurance, and legal sectors, which have seemed more internationally fungible than the distribution industry. Whether or not there is something objectively more "international" about banking than retailing, the perception of retailing as a domestic industry and even as culturally specific to each nation is also the product of deliberate political action. Small merchants in every country have fostered the idea that the existence of neighborhood communities, the vitality of local democracy, and even the survival of national identity are tied to their own well-being and prosperity. Although this rhetoric was originally employed against domestic competition, it has been equally useful in keeping distribution generally off the international trade agenda.

This insulation ended when the Americans targeted Japan's distribution industry as part of the Structural Impediments Initiative (SII) in the late 1980s. With significant help from powerful allies within Japan, the Americans succeeded in convincing the Japanese government to reform the implementation and later the provisions of the Large Scale Retail Stores Law (LSRSL), which protects independent merchants in Japan by restricting the opening of large stores. The streamlining of the opening process, an increase in the number of

stores opening, and special provisions for foreign applicants represent
a shift in retail regulation in Japan and have been cited as evidence of
the convergence of the Japanese and American economies in the new
global economy

These developments moved Japan away from the European model
of strict regulation of retailing and toward the American model of
relative laissez-faire. They may also represent a significant victory for
American trade warriors. It is less clear, however, that they are an
example of true convergence in the systems and processes of the Japanese and American economies. The pace of store openings and the
openness to foreign entrants resemble the U.S. pattern, but the process and language of regulation used in Japan have changed little if at
all. The results of the process may be much more to the Americans'
liking, but whether the SII leads to convergence or just another U.S.–
Japanese bilateral deal remains to be seen.

THE STRUCTURAL IMPEDIMENTS INITIATIVE

Japan's persistent and structurally distinctive trade and current account surpluses have convinced many Americans that Japan represents a different form of capitalism that is immune to ordinary market forces. Throughout the 1970s and 1980s the American
government tried every conventional technique to reduce its deficit
with Japan, and by 1990 Japan had lowered its formal barriers below
the level of most of its trading partners. The deficit persisted, and
Congressional pressure to take punitive action mounted.[1]

By 1989 the Bush Administration had concluded that the lines between "international" and "domestic" and "culture" and "economics"
were no longer sacrosanct. On the contrary, the argument went, the
expansion of free trade and hence global welfare depended precisely
on the creation of a universal trading culture and the dismantling of
parochial institutions and customs that hindered the interpenetration
of economies. And so Japan became the object of the first explicit
attempt to reshape a trading partner's domestic institutions in the
name of free trade.

American negotiators chose five targets for reform under the SII:[2]

[1] For a brief account of the way in which congressional pressure influenced the creation of the SII, see Abbott B. Lipsky, Jr., "Current Developments in Japanese Competition Law: Antimonopoly Act Enforcement Guidelines resulting from the Structural
Impediments Initiative," Antitrust Law Journal 60 (1991): 280–81.
[2] There was a sixth item, pricing mechanisms, that the parties agreed to study further
jointly. See Mitsuo Matsushita, "The Structural Impediments Initiative: An Example of
Bilateral Trade Negotiation," Michigan Journal of International Law 12 (Winter 1991):
444.

(1) macroeconomic and public expenditure policy that favored savings over private consumption or infrastructure development; (2) land policies, including tax policy favoring farmers and residential housing laws favoring tenants; (3) the distribution system, particularly the use of the LSRSL to limit the growth of large retail outlets; (4) antitrust enforcement and the elimination of a wide range of exclusionary business practices; and (5) the range of intercorporate relationships, including reciprocal dealing and interlocking shareholding, known as *keiretsu*. Each of these was considered by the Americans to be a structural barrier to the entry of foreign goods, services, and investment into the Japanese market.[3]

The SII began in May 1989 against a backdrop of intense congressional pressure on the Bush administration to act against the Japanese under Super-301.[4] Although initially created cooperatively by the Japanese and American negotiators to mollify Congress and avoid a trade war, the SII was not the relaxed exchange of views that the Japanese had hoped for. The negotiators met three times over the year; Congress kept up the heat with hearings; and Bush invited Kaifu to Palm Springs to convey in person the need for concrete Japanese reforms by the summer.[5] As late as February, however, the Japanese were resisting any significant concessions, claiming that the American demands were unreasonable and intrusive.

The Final Report included promises of reform by the Japanese, but the degree of specificity and depth of contemplated action varied greatly across the five targeted areas.[6] In a study of the effect of American pressure in the SII, Leonard Schoppa has characterized the Americans as being successful in two areas, as gaining ambiguous compromises in a third, and as having largely failed in two.[7] In the area of macroeconomic policy, perhaps the issue most hotly resisted initially by the Japanese and particularly the Ministry of Finance, the parties agreed that there had been inadequate investment in public facilities such as roads, parks, sewage disposal, and housing and that Japan would increase its public expenditure by ¥430 trillion over the

[3] Since the SII was formally a two-way dialogue rather than unilateral American demands, negotiators also chose a corresponding set of issues for structural reform in the American economy. No one took this side of the negotiations seriously as anything beyond cosmetic, however, and I deal only with the Japanese side. For a summary of the impediments identified on the American side, see ibid.

[4] 19 U.S.C. § 2420 (1988).

[5] Leonard J. Schoppa, "Two-Level Games and Bargaining Outcomes: Why *Gaiatsu* Succeeds in Japan in Some Cases but Not Others," *International Organizations* 47, no. 3 (Summer 1993): 357.

[6] The report also announced that the two countries would continue research on the Americans' contention that there exists unjustified price differentials between them. See Matsushita, "Structural Impediments Initiative," p. 444.

[7] Schoppa, "Two-Level Games," p. 353.

next decade.[8] This promise by the Japanese constituted a reversal of its fiscal conservatism of the late 1980s and was a substantial concession by the Ministry of Finance.

In distribution the promised reforms were also impressive. The Americans argued that the distribution system played a substantial role in making Tokyo 97 percent more expensive to live in than New York. The most important measures were the reforms in the implementation and structure of the Large Scale Retail Stores Law itself, which I discuss in detail, but the Japanese also agreed to improve import-related infrastructure and streamline import and customs clearance procedures, to change restrictions on marketing and advertising that disadvantaged new entrants,[9] to relax controls on liquor licenses, and to increase enforcement of the Antimonopoly Law against anticompetitive behavior in the distribution sector.

In land policy the issues were complex. The Americans wanted to reduce the price of land both to lower the cost of direct foreign investment in Japan and to allow Japanese consumers to save less by lowering the price of homes. Land use policy, however, does not lend itself to simple solutions. It comprises a wide matrix of regulations and policies, including welfare concerns for residential tenants, environmental concerns about access to sunlight, construction standards dealing with issues as disparate as earthquake damage and traffic control, and differential taxation of different uses of similarly situated land. Many of the Americans' suggestions had already been put forward in the domestic debate, and they found allies in the National Land Agency and the Construction Ministry. The range of the interests involved in land policy, however, meant a range of opponents as well, and in the end Japan agreed only to a series of regulatory reviews and to be "more active" in the appropriation of land for public facilities. In the next two years, however, there were reviews of the provisions and implementation of the statutes concerning residential housing and urban land, and significant measures were taken to deregulate land use and increase the supply of land. Although causality remains unclear, these steps have been credited with contributing to a dramatic drop in land prices in the early 1990s.[10]

[8] Joint Report of the U.S.–Japan Working Group on the Structural Impediments Initiative (hereinafter the SII Report) 1990, I (1–9).

[9] These reforms included relaxing control over premium offerings and advertisement under the Law to Prevent Unreasonable Premium and Representation. See Matsushita, "Structural Impediments Initiative," p. 442. The law enabled the FTC to set ceilings on the premiums that companies could offer consumers to try a new product. American companies complained that the ceilings were deliberately set unreasonably low in order to prevent new products from gaining market share.

[10] SII Report, II (1–5). The statutes involved are the Shakuchi hô (Land Lease Law),

The results in the two areas dealing broadly with competition policy were more modest. In antitrust enforcement the Americans had complained about a range of private-sector practices that included the bid rigging in public projects known as *dango*; collusive arrangements to postpone the purchase of technically advanced foreign products until Japanese equivalents were available; cartels among declining industries that fixed prices and excluded imports; and producer-dominated distribution networks that excluded new entrants. These practices flourished, the Americans argued, because of weak enforcement of the Antimonopoly Law (AML) by the FTC. According to their criticisms, it was understaffed and underfunded, the legal sanctions at its disposal were inadequate to deter collusive behavior, and it was reluctant to use the tools that it did have. Furthermore, there was no credible threat of private antitrust actions by either consumers or competitors that might counterbalance the weakness of government enforcement.[11]

The Japanese response was lukewarm. For some, the idea of the formal, arms-length business relationships that animated trust busting and an American-style market economy was un-Japanese. Because informality had served Japan well for over forty years, even the FTC, which had the most to gain in terms of bureaucratic power, did not see these practices as either illegitimate or inefficient. Furthermore, unlike the case of the distribution industry and the LSRSL, where a single sector could be portrayed as exploiting informality to the detriment of the general economy, this attack was broad based and truly threatened the structure of large segments of the economy.[12]

The Japanese finally agreed to beef up the FTC and review the AML with an eye toward increasing its teeth. The FTC agreed to issue guidelines on collusive practices in two areas of particular interest to the Americans, distribution and *keiretsu*. Despite some evidence of increased FTC activity,[13] the general response has not been encouraging

Law #49, 1921, as amended, and the Shakka hô (House Lease Law), Law #50, 1921, as amended. See Matsushita, "Structural Impediments Initiative," p. 441 and Schoppa, "Two-Level Games," p. 362, n. 22.

[11] See Mark Morita, "Structural Impediments Initiative: Is It an Effective Correction of Japan's Antimonopoly Policy?" *University of Pennsylvania Journal of International Business Law* 12, no. 4 (1991): 777, and Schoppa, "Two-Level Games," p. 362.

[12] Eventually, the construction industry was subjected to the same style of criticism as the distribution industry, however, because of a series of financial and political scandals that exposed the construction industry's illicit influence over the Liberal Democratic Party and the economic cost of the *dango* system. At the time of the SII, however, it would have been difficult to isolate the construction industry and *dango* in the same manner as the Americans were able to do with the distribution industry.

[13] For example, in May 1993, in an action instigated by the FTC, the Tokyo High Court convicted fifteen executives of wrapping film companies of violating the AML by

to the Americans. Indeed, the initial draft of the guidelines on collusive behavior in the distribution sector was directed at foreign companies' use of sole distributorships. Given that the purpose of the SII was to address fundamental issues in the Japanese domestic economy, one American commentator found it "both surprising and in a sense inconsistent for the Fair Trade Commission to issue a set of Guidelines aimed almost exclusively at practices of foreign firms attempting to export to Japan."[14] In other areas of competition policy, the FTC's approach was more acceptable, but it was clear that there remained substantial conceptual differences in the two societies' views.[15]

On the *keiretsu* issue the Japanese did not agree that *keiretsu* are illegitimate or a barrier to trade. Indeed, many Japanese who had sided with the United States on other issues argued that the *keiretsu* were economically rational and that the United States itself would be better served by imitating them than by forcing Japan to eliminate its own. The Final Report, therefore, committed Japan only to enforcing the AML against exclusionary dealing and anticompetitive practices among *keiretsu* firms. In other words, the FTC would investigate the *keiretsu* and take appropriate enforcement action if it found illegal behavior. When in 1992 the FTC looked at the six major *keiretsu*, however, it found no illegal behavior, and virtually none of the Americans' original demands has been effectively addressed.[16]

Because of the depth and complexity of its penetration into domestic issues, the SII has been called unique in the history of trade negotiations.[17] Precisely because the United States and Japan do not share a common culture or history, it has become for some a model for general trade negotiations and an example of both the need for and the possibility of convergence over a broad range of formal and informal practices. In the words of University of Tokyo professor Mitsuo Matsushita, "differences in taxation, technical standards, industrial policies, the regulation of business activities, and business customs and corporate behavior may hinder the expansion of transnational business activities. In the future, therefore, reduction of such differences and the harmonization of national economic institutions will, in a broad sense, become increasingly necessary."[18]

---

establishing price cartels in 1990. This was only the second criminal conviction of business executives under the AML. "Court Rules against Wrapping Makers' Cartel," Jiji Press, Reuters, May 21, 1993.

[14] Lipsky, "Current Developments," p. 285.
[15] Among other items the increased fines and penalties were still much too low by American standards. See Schoppa, "Two-Level Games," p. 363.
[16] Ibid., pp. 363–64.
[17] Matsushita, "Structural Impediments Initiative," p. 436.
[18] Ibid., p. 437.

THE NATURE OF JAPANESE RETAIL REGULATION

The focus of both the regulatory system in the Japanese distribution industry and of American criticism was the LSRSL.[19] In its attempt to protect small independent merchants from larger chain stores, it was a response to the same political forces that have engendered similar efforts in virtually all capitalist democracies. In the 1920s and 1930s most American states disproportionately taxed chain stores in an attempt to slow the expansion of A&P and other mass retailers, and there still remain remnants of such protection in Sunday closing laws, land use policies, and some antitrust doctrines. In Europe protection for small merchants is commonplace, and statutes such as the French *Royer* law are in structure if not implementation quite similar to the LSRSL.

What distinguished the LSRSL from similar practices elsewhere, besides its connection to Japan's trade surplus, was more the law's implementation than its content. The statute itself may be similar to political and regulatory culture elsewhere, but the manner in which regional offices of the Ministry of International Trade and Industry (MITI) and local governments implemented it contrasts sharply with American practice. Instead of applying the statute in a manner consistent with its language, which would have meant a balance of openness and protection, MITI delegated its power under the law to the retailers themselves in a manner that resulted in a series of overlapping local, regional, and national cartels and a virtual ban on contested new large stores in established commercial areas.

THE HISTORY AND STRUCTURE OF THE LARGE SCALE RETAIL STORES LAW

Retailing has been heavily regulated throughout modern Japanese history, but the usual method up to the 1930s had been the organization of merchants in particular product lines into cooperatives, which then controlled the marketing of that product, including entry into the cooperative. The move of the department stores into mass retailing after World War I rendered these cartels ineffective and prompted independent merchants to demand some form of restriction on the expansion of department stores into established commercial areas. After several false starts, the Diet in 1937 passed the Department Store

[19] *Daikibo kouritenpo ni okeru kourigyô no jigyôkatsudô no chôsei nikansuru hôritsu* (The law concerning the adjustment of retail business operations in large-scale retail stores), Law #109 of 1973 (October 1, 1973).

Law (DSL), which required a permit for the opening or expansion of any department store.[20] Although repealed during the Allied Occupation as inconsistent with the economic ideology of the Americans, it was reenacted in 1956.

From 1956 to 1965, the DSL helped structure Japanese retailing in a way that served the interests of department stores and small retailers alike. The permit system cartelized department stores by restricting new entrants and guaranteeing the territory of existing branches. It simultaneously protected small merchants outside of the established commercial centers from high-volume, high-status competitors.

By the late 1960s, however, a new form of retailing known as "superstores" (suupaa) was breaking down the system. Superstores were mass merchandisers offering a product mix similar to department stores but without the fashionable image. They developed independently of the preexisting retail groups and expanded rapidly in the 1970s by exploiting the niche between department stores and independent neighborhood retailers. By 1981 six of the ten largest retailers in Japan were superstores (the remaining four were department stores), and superstores held 53 percent of the retail sales handled by the 100 largest retailers.[21]

Superstore chains were able to build large stores in new areas because of the clever exploitation of a loophole in the DSL. The DSL defined department stores as single units of more than 1,500 m^2. A superstore, on the other hand, consisted of several legal entities, each of less than 1,500 m^2, operating under a common corporate identity within a single building. The new corporate form made the DSL ineffective in protecting either department stores or small retailers, and by the late 1960s both were lobbying for its revision. Department stores wanted the inclusion of superstores in a more relaxed regulatory regime. Small retailers wanted strengthened restrictions that would cover all retailing. The superstores were satisfied with the status quo. The resulting compromise was the LSRSL of 1973.

There were three significant differences between the LSRSL and its

[20] The language of the resulting Department Store Law (Hyakkatenhô), passed that August, states well the basic premise of Japanese retail regulation: "On the one hand, it goes without saying that department stores contribute to the rationalization of the retail system and to the interests of consumers. On the other hand, however, they are managed on a large scale and operate with abundant capital and huge amounts of credit, and their rapid advance inevitably results in a substantial impact on numerous small and medium sized retail enterprises."

[21] Retailing in the Japanese Consumer Market (JETRO Marketing Series 5, 1985), pp. 25, 16. The top six superstores in 1982 were Daiei, Itô-yôkadô, Seiyû, Jusco, Nichii, and Unii. They were still the top six, in the same order, in 1988. Yomiuri Shimbun (New York ed.), 20 October, 1988, p. 6.

predecessor. First, it added the protection of consumer interests and the rationalization of the retailing industry to the purposes of the act. Second, it replaced the direct regulation of the permit system with a notification and adjustment system. Large stores were to notify MITI of their plans and participate in a process that would require any adjustments to their operating plans necessary to protect the area's small retailers. Third, the LSRSL shifted the target of regulation from the type of store (i.e., department stores) to the volume of retail activity by focusing on the amount of retail floor space in a single building and disregarding the legal nature of the store or stores within it.

Although its passage might be adequately explained as the result of a political struggle among department stores, small and medium retailers, and superstores, official MITI commentaries on the LSRSL invariably cited strengthened consumer protection and industry rationalization as statutory goals.[22] Besides guaranteeing small merchants an "enterprise opportunity," articles 1 and 11 of the law specifically required due consideration to the interests of consumers and to the well-being of the retail industry as a whole, which contributed to a generally positive initial appraisal of the law by economists and large retailers.[23] Even though these goals were potentially contradictory, observers contemplated the bureaucratic creation of a set of criteria that would balance these various interests in each individual case.

The procedural structure of the LSRSL before its reform during the SII included three stages: notification of the intention to build and operate a store; the adjustment of the proposed commercial activities of the new store with those of the existing merchants in the area; and enforcement.[24] The process began with notification to the regional office of MITI of the store's plans, including opening date, floor space, hours and days of operation, and so on. Then MITI forwarded the notifications to two tripartite deliberative councils, first, the Commercial Activities Adjustment Board established within the local Chamber of Commerce, and then the Large Scale Retail Stores

[22] See, for example, Jun Arima, "Ima gyôsei wa rigai no tairitsu suru daitenhô ni dô torikunde iru ka" (How will the bureaucracy deal with the large stores law as it is now the object of interest conflict?)" *Shôgyôkai* (The journal of retailing) 41, no. 4 (April 1988): 146. (Arima was then a MITI official involved in LSRSL policymaking.) See also "Tsûshôsangyôshô [MITI], Daitenhô kankei shiryô" (Materials concerning the large stores law), (Tokyo: unpub. material, 1988), p. 3. Hereafter cited as MITI Materials.
[23] Toshimasa Tsuruta, "Kokusaikajidai no daitenhô wa dôarubekika" (What should the LSL be like in the age of internationalization?), *Ekonomisuto*, 13 December 1988, p. 47.
[24] Article 2 of the law distinguishes between class-one stores, those over 1,500 m², and class-two stores, those between 1,500 m² and 500 m². For purposes of simplicity, the following description deals primarily with the construction and operation of a new class-one retail outlet.

Deliberative Council at the prefectural level. Made up of merchants, consumers, and representatives of the public interest, these councils were to bring the sides together to determine whether the plans should be adjusted to lessen the impact on local merchants. They then submitted their opinion to MITI, which made its independent judgment based on the criteria of the statute. If it concluded that adjustment was necessary, it issued a recommendation (*kankoku*) that the store make the needed changes.

A recommendation had no legal force; a retailer could violate its terms without legal liability or being subject to MITI sanctions. If it did so, however, MITI had the power to issue a subsequent order, which did have compulsory force. The statute contemplated that the entire process from notification through enforcement would normally take no more than eight months.

Commercial Adjustment under the Large Stores Law

Implementation under the LSRSL during the 1980s had only a loose relationship to its formal structure. The shift from the licensing system of the DSL to the notification system of the LSRSL ostensibly meant that government intervention would be the exception rather than the rule, and an emphasis on free market principles played a role in convincing large retailers and others to support the law. At the same time that it was extolling free market competition to the large retailers, however, MITI and the Liberal Democratic Party were promising small retailers that the notification system would operate "almost like a permit system."[25] Throughout the 1980s MITI more than fulfilled this promise and oversaw the creation of a system that erected barriers to entry into the retail industry far surpassing those of the DSL in everything but formal legal authority.

Although MITI's creative interpretation of the draft legislation may have helped the LDP to pass it, it was not successful in preventing criticism thereafter. In the first five years of operation, almost 1,500 new large stores opened under the law, approximately doubling the number existing prior to 1974, and many chain retailers began avoiding the law altogether by shifting to stores of just under 1,500 m^2.[26] In response, local governments passed ordinances and administrative guidance restricting stores of less than 1,500 m^2, and independent retailers began pushing hard for extended coverage and tighter re-

[25] "'Gekishin' ima, ryûtsûga kawaru" ('Severe earthquake' now, distribution changes), *Shûkan Tôyôkeizai*, 6 August 1988, p. 8. "Kagirinaku kyôkasei ni chikai todokedesei ni suru," p. 9.
[26] Tsuruta, "Kokusaikajidai," p. 49.

strictions on new entrants into the industry.[27] By 1977 the Diet had passed a resolution urging action to protect small retailers, and MITI had established a series of study commissions on the "retail problem."[28] In 1978 the Diet extended the LSRSL's coverage from stores of more than 1,500 m² to all stores of more than 500 m², and small retailers began to call for the return to the permit approach of the DSL and a reorientation to regulate stores on the basis of type as well, thus targeting the new convenience store threat.[29]

Recourse to the Diet was unnecessary, for MITI restructured the regulatory scheme and met small retailers' demands without any legislative action. Part of MITI's efforts consisted of administrative guidance frontloading and extending the adjustment process so that large retailers had to begin negotiations with their rivals before officially notifying MITI of their plans.

Actual MITI practice, however, ignored both the statute and the ministry's own official guidance. One consistent feature was the removal of real power under the LSRSL from the regional MITI bureaus and their statutory advisory councils to local merchants operating under the umbrella of the chamber of commerce. Beginning in 1979 and accelerating in the 1980s, MITI refused to accept a retailer's statutory notification unless he or she appended a document setting forth the terms under which local merchants agreed to the new store's opening.[30] As a result, even the prenotification adjustment envisioned by the administrative guidance became a meaningless formality, replaced by an even more informal process known as "pre-prenotification adjustment."

At this stage, before any formal steps had been taken under the law, the large store and local merchants entered into negotiations on the conditions under which the latter would agree to the opening of the new store. Sometimes these negotiations were carried out by the members of the formal Commercial Activities Adjustment Board (CAAB) but more frequently by local merchants themselves organized as, for example, a "Large Store Countermeasures Task Force" or "Large Scale Retail Stores Policy Subcommittee" loosely affiliated with the local chamber of commerce.

---

[27] *Tsûshôsangyôshô sangyôseisakukyoku, daikibo kouri tenpo chôseikan* (MITI Industrial Policy Bureau, Large Scale Retail Stores Adjustment Office), *Shin Daikibo kouri tenpohô no kaisetsu* (New explanation of the Large Scale Retail Stores Law), p. 3.

[28] Ibid.

[29] See in general Ken'ichi Miyazawa, "Endaka keizaika de henyô suru ryûtsûkikô" (Changing structure of distribution under high yen), *Ekonomisuto*, 13 December 1988, pp. 58–59, and Masanori Tamura, "Chûshôgyôsha suitai saseta daitenhô" (The large stores law that causes small enterprises' decline)," *Nihon Keizai Shimbun*, 24 October 1988.

[30] Tsuruta, "Kokusaikajidai," p. 48.

FRANK K. UPHAM

A summary account of one large store's struggle to open illustrates the process.[31] On November 26, 1980, Summit Stores, a superstore chain related to the Sumitomo *keiretsu*, submitted its plans for an outlet in an area known as Higashi Nakano near the border of the Nakano and Shinjuku wards in downtown Tokyo. Ten days later local merchants formed two "countermeasures task forces" to oppose the opening. Over the next two years opponents repeatedly frustrated Summit's efforts to explain their plans and to negotiate with local merchants and with ward officials. Demonstrators picketed and disrupted public meetings and brought intense pressure on Summit's prospective landlord and his family—physically harassing him at public meetings, constantly telephoning his home, and eventually ostracizing his family to the extent that they were unable to shop in the area. When these efforts failed to dissuade the landlord and Summit, local merchants persuaded politicians to bring pressure on Sumitomo Shôji, Summit's parent company.

Eventually, two years after the initial announcement, negotiations with the countermeasures task forces began in earnest. By 1986 Summit had agreed to reduce its floor space, operating hours, and operating days and was able to persuade the Nakano ward merchants to agree. The Shinjuku opponents wanted further reassurances, however, and it was not until September 1986 that Summit filed its notification of proposed store opening as required by article 3 of the LSRSL. The Commercial Activities Adjustment Board discussed the Higashi Nakano Summit store for the first time at its monthly meeting on October 24, discussed it again on November 28, and approved the negotiated plan on December 19. Although by this time, construction was complete and the store ready for opening, further opposition meant that the store did not finally open until October 10, 1987, during which period Summit had to pay ¥150 million in rent for an empty building. According to Summit sources, the entire process included over 500 meetings with ward officials, task force representatives, politicians, and innumerable informal meetings with local notables.

There are three points to emphasize in this story. First, the length of the process. It became common for negotiations to take seven to eight years and delays of ten years were not unheard of, periods that are in stark contrast to the seven to eight months contemplated by the statute.

Second, it was not until six years into the process and after the agreement had been fully negotiated that the statutory procedure be-

[31] This account is taken from materials supplied to the author by NHK, Japan's national broadcasting company. It was confirmed in substance by an interview with Summit Store personnel.

274

gan with the discussions of the Commercial Activities Adjustment Board. The decisions were made not according to legal criteria by the regional MITI office in consultation with the local CAAB and the regional Large Stores Council, but by private bargaining among the large and small retailers themselves. The statutory procedure was essentially irrelevant to the result.

Third, the resulting agreements under the LSRSL reflected the veto power given to local power brokers by MITI more than legislative policy. They covered not only the four statutory items covered by adjustment (opening date, floor space, daily hours, and annual days of operation) but also frequently extended to matters wholly unrelated to the provisions of the law. They included, for example, requirements that the new store include specified local merchants as subtenants on favorable terms; make large "donations" to local merchants groups; not carry certain items or lines of products; reserve space in the store for community groups; or maintain prices or services at the same level as surrounding merchants.[32]

THE LEGAL NATURE OF THE ADJUSTMENT PROCESS

Given the gap between the goals of the LSRSL and the actuality of its operation, one might expect that one or more of the many individuals and groups injured by the process would have convinced the courts to force MITI to implement the statute in accord with its content and intent. Just as in the United States, if a Japanese plaintiff can show that a government act violates the statute on which it is based, a court will nullify it, and a common way to demonstrate illegality is to show that the government agency has used the wrong criteria or followed incorrect procedures in making a decision. Why no one successfully brought such an action against the implementation of the LSRSL can be illustrated by the litigation that grew out of the opening of a store in Etsurigo Village, Iwate Prefecture.[33]

On March 20, 1979, the Etsurigo Shopping Center Cooperative notified MITI of its plan to build a three-story shopping complex with the superstore Jusco as its anchor tenant but including also a coalition

---

[32] *Seifukisei nado to kyôsôseisaku ni kansuru kenkyûkai* (Research committee on governmental regulation and competition policy), *Kiseikanwa no suishin ni tsuite* (In regards to the promotion of deregulation) (Tokyo, 1989) (hereinafter cited as FTC Report). This research committee is a creation of the FTC. It contains several case studies of the operation of the LSRSL.

[33] For background on the litigation, see Tadashi Matsumoto, "Meikaku ni sareta daitenhô no fubi" (The clear defects of the large stores law), *Hanrei Taimuzu*, 1 May 1982: p. 71.

of local tenants. MITI recommended that Jusco reduce somewhat both its floor space and operating hours. Jusco accepted the terms, and the complex was clear to open by the beginning of 1980. The whole process took less than nine months.

In January 1981 one hundred and seventeen local merchants sued for the nullification of MITI's recommendation. They claimed that it did not preserve for local small merchants the "enterprise opportunity" guaranteed by article 1 of the LSRSL and that the process by which the recommendation was formed violated both the statute and the detailed regulations stipulating how adjustment was to be conducted. They argued that the advisory councils were packed either with persons with a financial interest in the proposed complex or who were chosen for pro–shopping center views. They supported their conflict of interest claim with allegations of procedural irregularities and a total lack of oversight by MITI.

Reports on practices elsewhere under the LSRSL leave little doubt that the plaintiffs' factual claims were largely accurate and that the facts amounted to a blatant conflict of interest on the part of the board members and a clear abdication of statutory duties by MITI. Such procedural abuses would probably have been enough to convince the courts to declare the whole process illegal. Because the doctrines of Japanese administrative law so restrict judicial review of government action, however, it made little difference what improprieties the plaintiffs might have been able to prove. In the end the District and High Courts had little trouble in either rejecting the local merchants as proper plaintiffs or finding that the MITI recommendation to Jusco was not the type of administrative act that could be challenged in court.[34]

The Administrative Case Litigation Law (ACLL), which governs judicial review of bureaucratic action in Japan, requires a plaintiff to show both that the allegedly illegal act is the type of official conduct that a court can review and that the plaintiff is the appropriate person to seek review. Based on an extremely rigid interpretation of the statutory language, Japanese courts have historically limited judicial review to a very narrow range of official behavior and have denied standing to bring an action to all but the most directly related parties. Under this interpretation, the only potential plaintiff under the LSRSL would be a prospective large retailer in the position of Jusco in *Etsurigo*, dissatisfied with the amount of space given him through the adjustment process. Even then, the retailer could not challenge the

---

[34] For a fuller discussion of doctrines governing judicial review of administrative action in Japan, see Frank K. Upham, "After Minamata: Current Prospects and Problems in Japanese Environmental Litigation," *Ecology Law Quarterly* 8 (1979): 213.

recommendation directly because he would not have had any legal obligation to follow it. He would have to defy the recommendation and wait until MITI issued a legally binding order under article 8.

The problem is that MITI has rarely, if ever, resorted to a formal order in the implementation of the LSRSL.[35] Large retailers invariably either reached a compromise with local merchants, waited it out, or gave up. According to the "pre-prenotification" procedures in effect during most of the 1980s and exemplified by the account of the Higashi Nakano Summit store, MITI did not even accept notifications from retailers without an appended agreement with local merchants. Under these circumstances there was no formal involvement in the enforcement of the statute until the deal had been cut. At this point, the prospective store would make the formal notification under article 3, and the CAAB and Large Stores Council would provide perfunctory screening and discussion. As in the Summit store instance, however, their involvement and that of MITI itself rarely amounted to more than a rubberstamp of a privately negotiated deal. Because of Japan's law governing judicial review of administrative action, both the private deal itself and MITI's delegation of public power to private parties that it represents remain virtually impervious to judicial review and therefore to citizen attack via judicial review.[36]

THE STRUCTURAL EFFECT OF THE LARGE SCALE RETAIL STORES LAW

The courts' tolerance of this regulatory approach meant that MITI could implement the LSRSL to respond freely to changing circumstances. Consequently, by the early 1980s barriers to entry into the retail market were stricter under the free market principles of the

[35] I have not found a single instance of MITI issuing an Article 8 order under the LSRSL.

[36] Two qualifications to the statement that judicial review is unavailable are necessary. First, in administrative law theory, a large retailer could have attempted to notify MITI without appending the required agreement with local merchants and, when MITI refused to accept the notification, sued to force MITI action. Second, a plaintiff could sue for monetary damages in a civil action, rather than for a declaration of administrative illegality in an administrative action. Even though neither of these types of litigation would have much immediate legal effect on its policies, MITI would consider either as a direct and political attack on its policies and would be likely to retaliate if possible. Although these circumstances make such suits rare, they also can make them politically effective when the plaintiff has the resources and independence to challenge the government openly and dramatically. In the LSRSL context, Life Stores, a superstore chain, did indeed sue MITI on the basis of its general implementation of the statute. Although legally ineffective, it may have had some minimal effect as political protest. (It was withdrawn after the SII reforms.)

LSRSL than they had been under the explicit government licensing of the DSL. The number of class-one stores making notification under the law dropped from a high of 576 in 1979 to 132 in 1982 and 125 in 1983. Thereafter it remained below 200 until the late 1980s. In 1990, after the law had become a trade issue and Japan had promised the United States that it would relax restrictions, it jumped to a pace of over 1,000 openings per year.

These figures demonstrate MITI's ability to respond to political pressure and its effectiveness in preventing specific commercial activity without recourse to formal legal measures. After independent merchants were successful in convincing the LDP and cabinet to tighten restrictions on new stores in the late 1970s, MITI was able to cut the number of notifications by 75 percent and then hold it steady through the 1980s. Then when the political pressure reversed and it became necessary to demonstrate good will to the Americans, it increased the number several fold in the space of months. To accomplish these shifts, MITI relied solely on administrative measures and negotiations with the leading chains.

Whatever its long-term social and economic contribution to Japanese social welfare, Japan's distribution system was woefully inefficient by conventional economic measures and was often cited as such by foreign and domestic critics alike. In its "Cost of Living '88" report, for example, the Economic Planning Agency estimated that the cost of living in Tokyo was 97 percent higher than in New York and traced part of the cause to the distribution system generally and to the LSRSL specifically. It attributed 40 and 59 percent of the retail prices of domestic and imported goods, respectively, to distribution costs and estimated that 30 percent of the savings theoretically achievable by the rise of the yen between 1985 and 1987 had been absorbed by the distribution sector rather than passed on to the consumer.

Many factors contributed to high prices, including a multilayered and inefficient wholesale sector and the range of government policies that facilitated producer domination of the distribution industry. But distribution costs were also attributed directly to the LSRSL and the fragmented and small-scale retail sector that it had helped to preserve. In 1982, for example, the number of retail stores per capita was 75 percent higher in Japan than in the United States, the next highest country, and the value added per employee was 28 percent less. Stores with only one or two employees accounted for 60 percent of all stores and yet generated less than 14 percent of all sales. Conversely, the 1,754 largest stores, with less than 400,000 employees, sold 40 percent as much as the almost 1.5 million smallest stores and their over 3 million employees. The annual sales per employee in the largest stores was more than four times that of those in the smallest.

Only the very naive, however, would have expected MITI's management of the LSRSL to contribute to either consumer interests or the healthy, in the sense of market-conforming, development of general retailing. The real test of the law and of MITI's management is whether it protected the small and independent merchants whose political clout helped to pass it in 1973 and convinced the LDP and MITI to strengthen it in the late 1970s. By this standard the results were mixed. Certainly, the small retailers who were included as tenants in new retail complexes or received direct payoffs benefited from the law. Those small retailers in areas where new stores were excluded entirely or were forced into price or merchandise cartels with local merchants also benefited at least in the short run. But the ability of the law to ensure "enterprise opportunities" for small independents was limited. The number of small retailers began to decline for the first time in Japanese history after 1982, a period of very tight restrictions under the LSRSL.

Few of those directly involved were dissatisfied with the LSRSL during the 1980s. Small merchants complained about its inability to protect them from a decline in absolute numbers, but they vigorously defended the law when it came under attack. Large retailers complained about the arbitrary power granted small merchants but did not generally oppose the law or call for its repeal. Besides its disguised shift of wealth from consumers to retailers, the law had helped large retailers to form an effective cartel.[37] During the late 1970s, when MITI had allowed large stores to open more freely, there had been intense competition, reduced profits, and frequent fluctuation in the ranking of the top ten stores. In the 1980s, by contrast, the ranking of the largest retailers remained essentially stable, and by 1988 the superstores had registered their highest profits in history.[38]

THE PROCESS OF CHANGE

Despite a general reluctance to embrace liberalization within the distribution industry, the Americans had allies when they chose the LSRSL to be part of the SII. In 1988–89 the *Nihon Keizai Shimbun*, the

[37] On the cartelization of large retailing, see Miyazawa, "Endaka keizaika," 60; "Kagirinaku," 11–12; Tsuruta, "Kokusaikajidai," 51; *Nihon Keizai Shimbun*, 21 October 1988; Tamura, "Chûshôgyôsha"; and *Nihon Keizai Shimbun*, 28 November 1988.

[38] "Taoreru daitenhô-jô (The toppling LSRSL-I), p. 6. *Yomiuri Shimbun*, 20 October 1988.

Keidanren, the Economic Planning Agency (EPA), the FTC, and the second Administrative Reform Commission (Shingyôkakushin) all called for varying degrees of relaxation of the law.[39] All cited the heavy toll on Japanese consumers, especially the gap between dropping import prices and high retail prices, and the unfairness and anti-import bias inherent in the implementation of the law.

Although most critics made only vague appeals for more flexibility or increases in permissible operating hours for large retailers, the EPA and the FTC both called for the eventual repeal of the LSRSL and total liberalization of the retail industry. By November 1988 the Administrative Reform Commission recommended a series of bureaucratic measures that together meant a thorough reform of MITI implementation of the LSRSL, eliminating required negotiations with small merchants, formalizing and shortening the process to represent better consumer interests, and easing local regulation.[40]

As the direct target of the small retailers' displeasure, MITI's views were somewhat different. In a December 1988 interview, Michinao Takahashi, MITI's councilor for commercial distribution, responded to American criticism by pointing to the rising share of imports in the total retail sales of superstores and department stores and by reiterating the special circumstances that made the current rate of about 200 new large stores per year appropriate for Japan: "Japanese retailing is characterized by many stores of extremely small scale densely packed into small land areas. If you look at it from this perspective, some adjustment of commercial interests is necessary within each area and the LSRSL is one way to accomplish that. If large stores were completely free to open, it would plunge local business into chaos."[41] Even Takahashi, however, recognized that the delays and conflicts currently

[39] See "Reform Distribution Now," *The Japan Economic Journal,* 25 March 1989, p. 10; Keizai Koho Center, "Deregulating Distribution: Keidanren Proposals for Transport, Trade, Retailing, and Farming and Food Processing," *KKC Brief No. 48* (The Japan Institute for Social and Economic Affairs, July 1988), hereafter cited as Keidanren Proposals; Keizaikikakuchô bukkakyoku bukkakanrishitsu (Economic Planning Agency Cost of Living Bureau, Cost of Living Management Office), *Kaihōgata ryūtsū shisutemu no kōchiku ni mukete* (Toward the construction of a liberalized retail system) (Tokyo: Shojihomu kenkyukai, 1988), table 2, p. 53, hereafter cited as EPA Report; Seifukisei nado to kyōsōseisaku ni kansuru kenkyūkai (Research committee on governmental regulation and competition policy), *Kiseikanwa no suishin ni tsuite* (In regard to the promotion of deregulation) (Tokyo 1989), hereafter cited as FTC Report. The salient points of the second Administrative Reform Commission's position are summarized in *Nihon Keizai Shimbun,* 13 November 1988, p. 7.
[40] "Gyôkakushin hôkokusho no yôshi" (The gist of the administrative reform commission report), *Nihon Keizai Shimbun,* 13 November 1988, p. 7.
[41] Michinao Takahashi, "Unyô no 'kaizen' de daitenhô wa sonzoku suru" (With "reform" in implementation, the large stores law will continue), interview, *Ekonomisuto,* 13 December 1988, p. 56.

caused by the LSRSL were excessive and that some reforms were necessary, although he took pains to stress that complete deregulation was premature.

MITI's draft of its "Vision of the Distribution System in 1990s" showed that it had realized that substantial reform was inevitable. The emphasis had shifted from protecting small merchants through the LSRSL to helping them to modernize and adjust to emerging technologies and new relationships between producers and distributors. Aid to small retailers was to come more through various subsidies and infrastructure improvements than through restrictions on their large competitors. One section even proposed measures to retrain merchants and ease their exit from the industry.[42]

It was not surprising, therefore, that the ministry announced a series of short- and long-term reforms in May 1990 as part of the SII package. First, steps would be taken under current law to make opening a large store quicker and easier. Next, MITI would submit to the 1991 regular session of the Diet amendments to the LSRSL that would further streamline the process. Finally, MITI pledged to reevaluate fundamentally its policy toward the retail industry within three years, including consideration of total liberalization.

The immediate measures meant substantial changes in the operation of the law. First, MITI announced that it would accept all notifications regardless of the area, an implicit acknowledgment of the illegality of its former system of "self-restraint zones," where authorities had refused to accept any notifications whatsoever. Second, MITI changed the process of commercial adjustment to limit the notification stage to four months and to eliminate the requirement of the local merchants' consent. If they remained dissatisfied, the formal process moved to the next stage nonetheless. The entire process from initial announcement of intention by the large retailer to the final decision was to take no more than eighteen months.

MITI also increased immediately the hours and days of operation for large stores and exempted retail space devoted to imports from the law in certain circumstances. It also initiated measures to increase the "transparency" of the process by requiring quarterly reports on the status of pending notifications, establishing a bureau within MITI to answer inquiries regarding notifications, and providing for limited disclosure of the results of meetings of the various entities involved in the adjustment process.

MITI explained these measures to the Americans as the maximum

---

[42] *Summary of MITI's Vision for the Distribution System in the 1990s* (provisional translation), received from MITI and on file with the author.

change possible under the LSRSL.[43] They were not. Not only was the eighteen-month deadline almost double the maximum time anticipated by the statute itself, but the liberalized hours and days of operation were well short of what MITI could have established by simply revising its ministerial order. Furthermore, true transparency remained impossible as long as the informal and nonstatutory prenotification explanation meetings were a significant part of the process. If MITI had simply decided to follow the formal process delineated by the law, the degree of liberalization and transparency would have been much greater, but to do so might have meant an unacceptable increase in the speed of reform.

Nonetheless, the results were dramatic. In the first six months following the measures over 900 prospective new large stores were announced, more than double that of the previous year and more than nine times the rate of 1982–85.[44] The American toy retailer, Toys R' Us, became the first foreign store to be allowed to open under the LSRSL and announced that it planned 100 stores by the end of the decade. Large Japanese retailers also reported that the adjustment process had become easier.[45] Small merchants and local governments accelerated the trend toward using large stores as the nucleus for the revitalization of established areas, and trade associations for small and medium retailers came to lobby on the national level for various forms of subsidies to replace the declining protection of the law.

In December 1990 MITI through a joint report by subcommittees of the Industrial Structure Council and the Small and Medium Enterprise Policy Council announced an amendment of the LSRSL to be submitted to the Diet in 1991. The eighteen-month period for store opening established in May was to be further shortened to one year and increases in floor space devoted to import goods further liberalized. To streamline the process prenotification explanation and negotiation, which had taken up to ten years in the mid-1980s, were eliminated. Most important to the shortening of the process and to increased transparency was the elimination of the local Commercial Activities Adjustment Boards. Initial deliberation on the impact on local retailers and consideration of reductions in size or operating conditions were to be performed by the regional Large Stores Council.

[43] MITI's exact language from its English-language explanation was, "These are the maximum measures which are legally possible under the current Large-Scale Retail Store Law."
[44] "Store Opening Announcements Double of Last Year," *Yomiuri Shimbun* (New York ed.), 6 December 1990, p. 1.
[45] "'Store Opening Adjustment Shortened,' Say Super Stores," *Yomiuri Shimbun* (New York ed.), 6 December 1990, p. 6.

In May 1991 the Diet passed a series of bills effective February 1992 that largely carried out MITI's proposals.[46] If implemented in accord with their spirit, these amendments would mean a significant change in the nature of retail regulation in Japan. The replacement of the boards and the elimination of the prenotification stage would mean that MITI and the Large Store Council would make the substantive decisions required by the statute. Instead of forcing large retailers to negotiate with their competitors, both sides would present their case to a supposedly neutral decision-making body in a process that would be considerably more open and accountable than its predecessor. In themselves these modifications may not necessarily mean a greater number of large store openings or any substantive change in the results of the process. Although the small retailers will no longer directly control the process, they may continue to wield considerable power in localities where they can convince the general population or the local government to oppose a large store's opening. In practice, however, the procedural regularity and the clear deadlines for action would likely mean that the retailing industry would develop in closer conformity with the "natural" demands of the market than under the LSRSL as it operated until 1990.

The first two years of operation under the revised statute gave some reason to conclude that the promise of a significant increase in store openings would be fulfilled. From February 1992 through April 1993 over 360 class-one stores and almost 1,400 class-two stores notified MITI of their intent to open. This annual rate of about 300 class-one stores was 50 percent higher than the average during much of the 1980s. Although lower than the rush of notifications immediately following the SII agreement, this figure was particularly noteworthy given the dismal state of retailing in Japan in the early 1990s. By August 1993 department stores and superstores had suffered eighteen and twelve straight months of declining sales, respectively. For them to expand at a rate 50 percent higher than five years earlier when the general economy and retailing in particular were booming is persuasive evidence at least that the regulatory scheme is no longer the barrier that it once was.

Initial data on the nature of the LSRSL adjustment process, as opposed to the absolute number of stores opening, show a somewhat more mixed picture. MITI officials report that the store opening process averages seven to eight months with the maximum being a year,[47] and a 1993 Keidanren evaluation of the reform agreed that the pro-

---

[46] "'Shortened Procedure' Expected of MITI," *Yomiuri Shimbun* 9 May 1991, p. 6.
[47] Interviews by the author in August 1993 in Tokyo.

cess was generally completed within one year.[48] The picture is murkier if we look not at the length of the process but at its results. One MITI official involved in the law's implementation in the Kanto Region, which includes greater Tokyo, noted in 1993 that 90 percent of notified changes under the law took place upon notification only, without any government action whatsoever. Most notifications are minor, however, and recommendations for reductions in hours or floor space for new stores reportedly remain common. In fact, reductions in floor space and operating hours are an increasing problem according to a 1994 survey of MITI's regional offices. The percentage of cases where proposed floor space was reduced had risen from less than a quarter in January 1992–March 1993, the first fourteen months of the revised LSRL, to almost 40 percent in the next year.[49]

A major factor in the acceleration of the process has been the elimination of the local Commercial Activities Adjustment Boards and the change in local merchants' role. The Boards' elimination was intended to take the deliberative process out of the control of the small retailers, the parties with the greatest personal stake in the outcome, and transfer it to the regional Large Store Councils, which were expected to be more sensitive to consumer interests and the demands of the market. Local merchants retain the right to appeal to the Councils, however, and the increasing number of forced reductions indicate that small retailers will presumably retain substantial power.

This type of political influence is at the heart of local democracy and necessary to preserving the "enterprise opportunities" of area merchants, one of the statutory goals of the LSRSL, and one would not expect controversial store openings to proceed without conflict. The problem, therefore, is not forced compromises per se but the unchanged legal nature of the consultative process, which raises questions as to the permanence and depth of the reform. One of the goals of the SII both generally and with specific reference to the LSRSL was administrative transparency, and many advocates for change had argued that only an open process could prevent the participation of local businesspeople from evolving into extortion and corruption. The statutory revisions, however, maintained the closed nature of the process to the extent that the record of consultation with the chamber

---

[48] Daikibo kouritenpohô kaisei no hyôka, Keidanren sangyôkibanbu (Evaluation of revision of LSRSL), Keidanren, August 1993. Because all "prenotification" requirements have been eliminated, these time periods are an accurate measure of the actual time from Article Three notification to completion. Previous official estimates of delays often ignored the prenotification negotiations, which could take years.

[49] "Hirogaru ōgataten funsō—I" (Spreading large store conflict—I), *Nihon Keizai Shimbun*, 22 November 1994, p. 15; and "Hirogaru ōgataten funsō—II" (Spreading large store conflict—II), *Nihon Keizai Shimbun*, 23 November 1994, p. 10.

of commerce is not open to public scrutiny, and the 1993 Keidanren analysis cautioned that there is the potential that the gathering of opinions by a compromised Large Stores Council could become a smoke screen for the kind of bartering among retailers that characterized the battle over the Higashi Nakano Summit store and that the revisions were meant to eliminate.[50]

As long as the Americans, the FTC, and the large retailers force MITI to supervise the process in conformity with the spirit of the reform, there is no reason to believe that such abuse will occur on a large scale. The problem with the 1980s practice, after all, was not MITI's role in mediating among interests, but the fact that MITI abdicated this role and left private parties to buy and sell public power—the right to deny or allow commercial activity—with no ongoing public oversight. In this light the elimination of the Commercial Activity Adjustment Boards becomes doubly important: it not only deprives the local merchants of a convenient organizing locus, but it also takes some of the most direct political pressure off local MITI offices.

The legal nature of the process, on the other hand, has not changed, and the continuing secrecy and unaccountability of bureaucratic action insulate the process from legal review and buffer it from public scrutiny to a degree that opens the door to other forms of abuse. The whole point of requiring a public record of the consultative process was to ensure that MITI and its satellite organs abide by the criteria of the statute and to open their interpretation and implementation of those criteria to public access and debate.[51] As long as they remain closed, outsiders remain blocked from the important information that will enable them to understand how and why a particular result emerges.

Furthermore, even when illegitimate motives or distorted procedures are exposed, they will be protected from judicial review by the same administrative law doctrines that prevented effective challenge to the implementation of the old LSRSL. The reforms did nothing either to expand standing to challenge biased decision making as occured in the *Etsurigo* case or to bring under judicial scrutiny legally informal bureaucratic acts such as article 7 recommendations to reduce floor space or operating hours. Even though the structural

---

[50] Daikibo kouritenpohô kaisei no hyôka.

[51] In this respect the 1994 *Nihon Keizai Shimbun* survey reported that the chair of one Large Stores Council in western Japan stated, "Unfortunately there is no objective basis for determining how far floor space should be reduced. Commercial data and the like are useless so we've never used them. In most cases we just follow local opinion, chiefly that of the merchants." *Nihon Keizai Shimbun*, 23 November 1994, p. 15.

weakening of the small retailers may prevent the store-by-store cartelization of the past, the continuing and perhaps enhanced influence of
the large chains may lead to different arrangements equally far from
the statute's language. Given that the locally bargained cartels of the
old LSRSL were accompanied by a national cartel of the large stores
orchestrated by MITI in Tokyo, there is reason to wonder whether
the natural inclination of the chains to seek the security of cartelization will be resisted by MITI in the long run. This concern is especially great when one notes that opportunities of *amakudari*, Japanese
bureaucrats' "descent from the heaven" of public service to lucrative
positions in the private sector, with leading retailers are considerably
more attractive than those offered by associations of small merchants.

INTERPRETING REGULATION UNDER THE LSRSL

The characteristics of MITI's implementation of the LSRSL in the
1980s reflect the general nature of Japanese economic regulation in
both its processes and its goals.[52] A fundamental characteristic of the
process is its legal informality: MITI uses legally voluntary administrative guidance in virtually all circumstances, including those where
there is formal legal power available to achieve the same end. It does
so when it is acting to enforce an agreement with a trade association
as when it enforced the petroleum refiners' gasoline import cartel in
the Lions Oil incident.[53] It does so when it is responding to the concerns of Liberal Democratic politicians, as was arguably the case in the
implementation of the LSRSL. And it does so when it is acting at the
behest of foreign governments, as in the voluntary restraint agreement in automobiles initiated in 1980–81.[54]

The implications of informality for the regulatory process are profound and complex. Most directly, informality insulates the bureaucracy and its clients from judicial review. If MITI were subject to legal
attack, it would have to defend both broad policy and each separate
action in the terms of legal formality. It would have to justify its policies by reference to the language of the statute and the disposition of
each individual case by reference to the rhetoric of the rule of law—

[52] Tamura, "Chûshôgyôsha." See Frank K. Upham, *Law and Social Change in Postwar
Japan* (Cambridge: Harvard University Press, 1987), chap. 5, for a fuller discussion of
these characteristics.
[53] Frank K. Upham, "The Man Who Would Import: A Cautionary Tale about Buck-
ing the System in Japan," *Journal of Japanese Studies* 17, no. 2 (Summer 1991).
[54] See exchange of letters among Senator Levin, Attorney General French, and Ambassador Odamura concerning the application of U.S. antitrust law to the Voluntary
Restraint Agreement (VRA), on file with the author.

of universal norms uniformly applied despite diverse circumstances and parties. Instead, it can respond to criticism of broad policy with ambiguous phrases such as "excessive competition," "self-restraint," or "self-sufficiency," and it need not respond at all to attacks on its decisions in individual cases.

Because it can avoid articulating its goals and methods in terms of universal rules, its actions can be extremely particularistic, and it can reach decisions via a series of ex parte meetings that are hidden from the view of not only the public but also of many of the parties themselves. Defenders of administrative guidance argue, I think convincingly, that informality gives the bureaucracy the flexibility to pursue the public interest aggressively without having to go through legislation or the lawyer-ridden procedures of American administrative law. But it must also be admitted that informality can allow the determining factors in both policy formation and policy implementation to become whatever is expedient for the influential actors at that time and place.

One important consequence of particularistic regulation is the increased cost of entry into the regulated industry. It was not a coincidence that the LSRSL was passed just as Japan was contemplating financial liberalization and the domestic retail industry feared a tide of foreign investment in Japanese distribution. To take this argument seriously, one need only note that no foreign-owned or -managed retail store opened under the LSRSL until the 1990s,[55] but particularistic regulation controls not only foreign entry but also entry by any outsider. It does so not only by enabling regulators to mask exclusionary decisions with opaque procedures but also by making it difficult for prospective entrants to acquire the information needed to open a store. Because the degree of difficulty increases with the applicant's lack of familiarity with the system, particularism has the added advantage over other forms of procedural barriers of most burdening the total outsider, the foreigner or the entrepreneurial Japanese seeking to introduce a new form of retailing.

Another aspect of particularism is localism. Under the LSRSL localism meant that except for those areas of "self-restraint" where MITI prohibited all new large stores, each locality had the ability to fashion the adjustment process to meet its own economic, social, and political circumstances. Thus, the opening of large stores was controlled not by centrally or even regionally determined policy but by the particular circumstances pertaining in each neighborhood. As a result the national retail market was replaced as object of regulation by the reality

[55] Tsuruta, "Kokusaikajidai," p. 45; Miyazawa, "Endaka Keizaika," p. 57.

of many fragmented and isolated markets, each of which was relatively easily manipulated by the players in the LSRSL process.

If particularism is the fundamental characteristic of the process of regulation in Japan, at least as exemplified by the LSRSL, the equivalent substantive characteristic is captured by the phrase "coexistence and coprosperity," which has dominated the rhetoric of retail regulation since it appeared in the debate on the prewar DSL in the 1930s. The ethos of coexistence and coprosperity rejects the market principle that only those who are able to compete should survive and replaces it with a convoy mentality, which in the LSRSL context meant that the most efficient large stores prospered and that relatively efficient small stores could survive regardless of their fundamental competitive disadvantages.

As the dwindling number of small retailers during the 1980s indicates, coexistence does not necessarily mean commercial immortality. Although the withdrawal from the industry of many small stores may have had as much to do with increased opportunities in other sectors for children of store owners as it did with bankruptcy, the coexistence part of the motto had limitations. When withdrawal was directly caused by the opening of a large store nearby, however, there was a good chance that the retiring small merchant did not leave the scene empty-handed. Instead of the bruising and often unsuccessful battle for survival of American main-street merchants against retailing innovators such as Wal-Mart, Japanese merchants did not withdraw after exhausting themselves financially. They were bought off before the competition began and so retired with both their savings and the equivalent of a golden parachute; and the new large store and its customers were forced to internalize some of the social cost of economic change.

The natural vehicle for economic regulation with the goal of coexistence and coprosperity and the method of particularism is cartelization, and the implementation of the LSRSL in the 1980s fostered cartels on the national, regional, and local levels.[56] Cartels by definition

[56] For prewar practices in retailing, see Yasuaki Suzuki, *Shôwashoki no kourishômondai* (Retail problems in early Shōwa) (Tokyo: Nihon keizai shinbunsha, 1980). For complementary interpretations of contemporary Japan, see Chalmers Johnson, *MITI and the Japanese Miracle: The Growth of Industrial Policy, 1925–1975* (Stanford: Stanford University Press, 1982), and Richard Samuels, *The Business of the Japanese State: Energy Markets in Comparative and Historical Perspective* (Ithaca: Cornell University Press, 1987). For postwar practice, also see Michael Young, "Judicial Review of Administrative Guidance: Governmentally Encouraged Consensual Dispute Resolution in Japan," *Columbia Law Review* 84 (1984): 923–83 (land use planning); Frank K. Upham, "Ten Years of Affirmative Action for Japanese Burakumin: A Preliminary Report on the Law on Special Measures for *Dowa* Projects," *Law in Japan: An Annual* 13 (1980): 39–73 (welfare programs); and "The Legal Framework of Japanese Declining Industries Policy: The Prob-

require barriers to entry, and the history of retailing regulation and legislation from before the prewar DSL through the 1978 amendment of the LSRSL is perhaps best interpreted as repeated attempts by established retailers to deal with either new entrants or new forms of retailing. Cartels are also ideal vehicles for a convoy mentality that both attempts to keep everyone in business and enables the most efficient to reap additional profits.[57] Finally, cartels are well suited to regional and local solutions to general problems. Once it was clear that the LSRSL was going to be implemented by groups of self-appointed local merchants unfettered by centrally developed criteria, the pace and nature of change in the retailing industry could be tailored to meet the peculiar requirements of each commercial neighborhood.

Once the centrality of cartelization in Japan's economic regulation is remembered, MITI's role under the LSRSL begins to make historical sense. Just as it was in the Sumitomo Metals incident in the 1960s, the petroleum refiners' production, price, and import cartels in the 1970s, the "naptha war" of the late 1970s, the declining industries cartels of the late 1970s and 1980s, and the automobile Voluntary Restraint Agreement of the early 1980s, MITI's role was to facilitate the cartel by serving as a clearinghouse for information and using its collateral powers to enforce its terms against firms that attempted to cheat. What somewhat differentiates the LSRSL story was the manner in which MITI chose to exercise this role. Previous exercises in cartelization have come without direct statutory authorization, but in most of these instances there have been connections to the public interest and MITI has retained an active oversight role. Even in the import cartel for gasoline, which raised the profit margins of domestic refiners, MITI was able to claim that it permitted the cartel in order to achieve a corresponding lowering of the price of kerosene, thus subsidizing home heating cost by burdening the use of private automobiles.

In its regulation of the retail industry during the 1980s, however, there is little plausible justification for either the substantive policy or the mode of implementation. Instead of developing a national plan for the retail industry that balanced the interests of consumers, large retailers, and small independents and then basing the criteria for local

---

lem of Transparency in Administrative Processes," *Harvard International Law Journal* 27, special issue (1986): 425–65 (declining industries); and Uesugi Akinori, "Japan's Cartel System and Its Impact on International Trade," *Harvard International Law Journal* 27, special issue (1986): 389–424 (cartels in general).

[57] There exists a similar situation in financial industry, as pointed out by Masaru Mabuchi, "Deregulation and Legalization of Financial Policy," in Gary D. Allinson and Yasunori Sone, eds., *Political Dynamics in Contemporary Japan* (Ithaca: Cornell University Press, 1993), pp. 130–54.

application on the goals and rationale of the plan in consultation with the Commercial Activities Adjustment Boards and the Large Stores Councils, MITI simply delegated its power to the local retailers themselves. In doing so, it effectively substituted the private interests of local merchants for the public interests embodied in the statute. Similarly at the national level, the annual allotments for additional floor space ensured high margins for the large chains without any corresponding or offsetting benefit to consumers, all in defiance of the terms of the statute and the legislative compromise that it represented.

The decision by MITI to delegate the process of adjustment entirely to a group of local merchants operating outside the tripartite structure of the Adjustment Boards, therefore, was a decision to gut the statute of much of its original meaning. The further decision to require unanimous consent among local merchants essentially granted each such merchant a property right in the competitive status quo; it completed the transformation of the LSRSL from an instrument of public policy to a tool of a limited number of private parties to use in their own self-interest with no reference whatsoever to the original political compromise that had shaped the statute.

There were several advantages to MITI in this course of action. In the first place, it was easy. To implement the statute as written would have required MITI to exercise its discretion based on its own investigation and the critical evaluation of the investigation and conclusions of the advisory councils. This in turn would have required both additional budget and personnel. One of the most telling aspects of the May 1990 reform of the LSRSL was MITI's immediate request for forty additional staff to carry out the reform. Government regulation consistent with the wishes of those to be regulated requires few personnel, but when the administration moves against those wishes, the call on resources is much greater. Although sold to the Americans and others as "deregulation," the reforms actually meant that for the first time in more than a decade MITI would have to regulate the retail industry in a manner that would create losers as well as winners among its members.

More important than the administrative burden of regulation, however, was the potential political cost if MITI had chosen to make the decisions itself. Although the political compromise at the level of the national Diet had included other interests, politics at the local level where the statute had to be applied were heavily weighted toward the protection of local merchants. Although the top level of the Liberal Democratic Party had the political leeway to refuse to pursue the interests of small merchants exclusively, the rank and file members frequently did not. They needed the support of the local chamber of commerce and its members to be reelected, and the recitation of the value of market discipline meant little to local merchants faced with the loss of their livelihood. In the 1970s MITI had learned the political cost of ignoring this reality, and there was no reason for it to make the same mistake twice. The satisfaction of large retailers with their increased profits in the 1980s meant that there was simply nothing to be gained by playing an active role.

The LSRSL gave MITI jurisdiction over the retail industry and created a set of criteria to govern its regulation. During the 1980s, however, MITI chose not to exercise the direct power that jurisdiction gave it and to ignore the statutory criteria. Instead, by granting local merchants a veto power over new stores in their neighborhood, MITI created an informal framework within which private parties worked out their own accommodation without reference to any rules whatsoever. Its refusal to accept notifications without the appended agreement of the local merchants forced large retailers into open-ended bargaining with their competitors. Whether or not the store opened and, hence, the direction and pace of change in the retail industry, depended not on MITI's regulation of the industry but on the results of private negotiations. No one, least of all an outsider using the law as a guide, could predict the outcome or understand the process, which could turn on factors as idiosyncratic as whether the prospective new entrant had correctly identified the bosses within the local merchant community.

THE STRUCTURAL IMPEDIMENTS INITIATIVE AND THE PROCESS OF CONVERGENCE

To discuss the SII-induced reform of the LSRSL as an example of forced convergence, we must first distinguish the underlying policy of regulating large stores from the mode chosen by MITI to carry out this policy. Even within the latter, a further distinction must be drawn between MITI's privatization of the process during the 1980s and the inclusion of private interests directly in the consultation process as contemplated by the statute. The former may be unique to Japan and perhaps to the LSRSL, but the latter is a standard form of regulation in Europe and is not unknown in the United States. Similarly the basic idea of restricting the opening and operation of large stores is virtually universal. Indeed, it is the relative freedom enjoyed by large retailers in the United States rather than their restriction in Japan that seems unusual from the comparative perspective. If Japan were to repeal the LSRSL and drop all regulation of retailing, therefore, it would raise the fundamental question of whether this was a part of a process of the general convergence of capitalist systems or merely Japan's choice to follow the American example.

Administrative Informality

Although in the aggregate these changes in MITI implementation of the LSRSL increase transparency and regularity, none affects the legal informality of the process. The particularism that existed under the old regime is gone, but there is no institutional barrier to its return. The process of consultation remains closed to the public, and, most important, the entire implementation of the law remains outside the scrutiny of the courts. Although anyone familiar with the intrusive role of American courts in the administrative process will perhaps find the exclusion of the judiciary a virtue rather than a vice, it has subtle but profound implications for the idea of convergence.

First, virtually total insulation from legal accountability is rare, if not unique, among OECD nations. The American example may be extreme in its degree of legalization, but administrative corruption as alleged in the *Esurigo* case and the procedural irregularities of the pre-prenotification adjustment era of the LSRSL would be cognizable by most if not all administrative courts in Europe. In France, for example, where the *Royer* law established a system of retail regulation not dissimilar from that of the LSRSL, the Conseil d'Etat has been available to check the extreme particularism, if not always the corruption, that thrived under the judicial laissez-faire of the Japanese courts.

Second, legal informality is conceptually incompatible with a fundamental premise of convergence. Unless convergence means simply similarity in results—the same number of large stores opening in Fukuoka, Provence, and Arkansas—the various processes of regulation in different societies must be mutually intelligible. To achieve mutual intelligibility, which is at the heart of the OECD's demand for transparency in governmental intervention in the economy, several of the attributes of the rule of law must be common, at least rhetorically, to all of the regulatory systems. First, the system must work on the basis of universal rules that are more or less uniformly applied. Second, there must be a clear-cut distinction between public and private spheres and public and private actors. Observers as well as participants must be able to tell who regulates and who is regulated.

The Japanese system, certainly as it operated under the LSRSL for most of its existence, was a system of ad hoc bargaining, not of the uniform application of rules, and MITI's delegation of its power meant that there was no distinction between public regulation of the industry and the decisions of a private cartel. As long as the process of regulation remains legally informal in Japan and the preferred form of statutory regulation is consultative, there is simply no way to guarantee procedural consistency, much less transparency.[58] At any given time, MITI may choose to centralize its regulation and promulgate and abide by clear standards and procedures. Similarly, at any given time, it may choose to emphasize flexibility and localism. Given the relative lack of penetration of the ideology and rhetoric of the rule of law into Japanese administrative processes, the only way that an outsider to the process can know which model prevails in a particular sector at a particular time (or more likely, what combination of the two) is to become an insider. Unlike in the United States, France, or the United Kingdom, the universal language of law (statutes, formal regulations, judicial decisions) may provide the outsider with little sense of the actuality of the regulatory process. Without the shortcut of rule of law ideology, mutual intelligibility remains elusive.

Rule of law rhetoric is a language of convergence in the same way that the language of market economics is. Perfect markets may be theoretically and practically impossible and widely recognized as such, but market rhetoric dominates the discourse of international trade and enables persons from different capitalist nations to believe that they can understand each other's economies. Similarly, rule of law rhetoric dominates the discourse of international trade disputes and specifically of the dispute mechanism of the GATT and the negotiations of the Uruguay Round. As long as the nature of Japanese economic regulation is not accessible through its own legal system, it is hard to interpret the SII reforms as convergence. From the point of view of law and ideology, therefore, Japan's agreement to allow more foreign stores to open and to make it easier for foreign firms to participate in the LSRSL seems more like the successful accommodation of two different systems than the creation of a unitary one.

[58] Note that the various administrative agencies could conceivably develop internal appeal processes that could achieve regularity. This system might in turn develop into a separate administrative court system like the Conseil d'Etat. Such a system would in theory remain "legally informal," but it would have all the characteristics of formality. In 1993, directly inspired by the discussion of administrative transparency during the SII, the Japanese Diet passed the Administrative Procedure Act. Although falling far short of what the Americans might consider transparency, the APA may be a significant first step in that direction. For an explanation of the passage of the act and a very preliminary appraisal, see Masaru Kaneko, *Gyōsei tetsuzukihō* [Administrative procedure law] (Tokyo: Iwanami Shinsho, 1994).

Retail Regulation or Community Preservation

In addition to reforming the process of large store opening, the SII took a significant step toward weakening protection for small retailers and toward deregulation of the industry. Continued movement in this direction is not certain, but a decision to allow small merchants to sink or swim on the currents of an unregulated retail market would be a dramatic departure both from Japanese history and from the pattern of economic regulation in most of the world.

Most democracies at various periods of history have shielded their merchants from destructive competition. Even the United States, which now has a relatively unregulated retail industry, has a long history of direct and indirect protection. In the 1920s and 1930s while Japanese merchants were demanding protection from expanding department stores, their American counterparts were targeting chain stores for legislative action and were by most measures considerably more successful than their Japanese counterparts. Their political champions in state legislatures and the U.S. Congress painted the chains as soulless agents of big-city capital and warned that they would relentlessly destroy the independent businesspeople that were the backbone of small-town democracy.

By the late 1930s more than two-thirds of American states had passed laws that discriminatorily taxed chain stores, and in the 1930s Congress passed the Robinson-Patman Act, which its original sponsors intended to protect small merchants from predatory and collusive practices of chains and manufacturers. These measures were in addition to the codes of fair competition for the distribution industry that were to be part of the New Deal's general attempt to revitalize the American economy by restraining what MITI bureaucrats refer to today as "excessive competition." Eventually all three of these efforts failed to provide effective protection. The Supreme Court found the underlying authority for the competition codes unconstitutional, although not on grounds directly related to cartelization; the chains and farmers allied politically to defeat the chain store tax laws at the polls and in the state houses; and the Robinson-Patman Act was so riddled with exceptions that it never achieved systematic protection for anyone.

As a result, the American distribution industry today is largely unregulated in most states. Opposition to the opening of large stores remains, but it is now couched solely or primarily in land use and city planning terms. The preservation of the independent retailer and small-town democracy has been replaced by issues of traffic, community, and historic preservation. Local retailers remain the object of protection, but they are not necessarily the leaders of the opposition and the rhetoric is not so much about protecting their livelihoods as it is about protecting a byproduct of their scale and mode of business. As one physician remarked at an anti–Wal-Mart rally in northern New England, "There are bad things about a massive marketing juggernaut coming in with such clout that it would disrupt the fabric of a small town, the Main Street character. It would break people away from the ferment of interacting with neighbors and colleagues downtown."[59]

City planning–based restrictions on large retailers are likely to remain sporadic and exceptional in the United States, but they are well established in most of Europe. Strict regulation of store hours in Germany is justified more in terms of life-style than as protection of mom-and-pop retailers, and France's *Royer* law, which is structurally similar to the LSRSL, is part of the law of city planning, not of commerce or industry. Consistent with this emphasis on a new store's impact on the locality in general rather than on its merchants alone, nine of the twenty members of the *commissions départementales d'urbanisme commercial* (CDUC), the French equivalent of the regional Large Stores Councils, are local elected officials. Rather than advising an administrative agency like their Japanese equivalents, the CDUCs make the final decision regarding store opening, and it is the role of the elected officials to represent their constituencies from the point of view of quality of life as well as the impact on either local retailers or consumers cum retailers or consumers.

Perhaps it is not coincidental, therefore, that the corruption that has bedeviled the *Royer* law has been of a different nature than that of the LSRSL. Instead of payoffs to local merchants, French retail chains have had to make disguised contributions to political parties and to the general infrastructure of the communities that they are entering. These contributions have not always been limited to measures that address the direct impact of their opening but have included the construction of police stations, stadiums, roads, and so on that are unconnected to and distant from the new store. In this way, the effect of the *Royer* law is similar to the contributions of land (or cash in lieu of land) for schools or parks demanded of residential developers by Japanese and American cities alike and the infrastructure "bribes" necessary to convince Japanese towns to accept nuclear power plants.

So far the LSRSL has not been part of Japan's city planning scheme, but the recent move by MITI to shift to revitalization of exist-

---

[59] "In 2 Towns, Main Street Fights Off Wal-Mart," *New York Times*, 21 October 1993, p. A16.

ing commercial areas as an alternative to direct restrictions on new stores may presage a similar shift in Japan. In fact, opposition to new stores has at times been couched in terms of traffic and other equivalent concerns as well as the statutory concerns of merchants' enterprise opportunities.[60] A true shift to an urban planning approach to large stores, however, is unlikely as long as the LSRSL remains under MITI's jurisdiction and the three goals of article 1 remain limited to issues of industrial policy. Any inclusion of city planning concerns would mean a jurisdictional overlap and perhaps conflict with the Ministry of Construction. What seems more likely, therefore, is the gradual deregulation of retailing as part of national industrial policy and more attention to the city planning issues of large stores by local governments.

It is certainly possible that independent merchants in Japan may be able to exploit their local political clout to turn the system to their advantage as easily in a city planning context as they were with MITI under the LSRSL umbrella. Despite any similarity in result, however, the shift in context may matter a great deal in international trade terms. The rhetoric of city planning is culture, quality of life, and grassroots democracy rather than efficiency, market access, and economic regulation. Although the SII demonstrated that even "culture" can be the subject of trade disputes, the shift from the rhetoric and processes of protection to those of architectural consistency, sense of community, traffic management, and historic preservation will make the result that much more difficult for Americans to attack. If the decision of a small New England town to reject a Wal-Mart or Home Depot is legitimate, after all, it is very hard to conclude that a similar decision by a Tokyo neighborhood is merely window dressing for protectionism.

The SII reforms have led to an expedited process that is more open to foreigners and other outsiders than the previous mode of implementation of the LSRSL. Local independent merchants have lost the veto over new competitors that they had in the 1980s, and it is possible that the current trend toward deregulation will continue in the 1990s until the retailing industry is largely unregulated by MITI.[61] If the LSRSL is eventually repealed and large retail projects become the

---

[60] The Keidanren Report at 6 notes the rise in land use planning conditions put on new stores, including traffic restrictions, donation of traffic lights, and the like. This may presage a shift to the American style of restricting large stores.

[61] An FTC Panel called for abolition of the LSRSL in June 1995, citing the continued lack of transparency and noting that "the incremental deregulation of the past has not brought a fundamental solution to the problem." *Nihon Keizai Shimbun*, 22 June 1995, reported in *Japan Digest*, 26 June 1995, p. 11.

focus of land use rather than economic debates, the superficial similarity with the United States will be striking. Even if the universal desire of businesses to cartelize and the long history of government toleration of cartels in Japan prevent a totally open scramble for location and floor space, these steps can be interpreted as a movement toward the American mode of retail regulation.

If convergence meant simply increased similarity between two systems, the SII could be said to have produced convergence at least between the two countries' retailing industries. Taking this reasoning further, however, may confuse a bilateral deal between the United States and Japan with a global trend. Although there has been movement recently with the *Royer* law and other European regulatory schemes, there is no indication that a fundamental move away from regulation is under way. Indeed increased transparency in the former has been aimed at preventing large chains from using their financial resources to corrupt the system as much as at facilitating their expansion. The inclusion of large retail projects under land use regulation in Japan would mean that retailers in all three areas would have to contend with a similar set of issues. This move might be evidence of a broad consensus of which areas should be regulated as economics and which as social life, but it does not follow that the level or process of regulation will be similar. Opposition to a recent attempt to liberalize, even marginally, the severe restrictions on hours of retail activity in Germany, for example, brings home the distance between Western European practice and the deregulation that the United States and perhaps Japan represent.

Convergence must mean similarity in process as well as result to mean anything about the nature of capitalism. Similarity in process in turn implies a similarity or at least mutual accessibility in legal systems. As discussed, the fundamental legal nature of Japanese economic regulation has not changed. The legal informality that allowed the privatization of the process in the 1980s remains throughout Japanese government activity and even within retailing regulation. The Americans' continued attention and the trend toward deregulation within MITI and the Japanese government make it unlikely that the pattern of the 1980s will repeat itself. However, the insulation of the government–business relationship from judicial scrutiny and the consequent parochialism of the regulatory system mean that any convergence will fall far short of the mutual intelligibility that deep convergence would require.

CHAPTER TWELVE

Trade and Domestic Differences

MILES KAHLER

On certain dimensions the international trading order of the 1990s could be described as the most liberal since the first decade of the century. Market integration across national boundaries advances, encouraged or at least tolerated by governments, from Europe's 1992 initiative, to NAFTA, to greater China. The borderless world has not emerged, but apart from recession years trade volumes have grown faster than world GDP; foreign direct investment, often associated with intrafirm trade, grew three times faster than merchandise trade from 1983 to 1989. In addition, more countries have endorsed broadly liberal orientations toward international exchange than at any other time since 1945. The post-1979 policies of China and the collapse of central planning in the former Soviet bloc are only the most dramatic policy turns; many large developing countries that had resolutely espoused statist controls on trade and investment have also opened their economies (Mexico and Argentina are only two examples).[1]

A somewhat different Spanish-language version of this paper has been published in *América Latina/Internacional*. The author thanks Suzanne Berger, Jeffrey Frankel, Lawrence Krause, John McMillan, and the participants in the Bellagio conference for their helpful comments. Barton Fisher and Sean Butler provided valuable research assistance.

[1] International Monetary Fund, *Issues and Developments in International Trade Policy* (Washington, D. C.: International Monetary Fund, 1992), p. 45, table 12, suggests at least limited trade reforms in a large sample of developing countries. Latin America has clearly moved further in this direction than other regions. See also the evidence from the 1990s in Naheed Kirmani, ed., *International Trade Policies: The Uruguay Round and Beyond, Vol. II: Background Papers* (Washington, D.C.: International Monetary Fund, 1995), pp. 35–40.

Despite the increasing scope of global markets and the apparent hold of liberal programs, the international institution that oversaw the liberal trade regime, the GATT, became the target of increasingly vehement attacks. Its critics argued that it was inadequate for the new post–Cold War, multipolar era, whatever its past accomplishments.[2] Ironically, as more developing countries joined the GATT, its most vociferous critics emerged in two regions that have benefited for decades from a liberal trading order: North America and Western Europe.

Several developments can be cited for the widely perceived "crisis" in a world trading system that appears increasingly integrated and open: American unilateralism, the decline of American hegemony, the failure of Japan to assume leadership, the growth of regional trading blocs (particularly the EC). The common theme of the crisis, however, is the expansion of conflict from trade to other dimensions of social and political life that had in the past been reserved as domestic and had not been connected to trade. For critics of the GATT and its successor organization, the World Trade Organization (WTO), removing barriers to trade at national borders has only revealed countless other barriers and distortions behind those borders. The decades-long process of lowering trade barriers resembles the draining of a lake that reveals mountain peaks formerly concealed or (more pessimistically) the peeling of an onion that reveals innumerable layers of barriers. The international trade regime has also been assailed by those who wish to defend a range of domestic practices and policies, from labor standards to environmental regulations, against those who view such domestic differences as barriers to international exchange. These critics of the WTO and international economic integration press to broaden the content of international rules governing trade by incorporating new issue areas that were previously regarded as national prerogatives.

These new, nontrade distortions and barriers, whether real or perceived, are not likely to diminish over time. The integration of the ex-socialist or reforming socialist economies into the world economy appears to be a gain for economic liberalization, but the introduction of hybrid forms of political and economic organization may add new lines of conflict. Even if transitional economies adopt one of the existing models of capitalist political economy, the existing models are likely to continue to exhibit variation in their policy regimes and pat-

---

[2] Lester Thurow, for example, has proclaimed that "the GATT–Bretton Woods trading system is dead," and that "a new system of quasi trading blocks employing managed trade will emerge." *Head to Head: The Coming Economic Battle among Japan, Europe, and America* (New York: Morrow, 1992), pp. 16, 65.

terns of organization. And those variations will continue to produce stress in the world trade regime.

These issues are fundamentally political, although their appearance on the international agenda may be influenced by a particular (mis)reading of economic prescriptions. As different political and economic systems have grated against one another, three contrasting political solutions, embodied in different international institutions, have emerged to address domestic differences and their effects on international exchange: (1) institutional competition (mutual recognition); (2) harmonization; and (3) managed trade. These solutions span a spectrum from greater confidence in market or marketlike solutions (institutional competition) to more "political" approaches that display little confidence in a stable "market" in institutions (managed trade).[3]

Mutual recognition, adopted as a means of accelerating market integration by the EC, implies a high degree of institutional competition among systems. Even this solution to the issue of domestic differences, however, has required some institutionalization at the international level to oversee the competition and to ensure that institutional competition, relatively free in some policy domains, is more restricted in others.

Harmonization of policies, the second solution to domestic differences, has appeared in two forms. The first, among trading partners relatively equal in bargaining power, characterized the dominant approach to domestic differences within the EC for much of its history. The inefficiency of this approach for deepening market integration eventually produced mutual recognition as an alternative. Equally significant is harmonization among partners with different bargaining power, exemplified by the NAFTA and the Structural Impediments Initiative (SII) negotiations. In these cases, harmonization, if not imposed by the more powerful partner, tends to be skewed in the direction of that partner's policy preferences. The weaker partners typically attempt to avoid linkages to policy areas outside a narrow definition of trade policy (with varying degrees of success).

Finally, some Europeans and North Americans argue that mutually beneficial market integration may be difficult in a world of radical domestic differences. Their arguments have been used in particular to define one side of the debate about relations with Japan and the East Asian NICs. Instead of institutional competition or even direct

[3] John H. Jackson proposes a somewhat different list of techniques to "manage interdependence": harmonization, reciprocity, and interface. This list confuses techniques (reciprocity) with end points (interface). Also, Jackson does not make clear the content of his "interface" category. *The World Trading System* (Cambridge: MIT Press, 1989), p. 305.

pressure to make trading partners "more like us," these critics, in particular the American revisionists, argue for "black boxing" domestic systems and relying on *managed trade* (results-oriented trade policy) to achieve more balanced economic relations, even at the risk of some international economic disintegration.

Each of these solutions entails a set of political prerequisites and institutional arrangements. Before examining the political context of each of these alternatives, reasons for the perceived crisis in the world trade regime, both institutional and intellectual, bear closer investigation. Three of these have been particularly important: perceived shortcomings of the multilateral trade regime in dealing with the new agenda, intellectual innovation in trade theory that has drawn attention to behind-the-border differences, and links between trade and investment that have expanded definitions of market access.

THE CRISIS OF THE LIBERAL TRADE REGIME IN AN ERA OF LIBERALIZATION

The 1980s witnessed a series of challenges to a model for organizing international trade relations that had been born with the GATT after World War II. This spare model of economic integration was embodied in the European Free Trade Association (EFTA); a similar model can be extracted from the GATT itself. Trade in this view is based on national differences; trade regimes in turn should be based on the principles of subsidiarity (the institutional "work" required should be done at the lowest political level possible) and diversity of national institutions.[4] The GATT regime was a model of this type of negative integration: it aimed to remove government intrusions of a particular sort (tariffs and quantitative restrictions) so that private agents could expand the scope of their activities and act according to a set of market signals relatively undistorted by governments. Because mainstream trade theory held unilateral liberalization of trade to be the preferred policy option in most instances, this view incorporated considerable skepticism about the use of interventionist trade policies to improve national economic welfare and the damage to trading partners even if such policies were employed. The GATT certainly permitted national action in response to some actions by corporations or governments (dumping, for example), but the list of domestic differences that were of interest, outside of commercial policy, was a

[4] Victoria Curzon Price, "Three Models of European Integration," in Sir Ralf Dahrendorf et al., eds., *Whose Europe? Competing Visions for 1992* (London: Institute of Economic Affairs, 1989), pp. 24–26.

short one. Jagdish Bhagwati, a leading supporter of the GATT system, has argued in favor of this restricted view of the scope of trade policy: "The problem with trying to include such things, and indeed most policies and institutions, as the natural target for objections that they affect trade and must therefore be scrutinized and changed to suit one's advantage if free trade is to be allowed, is simply that one is opening up a Pandora's Box. . . . If everything becomes a question of fair trade, the likely outcome will be to remove the possibility of agreeing to a rule-oriented trading system. 'Managed trade' will then be the outcome, with bureaucrats allocating trade according to what domestic lobbying pressures and foreign political muscle dictate."[5]

The GATT itself had cracked the lid of this Pandora's box. After its considerable achievements in lowering tariffs and removing quantitative restrictions to trade through successive multilateral negotiations, it was confronted with governments employing new "protectionist technologies" (in John H. Jackson's phrase) that it has had considerable difficulty in restraining. The GATT was pushed deeper into national institutions by its own core principles, particularly national treatment, enshrined in article III. At the same time, articles XX and XXI of the GATT explicitly incorporated a long list of exceptions to strict GATT obligations (including national treatment), so that governments could pursue other social goals, which ranged from national security, to "conserving natural resources," to the "protection of human, animal or plant life or health." These regulatory goals did not remove GATT obligations, but they softened them: they permitted departures from strict nondiscrimination and national treatment only to the extent necessary to achieve these alternative goals. "Arbitrary and unjustifiable discrimination" or regulation that is a "disguised restriction on international trade" is forbidden.[6]

The GATT's ability to construct rules to constrain national governments while still respecting national diversity has had a mixed record. The Subsidies Code completed during the Tokyo Round has been beset by a lack of consensus on the meaning of key elements in the code.[7] The Uruguay Round negotiations were devoted in part to clarifying and extending the GATT's reach over nontariff barriers to trade that are rooted in domestic institutional differences. Despite the fears of environmentalists and labor unions, in "approved" areas of domestic regulation (such as health regulations), enforceable rules

[5] Jagdish Bhagwati, "Multilateralism at Risk, The GATT Is Dead, Long Live the GATT," *The World Economy* 13, no. 2 (June 1990): 155.
[6] Jackson, *The World Trading System*, p. 207.
[7] Ibid., p. 388.

have been scarce, and panels have indicated little willingness to curb the discretion of governments.[8]

Rather than providing more detailed rules to constrain domestic differences, the new WTO embodies two strategies. On the one hand, it encourages or stipulates harmonization within broad "bands" of national discretion. (This is the approach taken in the General Agreement on Trade in Services, for example.) On the other hand, dispute settlement mechanisms are rendered more efficient and credible so that disagreement within the band of national discretion can be dealt with on a case-by-case basis within an agreed set of procedures.[9]

New Trade Theory and Ideological Erosion

Although the GATT attempted to take a narrow view of which domestic differences should be included in global trading rules, the emergence of new trade theory in the 1980s pointed in a different direction, reinforcing attention to behind-the-border barriers to goods and investment and, for some, undermining the intellectual basis for free trade. The literature elaborating, testing, and criticizing the new trade theory has grown too vast to be examined here in detail: one recent article includes a "survey of the surveys"![10] In very summary form, the new approach to trade no longer posits a world of perfect competition and constant returns. Instead, it links trade theory and industrial organization by introducing assumptions of increasing returns and imperfect competition. A second facet of the theory that is less innovative is its attention to externalities or spillovers, particularly the generation of knowledge in one sector that cannot be appropriated fully by the firms in question. Under certain conditions of imperfect competition (and the narrowness or breadth of those conditions is one point of controversy), a government may inter-

[8] Eliza Patterson, "International Efforts to Minimize the Adverse Trade Effects of Sanitary and Phytosanitary Regulations," *Journal of World Trade* 24, no. 2 (April 1990): 91–102.

[9] The results of the Uruguay Round negotiations, including the General Agreement on Trade in Services and dispute settlement procedures, are given in *The Results of the Uruguay Round of Multilateral Trade Negotiations: The Legal Texts* (Geneva: GATT Secretariat, 1994).

[10] J. David Richardson, "'New' Trade Theory and Policy a Decade Old: Assessment in a Pacific Context," in Richard Higgott, Richard Leaver, and John Ravenhill, eds., *Pacific Economic Relations in the 1990s* (St. Leonards, Australia: Allen & Unwin, 1993), pp. 86–90. Another recent and critical review is Richard Pomfret, *International Trade Policy with Imperfect Competition* (Princeton: Department of Economics, International Finance Section, 1992); see also Robert E. Baldwin, "Are Economists' Traditional Trade Policy Views Still Valid?," *Journal of Economic Literature* 30, no. 2 (June 1992): 804–29.

vene strategically to shift the excess returns or rents to its domestic firms and away from the firms of other countries. Its strategic goal, through protection or subsidy, is to deter foreign firms from entering in a sector that is characterized by excess returns. Similarly governments may subsidize sectors characterized by important spillovers that benefit other sectors of the national economy.

By introducing an additional set of domestic differences, as Paul Krugman points out, new trade theory strengthens the case for the benefits of trade rather than closure. Its prescriptions for government policy are far more controversial. Those who have elaborated the new theory argue that free trade is no longer an automatic optimum but rather a "reasonable rule of thumb."[11] Even its exponents, however, express skepticism regarding the support that the new theory offers to more activist government policies, in contrast to those (largely, though not exclusively, political scientists) who have used the theory to argue for "created comparative advantage" and detailed industrial policies.[12] Because of the tenuous economic assumptions built into strategic trade models, the small gains estimated from more activist policies, and the daunting political prerequisites, most mainstream economists continue to endorse free trade as the preferred policy regime. In a world of strategic trade competition, mutual governmental restraint—internationally monitored and backed with credible threats to retaliate—is the optimal strategy in most realistic contexts.

In two respects, however, strategic trade theory has contributed to discontent with the GATT regime and increased concern with domestic differences and their effects on trade. First, although removal of free trade's sacrosanct status is defended by some on intellectual grounds, the adherents of free trade lament the corrosive effects of the new views. Pomfret cites with approval Edgeworth's earlier statement on infant industry arguments: "Let us admire the skill of the analyst, but label the subject of his investigation POISON."[13] Equally important, the wedding of trade policy and industrial organization reinforces concern with elements of national policy that used to be hidden in the Pandora's box of Bhagwati. The attitudes of old and new trade theorists on this score stand in stark contrast. Although arguing that new trade theory on balance strengthens the case for free trade, J. David Richardson also contends that it provides an endorsement for scrutiny of nonborder policies that restrict entry and competition. In

[11] Paul Krugman, "Is Free Trade Passé?," in Philip King, ed., *International Economics and International Economic Policy* (New York: McGraw-Hill, 1990), p. 91.
[12] For an example of the latter (not by a political scientist), see Thurow, *Head to Head*, p. 40.
[13] Pomfret, *International Trade Policy*, p. 52.

contrast to Bhagwati's protests about expanding the scope of trade policy, for example, Richardson lauds "constructive experimentation" such as the SII negotiations between the United States and Japan.[14]

INVESTMENT AND TRADE: DEEPENING LINKAGE

Strategic trade theorists suggest a final reason for questioning GATT's role and devoting more attention to government policies outside a narrowly defined sphere of commercial policy: deepening linkages between trade and investment as production in many sectors is organized globally. The U.S. response to Europe's 1992 Single Market initiative marked a clear-cut shift in perspective for the largest American firms: "European" treatment for American investments in Europe was far more significant than the threat of a "fortress Europe" that raised barriers to American exports.[15] The investment asymmetry between Japan and its major industrialized trading partners has become a key element in the perceived "Japan problem," spilling over into conflict regarding Japan's competition policies, obstacles to mergers and acquisitions, and informal networks of firms that restrict foreign competition.[16]

The manipulation of investment rules is not only about protection of domestic producers or preserving the advantages of national champions, however. Governments in the 1980s, particularly in the developing world, radically altered their attitudes toward foreign investment. Many governments moved from restricting foreign entry to wooing it, offering incentives to overseas investors. Openings to foreign investment remained controlled in most instances, however: governments were interested in investment of a particular kind—export intensive, research-and-development intensive, or high-wage employment intensive. Particular types of foreign investment were encouraged, in part because of a concern (perhaps misplaced) over externalities that might result from siting production on national territory. Needless to say, the proliferation of such restrictions in unpredictable ways is disliked by both foreign investors and by competing governments. The effort to create competitive advantage through national investment rules often exacerbates international conflict.

Once again, the GATT regime was able to respond only modestly to

---

[14] Richardson, "'New' Trade Theory," pp. 102–3.

[15] Gary Clyde Hufbauer, "An Overview," and Kenneth Flamm, "Semiconductors," both in *Europe 1992: An American Perspective* (Washington, D.C.: Brookings, 1990), pp. 39–40, 271–78.

[16] The best documented account of this issue is Dennis J. Encarnation, *Rivals beyond Trade: America versus Japan in Global Competition* (Ithaca: Cornell University Press, 1992).

a set of issues that had not been central to its mandate; the Havana Charter had confronted investment-related issues much more squarely. The Uruguay Round negotiations dealt directly with investment only in the area of trade-related investment measures (TRIM). The Agreement on Trade-Related Investment Measures prohibits certain TRIM, such as local content requirements and requirements to balance imports and exports, that violate the GATT principle of national treatment or its rules on eliminating quantitative trade restrictions. The OECD has also attempted to ensure both freer entry for foreign investors and national treatment of foreign firms within the industrialized country group. Its principal fora have been the Committee on Capital Movements and Invisible Transactions (responsible for implementation of the Codes of Liberalization) and the Committee on International Investment and Multinational Enterprises (responsible for the voluntary National Treatment Instrument designed to ensure nondiscrimination).[17] Like the GATT, the OECD has attempted harmonization of national policies within wide bands and without significant sanctions.

Beginning in the 1970s and intensifying in succeeding decades the global trade regime has been pressed to devote more attention and rule making to behind-the-border obstacles to trade. The growing membership of the GATT, a testimony to a broader acceptance of liberalization for some, is viewed as an added weakness for others, ensuring that negotiations on harmonization will be slow and that the bands of harmonization will be wider rather than narrower, that the lowest common denominator will become even lower among increasingly diverse systems. In the best of circumstances, then, the "level playing field" under the GATT will continue to display bumps that are too large for some participants, the rules will remain too general, and the umpire too weak. As a result, those players concerned about domestic differences and their effects on trade have moved to deal with those differences within groups of smaller number. The record of these recent experiments in mutual recognition, harmonization, and managed trade offer one estimate of the likely benefits and costs of using these strategies to deal with domestic differences in an integrated world economy.

MUTUAL RECOGNITION AND INSTITUTIONAL COMPETITION IN THE EUROPEAN COMMUNITY

A commitment to the Common Market, the free movement of goods within Western Europe without regard to national borders, has

[17] For a summary of OECD trade– and investment–related activities, see IMF, *Issues and Developments in International Trade Policy*, p. 18.

been at the center of the EC from the start. In practice the Community discovered the same national ingenuity in retreating from one set of (more transparent) barriers to other, less perceptible, barriers, despite countervailing action by the Commission and the European Court. Differing national regulatory environments, whether designed for protection or not, became major impediments to implementing the common market. By the mid-1980s the complicated task of harmonization of national differences and devising common European standards had nearly ground to a halt: "In the end, little 'harmonization' was achieved and few Community-wide standards were even drafted, let alone enacted."[18] As Jacques Pelkmans describes, the old approach to technical harmonization in the Community was inefficient, excessively uniform, and ultimately ineffective, because new national regulations were introduced at a rate that exceeded the establishment of Euro-standards.[19]

The European Court provided a new template for removing national restrictions on the free movement of goods in its 1979 *Cassis de Dijon* decision.[20] The Court found that "a product lawfully produced and marketed in one member state must have access to the other. Refusal to do so violates the clause providing for the free movement of goods."[21] The Court thus established the principle of mutual recognition that would accelerate trade liberalization within the Community. The Court's jurisprudence hedged the principle, but states had to have good reason to impede imports through imposing their own national standards. As Shapiro points out, the Court's reasoning in this regard has run parallel to American jurisprudence on the interstate commerce clause. States could maintain their own standards if the Court found that the Community had not indicated that its own regulations or standards overrode national ones or that the national regulations did not discriminate against imported goods. To determine discrimination the European Court relied in part on the historical context to ascertain the intent of the national regulations and in part on a test of proportionality, whether legitimate goals (health or

[18] Martin Shapiro, "The European Court of Justice," in Alberta M. Sbragia, ed., *Europolitics: Institutions and Policymaking in the "New" European Community* (Washington, D.C.: Brookings, 1992), p. 128.
[19] Jacques Pelkmans, "The New Approach to Technical Harmonization and Standardization," *Journal of Common Market Studies* 25, no. 3 (March 1987): 249–69.
[20] The actual title is *Rowe-Zentral AG v. Bundesmonopolverwaltung für Branntwein*, Case 120/78 (1979) ECR 649. The specifics of the case illustrate the types of barriers that obstructed trade within the EC. The case involved a German importer who wished to import the well-known French liqueur crème de Cassis. Since under German regulations, the liqueur was neither wine nor liqueur, its importation was essentially banned. The Court found in favor of the importer.
[21] Shapiro, "European Court," p. 129.

environmental protection, for example) could be satisfied by policies that distorted trade less.[22]

The Single European Act adopted the logic of mutual recognition and in certain respects broadened it to expedite the removal of the remaining barriers to a common market. Emile Noël has labeled "differentiation" one of the four key innovations in the 1992 process.[23] Instead of a centralized model relying on painstaking harmonization achieved and enforced by supranational institutions, the new high-speed model of liberalization was "mutual recognition and equivalence." Member states agree to the same general goals whatever their domestic differences and recognize that "there are many different and equally valid means of achieving [these goals]. The ends are common but the means can differ."[24]

Harmonization was not set aside under the new logic, of course, but harmonization "bands" were often very wide, and the possibilities for national variation considerable. "Essential requirements" were typically embodied in broad Community Framework Directives; if covered by such a directive and by a country's own laws, then a product was deemed free to circulate throughout the Community. An additional motor driving the pre-1992 process was the adoption of qualified majority voting (rather than unanimity) for much of the single market program. The principal exceptions occur outside the area of goods and services, where harmonization is accomplished by unanimity on the old model, not by qualified majority voting. In addition, even after harmonization, the new article 100a of the Treaty of Rome permits states to continue national regulation and even to introduce new regulations to protect health, safety, or the environment. Such exceptions are, however, subject to review by both the Commission and the Court for discriminatory intent or restrictive effects on trade.[25]

For some, the mutual recognition route to removing trade barriers held out the promise or threat of institutional convergence toward a less regulated norm. A more careful examination of the underlying models that might produce such a future casts considerable doubt on this outcome. One route is exit by consumers or by capital and labor. The assumption that consumers will base their choices primarily on price, disadvantaging products made in high-cost (high-regulation)

[22] An excellent account of the jurisprudence of the European Court in this area is given in ibid., pp. 130–31.

[23] Emile Noël, "The Single European Act," *Government and Opposition* 24, no. 1 (Winter 1989): 13.

[24] Price, "Three Models," pp. 30–31; see also David Cameron, "The 1992 Initiative: Causes and Consequences," in Sbragia, ed., *Euro-politics*, pp. 31–35.

[25] Noël, "The Single European Act," p. 14; Shapiro, "European Court," pp. 136–37; and Price, "Three Models," p. 31.

environments is undermined by the success of German consumer products, made to high standards of reliability and design and inspiring considerable consumer loyalty. A second engine of competitive pressure (and a constraint on national choices) could be factor mobility. Capital or labor desiring a different regulatory or taxation environment could vote with its feet: after the creation of the single European market not only capital, historically the most geographically mobile factor, but increasingly labor as well could make such choices. Here, too, however, pressures exerted under institutional competition may be less demanding in the short run than some proponents believe. Although British shoppers are already responding to lower indirect taxes across the Channel, movement of labor in response to direct taxes is likely to be much slower to take effect. Social security legislation, for example, may need little harmonization in the Community, since most workers are unlikely to be motivated to move by tax differentials alone.[26]

Linked to the possible competitive pressures exerted by threat of exit is the exercise of voice by voters. Voters, concerned about the economic effects of firm or worker exit or the longer run consequences of higher levels of regulation, might elect governments that promise lower regulation. Even if the trade-off is posed so clearly to an electorate, the implicit political assumption that voters will uniformly choose lower regulation and higher growth is as questionable as the assumptions about consumer choice and factor exit. One can easily imagine different national choices being made regarding the mix of regulation and economic growth among European societies. As one proponent of the deregulatory pressure imposed by the mutual recognition model argues, in issue areas without cross-border externalities, "each country should remain free to decide how to allocate national income between competing objectives."[27] There is no reason to predict that a "market" in policy regimes will produce an undifferentiated set of social "products": product differentiation to match a wide variety of individual and corporate tastes is equally likely.[28]

The threat of a race to the bottom—convergence on the least regulated social model under competitive international pressures—is overstated in Europe, because the motors of competitive pressure will only work slowly and over the long run or they may not work at all. To the degree that societies are linked systems of norms and practices, the effects of competitive pressure will be circumscribed by those link-

---

[26] Jorn Henrik Petersen, "Harmonization of Social Security in the EC Revisited," *Journal of Common Market Studies* 29, no. 5 (September 1991): 505–26.
[27] Price, "Three Models," p. 34.
[28] I owe this observation to John McMillan.

ages: one institutional change may imply a widening cascade of other changes. The perceived risks to EC members are also reduced because competition would take place within wide bands set through an expedited process of harmonization (itself affected by the threat of mutual recognition). Finally, the process of institutional competition also occurs within a highly institutionalized international environment, one that includes well-elaborated processes of dispute settlement and adjudication. Shapiro notes that the apparent deregulation will probably result in an increase in the workload of the European Court. The Court will now be called upon to make difficult judgments regarding the relative weight to assign "good" regulation (to protect health, safety, and the environment) on the one hand and the free movement of goods, services, capital, and labor on the other. It may also be asked to determine whether lower regulation or standards represent "social dumping."[29] Active participation by strong international institutions, the Court and the Commission, seems likely to soften further the effects of deregulatory competition.

HARMONIZATION: SYMMETRIC AND ASYMMETRIC BARGAINING

The Single European Act's adoption of mutual recognition as a means to accelerate market opening in the presence of domestic differences was widely regarded as a challenge to the traditional mode of integration in the EC: harmonization. To supporters, the new model improved on the old not only in speeding the removal of internal barriers but in two other ways as well. Instead of the top-down, centralized model in which common standards for domestic arrangements were negotiated and then enforced from Brussels, the new model permitted diversity developed from the national (or even local) level up within an environment of similar social goals. As Petersen declares, "spontaneous competitive adaptation may lead to differentiation by reform and innovation. This might be an advantage, because it creates opportunities to fit the institutional systems to the multitude of political preferences in Europe."[30] Even in those cases where European harmonization was recognized as necessary, considerable power to set standards was delegated to private organizations.[31] More significantly the new model called into question *how much* harmonization or convergence was necessary for an integrated market.

[29] Shapiro, "European Court," p. 140.
[30] Petersen, "Harmonization of Social Security," p. 524.
[31] Jacques Pelkmans, "The New Approach to Technical Harmonization and Standardization," *Journal of Common Market Studies* 25, no. 3 (March 1987): 255.

Supporters of old-style harmonization tended to argue that harmonization was required across a broad range of policy interventions to obtain the full benefits from a common market.[32] The new strategy takes a far more agnostic view of the degree of eventual policy convergence required and the areas in which it is required.

Despite the shift represented by the Single European Act, harmonization was acknowledged as necessary in certain spheres, and the notion of "Euro-standards" still had strong supporters in the Commission and among those who aimed at a federal Europe. The course toward monetary integration was very much in the old model: British efforts to win consent for competition between national currencies and a European currency found few supporters. In another sensitive area, however, the "social dimension," an apparent agreement on harmonization rather than institutional competition was challenged by Britain once again, producing the unique settlement at Maastricht in 1991 that permitted Britain to opt out.

The Maastricht settlement seemed to signify victory for "tight" harmonization on the social dimension "up" to the standards to northern Europe rather than harmonization on a narrowly defined range of issues (such as child labor), or harmonization within very wide bands. Peter Lange argues, however, that even in this sphere, sectoral and individual firm interests in competitiveness will override class interests and undermine serious harmonization to high European standards. Earlier, ideologically based rhetoric was cheap talk so long as British opposition was clear; with Britain removed from the bargaining, positions will be determined by narrower and carefully calculated economic interests.[33]

Lange suggests reasons for the willingness of highly regulated northern Europe to move toward institutional and regulatory competition even in this politically sensitive area. As in other areas of regulation, close, negotiated harmonization within the Community seemed less necessary than it might have in other international contexts. Fears of "social dumping" by other members of the Community were allayed by beliefs that all EC countries exemplified variants of a "European model" of production that incorporated a high level of protection (and considerable political power) for labor.[34] In other words, in this realm as in many others the pressures for negotiated harmonization at the Community level diminished as countries in the EC devel-

---

[32] See, for example, Jacques Pelkmans and Peter Robson, "The Aspirations of the White Paper," *Journal of Common Market Studies* 25, no. 3 (March 1987): 183.

[33] Peter Lange, "The Politics of the Social Dimension," in Sbragia, ed., *Euro-politics*, pp. 236–37, 244–45.

[34] Ibid., p. 253.

oped familiarity with each other's domestic systems and confidence in underlying social preferences. Contrary to the predictions of federalists, development of "habits of cooperation" (Dahrendorf's phrase) did not entail heightened joint decision making and standard setting in every instance. Instead, decentralization and competition were more acceptable because the implicit boundaries of that competition were clear.

THE UNITED STATES: HARMONIZATION THROUGH LEVERAGE

The United States typically approached its concerns over the trade-distorting effects of domestic differences through multilateral negotiations within the GATT. The negotiation of codes governing non-tariff barriers produced by different domestic regulatory and political contexts was one solution pressed by the United States during the Tokyo Round. The massive current account deficits induced by the Reagan Administration economic policies during the 1980s placed greater strain on the American pattern of trade politics and encouraged Congress to seek bilateral solutions to "unfair" practices abroad by threatening access by unfair traders to the American market. The culmination came in the 1988 Omnibus Trade and Competitiveness with the strengthening of Section 301 of the 1974 Trade Act, creating "Super 301," which authorized the identification of "priority foreign countries" that displayed "major barriers and trade distorting practices," and "Special 301" to deal with violators of intellectual property rights. Super 301 raised the issue of domestic differences that were perceived as systemic and anticompetitive in character to the top of the trade agenda.

These extensions of American trade law were controversial, because the United States unilaterally determined the existence of "unfairness" and threatened retaliation outside of the GATT if its determinations were not negotiated away. The negotiations took place under a deadline. Super 301 also extended American demands to policy areas and practices in which there were no GATT obligations and in which the link to trade in particular cases (such as denial of worker rights, export targeting, and anticompetitive business practices) was arguable.[35] In other words, the United States set out to harmonize domes-

[35] See the account by Jagdish Bhagwati, "Aggressive Unilateralism: An Overview," and Judith Hippler Bello and Alan F. Holmer, "The Heart of the 1988 Trade Act: A Legislative History of the Amendments to Section 301," both in Jagdish Bhagwati and Hugh T. Patrick, eds., *Aggressive Unilateralism* (Ann Arbor: University of Michigan Press, 1990), pp. 1–4, 65–75. Super 301 lapsed in 1990. A "kinder and gentler" version

tic differences by threatening trade retaliation (some closure of its domestic market). Bilateral negotiations over domestic differences took
place in the shadow of that mandated retaliatory threat.

STRUCTURAL IMPEDIMENTS INITIATIVE:
THE UNITED STATES AS "OPPOSITION PARTY"

Growing out of this pattern of American policy and carried out
under threat of Super 301 action was a set of negotiations that represented the most intensive effort to date outside the EC to place virtually any domestic practice or national policy on the table as possible
impediments to international exchange: the Structural Impediments
Initiative (SII) between the United States and Japan. These negotiations symbolized a growing consensus in the United States that there
was a "Japan problem," defined as systematic barriers to entry in the
Japanese market that prevented a "level playing field" in trade and
international competition.[36] In the case of Japan, domestic differences
were viewed as deeper ("structural") and not entirely governmental,
including "private" arrangements that restricted trade, entire sectors
that served as impediments (retailing), and most radically, patterns of
savings and investment (normally treated as part of macroeconomic
policy) that produced persistent external imbalances. For defenders
of the SII these new negotiating items represented a shift away from
narrow and relatively unimportant sources of trade conflict, such as
Japan's remaining explicit trade barriers, and toward a new emphasis
on domestic differences between the two countries that actually accounted for the persistent imbalance in their trading relationship.

The SII also had the benefit of being, at least superficially, less
asymmetric than other market-opening measures: both the United
States and Japan presented suggestions to the other side that would
reduce external imbalances. In practice, the United States posed most
of the demands, and Japan made most of the concessions. Some of
the U.S. demands dealt with barriers to imports, such as its claims
concerning the anticompetitive practices of Japanese industrial
groups (*keiretsu*). Other American agenda items, such as the Japanese
distribution system, were believed to lower the volume of Japanese

was revived by the Clinton Administration in 1994. See Thomas O. Bayard and Kim-
berly Ann Elliott, *Reciprocity and Retaliation in U.S. Trade Policy* (Washington, D.C.: Institute for International Economics, 1994), pp. 44–45.

[36] For recent summaries of the evidence for Japan as outlier in trade and investment,
see Encarnation, *Rivals beyond Trade*, pp. 75–96, and John Ravenhill, "The Japan Problem in Pacific Trade," in Higgott, Leaver, and Ravenhill, eds., *Pacific Economic Relations
in the 1990s*, pp. 106–32.

imports, but also, through driving up the price of consumer goods, to serve as yet another "tax" on consumption. (In other words, rationalizing the distribution system might be expected not only to shift the composition of consumption toward imports but also to increase the level of household consumption.) Still other agenda items, such as changes in Japan's land policy to lower the price of land (and housing) were more clearly directed toward one element in the explanation for high household saving. Many of these proposals had been urged by American analysts, particularly measures to render Japanese government policies less supportive of saving and more favorable toward consumption and public investment.[37] Although the Japanese side proposed measures to improve American competitiveness and education and to improve the American savings rate (including an early suggestion to limit the number of credit cards that Americans could hold), the weight of Japanese pressure fell, predictably, on the American fiscal deficit.

The SII represented an unprecedented effort by industrialized countries to influence structural adjustment in each other's economies and societies. The American task was even more difficult than other external attempts to influence economic policymaking, given the novel character of much of its agenda. The United States hoped that *gaiatsu* in this instance (as on past occasions) would mobilize its tacit allies within the Japanese political economy. Unfortunately, the changes that it sought challenged a deeply embedded set of interests that had dominated and profited from export-led growth for decades. Bureaucratically, the SII divided some potential internationalist allies of the United States: for example, MITI was responsible for the protection of small retailers and resisted revision of the Large Scale Retail Store Law, which blocked the opening of large department and chain stores. Other ministerial patrons of "impediments" were not at all internationalist and had no organizational interest in conceding the demands of the United States. The key bureaucratic players in land policy did not have interests that meshed with those of the United States, and those that did were notoriously weak. The Construction Ministry backed large infrastructure projects that could be bargained for political support and electoral finance by Liberal Democratic Party (LDP) politicians; housing was not one of its priorities. The National Land Agency, established in 1974 to restrain land prices, was a virtual nonplayer bureaucratically.[38] In general, this exercise in structural eco-

---

[37] See, for example, the suggestions of Edward J. Lincoln in *Japan: Facing Economic Maturity* (Washington, D.C.: Brookings, 1988), chap. 5.
[38] Bruce Roscoe, "Japan's Housing and the Rabbit-Hutch Mentality," *Far Eastern Economic Review*, 16 January 1986, p. 95.

nomic reform, like others, was likely to confront bureaucratic and political players who had little ambivalence in sacrificing international agreement for particularistic economic interests.

The key groups that might have supported the U.S. position were Japan's long-suffering consumers and its workers, whose wages had failed to keep up with productivity increases in the 1980s. Why Japanese consumers did not demand greater levels of public investment to raise their quality of life to levels comparable with other industrialized countries remained a mystery to outsiders. The immediate causes for low consumer influence were clear-cut, however, and they resembled, in exaggerated form, the portrait in other industrialized countries. Responsibility for consumer interests was spread among eighteen different government bodies in Japan. The Japanese consumer movement, fragmented into more than 4,000 groups, remained divided on the SII, in part because its membership included many small retailers.[39] In addition, conceptions of economic security that are deeply embedded in Japanese institutions find some resonance among Japanese consumers.[40] Survey data demonstrated surprising levels of support for the U.S. positions during the SII negotiations, however, suggesting an audience for American claims that the SII was in the best interests of the Japanese.[41] Nevertheless, without political entrepreneurship to mobilize this latent consumer discontent, the United States could count on little positive support. Leonard Schoppa has documented U.S. success in the SII on precisely those issues in which domestic political actors with preferences closer to those of the American negotiators, in the bureaucracy and the wider public, could be mobilized. This strategy was particularly successful in the case of changes in the Japanese retail distribution system, one of the successes of the SII.[42]

Final agreement in the SII negotiations was reached in June 1990. The United States received commitments from Japan for a ten-year public investment program, measures to reduce the cost of land, a revision of the Large Scale Retail Store Law, a more activist antitrust policy, and, more broadly, renewed commitment to reduce its current

[39] Shigeru Wada, "Buyer Interest Push Meets Public Apathy," *Japan Economic Journal*, 19 May 1990, p. 3.
[40] Richard Samuels, "Consuming for Production: Japanese National Security, Nuclear Fuel Procurement, and the Domestic Economy," *International Organization* 43, no. 4 (Autumn 1989): 625–46.
[41] "Many Japanese Support U.S. Trade Stance," *Japan Economic Journal*, 7 April 1990, p. 6.
[42] Leonard J. Schoppa, "Two-Level Games and Bargaining Outcomes: Why *Gaiatsu* Succeeds in Japan in Some Cases but Not Others," *International Organization* 47, no. 3 (Summer 1993): 353–86.

account surplus. The United States agreed to extend the Gramm-Rudman-Hollings deficit reduction legislation beyond 1993 and endorsed a number of other, less specific measures to enhance American competitiveness.[43] Even proponents of the negotiations argued that any effects would take several years to become apparent. Within one year, Japan had revised rules on the opening of large retail outlets and had implemented the first stage of its increase in public works spending. Despite the American deficit reduction agreement of 1990, the Japanese were less impressed with implementation of American commitments under the SII: as one Japanese official stated, "we appreciate the effort, but the result was nonsense."[44]

The ability of the two sides to reach agreement in 1990, whatever questions remained concerning the implementation of that agreement, was remarkable given the range of "domestic" issues that were part of the negotiations. Both sides seem to have accepted Edward Lincoln's blunt dismissal of the relevance of national sovereignty in these issues of economic policy: "When domestic policies have an important impact on international relations, they become a proper item for discussion and negotiation."[45] Despite surprising acceptance of external scrutiny of domestic differences between the two economies, the SII experiment documents clear limits to harmonization negotiations of this kind.

First, great uncertainty surrounds the ultimate effects of many of the changes urged on Japan (less regarding those pressed on the United States). The causal models are complex and poorly understood. The degree of uncertainty was demonstrated by contrasting arguments made by mainstream economists, who argued that the United States was helping the Japanese to become *more* competitive and by revisionist Japanologists who believed that the SII would never succeed because the Japanese knew that it would *reduce* their competitive edge.[46] If the underlying models are wrong, the results of an implemented agreement of this kind would necessarily be a disappointment and could even intensify the level of bilateral economic conflict.

Equally apparent from the SII episode is the need for firm transna-

[43] On the contents of the agreement, see Yuko Inoue, "SII Talks Shift Emphasis to Savings Imbalance," *Japan Economic Journal*, 7 July 1990, p. 3; David E. Sanger, "U.S. and Japan Set Accord to Rectify Trade Imbalances," *New York Times*, 29 June 1990, p. A1.

[44] Steven R. Weisman, "Trade Talks with Japan Face Stormy Reopening," *New York Times*, 13 January 1991, Section 1, Part 1, p. 14.

[45] Lincoln, *Japan Faces Economic Maturity*, p. 286.

[46] For an example of the former, see Jeffrey A. Frankel, "The SII Outcome: In Whose Best Interest?," *International Economy*, October/November 1990: 70–72; for the latter, see below.

tional coalition building in order to consolidate an agreement and ensure its implementation. As American demands reached deeper into the Japanese political economy, the likelihood of constructing such a coalition diminished, particularly for the long-run policies that would be required to shift Japan to a more consumption-oriented economy. For policy initiatives of the SII variety, coalition building is arduous: the beneficiaries of such structural reforms are often weakly organized; the opponents have entrenched political positions built up over years in pursuit of a national economic strategy, whether import-substituting industrialization in Latin America or export-oriented industrialization in Japan. Schoppa's account of the SII suggests that the informational requirements for a successful strategy are formidable: a keen awareness of the latent preferences of groups within the bureaucracy and the wider public that might be mobilized on behalf of the goals of the external negotiator.[47] The strategy must aim at mobilizing such sympathetic allies into the negotiating process on the other side without arousing nationalist hostility to external pressure or foreign meddling in domestic politics.

Finally, the SII negotiations were about more than harmonization of domestic differences to the American model or joint gains from mutual economic adjustment. They also concerned international influence. The structural changes demanded by the United States could also be read as an attempt to rein in Japanese economic advance and deflect the rise of Japan as a major economic and financial power. As symmetry between the two economies increases, Japanese willingness to undertake this style of one-sided harmonization is less and less likely.

HARMONIZATION AND THE NORTH AMERICAN FREE TRADE AGREEMENT: LABOR STANDARDS AND THE ENVIRONMENT

The original plan for the U.S.–Canada Free Trade Agreement and the North American Free Trade Agreement (adding Mexico) was minimalist. Few expected institution building along the lines of the EC; little policy coordination was predicted or required. This was to be economic integration on the old model, a clearing away of barriers—principally barriers at the border—to trade and investment. American goals were in part economic (lowering barriers to American exports and investment) and in part political (locking in policies to the south that were more likely to create a stable Mexico). For Mexico and Canada, ensuring access to the American market in the face of in-

---

[47] Schoppa, "Two-Level Games."

creasingly capricious anti-dumping and countervailing duties cases
was a prime objective; in addition, the Salinas government in Mexico
sought an external means of embedding its economic reforms in Mexican politics. Each of the participants in the negotiations for NAFTA,
however, were also interested in increasing their competitiveness
against third parties.[48] Given strong domestic preferences that ran
counter to American policies in areas outside commercial policy, both
Canada and Mexico were concerned that the trade negotiations not be
broadened. Both were interested in retaining their domestic differences vis-à-vis the United States, and both resisted any American efforts to link such policies to the trade agenda.[49]

The Bush Administration shared this preference for a narrow
agenda, but the administration's request for fast-track negotiating authority in 1991 dramatically shifted the debate in the United States.
Organized labor and environmental groups pressed to include
broader policy harmonization on the agenda. Four types of argument
were used by environmental and labor advocates to oppose NAFTA
or to seek modifications in it. First, those who wished to end the negotiations for NAFTA simply argued against expanded cross-border
trade, because it increased economic activity of traditional (environ-
mentally unsound) types in Mexico. Second, certain environmental
and to a lesser degree labor issues were directly related to industrialization along the border under the pre-NAFTA maquiladora program. Many of these issues were classic environmental externalities.
The Reagan and Bush administrations had already taken some steps
to address transborder pollution issues in bilateral agreements such as
the La Paz Accord of 1983. These measures were regarded by environmentalists, with justification, as inadequate. Third, environmentalists were concerned that American regulations designed to protect
health and the environment might be challenged as nontariff barriers
under NAFTA. Although the Bush Administration had offered assur-
ances that this would not take place at the national level, state and
local regulations, often stricter than national ones, could be pre-
empted. A regulatory race to the bottom through NAFTA mecha-

[48] Gary Clyde Hufbauer and Jeffrey J. Schott, *North American Free Trade: Issues and
Recommendations* (Washington, D.C.: Institute for International Economics, 1992), pp.
6–12.
[49] See, for example, comments by Gustavo Vega-Canovas in Nora Lustig, Barry P.
Bosworth, and Robert Z. Lawrence, eds., *North American Free Trade: Assessing the Impact*
(Washington, D.C.: Brookings, 1992), pp. 200–201, and Lorraine Eden and Maureen
Appel Molot, "From Silent Integration to Strategic Alliance: The Political Economy of
North American Free Trade," Occasional Paper in International Trade Law and Policy
no. 17, 1991, Centre for Trade Policy and Law, Norman Paterson School of Interna-
tional Affairs, Carleton University, Ottawa, pp. 24–25.

nisms was therefore a concern. Finally, harmonization to a lower level of labor or environmental regulation through a more indirect route (competition from less-regulated Mexican exporters and exit by American firms seeking a less-regulated environment) also received a great deal of attention in the debate over NAFTA. This route to lowering American environmental standards was labeled "environmental dumping."[50]

As Grossman and Krueger have noted, these arguments were seldom stated in terms of clear causal linkages, and they were even more rarely supported with strong empirical evidence.[51] The absence of strong evidence for some of the posited effects, particularly environmental dumping through foreign investment in Mexico, suggests that the environmental opposition to NAFTA was in part opportunistically driven. In other words, NAFTA was a useful hostage with which to pursue a strategy of issue linkage, in which environmental demands on Mexico were connected to the trade agreement and Mexican desires for guaranteed market access to the United States. In part, however, the arguments of labor and environmental groups, particularly about effects on American regulation, did not assume a fixed policy environment. A central anxiety was that NAFTA, either institutionally or through increasing the incentives for exit, would reduce their domestic bargaining power in perennial battles with business and "progrowth" interests. The use of access to the American market to impose, in effect, American environmental and labor standards was seldom questioned. One supporter of linkage was straightforward: "while import standards may be intrusive and paternalistic, they are not coercive. They do not force trading partners to take action. What they do is to set conditions for voluntary exchange."[52]

Other participants in the NAFTA debate argued for greater tolerance of national preferences and limiting negotiations to those environmental issues with either genuine cross-border spillovers or close and clearly identified connections to trade. Gary Hufbauer and Jeffrey Schott argued that "the huge disparities in income between the United States and Mexico argue for tolerance toward Mexican

---

[50] For a consideration of the links between environmentalism and NAFTA, see Mary E. Kelley, Dick Kamp, and Michael Gregory, "Mexico–U.S. Free Trade Negotiations and the Environment: Exploring the Issues," discussion paper, Texas Center for Policy Studies and Border Ecology Project, January 1991, and Udi Helman and Ben Tonra, "Free Trade and the Environment," CSIS Policy Papers on the Americas, Vol. 2, Report 8, Center for Strategic and International Studies, Washington, D.C., 23 May 1991.

[51] Gene M. Grossman and Alan B. Krueger, "Environmental Impacts of a North American Free Trade Agreement," discussion paper in economics no. 158, Princeton University, November 1991.

[52] Steve Charnovitz, "Environmental and Labour Standards in Trade," *The World Economy* 15, no. 3 (May 1992): 347.

priorities in addressing local pollution problems (i.e., problems that do *not* spill across the border)." Instead of harmonization through American leverage to American standards, they suggested an approach closer to mutual recognition in the short run. Members of NAFTA should be free to maintain their existing environmental standards and regulations subject to challenge only on the basis that they are "disguised restrictions" on trade (thus narrowing one route in a regulatory race to the bottom). On the other hand, parties to NAFTA would commit initially only to rigorous enforcement of their existing environmental standards.[53]

Labor and environmental objections to NAFTA grew more important with the election of Bill Clinton as president of the United States, because as a candidate Clinton had made support of NAFTA conditional on the completion of side agreements to deal with these issues. The labor and environmental side agreements announced in August 1993 were relatively modest in scope, embodying mutual recognition with international surveillance of implementation, rather than harmonization to U.S. standards. The position of the U.S. government (under pressure from Republicans in Congress) had retreated from any hint of supranational authority for the commissions established in the side agreements. The Canadian and Mexican governments apparently resisted encroachment in the sphere of labor market policies more assiduously than in environmental policy. The side agreements attempted to bridge the sovereignty concerns of Mexico and Canada (and some in the U.S. Congress) on the one hand, and the demands for rapid harmonization from U.S. labor and environmental organizations on the other through an innovative formula. On paper standards in the three countries were not dissimilar: concerns centered on enforcement of those standards. The side agreements established *international* oversight (and possible sanctions) of *national* enforcement of *nationally* determined standards. This mix was weighted differently in the environmental and labor spheres, with national governments awarded more latitude in enforcing labor standards.

The NAFTA debate demonstrated that "domestic" issues with only tenuous connections to trade could be linked to trade negotiations through the power of political groups that could enforce the linkage. In the course of the NAFTA negotiations, a GATT panel decision ensured that the connections between environment and trade at the global level would be scrutinized carefully. The dispute settlement panel found an American ban on imports of Mexican tuna imposed under U.S. environmental legislation (the Marine Mammal Protection

[53] Hufbauer and Schott, *North American Free Trade*, pp. 147–53.

Act) in contravention of GATT obligations. The case was an interesting test of yet another effort by the United States to extend the reach of its environmental legislation through restrictions on market access.[54] Of greater political significance, the panel findings heightened anti-GATT sentiment in the environmental movement. The trade organization was portrayed as simply another minion of free markets and deregulation, whatever the costs to the environment. The GATT seemed to lean heavily against the unilateral use of trade measures to force international regulatory conformity. This position was likely to produce new collisions with environmentalists who seemed eager to use unilateral national means, including trade leverage, to influence the environmental policies of other countries. Making judgments about the primacy of environmental regulations or international trade rules when they clash will be all the more difficult as tougher environmental standards affect products that are important in world trade and as protectionists discover the benefits of aligning themselves with an increasingly powerful domestic interest group.[55]

Managed Trade and System Conflict

Mutual recognition addresses domestic differences in economic integration by accepting national diversity and permitting competition to determine the shape of national institutions. Harmonization attempts to reach a greater or lesser degree of institutional convergence through intergovernmental negotiation or unilateral leverage. In the first instance it is assumed that economic exchange will not be seriously skewed or blocked by the institutional differences that emerge; in the second that barriers to economic exchange can be effectively dealt with through international negotiation and monitoring, ideally in a multilateral forum.

For an increasingly vocal band of skeptics, however, these core assumptions are rejected, at least in the case of Japan and other East Asian economies. Proponents of managed trade base their skepticism of both mutual recognition and harmonization on a revisionist account of the Japanese economy.[56] Despite their very different descrip-

---

[54] For a summary and analysis of the case and report of the GATT dispute settlement panel, see Joel P. Trachtman, "GATT Dispute Settlement Panel: United States—Restrictions on Imports of Tuna," *The American Journal of International Law* 86, no. 1 (January 1992): 142–51. The production process in question was the use of fishing methods that produced an excessively high kill rate of dolphins.

[55] Gilbert Winham, "The GATT after the Uruguay Round," in Higgott, Leaver, and Ravenhill, eds., *Pacific Economic Relations in the 1990s*, pp. 192–93.

[56] The revisionists are generally taken to include James Fallows, Chalmers Johnson,

tive accounts of Japan, revisionists agree that Japan's political economy is fundamentally different from that of the United States and Western Europe, that international economic competition confirms those institutional differences rather than produces institutional convergence, and that bilateral and multilateral efforts at harmonization are too slow, too difficult to enforce, and generally unsuccessful at creating open markets. Rather than complex and carefully calibrated negotiations that attempt to harmonize institutions in order to obtain the fullest gains from market integration, managed trade in this view is an appropriate outcome—at least in the medium term—for exchange among radically different socioeconomic systems. Under this results-oriented trade policy, access is measured by quantitative targets negotiated bilaterally by governments.

Because this approach has become a prominent element in the Clinton administration's trade negotiations with Japan, it is important to tease apart the points of agreements and disagreement among those who advocate managed trade as at least one element in American trade strategy. First, proponents agree that managed trade as a *policy* is made necessary by managed trade as a *fact* of international economic life. Managed trade is not novel; trade in certain sectors has seldom taken place in a competitive setting dominated by private actors. When the prevalence of managed trade is cited, however, analysts may adopt a broad or a narrow definition. Lawrence Krause argues that managed trade is "trade that is not priced at marginal cost to ultimate consumers, that is not under competitive conditions."[57] This definition includes most trade internal to multinational corporations or linked combinations of firms, such as the Japanese *keiretsu*. Laura Tyson endorses a more conventional definition that emphasizes government intervention and distortion of trade, although even in this narrower portrait there is some confusion: at one point, Tyson declares that "strategic interaction between firms and governments manipulates competitive outcomes in high-technology products"; at another, she describes "a world in which trade is manipulated by government intervention, and structural differences impede competition between producers from different nations." "Strategic interaction" and "manipulation" are not equivalent, and it is difficult to tell how

Clyde Prestowitz, and Karel van Wolferen. Arguments in support of managed trade (in the sense of quantitative targets for imports) have been advanced by certain "mainstream" economists as well: see, for example, the contributions by Rudiger Dornbusch and Laura Tyson in Robert Z. Lawrence and Charles L. Schultze, eds., *An American Trade Strategy: Options for the 1990s* (Washington, D.C., Brookings, 1990), pp. 106–94.

[57] Lawrence B. Krause, "Managed Trade: The Regime of Today and Tomorrow," *Journal of Asian Economics* 3, no. 2 (Fall 1992): 302.

much strategic calculation (as opposed to political responsiveness or unanticipated consequences) is involved in the high-technology cases described by Tyson. Whatever the extent of managed trade within the international economy, however, she clearly defines managed trade as policy: "any trade agreement that establishes quantitative targets on trade flows."[58]

Second, if those who accept managed trade as a policy are divided on the extent of (relatively) free trade in the existing international economy, they also disagree on the desirable and plausible outcomes that they foresee for a more successful trade policy. Some proponents endorse garden-variety neomercantilism, a simple repudiation of what they regard as the naive American view (shared by few others in the world) that free exchange produces mutual economic benefits in favor of a more power-oriented and conflictual view of trade.[59] Rather than defining national economic welfare as increasing the standard of living of the citizenry, neomercantilists come close to arguing for export promotion over almost any other national economic goal. For others in the managed trade camp, the image of the future is much less conflictual: endorsing managed trade is simply becoming "more like them" (the Japanese). Krause, for example, suggests that a trading system based on "orderly change" and managed by stable oligopolies would match the preferences of populations on both sides of the Pacific without impairing the dynamism of Pacific economies.[60] Managed trade in this view permits the maintenance of valued domestic differences in a negotiated setting.

Others who accept managed trade as a policy do not endorse it as a necessary or desirable future. Although Tyson sees pervasive government intervention in high-technology sectors, the setting of quantitative or other outcome-oriented targets for trade is a means to a more competitive future: in Japan, managed trade is required to reach "something akin to a market outcome."[61] Tyson's ultimate goal appears to be a gradual opening of the Japanese market and a change in the behavior of key Japanese players, particularly corporations. She argues that such change could be detected following the 1986 Semiconductor Agreement (SCTA), but despite the increase in market share for American semiconductor firms in the Japanese market, her evidence for a permanent change in Japanese corporate behavior is

[58] Laura D'Andrea Tyson, *Who's Bashing Whom?: Trade Conflict in High-Technology Industries* (Washington, D.C.: Institute for International Economics, 1992), pp. 294, 295, 133.
[59] See, for example, Clyde V. Prestowitz, Jr., Alan Tonelson, and Robert W. Jerome, "The Last Gasp of GATTism," *Harvard Business Review*, March–April 1991: 134–36.
[60] Krause, "Managed Trade," 306.
[61] Tyson, *Who's Bashing Whom?*, p. 262.

anecdotal at best.[62] Fred Bergsten and Marcus Noland are even more hesitant in recommending results-oriented agreements. They accept voluntary import expansions (VIEs) as useful in particular circumstances, however: intermediate or capital goods sectors in which entry is blocked by vertical *keiretsu*. Bergsten and Noland do not contest the possible efficiency of such Japanese arrangements, but they argue that such corporate groups developed in a peculiar setting of government-imposed closure to international competition. In such cases results-oriented policies "may make some sense as a mechanism to force the adaptation of a system that was developed in the closed, policy-distorted environment of Japan in the 1950s and 1960s."[63] The degree of change to a more internationalized market structure (minimal test) or more market-oriented behavior is crucial in evaluating the managed trade case and in comparing its efficacy with other instruments, multilateral and bilateral.

A final distinction among managed trade proponents concerns those alternative instruments. Managed trade advocates discount mutual recognition of institutional differences: the international economic stakes in permitting market closure or unchallenged trade distortions are simply too high. Their disagreements center on the relative weight assigned to multilateral mechanisms and bilateral, results-oriented negotiations. For Clyde Prestowitz and others more pessimistic about internal change in Japan, the GATT has simply attempted "a series of unenforceable rules applied to currently ungovernable areas of international economic competition."[64] Despite their harsh criticism of the GATT, however, advocates of managed trade have not argued for its overturn; indeed, in some cases, they urge the creation of stronger international institutions that can deal with domestic differences more effectively among smaller groups of "like-minded" countries.[65]

Those who see results-oriented agreements as a temporary measure in pursuit of greater market access are clearer on the place of managed trade in their portfolio of trade options: it is a second-best solution when efforts at multilateral harmonization are unlikely to succeed in the short run. Bergsten and Noland make clear their preference for identifying and dismantling the source of market clo-

[62] Tyson focuses on the EPROM market in Japan but also notes that only one American company, Motorola, re-entered DRAM production during the period of the SCTA and NSCTA. Ibid., p. 126.
[63] C. Fred Bergsten and Marcus Noland, *Reconcilable Differences? United States–Japan Economic Conflict* (Washington, D.C.: Institute for International Economics, 1994), p. 196.
[64] Prestowitz, Tonelson, and Jerome, "The Last Gasp of GATTism," p. 131.
[65] See ibid. on "super-GATT," p. 137.

sure, whether through bilateral negotiation or international agreement on competition policy or subsidies.[66] In each of the cases that Tyson presents, she tends toward pessimism about the prospects for negotiated, multilateral harmonization of the domestic practices that present barriers to entry or threats to the competitive success of American firms. The GATT may not be dead in her view, "but in its present form it is largely irrelevant to many of the government practices and structural impediments that give rise to high-technology trade friction."[67] In other cases, bilateral harmonization negotiations are thwarted by successive layers of barriers presented by the Japanese "onion"; the major barriers are deeply embedded in Japanese business organization, and negotiated change is unlikely. In yet other instances, rules-based frameworks that would capture the many obstructions to foreign entry are difficult to conceive.[68] Tyson's pessimism is difficult to evaluate, because the degree of harmonization that would be acceptable is seldom made clear. Her own evidence also suggests that harmonization agreements without quantitative targets have worked successfully in key instances.[69] Clearer criteria are required for determining when to persist in efforts at harmonization and when to move to the second-best alternative of managed trade.

The Clinton Administration has made results-oriented bilateral trade negotiations a centerpiece of its economic diplomacy with Japan. From its earliest months the Administration has made clear that quantitative targets for American imports in the Japanese market would be a central measure of success in its dealings with Japan.[70] Even though these initiatives were resisted by the Japanese government and condemned by many outside Japan, it is unlikely that managed trade will disappear as an option for the United States and other industrialized countries. As a means for dealing with domestic differences, therefore, its claims deserve careful evaluation.

The principal shortcoming of managed trade as an instrument for addressing domestic differences lies in its uncertain efficacy in inducing institutional change, efficacy that is likely to decline with American bargaining power. The anticompetitive effects of results-oriented

[66] Bergsten and Noland, *Reconcilable Differences?*, p. 196.
[67] Tyson, *Who's Bashing Whom?*, p. 5.
[68] See her argument in the Motorola case. Ibid., pp. 73–74.
[69] The 1992 bilateral agreement on civil aircraft between the United States and the European Community is the most prominent example; Tyson also suggests that a plurilateral agreement governing semiconductor trade is also feasible and desirable. Ibid., p. 151.
[70] Keith Bradsher, "For Clinton, 'Managed Trade' Is Emerging as Policy Option," *New York Times*, 30 March 1993, pp. A1, C9; Andrew Pollack, "U.S. Steps Up the Pressure in Tokyo," *New York Times*, 24 April 1993, pp. 17, 18; James Risen, "Clinton Frustrated with Japan on Trade," *Los Angeles Times*, 30 September 1993, p. A14.

trade agreements have long been argued by their critics. If voluntary export restraints (VERs) encourage cartellike behavior on the part of exporters as well as assigning them massive rents, the same can be suspected concerning the VIEs of managed trade. If managed trade encourages anticompetitive practices and government intervention, some proponents of managed trade with Japan would hardly be alarmed: in their view the Japanese political economy is pervaded by such practices and they are not likely to change. For those who argue that managed trade provides an acceptable second-best to other trade options and serves to enhance competition in the Japanese economy in the long run, anticompetitive effects from managed trade are a more damaging side effect. Managed trade, through encouraging producer collaboration to meet import targets, could deepen one set of domestic differences that are of central concern as barriers to market access.

The treatment of bargaining power by proponents of managed trade is even more plagued with contradictions. Aggressive unilateralism on the part of the United States has been based on a perceived asymmetry in bargaining power between the United States and its trading partners: as SII demonstrated, however, it was not bargaining asymmetry that provided the most satisfying explanation for success and failure in those negotiations. On the one hand, managed trade is endorsed because the GATT is portrayed as incapable of sustained enforcement of harmonization in key policy areas; part of the GATT's weakness is also assigned to a relative decline in American power. Declining American leverage also seems to be one reason for skepticism regarding the SII and other harmonization efforts: the United States simply does not possess the leverage vis-à-vis Japan that it once had. Nevertheless, the United States is expected to negotiate (impose?) bilateral, market-opening deals that seem to require as much leverage or more. Apparently, using market access as its principal instrument, an America in decline can still work its will in one corner of the international arena.

STRATEGIES FOR DEALING WITH DOMESTIC DIFFERENCES

Conflict over divergent political and economic models and their effects on international exchange has grown since the mid-1970s. The United States and Western Europe have been joined by highly competitive trading nations that do not display the same institutional landscape. Even after a decade of apparent global advance for market prescriptions, these anxieties over attributes that seem to hinder entry or offer "unfair" advantage are likely to grow. As Shapiro shrewdly notes with regard to the EC (and his finding could be extended), some forms of rent-seeking domestic regulation have become less legitimate, but other forms of restriction on exchange, such as regulations to protect health, safety, and the environment, have become more potent.

As economic integration has deepened and domestic differences behind borders have assumed greater political salience, each of the strategies described—mutual recognition and institutional competition, harmonization (through symmetric and asymmetric bargaining), and managed trade—has found proponents in the new order of international trade. Most of the examples discussed involve regional trading arrangements in which a choice between strategies of harmonization and mutual recognition is most likely. Each strategy displays certain political prerequisites for its adoption and success; each has particular shortcomings when compared to the alternatives.

Mutual recognition calls into question a familiar argument in much of the writing on economic integration, a functionalist claim that removing barriers to economic exchange at the border (negative integration) will necessarily lead to convergence through a negotiated process of positive integration, institution building, and policy coordination. The turn toward mutual recognition within the EC was in part a response to the failure of a previous model of harmonization under symmetric bargaining, symmetry enforced through the mechanism of unanimity. Acceptance of mutual recognition was also dependent on the success of previous integration.

Mutual recognition and institutional competition are favored by those who incline toward marketlike and competitive solutions to international differences. The strategy has stiff political prerequisites as a mechanism for managing conflict over domestic differences in a setting of deepening economic integration, however. A willingness to accept institutional competition is far more likely if societies display a high degree of comity. Members of the EC have been willing to credit one another with fundamental similarity in their national preferences over key policies. They effectively endorsed the existence of a "European model" for organizing national political economies with basic similarities across EC members.

Contributing to these perceptions was the EC's stipulation that only democracies could be members. Democratic governance guaranteed a high degree of transparency in policymaking, enhancing the levels of trust among member states. Democratic governance also provided some insurance that preexisting domestic imbalances in power would not distort the expected results of institutional competition. Authoritarian systems such as those of China or Mexico may tilt the domestic balance more readily against particular interests, repressing their abilities to organize or to vote. The social equilibrium in these cases may be sustained in ways that muffle the competitive pressures arising from the international economy: a "level playing field" internationally may require a more level playing field in domestic politics.

If European experience is a guide, another prerequisite for a mutual recognition strategy is belief in relatively weak competitive effects when institutional diversity is permitted within wide bands of harmonization. The policy differences that survive within the EC in the 1990s are not likely to produce widespread dislocation in the short run, only gradual pressure for change that can easily be met through political accommodation. Given these conditions, the transparent and relatively slow process of institutional competition allows the possibility of widespread social learning among members of the Community: borrowing ideas and institutions in policy areas such as taxation or health care is possible.

Finally, although mutual recognition seems to eliminate the need for cumbersome international negotiations to ensure harmonization, it is unlikely to remove the need for dispute-settlement devices, a role played by the European Court and the Commission within the EC. In the absence of such quasi-judicial mechanisms, even in a highly institutionalized international setting, political pressure could lead to a spiraling proliferation of new restraints to economic exchange in the guise of "permissible" regulation.

The mutual recognition model and its acceptance of institutional competition might appear to be the most efficient means of dealing with domestic differences. The political prerequisites noted, however, suggest circumstances under which it may be unacceptable to partners in international economic exchange. On the one hand, a regime of mutual recognition must be perceived as free from disguised protectionism: institutions alleged to serve important social purposes may also (or primarily) impede inward access to domestic markets or discriminate against non-nationals. The obverse of this concern is anxiety that intensified economic integration will produce a Darwinian process of institutional competition, impose insupportable adjustment costs, and force the abandonment of important social goals, whether it is protection of the environment or defense of labor standards. These anxieties are based as often on perceptions of other societies as on clear evidence or causal models of the effects of institutional competition. That fact does not diminish their political potency, however. As a result, two other strategies are advanced for dealing with domestic differences when mutual recognition is politically impossible.

Harmonization, once widely accepted as a solution to conflict over domestic differences in the EC and in the global trading system, is viewed more skeptically today. Negotiated harmonization under conditions of relative symmetry in bargaining power proved less and less efficient over time in the EC. Decision rules based on unanimity explain a part of that record, but the Community also undertook harmonization in areas in which the payoff in terms of enhanced efficiency and increase in market scope was slender. In any case, harmonization on "Euro-standards" was more than a simple strategy for market integration; for some within the Community it remains a means for building a federal Europe.

The attachment of such issues to harmonization programs can be seen even more clearly in harmonization that occurs under conditions of unequal bargaining power. In most negotiations over harmonizing domestic differences, the issue of what is a legitimate, "trade-related" linkage is in fact one of the core disagreements. For some, the boundary is clearly demonstrated nontariff barriers to imports; for others, it is, more broadly, restrictions on entry, particularly in the area of investment and services; for still others, it is any policy difference that might convey an "unfair" competitive advantage. The latter category, encompassing labor standards and environmental regulations, is most controversial politically. Such unrelated or distantly related linkage also becomes more and more attractive to policy proponents of different stripes: as more countries liberalize their economies and other means of influence (such as military force) decline in utility, trade leverage becomes an appealing tool if some association with "unfairness" can be established.

In examining the record of harmonization negotiations, particularly the SII, the disadvantages of this model are clear and the gains often seem slight. The achievement most often cited for such exercises is that they remove political pressure to implement even more unappealing and damaging policies, such as legislated protection. The principal prerequisite for success seems to be the presence of powerful domestic allies in the target state, both to ensure effective implementation of agreed policy changes and to guard against a nationalist backlash. As Takatoshi Ito argues, Japanese resentment increased as the United States has moved from VERs to market-oriented, sector specific (MOSS) and SII negotiations to Super 301 pressure, in large measure because the gains to domestic Japanese economic interests declined with each new set of American demands. Many Japanese consumers viewed much of the SII program as beneficial to their interests and essentially supported the American negotiating position.[71]

[71] Takatoshi Ito, "U.S. Political Pressure and Economic Liberalization in East Asia," in Jeffrey Frankel and Miles Kahler, eds., *Regionalism and Rivalry: Japan and the U.S. in Pacific Asia* (Chicago: University of Chicago Press, 1993), pp. 391–422.

Active and visible environmental and labor support in Mexico alleviated the intrusiveness of American demands on these issues during the NAFTA negotiations. The need for internal support is particularly important given the types of domestic differences that are under negotiation and implementation. Unlike in earlier trade negotiations, the focus is no longer on government policies exclusively. The style of threat is to compel, rather than to deter, and it is a two-step strategy to compel: governments are asked to change "private" practices, often over great resistance. Monitoring such agreements from the outside is difficult; internal allies may also provide a reliable monitoring device.

Managed or results-oriented trade agreements are advanced as an alternative to the shortcomings of bilateral or multilateral harmonization. Proponents argue that multilateral harmonization in the WTO will occur only within unacceptably broad bands of harmonization; enforcement of even these weak constraints will be ineffective. Bilateral harmonization requires information about domestic practices that distort trade and investment and confronts even greater obstacles to monitoring and enforcing agreements that are reached. Underlying the skepticism of revisionist proponents of managed trade is a belief that some economies in the trading system, particularly Japan, are not "like-minded" enough to risk mutual recognition or to implement harmonization credibly.

For some proponents managed trade strategies, in contrast to harmonization, can claim to avoid intruding in other societies in ways that inevitably provoke resentment. The political economy in question can achieve the targeted changes in any way that it likes. For others, however, managed trade is simply a more palatable and efficacious means to the same ends as harmonization: a political economy "more like us." In both variants, the route to achieving such quantitative targets (establishing cartels, for example) might well make future conflict between competing systems even worse. Assumptions of a high degree of government influence over private actors might become a self-fulfilling prophecy. In any case, proponents of managed trade assume considerable bargaining power on the part of the United States or other outsiders in settings where domestic political allies are likely to be nonexistent. The sources of this bargaining power remain obscure, particularly after the end of the Cold War.

International conflict over domestic institutional differences within the trade regime are unlikely to disappear and will probably intensify: the growing importance of trade to most economies, the integration of an increasingly diverse group of societies into the GATT system, and the continued commitment of governments to domestic intervention on behalf of a wide array of social goals all portend a lengthening agenda. Even benign regulatory goals, such as protection of the environment, may conceal protectionist intentions: none of the models here offers a satisfactory means for deciphering the motives of states, although each offers some clues or rules of thumb.

It is unlikely that any of these strategies will become the dominant strategy in managing the political conflicts arising from deeper economic integration, but it is worth contemplating the consequences for global welfare of alternative worlds organized along the lines of one or another of these models. Mutual recognition and institutional competition favor national diversity at the risk of disguised obstacles to economic exchange on the one hand and a "race to the bottom" that undermines desirable social ends on the other. The widespread adoption of harmonization risks eliminating institutional innovations that may be more efficient than existing practice and removing national differences that have beneficial global effects. A system based on managed trade could impose high costs in further fragmentation of the trading system and weakening of multilateral constraints on national behavior. In addition, apart from the market openings imposed by more powerful trading partners, external pressures to enhance competition would either be muffled or disappear. National systems could live happily in a relatively static and inefficient relationship with one another.

Each of these strategies is likely to remain in competition as a means of dealing with domestic differences in the context of deepening international economic integration, as each represents important strands within a broader liberal outlook and each finds echoes in other spheres of political discourse. Mutual recognition and institutional competition place liberal desires for diversity of national systems in a preeminent place. Social advance in this view is grounded in an evolutionary process of competition and selection that produces more efficient and desirable social outcomes. It is a liberal image open to the future, but utterly unconcerned about the past endowments that societies, groups, and individuals bring to the process.

Harmonization, on the other hand, satisfies liberal beliefs in universal norms. It poses more difficult requirements on policymakers and the public in not only determining the content of those norms but also assessing which are essential in any process of international economic integration. Distinguishing an international consensus on those norms from the peculiarities of individual liberal nations, such as those of the United States, is particularly daunting. Although harmonization may seem arrogant and ethnocentric, whether in trade, human rights, or environmental issues, it may also strengthen groups and interests in less liberal societies who might otherwise not have the power to achieve their goals. Harmonization, then, also satisfies the liberal belief in transnational alliances of the like-minded.

Finally, although it rejects many of the presuppositions of both mutual recognition and harmonization, managed trade also appeals to a particular strand of American national ideology: distrust and dislike of foreign entanglements, an unwillingness to believe that the United States, whatever its good intentions, can understand or shape other societies, a suspicion that some of those societies do not have the best interests of the United States at heart. Unfortunately, this viewpoint also represents an American desire to have the benefits of economic interdependence without paying the full costs.

The new and untested WTO confronts an international economic agenda driven by domestic differences and increasing openness to trade and investment. In future debates over competition policy, labor and environmental standards, and international investment rules these competing variants of liberal prescription and strategy will set the political limits of international economic exchange.

CHAPTER THIRTEEN

Policy Approaches to System
Friction: Convergence Plus

SYLVIA OSTRY

Over the 1980s two powerful forces created pressure for convergence in harmonization of national policies. One stemmed from globalization, characterized by the enormous surge of foreign direct investment (FDI) and the growing importance of the multinational enterprise as an actor in the international economy. The other, spurred by the prominence of Japan as a strong competitor in technology-intensive sectors, arose from U.S.–Japanese rivalry and from important changes in American international economic policy.

In this essay I briefly review these background developments and then turn to international policy issues. The priority target for harmonization is competition policy, which affects both trade and innovation. It is argued that harmonization of competition policy will be necessary but not sufficient to mitigate the system friction that has emerged from the more intense competition within the Triad (the EC, the United States, and Japan) in high-tech sectors.

GLOBALIZATION

The term *globalization* became fashionable in the late 1980s, but no one definition exists. There is agreement, however, that the globalization of the 1980s, driven by a surge of FDI, represents a new phase in the tightening of the trade and financial linkages among countries that began after World War II. As linkage deepens, the scope for effective independent policy action by individual countries narrows

333

or, to put it differently, the international spillover of domestic policies increases. Further, as linkage deepens, international rivalry among the advanced industrialized countries has become more intense and increasingly focused on technology-intensive goods and services.

Between 1985 and 1990 FDI grew at four times the rate of world output and three times the rate of trade. Eighty percent of the investment was controlled by multinational enterprises (MNEs) from the EC, the United States, and Japan. Unlike in previous postwar patterns, the United States was the main recipient country and Japan the dominant source country. Japan was a latecomer to globalization. A reflection of this is seen in Table 13-1, which shows the striking disparity between inward and outward stocks of FDI in Japan as compared with Europe and the United States. Whereas by 1990 Japanese MNEs controlled 12 percent of world FDI, foreign investment in Japan represented only 1 percent of the total world stock. The comparable figures in 1980 were 4 and 1 percent.

Manufacturing investment, especially in capital- and technology-intensive industries, grew faster than that in natural resource- and labor-intensive sectors. By 1990 the share of the former in manufacturing's inward stock of FDI had increased to 40 percent, from 27 percent in 1975, as a result of increased flows to the OECD countries and the NICs of East Asia. Within these industrial sectors, the fastest growth has been in research-intensive industries within the triad of Europe, the United States, and Japan.[1] Such developments reflect the need for firms in technology-intensive sectors to locate in countries with strong research capacities, in order to access knowledge globally and also better to serve sophisticated buyers through customization of products. More generally FDI has become a two-way channel for the flow of technology as well as trade.

This link between investment and technology is also illustrated by the growth over the 1980s of joint R&D agreements among firms in the major industrialized countries. Many forms of joint agreements among OECD MNEs proliferated in the 1980s and should be regarded as a new form of foreign investment, but the increase in joint R&D agreements was the most rapid, reflecting, among other forces, increased R&D costs and the need to monitor a growing spectrum of technologies. From near zero in 1980 there were well over 4,000 such agreements by the end of the 1980s.[2]

Even though foreign investment flows slowed down in 1991 and

[1] *World Investment Report, 1993* (New York: United Nations, 1993), pp. 70–74. For U.S. data showing the growth of inward and outward FDI stock in research-intensive manufacturing, see p. 74.
[2] See John Hagedorn, "Organizational Modes of Inter-Firm Cooperation and Technology Transfer," *Technovation* 10, no. 1 (1990).

Table 13-1. Inward and outward stocks of FDI by regions and countries, 1980, 1985, 1990 (billions of dollars and world shares)

Country/region	1990 Inward $	%	1990 Outward $	%	1985 Inward $	%	1985 Outward $	%	1980 Inward $	%	1980 Outward $	%
World	1,638.9	100.0	1,644.0	100.0	727.1	100.0	678.2	100.0	505.3	100.0	516.9	100.0
Developed economies	1,328.9	81.1	1,593.0	96.9	544.5	74.9	656.3	96.8	394.1	78.0	503.6	97.4
Triad	1,053.2	64.3	1,342.7	81.7	413.9	56.9	563.1	83.0	273.2	54.1	440.0	85.1
European Community	646.6	39.5	714.8	43.5	224.6	30.9	268.1	39.5	186.9	37.0	200.2	38.7
France	71.8	4.4	114.8	7.0	31.9	4.4	31.5	4.6	21.1	4.2	20.8	4.0
Germany	132.5	8.1	155.1	9.4	49.5	6.8	59.9	8.8	47.9	9.5	43.1	8.3
United Kingdom	205.6	12.5	244.8	14.9	62.6	8.6	101.2	14.9	63.0	12.5	79.2	15.3
United States	396.7	24.2	426.5	25.9	184.6	25.4	251.0	37.0	83.0	16.4	220.2	42.6
Japan	9.9	0.6	201.4	12.2	4.7	0.6	44.0	6.5	3.3	0.7	19.6	3.8
Triad/World	64.3		81.7		56.9		83.0		54.1		85.1	

SOURCE: John Rutter, "Recent Trends in International Direct Investment," U.S. Department of Commerce, August 1992, Appendices 3 and 8.

1992, largely because of slower growth in the advanced countries, globalization is not over. The bulge of the 1980s is unlikely to be repeated because it was in part due to special factors, including trade policy developments in both the EC and the United States. But broad and pervasive underlying forces will continue to influence the MNEs to extend their presence abroad. In any case, even if flows were to cease for a period of time, the size of the underlying stock (estimated at nearly $2 trillion in 1991) ensures continued growth of the international corporations because of the investment of retained earnings.

The main structural force pushing globalization is the revolution in information technology (ICT) that is transforming the nature of production of both goods and services and facilitating major changes in the organization of the enterprise. The ICT revolution has acted as both an enabling factor and a pressure for continuing globalization. Indeed, through effective use of technology in a number of sectors as well as major innovation in enterprise form, the Japanese have emerged as powerful new transnational actors. Intensified international competition has pushed firms to adopt new locational strategies in order to capture economies of scale and scope; customize products to satisfy changing consumer tastes and manufacturers' needs; access technology internationally; and develop new forms of enterprise organization. Finally, globalization is changing the nature of trade, as intraindustry and intrafirm trade in high and medium R&D intensity manufacturing is increasing trade among advanced countries. Globalization is also changing the context of trade policy, blurring the boundaries between trade, investment, and technology issues as well as those between the international and domestic domains. These changes are most evident in industries such as autos and electronics that have been the earliest users of the new ICT technologies.

As a result of globalization the role of the MNE (which is seriously underestimated by our current information focus on trade flows) has been greatly enhanced. In 1988 MNEs undertook more than 80 percent of U.S. trade. But when sales as a whole are measured (i.e., worldwide sales of foreign affiliates of MNEs in host countries, which includes sales to third countries), they amounted to $4.4 trillion in 1989, nearly twice the value of world exports of goods and services.[3] In 1989 the total of sales of U.S. multinationals in Japan were $8 billion, whereas the sales of Japanese firms in the United States were $86 billion, reflecting the asymmetry of foreign investment presence in the two countries.

Even this brief review highlights the key role of the multinational

[3] *World Investment Report, 1992* (New York: United Nations, 1992), p. 55.

enterprise. Trade and investment continue to be seen by many governments as *alternative* routes to access foreign markets, but for MNEs, especially in technology-intensive sectors, trade as well as investment, including joint ventures, have become part of an *integrated strategy* to gain or maintain market share. Among the many consequences of this integrated strategy has been pressure by corporations for harmonization of regulatory policies. Harmonization is a way of reducing the costs associated with different standards and practices as corporations spread their production globally. Harmonization may also be a way of preventing standards and regulatory practices from being used as nontariff impediments to market access. Further, corporations perceive differences in either the substance or enforcement of competition policy both as an impediment to access and a possible impediment to transborder mergers.

AMERICAN–JAPANESE RIVALRY

During the 1980s there was a significant increase in international conflict centered on high-tech products (for example, supercomputers, medical equipment, pharmaceuticals, telecommunications products, aircraft) and key components in a number of systems-products sectors (for example, semiconductors). Except for aircraft (the dispute with the EC over subsidies), all these were U.S.–Japanese disputes handled by bilateral sectoral negotiations. At the end of the 1980s the U.S.–Japanese bilateral Structural Impediments Initiative (SII) moved away from sector-specific discussions and focused on a range of "generic" policies, both at the macro and micro levels. Micropolicy was the heart of the American agenda and included, for example, regulation of the Japanese distribution system, land use policy, patent law standards, and competition policy, especially the role of the Japanese *keiretsu*. The *keiretsu* was also an American concern in discussions on high-tech sectoral and auto issues.[4]

One major cause of the heightened U.S.–Japanese conflict stems from the relative decline of the United States. Following World War II the United States was the undisputed economic and technological leader.[5] The rise of Japan as a technological power, at least equal to

---

[4] For a review of the U.S.–Japanese conflict of the 1980s, see Laura Tyson, *Who's Bashing Whom? Trade Conflict in High Technology Industries* (Washington, D.C.: Institute for International Economics, 1992), and C. Fred Bergsten and Marcus Noland, *Reconcilable Differences: United States–Japan Economic Conflict* (Washington, D.C.: Institute for International Economics, 1993).

[5] See R. R. Nelson, "U.S. Industrial Competitiveness: Where Did It Come From and Where Did It Go?," *Research Policy* 19 (1990): 117–32.

the United States in a number of industries, came as an unpleasant surprise to many Americans. Technological convergence with Europe was also a feature of postwar developments, but there was less conflict generated in the high-tech area, both because European firms were less threatening and because the trans-Atlantic political and security relations were so powerful that overt conflicts were often constrained. Finally, another reason for the greater U.S.–Japanese friction was the significant differences between the American and Japanese styles of capitalism, with their markedly different regulatory infrastructure and cultural and historical legacies. Increasingly, both economists and policymakers acknowledged that the competitiveness of the corporation, especially in leading-edge sectors, depended not only on internal capabilities but also on systemic factors. Thus the rivalries in high-tech sectors were also rivalries among different capitalist systems, causing system friction. One way of reducing system friction and of achieving a level playing field, or *fairness* (a powerful factor in American economic and foreign policy), is to harmonize, that is, to establish one brand of capitalism.

Hence the U.S. role was paramount in launching and sustaining pressure for harmonization of domestic policies, although the precise scope and nature of harmonization are by no means clear. Further, the idea of "fair competition," embedded in the American Constitution and exemplified in antitrust laws,[6] linked harmonization with fairness. Finally, U.S. trade policy changed in a fundamental fashion over the 1980s. From a singular overriding commitment to multilateralism, the United States adopted a multitrack policy: continuing efforts in the Uruguay Round; bilateral free-trade agreements where appropriate; and unilateralism, through more active use of section 301 of the 1974 Trade Act, later extended in the 1988 Omnibus Trade Act. Unilateralism, unique to the United States, involves unilateral definition and evaluation of unfair trade practices and the use of sanctions to remove them if necessary. One risk in an American-led push for harmonization, then, is that the alternative to multinational policy approaches is likely to be unilateralism.

POLICY OPTIONS TO MITIGATE SYSTEM FRICTION

As pointed out, the current priority candidate for harmonization is competition policy, where differences in substance and enforcement

[6] For a comprehensive account on the concept of fair competition, see Robert E. Hudec, "Mirror, Mirror on the Wall: The Concept of Fairness in United States Trade Policy," Canadian Council on International Law, Proceedings of the XIXth Annual Conference, Ottawa, 1990.

affect both trade and innovation at the level of the firm. Indeed, as a consequence of a major OECD project on technology and the economy (the TEP), OECD ministers in 1991 recommended that proposals for convergence of competition policy be presented by June 1994. Similarly, a number of experts and policymakers have placed competition policy high on the agenda for post-Uruguay negotiations at the GATT.[7] An account of the harmonization process lies outside the scope of this present study, but it is worth making some observations to indicate the links with our subsequent discussion.

Substantive convergence must first confront the fact that the overall objectives of competition policy vary from country to country and, indeed, have varied within the same country over time. For example, although most countries include efficiency as an objective, a distinction is made between static and dynamic efficiency in only a few jurisdictions. The changes in U.S. antitrust law over the 1980s to facilitate joint research and more recently joint production seem to indicate a shift in orientation to the idea of dynamic efficiency. As transnational consortia and joint ventures spread and proliferate, this issue will have to be dealt with more explicitly if convergence is to be achieved. Moreover, objectives other than efficiency are included in many countries, but these social and political objectives vary across countries and may often conflict with the target of promoting efficiency. Many European countries after the war granted exemptions to antitrust action to protect their weakened industries, but these exemptions have not survived under the EC competition regime. In Japan, however, the number of legal cartels is still well over 200 today, although most are to be abolished by 1995. In addition, resale price maintenance was abolished (because of American pressure) only in 1992. These differences in Japanese policy act as an impediment to imports and are thus linked with trade conflict.

Substantive convergence is only half the battle. The variation in enforcement of both the structural and behavioral instruments of competition policy is probably greater than the differences in objectives. Whereas American pressure has resulted in a strengthening of the Japanese FTC (which undertook its first prosecution of a price cartel in November 1991), the FTC has some way to go if reasonable convergence in enforcement with most other OECD countries is to be achieved. On the other hand, differing legal traditions among countries are also an important factor in divergence, with the United States being unique in its emphasis on private avenues of enforcement, triple-damage suits, and a greater predisposition to extraterritorial application.

---

[7] See, for example, Geza Feketekuty, *The New Trade Agenda* (Washington, D.C.: Group of Thirty, 1992). Sir Leon Brittan has made the same suggestion (ibid., p. 10).

Finally, assuming that the OECD convergence project achieves success, or at least significant progress, by 1994, there would still be a need to consider a supranational authority for dispute settlement and monitoring. Moreover, transnational mergers and joint ventures are likely to continue to proliferate, and national governments may hold quite different views on the trade-off between efficiency and competition, so that disputes will also proliferate.

While harmonization is one means of reducing system friction, a less "extreme" approach is *mutual recognition* of national differences. This can be especially applied to the setting of industry standards. The EC has pioneered the mutual recognition option that includes three distinct elements: (1) minimal harmonization (equivalence) of national standards and regulation; (2) mutual recognition of different country standards and regulation; and (3) a binding dispute settlement mechanism.[8] Despite the considerable difficulties in establishing equivalence—again because of deep-seated national systems differences—a multilateralization of mutual recognition policy in the GATT, involving industry participation, would be the most appropriate policy to reinforce and update the GATT code on technical barriers to trade (TBT).

Thus harmonization of competition policy and mutual recognition in the area of technical standards are two important feasible multilateral policy options that would preserve and reinforce the liberal multinational trading system. But more would be needed, because neither form of convergence would fully resolve the ongoing debate about fairness, that is, the level playing field. The remainder of our discussion is devoted to this issue.

THE NEW LEVEL PLAYING FIELD

One outcome of the experience of the 1980s has been to introduce some new concepts into today's trade policy discourse. These concepts are derived both from the Uruguay Round (especially the negotiations on services) and the bilateral negotiations between the United States and Japan. Essentially they extend trade negotiations inside the border to include domestic policies. The idea of *effective access* extends the category of barriers to imports to include, in addition to tariff and nontariff barriers such as subsidies and voluntary export restraints (VERs), domestic regulatory policies that are not necessarily designed to protect against imports but have that effect and other structural

[8] See Jacques Pelkmans and Niall Bohan, "Towards an Ideal GATT TBT Code?," mimeo, Centre for European Policy Studies, Brussels, December 1992.

impediments that limit competition or transparency. A related concept, *effective presence*, refers to access via investment, which will be discussed. Effective access and presence, it is argued, are more appropriate concepts for a globalizing world where factors such as economies of scale and scope, customization, and access to technology require broadly comparable penetration of all three triad blocs to sustain competitiveness. This notion implies an approximate reciprocity, in the sense of a broad balance of benefits among countries similar in concept to the principles of the GATT, which underlay the successful multilateral negotiations in the postwar decades.

In tackling structural barriers to effective access a fundamental distinction should be made between government and private barriers. In the case of the former, the main impediments arise from government regulation in areas such as financial and other (for example, telecommunications) services and government procurement practices and could be handled by post-Uruguay negotiations in the GATT.

Handling private barriers to effective access presents different and more complex problems. Attention has centered on the Japanese *keiretsu* as a result of the U.S.–Japanese auto disputes and of the SII negotiations. The conflict over auto parts centered on the role of the vertical production *keiretsu*. In the SII the vertical distribution *keiretsu* were cited as a barrier to American imports.

The United States argued that both the production and distribution *keiretsu* were exclusionary (i.e., impeded effective access and should be subject to tougher antitrust enforcement by Japanese authorities). The effect of vertical *keiretsu* is to impede access, but there is no agreement among antitrust authorities that these vertical arrangements, which are not confined to Japan, violate competition policy norms. Indeed, neither U.S. nor EC policy prohibits vertical agreements. In the case of the EC there are block exemptions for certain types but an overall policy approach that considers market structure as well as efficiency on a case-by-case basis.

It is useful to look at the production and distribution *keiretsu* as separate cases (we will discuss horizontal *keiretsu* in connection with investment). In the case of production *keiretsu* many studies, especially of the automobile industry, have demonstrated that the long-term supplier–assembler relations of the Japanese *keiretsu* are a more efficient organizational form than vertical integration or spot-type procurement from external suppliers.[9] The issue of collusion should be directed at the final product market and essentially involves *horizontal*

[9] See, for example, J. P. Womak, D. T. Jones, and D. Roos, *The Machine That Changed the World* (New York: Harper, 1991), and OECD, *Globalisation of Industrial Activities* (Paris: The Automotive Parts Industry, 1992).

behavior. So long as competition in final products exists, the efficiency gains outweigh the exclusionary consequences. Indeed, the diffusion of the *keiretsu* innovation through Japanese investment in the United States has improved American industry performance. A recent study of the impact of Japanese transplants in the United Kingdom details the process of the "Japanization" of British industry by direct transplant practices and indirect (emulation by British firms) means.[10] The diffusion process has spread beyond the auto industry and is affecting a range of domestic suppliers. Ironically, Japanization, which is described as a high-dependence organization strategy, is the opposite of Taylorism, the low-dependence organizational innovation introduced by American investment after World War II.

Although there is no case for the use of competition policy, the exclusionary effects remain as a source of friction. But these are likely to diminish over time as Japanese firms develop more transparent and inclusive procedures for intercorporate linkages.[11] Organizational innovation is best diffused by FDI since the knowledge is largely tacit and centered on interpersonal relations. In sum, in the case of production *keiretsu* the problem of effective *access* is essentially a problem of effective *presence*, that is, of FDI in Japan.

The vertical distribution *keiretsu* are much more clearly a barrier to effective access to the Japanese market. Moreover, although there may be some efficiency gains from exclusive dealing arrangements that provide customer services and information (largely nonappropriable and therefore subject to free riding by competing distributors), such gains are outweighed by the very significant exclusionary impact on imports. The distribution *keiretsu* may provide an example of a case where domestic antitrust policy as presently interpreted is at odds with trade policy.

The distribution system in Japan, as in other countries, is now in a process of significant structural transformation as a consequence of changes in government policy and in information technology. Reform of the Large Retail Store Law (as a consequence of the SII), tougher action by the FTC on resale price maintenance, and changing consumer attitudes have weakened the link between manufacturers and distributors and will rationalize the inefficient, multilayered system and open the market to large and efficient discounters. More fundamentally, the spread of computer-driven ordering systems should eliminate layers of middlemen and open the door to foreign ex-

[10] Nick Oliver and Barry Wilkinson, *The Japanization of British Industry* (Oxford: Blackwell, 1988).

[11] This is recommended by Japanese industry associations clearly as a response to American complaints. See, for example, the comprehensive analysis and proposals of the Tokyo Chamber of Commerce and Industry, *Building a New Corporate Network: Report on Research into Corporate Keiretsu* (Tokyo: Tokyo Chambers of Commerce, 1993).

porters. Recently MITI has announced a new project to unify ordering and settlement systems for the distribution industry. It is essential that foreign participation be encouraged, but early signs are not encouraging.[12] If these ongoing structural changes do not result in a significant reduction in impediments to effective access, further changes in antitrust enforcement may be required. The cumulative effect of distribution *keiretsu* on export foreclosure would have to be given significant weight in any such changes. This would be an appropriate issue for a supranational authority. If that option does not exist, extraterritorial application of domestic competition policy seems the most likely alternative.

Although there has been a great deal of debate about impediments to effective access via exports, there has been remarkably little attention paid to effective presence via investment. This is now beginning to change,[13] and both investment and technology issues are likely to move to the top of the international agenda in the coming years.

There is a striking disparity between the inward foreign investment stock of Japan and those of Europe and of the United States (see Table 13-1). This low level of foreign investment in Japan is in part a result of many decades of official restrictions, most of which were removed during the 1980s. Yet there was still an enormous disparity between the inward flows of investment to Japan and other OECD countries during the wave of transnationalization in the 1980s. As stressed, trade and investment are complementary routes to market penetration, and investment is usually a necessary condition for technology access. For these reasons the low level of FDI in Japan will become central to the "level playing field" debate.

There are a number of reasons for the low level of foreign investment in Japan. One is clearly the after-effects of the pre-1980 protection and industrial policy, which in some sectors, such as semiconductors, entrenched domestic oligopolies and created significant barriers to entry for both domestic and foreign firms. Another is rising land prices and the generally higher costs due to the asset price inflation at the end of the 1980s. Cost factors will continue to impede entry as the yen rises in large part because of American policy (which is designed to improve market access!). But the major *structural* impediment to effective presence is the horizontal *keiretsu* or, more broadly, the Japanese corporate governance model.

[12] See *International Trade Reporter*, Current Reports, 12 May 1993, p. 793.
[13] For recent analyses, see Robert Lawrence, "Japan's Low Levels of Inward Investment: the Role of Inhibition on Acquisitions," *Transnational Corporation* I, no. 3 (December 1992): 47–76; Dennis J. Encarnation, *Rivals beyond Trade: America versus Japan in Global Competition* (Ithaca: Cornell University Press, 1992); and Mark Mason, "United States Direct Investment in Japan: Trends and Prospects," *California Management Review* 35, no. 1 (Fall 1992): 98–115.

The intermarket or horizontal *keiretsu*, which involves groupings of firms in diverse industries around a major bank, are a fundamental aspect of Japanese capitalism.[14] The lead bank is not only an important source of capital (though less so now than in the early 1980s) but also performs other functions for client firms such as facilitating access to other banks, assisting in restructuring if required, and providing management assistance if necessary. In addition to this long-term reciprocal relationship with the lead bank in the *keiretsu*, cross-shareholding among intermarket *keiretsu* members is very extensive, although it has been somewhat eroding as a result of the bursting of the asset price bubble of the 1980s. Nonetheless, the tradition of cross-shareholding makes members resistant to takeover bids. This resistance is strengthened by the long-term stable investment strategies of insurance companies and pension funds that also reduce the pool of publicly traded shares. The corporate governance model of Japan is thus strikingly resistant to mergers and acquisitions (M&As), the dominant mode of inward foreign investment in other countries, especially in the United States, where equity markets and other phenomena such as takeovers, shareholders' rights, and extensive disclosure regulations create active markets for corporate control.

Is the Japanese corporate governance model, so clearly exclusionary, also more efficient? Is there, in other words, a parallel with the production *keiretsu*? A judicious answer would seem to be yes and no. A reasoned judgment suggests that the Japanese governance model and the Anglo-Saxon model are alternative "economically rational attempts to resolve traditional universally typical problems of coordination and control."[15] The Japanese model seems more effective in reducing transactions costs and is particularly suited to encouraging a long view that facilitates innovation. The Anglo-Saxon model, by contrast, maximizes exposure to market discipline, which is essential to the resolution of problems arising from the separation of ownership and control. The Anglo-Saxon model centers on the game; the Japanese model centers on the players. An "ideal" model would include elements of both, and policy proposals to promote convergence have, indeed, been suggested by both American and Japanese experts.[16]

[14] For a comprehensive analysis of all types of *keiretsu*, see Michael L. Gerlach, *Alliance Capitalism: The Social Organization of Japanese Business* (Berkeley: University of California Press, 1992).
[15] W. Carl Kester, chapter 4 in this volume, p. 108.
[16] Ibid. In the United States a comprehensive reform of financial regulation would be required. In Japan the bursting of the asset price bubble of the 1980s has revealed the dangers of ignoring shareholder interests. See Shigeru Watanabe and Isao Yamamoto, "Corporate Governance in Japan: Ways to Improve Low Profitability," *Nomura Research Institute Quarterly* 1, no. 3 (Winter 1992): 28–45.

Convergence of governance models may be desirable and even probable, but it will not be achieved quickly. Nonetheless the problem of Japanese structural barriers to effective market presence will remain for some considerable time, and other policy actions will be required if the marked asymmetry is to be reduced.

The Japanese are now well aware of the serious nature of the deep-seated structural impediments to foreign investments. The government has launched a number of projects to facilitate greenfield investment, including tax incentives to offset the high cost of land. The Keidanren issued a special report on investment prepared by an ad hoc committee, in consultation with foreign business, that produced a series of recommendations involving deregulation and liberalization of key sectors, including legal services. Investment issues were included—for the first time—as one of the "baskets" in the U.S.–Japanese trade negotiations launched at the Tokyo Summit in July 1993.

Because mergers and acquisitions will not become a significant "port of entry" for foreign investment into Japan for the foreseeable future, government policy over the past few years has focused on greenfield incentives. More recently, there appears to be a shift to encouraging joint ventures. As seen, joint ventures are proliferating for many reasons, and promoting them may provide MITI with the easiest and fastest policy response to foreign pressure.

There is a strong link between foreign investment and knowledge flows. Today in high-tech sectors these are two-way flows. Japanese investment in Europe and in the United States has served not only as a diffusion mechanism for enterprise innovation but also as an access mechanism to U.S. science and technology, especially through university research funding. To ensure that the knowledge is effectively integrated within the firm, many Japanese corporations have established R&D facilities in the United States. Then, later in the 1980s, a number of R&D bases were established in Europe, in part to gain access to EC technology consortia.[17] Access to Japan's considerable technological infrastructure will require foreign firms to do the same. Yet, few have done so. Structural barriers to investment are one factor explaining this behavior, but the Japanese have also argued that another is the attitude of foreign firms who have been slow in seeing the advantages to be derived from establishing a base in Japan.

But whatever the balance of these factors the fact remains that investment barriers in Japan do have the effect of reducing technology access. As may be seen in Tables 13-2 and 13-3, even though Japan is

---

[17] See Shuji Asami, "Companies Set Up Overseas R&D Bases," *Nikkei Weekly*, 9 November 1992, p. 13.

Table 13-2. Japan's corporate technology trade by country, exports, fiscal years 1986–89 (number of cases and value in billions of yen)

	FY 1986		FY 1987		FY 1988		FY 1989	
	Cases	Value	Cases	Value	Cases	Value	Cases	Value
Asia	2,748	86.5	3,152	86.4	3,264	101.4	3,965	108.0
China	454	19.7	405	0.4	339	8.4	473	8.1
Taiwan	532	8.5	590	12.3	660	13.2	609	16.3
S. Korea	732	21.1	816	27.5	888	30.6	1,350	38.5
Thailand	203	5.4	294	7.3	331	9.9	364	17.6
Philippines	89	0.6	133	2.0	n.a.	n.a.	n.a.	n.a.
Indonesia	196	4.4	182	3.2	228	13.6	304	10.9
Malaysia	128	3.2	147	3.1	128	4.0	221	6.3
India	196	4.4	182	3.2	211	5.4	245	6.2
West Asia	94	10.5	52	1.6	59	2.3	72	2.4
N. America	1,006	62.3	1,058	72.5	1,225	77.0	1,671	115.1
United States	869	57.7	912	65.9	1,080	71.1	1,445	107.7
S. America	216	5.2	198	4.5	195	4.4	182	4.6
Brazil	127	3.8	107	2.5	114	2.5	n.a.	n.a.
Europe	1,040	43.6	1,184	40.3	1,281	49.3	1,342	65.1
United Kingdom	161	7.6	190	10.6	221	13.9	251	20.0
W. Germany	247	7.8	297	7.4	301	10.7	328	13.7
France	145	5.9	162	5.2	137	4.4	149	7.1
Netherlands	41	2.5	53	2.1	86	2.2	71	2.1
Switzerland	53	3.8	52	2.3	63	1.4	51	1.6
Africa	189	9.5	147	5.0	141	6.0	136	6.8
Oceania	176	6.6	164	5.3	187	5.9	191	6.5
Australia	139	5.8	116	4.2	134	5.2	143	5.7

SOURCE: Japan Economic Institute Report, 27 September 1991, p. 19.

Table 13-3. Japan's corporate technology trade by country, imports, fiscal years 1986–89 (number of cases and volume in billions of yen)

	FY 1986		FY 1987		FY 1988		FY 1989	
	Cases	Value	Cases	Value	Cases	Value	Cases	Value
Asia	15	0.3	12	0.1	29	0.2	26	0.3
China	4	*	2	*	0	0.0	3	*
Taiwan	0	0.0	2	*	15	0.0	4	*
S. Korea	4	*	4	*	4	*	7	0.1
West Asia	94	10.5	2	*	0	0.0	8	0.1
N. America	4,926	174.6	4,747	179.3	5,591	198.1	4,118	210.7
United States	4,825	173.8	4,667	178.6	5,495	196.9	4,029	209.5
S. America	4	*	3	*	1	*	1	*
Europe	2,516	85.1	2,568	103.4	2,706	113.6	2,903	118.2
W. Germany	903	20.7	847	21.4	835	18.4	1,104	24.3
United Kingdom	477	13.0	512	10.3	451	9.3	487	10.8
France	298	7.3	313	22.1	432	26.2	354	25.5
Switzerland	241	17.5	273	17.4	277	18.4	256	19.0
Netherlands	163	15.6	173	20.8	182	27.6	202	21.1
Africa	3	*	3	*	0	0.0	0	0.0
Oceania	28	0.4	38	0.3	29	0.3	53	0.7

SOURCE: Japan Economic Institute Report, 27 September 1991, p. 19.
*Less than ¥ 50 million.

Table 13-4. Indicators of asymmetry in technology flows between the United States and Japan

Japanese R&D facilities in the United States (1990)[a]	119
U.S. R&D facilities in Japan (1990)[d]	71
Value of Japanese purchases of technological know-how through new sales agreements in the United States (1988, millions of yen)[b]	32,893
Value of U.S. purchases of technological know-how through new sales agreements in Japan (1988, millions of yen)[b]	5,500
Percentage change in the value of Japanese purchases of technological know-how through new sales agreements in the United States (1984–88)[b]	40
Percentage change in the value of U.S. purchases of technological know-how through new sales agreements in Japan (1984–88)[b]	−55
Percentage of Japanese students studying sciences in the United States (1987–88)[c]	11.9
Percentage of U.S. students studying sciences in all foreign countries (1987–88)[c]	5.9
Share of cases in which flow of technology was from the United States to Japan[d]	90
Share of cases in which flow of technology was from Japan to the United States[d]	5
Approximate share of alliances in semiconductor industry in which the Japanese partner is substantially larger than its U.S. counterpart (1990)[e]	67

SOURCES:

[a]Donald H. Dalton and Manuel G. Serapio, Jr., *U.S. Research Facilities of Foreign Companies* (Washington, D.C. U.S. Department of Commerce, 1990); Technology Administration, Japan Technology Program.

National Science Foundation, *Survey of Direct U.S. Private Capital Investment and Research and Development Facilities in Japan*, NSF 91-312 (Washington, D.C.: 1991).

[b]National Science Board, *Science and Engineering Indicators*, 10th ed. (Washington, D.C.: National Science Board, 1991).

[c]National Science Foundation, *International Science and Technology Update* (Washington, D.C.: National Science Foundation, 1991), pp. 67–68.

[d]National Research Council, *U.S.–Japan Technology Linkages in Biotechnology: Challenges for the 1990s* (Washington, D.C.: National Academy Press, 1992), p. 22.

[e]National Research Council, *U.S.–Japan Strategic Alliances in the Semiconductor Industry* (Washington, D.C.: National Academy Press, 1992), p. 40.

now an overall net exporter in technology trade because of increasing exports to developing countries, the share of United States and other OECD countries is still very high. Further, these balance of data, based on royalty and licensing fees, capture only one aspect of technology flows. As Table 13-4 shows, other measures suggest very large deficits with the United States.

The Japanese are aware that the "knowledge deficit" will add to the growing international friction with the United States. One response has been to invite foreign firms to join some government industry consortia and to pressure private Japanese firms to open up their research facilities to foreign participants. Another policy response has been to launch two international projects, one in basic science (the Human Frontiers Science Program), and the other in precompetitive research, the Intelligent Manufacturing System (IMS). Serious difficulties were encountered in the launch of both, perhaps because of suspicion about Japanese motives but also because of the lack of experience in the field of international science projects, where both the EC and the United States have played a more active role.[18] The Japanese experience illustrates the need for developing new international rules for public–private research cooperation. Promoting and subsidizing international research is a means of "compensation" for a structural asymmetry that will not be easily reduced.

We have argued in this analysis that there are two major forces pushing for convergence of a range of domestic policies: the multinational corporations and governments, especially the U.S. government. Multilateral approaches are preferable to bilateral negotiations in a globalizing international economy. Thus both harmonization and mutual recognition should be pursued in multilateral institutions such as the OECD and the GATT. In addition, both for political and economic reasons, it would be unwise to ignore the fairness or level playing field disputes. One of the basic principles of the GATT is overall reciprocity or balance of benefits. The same idea, adapted as appropriate, will have to apply to investment and technology.

[18] For an American view of IMS, see Deborah Wince-Smith, "Perspectives on U.S. Technological Competitiveness," *Business and the Contemporary World*, Autumn 1991: 25–26.

PART IV

RESISTING CONVERGENCE

CHAPTER FOURTEEN

Free and Managed Trade

PAUL STREETEN

The task set for me by the editors of this book is to identify government interventions in free trade ("trade management") that can be justified in the light of the desire to preserve particular national institutions and, beyond that, a particular way of life, a particular set of values, a particular community, a particular culture. I will therefore not say anything about the many other arguments for intervention but concentrate on those for the preservation of institutions, practices, and lifestyle.

Four brief preliminary remarks are in order. First, free trade is not, as is sometimes thought, the result of laissez-faire, but it has to be "managed." In the absence of international cooperation and enforceable agreements or accepted rules, which amount to some sacrifice of national sovereignty, each country has powerful incentives to interfere with free trade, whether other countries do the same or not. This can be (according to conventional doctrine) for "good" economic reasons, such as the terms-of-trade argument for intervention,[1] or for "good" noneconomic reasons, such as military power, or for "bad" reasons, such as yielding to the pressures of a protectionist lobby. The argument is parallel to that for the maintenance of competition. Just as the natural outcome of laissez-faire is monopoly or oligopoly and restraints on competition domestically, so the natural outcome of laissez-faire is restraints on free international trade internationally. Competition, like free trade, has to be enforced.

I am grateful to Ronald Dore for his helpful comments on an earlier draft.
[1] Tibor Scitovsky, "A Reconsideration of the Theory of Tariffs," *Review of Economic Studies* 9 (1942): 89–110.

Second, a prima facie argument for government intervention is not necessarily an ultimate argument. Free trade may fail to achieve a particular objective, but government intervention may be even worse. For example, by trying to insulate a country from alien influences, intervention may raise the costs of production, encourage inefficiencies, destroy the product basis of its society, and render it wholly dependent on foreign aid and the conditionality that goes with it. On the other hand, even if government intervention may not achieve its objective, or have undesirable side effects, the free market may do even worse. Opening the economy to foreign transnational corporations may lead to a drain on resources and a change in consumers' preferences in line with the companies' advertising. The poorly performing, often corrupt, African public marketing boards have had a bad press. But privatization may hand marketing over to monopolistic, exploitative foreigners (Asians in East Africa, Lebanese or Greeks in West Africa).

Third, it is sometimes argued that, although there may be a case for government intervention in particular instances, the simple rule of free trade is best, because otherwise the floodgates are opened for all sorts of bad arguments for protection. In complex situations, in which the "new," sophisticated arguments for trade intervention are difficult to implement, yield uncertain returns, and may be captured and abused by special interests, simple rules are best "in a world whose politics are as imperfect as its markets."[2] The argument is similar to that for rule utilitarianism that attempts to combine our respect for deontological rights with moral justification by results. But it should be remembered that there are simple rules other than that of free trade, if simple rules are needed, such as an across-the-board 20 percent tariff. Moreover, the principle of simple rules is not applied to other spheres subject to political pressures, such as our tax system. Those who advocate "simple rules" may be confusing simplicity with universality. Universality allows for differences according to different circumstances. In the tax system age, size of family, disability, whether the income is earned, and other such factors are relevant. A poll tax would be a simple tax. The rules should not relate to uneliminable individual cases or to pressures from self-interested groups, but universality can, indeed must, allow for differences in countries and circumstances.

Fourth, we hear and read everywhere that "interdependence among nations (sometimes wrongly equated with integration) has in-

[2] Paul Krugman, "Is Free Trade Passé?," *Journal of Economic Perspectives* 1, no. 2 (1987): 143.

creased dramatically. This can be seen in the spectacular growth of the trade-to-GNP ratio, which, for some countries, has doubled since the mid-1980s. It can also be observed in the globalization of production through foreign investment by transnational corporations; in the integration of international capital markets and portfolio investments; in the growth of international migration; and in the spread of cultural impulses such as television, styles in clothing, music, sport, sexual mores, and even crimes. At the same time, there is a rise of religious fundamentalism and of the assertion of national identities by potentially 5,000 different peoples in the already proliferating 182 states. The main lessons are (1) that trade cannot be considered in isolation, but must be accompanied by an analysis of the flow of information, capital, people, and educational and cultural impulses, in addition to monetary and fiscal policies; and (2) that economics no longer can be isolated from political science, philosophy, law, and other disciplines.[3]

EXTERNALITIES OF CONSUMPTION AND ACQUIRED TASTES

Economic welfare is not just a matter of command over resources: the greater the command, the higher the welfare. It is a matter of command in connection to wants. Gains from international trade have to be assessed in relation not only to additional income (and output) but also to additional wants, expectations, and aspirations generated by the extra income. It is then quite possible, indeed likely, that gains in income are accompanied by losses in welfare, because wants grow faster than command over resources. The appetite grows faster than what it feeds on. This phenomenon occurs not largely because of advertising and sales promotion; it is mainly the result of the unequal division of the gains from trade. Even with an equal division between countries, there can be greater inequalities within countries. The lower income groups take as their reference group the higher income groups. When the lion's share of the gains go to these higher income groups, the poorer are worse off. It is then possible that the countries with large gains from trade fail to benefit because their internal inequalities are great, and those with small or no gains do not benefit because international inequalities are great. Ronald Dore has pointed out another possibility. The gainers from trade may be people who represent one set of values, for example, those of speculative financial gains, whereas the remainder represent other values, such as hard

[3] For an elaboration of this point, see Jagdish Bhagwati, "Economics beyond the Horizon," *Economic Journal* 101, no. 404 (January 1991): 9–14.

work with its rewards. They may judge the costs of free trade to be too high.

It is, of course, possible to define welfare in a different way, such as a widened range of choice. But this definition has been disputed by psychologists.[4] Moreover, disagreements over the distribution of additional income can be almost as acrimonious and divisive as disputes over the distribution of a constant income, implying absolute lowering of some people's income.

The classical advocates of free trade, and most explicitly John Stuart Mill, wished to bring out the educational effects of free trade and did not assume, as is commonly done by economists today, constant tastes. They included in their analysis the receptivity to new ideas and new techniques; the stimulus to the creation of new wants, new incentives to work and save, and new rewards; the growth of new forms of organization. It is worth quoting Mill at some length, to show that he believed in the possibility of learning by trading:

There is another consideration, principally applicable to an early stage of industrial advancement. A people may be in a quiescent, indolent, uncultivated state, with all their tastes either fully satisfied or entirely undeveloped, and they may fail to put forth the whole of their productive energies for want of any sufficient object of desire. The opening of foreign trade, by making them acquainted with new objects, or tempting them by the easier acquisition of things which they had not previously thought attainable, sometimes works a sort of industrial revolution in a country whose resources were previously undeveloped for want of energy and ambition in the people: inducing those who were satisfied with scanty comforts and little work, to work harder for the gratification of their new tastes, and even so save, and accumulate capital, for the still more complete satisfaction of those tastes at a future time.

But the economical advantages of commerce are surpassed in importance by those of its effects, which are intellectual and moral. It is hardly possible to overrate the value, in the present low state of human improvement, of placing human beings in contact with persons dissimilar to themselves, and with modes of thought and action unlike those with which they are familiar. Commerce is now, what war once was, the principal source of this contact. Commercial adventurers from more advanced countries have generally been the first civilizers of barbarians. And commerce is the purpose of the far greater part of the communication which takes place between civilized nations. Such communication has always been and is peculiarly in the present age, one of the primary sources of progress. To human beings, who, as hitherto educated, can scarcely cultivate even a good quality without running it into a fault, it is indispensable

[4] According to a German proverb, *Wer die Wahl hat, hat die Qual*, "He who has to choose is tormented."

to be perpetually comparing their own notions and customs with the experience and example of persons in different circumstances from themselves: and there is no nation which does not need to borrow from others, not merely particular arts or practices, but essential points of character in which its own type is inferior.[5]

Mill's argument can easily be reversed if it is decided that the generation of tastes, wants, and incentives should be restrained, or of a different nature and in a different direction. A particular country may see a danger in opening trade too indiscriminately to a world in which demand and production patterns are different from the ones it would like to pursue. It may choose as its model specific, like-minded other cultures and open its trade relations selectively to these countries. But the assumptions of contemporary economic theory are not sympathetic to this approach. The spirit of this conference reflects a return to Mill's view of trade as an instrument for the convergence of attitudes.

A QUIET LIFE

Sir John Hicks said that the best reward of a monopolist is often a quiet life. The effort to maximize profits by equating marginal returns is itself subject to diminishing marginal psychic returns. The free-trade gospel, based on the doctrine of comparative advantage, bids us always to strive for higher incomes from the international division of labor. But adjustments in response to changing comparative advantage are costly. They involve changing occupations, often changing residence, periods of unemployment and uncertainty, and generally upheaval and disruption. In an international environment in which comparative advantage changes rapidly, trade policy can become a policy for tramps: it imposes the imperative to move from one occupation to another, from one residence to another. The citizens of an already fairly rich country, or a like-minded group of such countries, may say: We already enjoy many earthly goods. We wish to forgo some extra income from international trade for the sake of a quieter life, for not having to learn a new trade, for not being uprooted from our community. There is nothing irrational or "noneconomic" in such a choice.[6]

[5] John Stuart Mill, *Principles of Political Economy* (London: Longmans, Green, 1902), pp. 351–52. It is interesting to note that the demonstration effect, applied in the postwar years to consumption, was thought by Mill to apply to work and savings.

[6] Another option would be to train a force of workers who must be ready to move to

A quiet life will, of course, depend on how important international trade is in the economy of the country. Reductions in income resulting from having opted out, even only at the margin, of remaining internationally competitive must be avoided. A quiet life also depends on not permitting the vested interests benefiting from protection (which include capitalists and managers, as well as workers) to become so powerful as to drive the economy beyond the point where forgone income from international specialization just balances the benefits of a somewhat less disruptive life. It is probably true that many countries have sought protection beyond this optimum point, and the real costs to the community of keeping workers employed in industries that should be shrunk greatly exceeds the benefits that could be reaped by a redeployment of labor.

The qualification introduced for countries heavily dependent on international trade would, in turn, have to be qualified if international cooperation could be implemented on the optimum rate of technical progress, where such progress involves disruption. In most other lines of advance we accept the application of some form of benefit/cost calculus. Only where advances in knowledge and its technical and commercial application are concerned do we not ask questions about its social and human costs. When technological progress in synthetics knocks out lines of raw material exports on which a country is heavily dependent for foreign exchange, the costs of adjustment of the exporting country may greatly exceed the benefits to the buyers in the importing countries, quite apart from the evaluation of the distributional impact. It would then be reasonable either to ask for some form of international agreement to slow down the pace of scientific and technological progress or to contract out of the international competitive rate. The issue here is not to forgo some income for a quiet life, but by international cooperation to avoid impoverishment through deteriorating terms of trade or growing unemployment.

There is a literature on the so-called noneconomic objectives of policymakers, such as the desire to maintain a large agricultural sector (or industrial sector) as an end in itself and on how to modify free-trade policy to accommodate them.[7] But my point is not to introduce noneconomic objectives. Leisure is part of conventional economic ob-

---

new places and learn new skills in response to the changing international scene. These "commandos" would get higher pay and better conditions than the ordinary work force in return for accepting these disruptions. The life might appeal to young bachelors or people keen on frequent change. But, as Ronald Dore has pointed out, with the reduced importance of unskilled and semi-skilled labor and the growing importance of highly skilled people, retraining is difficult or impossible.

[7] Among the contributors to this literature in the 1950s and 1960s are Max Corden, Harry Johnson, Jagdish Bhagwati, and T. N. Srinivasan.

jectives, as are both the psychological and financial costs of disruption, such as the costs of resettlement, of rehousing, of retraining. These benefits and costs are entirely within the domain normally surveyed by economists, have been largely ignored, but lead to a modification of the doctrine of free trade.

In the EC the people's preferences are for greater leisure, longer vacations, more generous social security provisions, higher minimum wages, and greater participation in the management of firms by their workers. Insofar as these preferences do not interfere with the ability to compete with the outside world, free trade can be pursued. But insofar as they are bought at the cost of some competitive efficiency and therefore some reduction in income compared with free trade, some closing off and some management of trade relations would be legitimate if such closing off can avoid or reduce the losses from free trade.

It could be that the social harmony and homogeneity achieved by maintaining similar values adds to efficiency and makes for higher economic growth. If so, the interventions with trade that lead to the formation of Orwellian trading blocks can lead to a *higher* volume of trade between the blocks. The ratio of trade to national income would be reduced, but as a result of higher incomes there would be *more* trade.

COMPARATIVE ADVANTAGE:
CREATED, ARBITRARY, AND TEMPORARY

The textbooks speak of "factor endowments." These and other God-given natural phenomena such as climate are said to determine comparative advantage. In the Ricardo version, different countries have different production functions, but the same endowment with a single factor, labor. In the Heckscher–Ohlin version, production functions are the same everywhere, but factor endowments vary between countries. Ricardo's production possibility curve exhibits constant unit costs, Heckscher–Ohlin's increasing unit costs. Both are given and unchanged over long periods. Several authors have extended the Heckscher–Ohlin model to the long run, allowing for the production of a capital good, for savings and investment, and growth.[8]

This model has dominated the minds of trained economists for a

[8] See, for example, Ronald Findlay, "Factor Proportions and Comparative Advantage in the Long Run," *Journal of Political Economy* 78, no. 1 (January/February 1970): 27–34.

long time. But with the growing importance of science and technology, the capacity to shape human capital, and the increasingly systematic relation between expenditure on research and development, and commercial results, comparative advantage has become something created and manipulated. At the same time scientific research expenditure and human capital formation are outstanding cases of activities subject to scale economies and increasing returns. These economies of scale are not God-given but accrue to whomever devotes resources and ingenuity to the task. The same goes for cost reductions from learning by doing. Textiles may initially have been a labor-intensive industry, but a fully automated textile plant uses hardly any labor. The direction of R&D expenditure can shift the comparative advantage of different countries in growing different crops. Japan's strategy has been to build up one industry after another behind protective barriers and then to sell the products in excess of domestic requirements abroad at low prices.

South Korea did not so much select or pick winners as create winners. In shipbuilding the country had neither the skills nor the materials, yet it is now replacing Sweden, the previously preeminent shipbuilding country. The same is true of steel. The country has neither coal nor iron ore, yet it has become one of the most competitive producers of steel.

In the world just described government intervention in the form of export subsidies or import restrictions can play the role of cost-reducing technological innovations by the firm and give it the initial advantage required to establish its "comparative advantage" in the chosen field. Such interventions can also determine the thrust of scientific and technical innovations and with them the whole culture. It may, of course, be that these incentives are better given through subsidies to R&D expenditure, education, training, credit, employment, or production than through direct interventions in trade.

INTRAFIRM TRADE

A large and growing proportion of world trade is conducted between affiliates or branches of multinational or transnational firms. At least one-third of world trade in manufactured goods is now intrafirm trade. It has been estimated that more than two-thirds of all American imports from Japan are intracompany transactions.[9] The considerations that guide these firms in their pricing, output, and investment

[9] Dennis Encarnation, *Rivals beyond Trade: America versus Japan in Global Competition* (Ithaca: Cornell University Press, 1992).

decisions are likely to be different from those guiding arms-length transactions. It could be argued that the allocation of real resources will still be governed by the doctrine of comparative advantage (assuming prices reflect real costs), although the decline in the dollar against the yen since 1985 has done little to improve the bilateral trade balance. Such devaluations do not seem to affect intrafirm trade between Japanese parent companies and their overseas subsidiaries.[10] Firms are reluctant to drop their own subsidiaries as suppliers in favor of a domestic rival, unless the devaluation is large and sustained. In any case, the allocation of shown profits between countries will be quite different for intrafirm trade than for arms-length trade. It will be guided by considerations of taxation, of trade union pressures, of price controls, of insistence on joint ventures, on public image, and all other considerations that give rise to transfer pricing.

Analogous arguments apply to the growth of the shrinking number of public enterprises conducting international trade. If efficiently managed, they will produce in the lowest cost conditions. But extraneous considerations of power, national prestige, or social objectives also enter.

Trade policies and exchange rate policies are greatly weakened by the ability to locate firms abroad. If Japan wishes to maintain its export surplus to the United States, even in a period of a depreciating dollar, firms should put their manufacturing plants in Korea and Taiwan, whose currencies have depreciated with the dollar. In this way the reduced comparative advantage of some Japanese industries resulting from the relatively appreciating yen is frustrated. As foreign direct investment by the multinational firm is increasingly replacing arms-length trade transactions, the rules that apply to trade will apply less and less. Or as the dollar depreciates relatively to the yen the Japanese find it cheap to invest heavily in the United States, swelling the Japanese surplus by earning more profits. The current account balance, far from improving, further deteriorates.

The implications of this for convergence is that the growing "management" of trade by transnational corporations (1) violates some of the principles of comparative advantage; (2) reduces the power of governments to regulate trade; (3) is likely to have some influence over the convergence of styles of management, labor relations, and industrial structure. The style of Japanese transnational corporations is quite different from that of Anglo-American ones. Being large, powerful oligopolies, they can resist the forces of convergence to which smaller firms would be subject.

[10] Ibid.

Free Trade in Services?

Free trade in services has been pushed hard in the Uruguay Round by what might be called postindustrial or service countries such as the United States, Great Britain, and Switzerland, joined by some developing countries such as Hong Kong and Singapore. Yet, some considerations should make one hesitate. These have nothing to do with infant industry arguments, balance-of-payments losses, restrictive business practices, national sovereignty, cultural autonomy, externalities, infrastructure, or "commanding heights," but I have not come across them in the literature. I consider two.

The first consideration springs from a specific characteristic of services: they are not storable. There are exceptions, such as software messages stored on a recording machine, but by and large services cannot be stored. They have to be consumed at the same time as they are being produced. They have been defined as those fruits of economic activity that you cannot drop on your toe. This gives added power to the provider of the service, if the service is important and if there are no adequate alternatives. Electricity workers, railway workers, and postal workers have greater bargaining power than coal miners, because coal can be stocked and used up while miners are on strike, whereas electricity, transport, and mail delivery cannot. The bargaining power of the providers of services is greater than that of the producers of storable goods. Whether this is important in international trade, say, in the case of trade embargoes and sanctions, remains to be seen. In addition to storability, the access to alternative sources of supply is also important. If a country became dependent on another country's essential service, say shipping, this could lead to greater dependence than, say, imports of grain. In this way, the growing international trade in services would reinforce a tendency already at work in the international economy, to wit the growing inter*dependence*. By this I mean the growth not only of benefits from international relations but also of possible damage, should these relations be disrupted. A strategy that is risk-averse might forgo some of the benefits of international exchange and provide the service domestically at higher costs for the sake of avoiding the risk of damage, should trade be terminated.[11]

The second consideration is concerned with equality. The international division of gains from free trade in services may be unequal, and, moreover, may make national policies for greater equality or an

[11] It may be possible in some cases to provide the potential for expansion of some of these services, should the need arise, while permitting international trade. Or it would be advisable to diversify the trade, so as to have access to alternative sources.

income policy more difficult. Consider a model in which two types of services have to be combined, one of which is highly skilled, the other unskilled. Take, for example, air transport. The providers of the skilled service, pilots, are in relatively scarce total supply but highly mobile between countries in response to financial incentives. On a clear day, an airline pilot can see the world. The unskilled factor, ground personnel, is in highly elastic local supply, but immobile between countries. The result is that pilots earn large rents and ground personnel get the bare minimum wage. Any country wishing to have an airline has to pay its pilots something not too far below the high international salaries, or it will lose them. A policy to achieve greater income equality domestically will be impossible. Both international and domestic inequalities will tend to increase. Other examples are transnational advertising, hotel chains, tourist enclaves, and so on. The cause of the problem is differential elasticities of supply and types of service that have to be combined. These can cause more serious problems in pursuing a policy of national integration than the direct effects of the brain drain. Gunnar Myrdal wrote about how national integration makes for international disintegration.[12] Every country, attempting to achieve full employment, price stability, and high growth, casts its problems by regulation of exchange rates, trade, and foreign investment on to other countries. The situation described here is the reverse: it shows how (partial) international integration makes for national disintegration. Total integration would imply a global system of progressive taxation and social services: a Utopian vision.

OLIGOPOLISTIC GOVERNMENT RELATIONS
AND INTERNATIONAL COOPERATION

Much of trade theory and the theory of policy takes the interest of the nation-state as its starting point. In the letter inviting authors to participate in this volume, Suzanne Berger and Ronald Dore wrote: "About the tendency of free trade to maximize world welfare, conventional economic theory leaves us in little doubt. About *how that welfare gets distributed among nations, however, dispute rages*" (my italics). The textbook trade theory says that the only legitimate economic exception to advocating free trade is the optimum tariff argument for intervention, according to which a country that can influence its terms of trade can improve them by import or export restrictions. But retal-

[12] Gunnar Myrdal, *International Economy: Problems and Prospects* (New York: Harper and Brothers, 1956).

iation by others can land every country in a worse position than if it had not sought to snatch this advantage at the cost of others. However, the fear of such retaliation is no reason for refraining from intervention, for in the absence of a general agreement the country will gain whether others retaliate or not.

It has become a truism to say that the world is now more interdependent. But interdependence has been scrutinized much more in the relations between multinational corporations, financial markets, and activities in the marketplace than between policies adopted by governments. The challenge, then, is to formulate both a positive and a normative trade theory of government interaction in an interdependent world.

The positive theory would apply the theory of oligopoly, especially aspects of game theory, to the relations between government policies. This is a relatively unexplored area. Yet, there are clear analogies between the way governments react to one anothers' tariff, subsidy, and exchange rate policies and how oligopolistic firms react to one anothers' price and output policies. For example, whether a duopolistic firm will match a rival's price reduction or increase will depend on whether it is faced with excess demand or excess capacity. Similarly, whether a government will match a rival's devaluation will depend (in the absence of binding rules) on whether it has large foreign exchange reserves, or whether it is faced with inflationary pressures or large unemployment. It is easy to think of other similarities.

The normative theory would analyze the gains from tacit or explicit international cooperation and the principles for the distribution of these gains. It would be concerned with the avoidance of prisoner's dilemma outcomes and free-rider problems and would formulate the incentives for moves toward an efficient and equitable allocation of resources from a global point of view while respecting the diversity and autonomy of different societies. It should be accompanied by an exploration of the political economy of reform: How can interest groups be mobilized to move toward desirable outcomes? How can nongovernmental coalitions or constituencies be formed to promote the policies that the normative theory indicates? What are the present obstacles and inhibitions, and how can they be removed? Such alignments will normally be across national frontiers, such as independent retail chains or consumers' associations and labor-intensive exporters, or advanced country banks and developing debtor countries, or even economists, the "guardians of rationality," as well as the "trustees for the poor,"[13] and the global international civil society. In the past the

[13] See G. M. Meier, "Introduction," in *Emerging from Poverty: The Economics That Really Matters* (New York: Oxford University Press, 1984).

self-interest of the dominant power—Britain in the nineteenth century and the United States for a quarter-century immediately after the last war—ensured that some rules of international conduct were obeyed. With the disappearance of a single dominant power, we have, for the first time, to formulate rules and create institutions for a pluralistic world. Such an approach would be a far cry from the doctrine of comparative advantage with its assumption of atomistic agents and a specified government's action in the face of fixed policies by other governments, but it would be a step toward our present reality.

COMPETITIVE SUCCESS REQUIRING
THE MAINTENANCE OF DIVERSITY

It is quite possible for institutional *divergence* to be the result of free trade. Ronald Dore, Michael Albert, David Soskice, and others have analyzed different "types," or "families," or "styles" of capitalism. One type, the Japanese and German, is (or at least was until recently) characterized by close coordination between different firms, between firms and banks, between government and business, and between employers and workers; the other exhibits little coordination and conducts its relations at arms' length between firms, does not involve banks in the management of firms, and hires and fires within the firm. One commits its resources to long-term goals, the other is more concerned with short-run financial flexibility. One emphasizes "flexible specialization" and product innovation, the other preset machinery whose performance does not depend on the skill of the workers, who are tightly controlled financially.

I would suggest that it would be perfectly possible for trade to provoke different reactions to the challenge of productivity growth and international competition. Productivity growth can be achieved in a variety of ways, and it is possible for it to converge as a result of divergent institutional arrangements. The situation would be the reverse of that in which economic gains are sacrificed for the sake of noneconomic objectives, such as protecting agriculture as a "way of life," industry as a demonstration of modernity, or protecting for the sake of military strength or cultural autonomy. Dismantling trade barriers provides the challenges that reinforce the indigenous, different styles. Whether such policies achieve their alleged objectives, whether there are not more effective ways of achieving them, or whether the economic costs are excessive, raises important questions. But this is another story, which I leave for others to tell.

CHAPTER FIFTEEN

Convergence in Whose Interest?

RONALD DORE

Perhaps the last essay in the volume may be permitted to reflect briefly on what we thought we were about when we got together to discuss whether or not economic internationalization leads to institutional convergence. Were we just curious to find out how the world works, as an oceanographer might be curious about the factors determining climatic change? Were we drawn to the subject because we had certain intellectual theories for which convergence or nonconvergence might offer crucial evidence? Or were we drawn to the question because we were hoping for more convergence or less convergence? Were we looking for ways to promote or stop it? Were we beating some drum either of conviction or of personal taste—an ideological, a national, a personal-ethical, or whatever sort of drum?

Clearly, our motives were mixed. It seems to me that one can crudely classify the approaches adopted by the essays in this volume under three heads:

The Analytic;
The Implicit Normative;
The Explicit Mandarin Normative.

I would like to elaborate briefly on the differences as I see them, declare my allegiance in this particular context to the explicit mandarin normative mode, and present one particular example of the sort of messy dilemma such thinking gets one into.

As particularly pure and consistent examples of the analytic mode I would cite the essays by Gourevitch and Boltho. They are concerned, above all, with teasing out causal connections, with showing the multi-

366

plicity of forces that cause economic institutions to be different in different countries and might in the future cause them to converge or diverge, and with seeking generalizations about the way those forces interact and which are likely to be stronger.

As good representatives of the implicit normative category I would choose the papers by Ostry and Kester. Although the one expresses her norms more frequently in the form of prescriptive "shoulds" and the other in predictive "wills," it does not take much reading between the lines to infer that the values that direct their analysis are similar. The two goods on which both agree are "fairness" and "efficiency." But because "fairness" turns out to be defined as that which maximizes the openness of competition by giving everyone an equal chance to take part in it, and competition is valued because it leads to greater efficiency, eventually it is efficiency that is king—the ur-value from which all other values are derived.

But when the underlying values of normative reasoning are left unargued and implicit, they can be more easily partisan. Efficiency, which presumably means improving the ratio of outputs to inputs, is all very well, but outputs for whom from inputs by whom? Consider the questions Kester asks and the questions he does not ask about the two systems he compares, the American system, which emphasizes the reduction of agency costs, and the Japanese system, which reduces transaction costs. The question he asks is which offers "genuine economic efficiency," which the least "unfair restraint of trade that ultimately reduces global economic welfare". The questions he does not ask are "which leads to a more equal or a more equitable distribution of income in society," "which to a more democratic distribution of political power," "which to an atmosphere more conducive to the peaceful and costless resolution of clashes of interest."

I say "partisan" because the viewpoint taken is that of the owner of capital. The fact is that agency costs—the costs to shareholders of managerial behavior not wholly devoted to their interests—may well, in the United States, take the form of the famous fleet of jets run by Mr. Johnson of RJR Nabisco,[1] whereas in Japan they are more likely to take the form of keeping underemployed workers on the books in a recession instead of laying them off. But such considerations do not appear in Kester's paper because they are irrelevant to the argument. They are, indeed, irrelevant from the point of view of the owner of capital who bears those costs and has no interest except in minimizing them.

I called this approach "partisan" because there is a long-standing

---

[1] See Bryan Burrough and John Helyar, *Barbarians at the Gate: The Fall of RJR Nabisco* (New York: Harper and Row, 1991).

debate, and in some quarters ongoing debate (particularly quarters where very little capital is owned), as to whether the owners of capital actually deserve such exclusive consideration.[2]

It is in making its partisanship explicit that the third category, what I called the explicit mandarin normative category, differs. I would put the paper of Streeten in this category. Because my own brief discussion of trade policy which follows falls into the same category, it is perhaps worthwhile to spell out the assumptions of this approach.

(1) It is not meaningless to speak of a "public interest" and of "fair" criteria for adjudicating between clashing private interests, even though any definition of that interest must be a reflection of the definer's own values.

(2) The values of people who talk about the public interest and about fairness do frequently go beyond the Pecksniffian rationalization of private interest. This can happen even for those who have not had the training in detachment given to mandarins in the best civil services, whose role is explicitly defined as guardians of the public interest, and a fortiori for those who have.

(3) Where there is a consensus on what public interest or criteria of fairness mean (and therefore by definition on the values that define them) within a society or among the politically active members of society, this consensus can have an effect on policy that is not always and necessarily overwhelmed by the self-interest maximization of group lobbies (the more so, obviously, in more socially cohesive societies).

(4) Seeking to create such a consensus by persuading others to accept one's own values (frequently described as the political process par excellence in ideal or idealistic conceptions of democracy) can actually occur in practice. Politics in the industrial democracies are not all about interest assertion and horse trading. There are competing altruisms as well as competing egoisms.

(5) There is reason to think that the altruism quotient may be steadily diminishing in most industrial societies, a thesis encapsulated in Fred Hirsch's phrase about the "depleting moral legacy of capitalism."[3] Capitalism may be undermining itself because it depends for its functioning on the force of certain moral constraints that derive from precapitalist society and that capitalism itself works steadily to erode. Part of that notion, its relation to politics and the conception of a "general interest," is neatly summarized by Hirschmann: "With macromanagement, Keynesian or otherwise, assuming an important role in the functioning of the [capitalist] system, the macromanagers must be motivated by the 'general interest' rather than by their self-interest, and

[2] See, for example, L. E. Preston, H. J. Sapienza, and R. D. Miller, "Stakeholders, Shareholders, Managers," in A. Etzioni and P. R. Lawrence, eds., *Socio-economics: Toward a New Synthesis* (Armonk, N.Y.: M.E. Sharpe, 1991).

[3] Fred Hirsch, *Social Limits to Growth* (London: Routledge, 1977).

the system, being based on self-interest, has no way of generating the proper motivation. To the extent such motivation does exist, it is a residue of previous value systems that are likely to "erode.'"[4]

(6) The tendency to nail one's colors to the mast is exacerbated by a contemporary *trahison des clercs*, the propensity among academic analysts to elevate the importance of self-interest among the factors that make the world go round. This seems to spring either from the pursuit of some hard-nosed macho self-image or from the envious desire to do game theory just like the economists.

(7) Even if one is fighting a losing battle and the world is going to the dogs, it is worth trying to resist these tendencies, even if all one gains is temporary respite from the inevitable.

(8) Any definition of the public interest or of fairness is properly open to attack on the nonintellectual, moral-judgmental grounds that they are repulsive/uncongenial/ fascist/infantile/*fin de siècle*/neoliberal/unregenerate-Marxist, or whatever. But we make those judgments as citizens. The only intellectual job to be done is that of uncovering the underlying value judgments and assessing their logical consistency.

(9) But that job of sorting out the logical consistency or otherwise of different value positions and the policy prescriptions that follow from them are indeed useful intellectual or academic activities—as useful as the (different) intellectual activity of causal analysis.

(10) Any intellectual's selection of the value positions to be analyzed is bound to be (and, alas, his or her conclusions about their consistency may well be) affected by what her or his own values are, so that Trade Description Act considerations require one to make one's values explicit (quite apart from any proselytizing zeal to make converts). The frequent use of the first-person singular that this entails may give such writing a certain let-it-all-hang-out, me-decade air that not everyone will find tasteful, but that cannot be helped.

In principle there is no reason why the causal analysis of political economists and mandarin normative analysis of value consistency should ever be in conflict. The latter also requires causal analysis, insisting only that it should be kept separate from the normative consistency analysis.

However, in practice, when mandarin normative analysts do such causal analysis, their sensitivity to (and wish to believe in the causal efficacy of) public interest and fairness arguments may cause them to give slightly different causal interpretations from those of full-time political economists of the same situation.

This reflection occurred to me when I read Gourevitch's account of

[4] A. O. Hirschmann, *Rival Views of Market Society* (Cambridge: Harvard University Press, 1992), p. 111.

the Structural Impediments Initiative Talks in Japan and found my-
self balking slightly at his suggestion that the success of the attempts
of U.S. negotiators to urge institutional reforms on Japan were determined by whether or not they were supported by articulate domestic
interest groups. I would suggest, however, that what one might call
"strength-of-the-argument" considerations also played a part in determining outcomes. Examples include: (1) A widely shared sense that it
was in the public interest to mollify the Americans lest worse
(Super-301, etc.) befall; hence some especially rapid concessions in
areas that seemed dearest to American hearts, such as quick licenses
for Toys-R-Us. (2) A sense that the institutionalized deviations from
legal procedures involved in the Large Retail Stores Law (see chapter
11) were an affront to administrative rectitude and could not be defended. (3) On land taxation a sense that the redistribution of wealth
through phenomenal land price rises was inequitable (I mean inequitable, not just bad for the losers)—a sense made all the stronger by
the dominance of a "productivist" ethic that looks suspiciously on un-
earned speculative gains of any kind. (4) An "absurdity level" effect.
Defending a domestic rice price that is five times the international
level is harder than defending one that is only three times higher
through mechanisms that have nothing to do with the rice-eaters' assessment of the consumer surplus they are being denied.

The point is that the coincidence between foreign and domestic
pressures involves something wider than domestic pressures driven by
group self-interest. To put it in Weberian terms, democratic pluralism
involves a plurality of ideal as well as of material interests.

But Whose Public?

One problem with notions such as the "public" interest is to define
one's public. Should it be fellow-citizens or fellow-human beings everywhere? Real mandarins have no difficulty: the answer is that public who pays their salary, whose civil "servant" they are. But for free-
floating would-be ventriloquist mandarins in academia and the media,
the dilemma is real. One could see it lurking in the background to
many comments on NAFTA during the American debate in the fall of
1993. Is an extra dollar's welfare to a citizen of Chiapas to be treated
as of equal or less value than an extra dollar for a citizen of Peoria? It
was not a question that made much difference to the American debate, but in a similar debate in, say, Norway, where the aggressive
assertion of national self-interest is less admired as an expression of
proud masculine patriotism, it would have been frequently heard.

The Dilemma Where It Hurts

What public? is a question that must be confronted in any reasonable argument about protectionism and free trade. I have long been an advocate of protectionism against Japan. Not at all because I think the Japanese unfair. It is one of the follies of the GATT system that the only way it allows an industry threatened by Japanese imports to fight even for the temporary protection it needs to survive at all is by hurling charges of unfairness—trumped-up charges of dumping, collusive targeting, and so on—to justify anti-dumping duties or the demand for VERs, "voluntary" export restrictions.

I am in favor of protection against Japanese exports and of the Japanese defending themselves against us by refusing to deregulate in fields such finance and insurance where they might feel threatened by our superior ruthlessness or expertise in inventing arcane derivatives and by our tendency to turn the insurance industry into something less like a means of socializing risks and more like a means of speculative gambling. I take this position not on any grounds of unfairness, because the playing field is tilted, or whatever, but because of the need for mutual recognition of different definitions of the public interest, deriving from different value conceptions of what life is about. To take our case in Europe and North America—theirs, with respect to finance, would be somewhat different—it seems to me that the Japanese expand their market shares so rapidly in our markets as well as in third markets partly because they are more clever and efficient (in organizational as well as material technology) but also partly because they work harder, give more of their time and loving care to their work life, and have fewer and less dominant outside interests beyond their work lives than we do. (The competitive advantage this confers is not a question of "wage costs per hour" but, rather, of the total "put-work-demands-first" flexibility with which the hours are offered. The debate on "lean production" among German unions recognizes how much this is an ingredient of Japanese success, something glossed over in the MIT book[5] that gave that concept such wide diffusion.) The Japanese often *seem* to be happier that way than we are, leading a more "balanced" life, seeing more of our friends and families, spending more time in front of the television or whatever. But that's their affair. We would, on the whole, not like to sacrifice our weekends whenever our job required it the way they seem to do,

[5] J. Womack, D. T. Jones, and D. Roos, *The Machine That Changed the World: The Story of Lean Production* (New York: Harper, 1991). For the German debate, see G. Schienstock and B. Steffensen, "Lean Production: The German Debate," mimeo, Akademie für Technikfolgenabschatzung, Stuttgart, n.d.

and we have all kinds of domestic institutions to keep it that way, such as public holidays, hours of work legislation, Sunday closing laws and the like, and, more important, established nonstatutory norms about what it is fair and reasonable for employers to expect of their workers.

So, if the only way we can obey the dictates of free trade and simultaneously prevent ourselves from getting poorer while the Japanese get richer is to compete both in the efficiency *and* in the workaholic dimension, then we should not let free-trade dogma stand in our way of saying, "No, thank you."

I think the answer to the Japanese is precisely the answer our mandarins (our real mandarins, I mean, not our treason-prone academic clerks) have been introducing *sub rosa* since the 1980s—all those barely-GATT-legitimate devices such as the threat of phoney anti-dumping charges and "level playing field" retaliations, which provide just enough protection, or noncalculable threat of protection, to force the Japanese to substitute direct investment for exports. That way they bring their factories over here, teach us the clever efficiency bits of their secrets, use their stringent recruitment tests to sort out the most workaholic Europeans and Americans to work with them, and make net additions to the value added on our territory and the income going into the pockets of our nationals. They also compensate the Japanese for the pain of having to work amidst the alien corn with a sense of their own moral superiority (recently expressed in the MITI report on the unfair protectionist trading practices of Japan's trading partners) and possibly with dreams of eventually owning half the world and establishing a Pax Japonica (almost certainly false dreams because in the end affluence will surely erode their hard-working advantage well before they have learned how to translate manufacturing competitiveness into world power and prevent the Chinese from overtaking them).

But instead of having to justify that protectionism by silly charges of "unfairness," why not accept it as the sensible device it is and write it into the GATT? Why not make it legitimate under some such rubric as Investment Inviting Import Quantity Restrictions or Triple IQRs? Make it possible, that is to say, for countries to declare to their technologically superior competitors: "We shall import only x of your cars/ machine tools/biscuits per annum for the next ten years, but if you build your factories here we will give you all the facilities we give domestic producers. Any domestic content rules, for instance, if they prove desirable, will be imposed on existing domestic producers as well as on you."

AND DEVELOPING COUNTRIES?

Triple IQRs, I would argue, should only be applied to technologically superior competitors. It should *not* be available for protection against Mexican textile producers, Mauritian sugar producers, Chinese automobile firms, and so on whose competitive advantage lies in the cheap wages of their workers. The GATT formulation would probably have to make the distinction in terms of differences in the per capita income levels of exporting and importing countries, perhaps in terms of the labor intensitivity of the production chain.

Let us explore the principles of fairness that underlie my use of the last paragraph of that mandarin "should." I accept as a starting point that free trade is an international public good that would cease to exist if too many free riders defected, thus starting the chain reaction usual in such circumstances. It may not be a good the benefits from which are equally distributed, but then neither, for example, are the laws protecting property, which disproportionately benefit, as Proudhon used to say, those who have a lot of it. But free trade can still make it Pareto optimal to have rather than not to have that good. The good procured by free trade, moreover, is not only its economic growth-enhancing effects but also (the *doux commerce* arguments) a means toward the erosion of nationalism, the scourge of the last two centuries.

So one should be careful about using frontiers and the legislative power of the nation-state for any sort of defection from free trade. Certain considerations do, however, justify it, such as preserving ways of life one would otherwise have to give up—leisure in the Japanese case or, in the case of a different contemporary Uruguay Round debate, French television productions threatened by Hollywood's economies of scale. But they may only be used when the cost from diminished trade would be borne by producers in richer or equally rich countries, not by producers in poor countries. The reason? Because trade is the only way poor countries can get richer; those who have arrived should not pull up the ladder. That (arbitrary) principle of fairness would not claim universal acclaim, using, as it does, a conception of the "public interest" that envisages a wider "public" than that of one's fellow-citizens alone. But it is one to which I would adhere, one that in some countries would find quite wide support, and one that might provide a compromise principle in international gatherings of rich and poor countries—especially if the delegates had been given a preliminary brainwashing by John Rawls.

RONALD DORE

THE DILEMMA

So far, so good. But consider some of the implications. Among the other issues that occupy media and academic discussion today are the widening of wage differentials, growing unemployment and the increasing dispersion of personal and household income levels—the increasing gap between rich and poor—in the advanced industrial countries. There is little doubt—and Wade's essay cites a calculation that supports the thesis—that a major cause of this pretty universal trend (in addition to the probably much more important factor of technological change) is the growth of imports from low-wage countries.

For those of us who dislike and fear this trend (either from rich man's guilt or fear of mugging) more than we value the chance to earn an ever-higher income, there is, then, a painful dilemma. One (international) argument from fairness says that it is precisely against poor countries that one should not use protectionist weapons; the other (domestic) argument for fairness says that in order to avoid an unfair distribution of the costs, it is precisely against the poor countries that one should discriminate.

RESOLUTION

It is tempting to end by observing that this is the sort of mess one gets into when one adopts mandarin pretensions; better to stick to political economy. I would rather end, though, still in mandarin vein by holding out the hope that the rich countries will eventually find some way of reconciling the two goods.

Clearly it cannot be done by internal income distribution alone (even if the tax allergies of modern democracies could be overcome sufficiently to make that possible), given the extent to which citizen dignity, and not just income, depends on having a meaningful job and not being a welfare scrounger. One idea is somehow to engineer a reevaluation of the meaning of work. One should seek, this recipe goes, to alter the connection between income rights and work contribution through some sort of universal citizen income. This is an idea that, with unemployment rates still hovering only around 10 percent, still seems utopian.[6] I hope there are better ones.

[6] For elaborations of this idea, see my *Taking Japan Seriously* (Stanford: Stanford University Press, 1987), and, more recently, "Incurable Unemployment: A Progressive Disease of Modern Societies?" *Political Quarterly* 65 (July–September 1994).

Contributors

SUZANNE BERGER
Raphael Dorman and Helen
Starbuck Professor of Political
Science
Massachusetts Institute of
Technology
Cambridge, Massachusetts

ANDREA BOLTHO
Professor, Magdalen College
Oxford University
Oxford

ROBERT BOYER
Professor, Centre d'Etudes
Prospectives d'Economie
Mathematique Appliquées à la
Planification
Paris

RONALD DORE
Senior Research Fellow
Centre for Economic Performance
London School of Economics and
Adjunct Professor of Political
Science
Massachusetts Institute of
Technology
Cambridge, Massachusetts

HERVÉ DUMEZ
Professor, chargé de recherches
Centre National de Recherche
Scientifique
Centre de recherche en gestion
Ecole Polytechnique
Paris

PETER A. GOUREVITCH
Dean of the School of International
Relations and Pacific Studies
University of California, San Diego
La Jolla, California

ALAIN JEUNEMAÎTRE
Professor, chargé de recherches
Centre National de Recherche
Scientifique
Centre de recherche en gestion
Ecole Polytechnique
Paris

MILES KAHLER
Professor of International Relations
Graduate School of International
Relations and Pacific Studies
University of California, San Diego
La Jolla, California, and
Senior Fellow, Council on Foreign
Relations
New York, New York

CONTRIBUTORS

W. CARL KESTER
Professor of Business
Administration
Harvard Business School
Cambridge, Massachusetts

YUTAKA KOSAI
President, Japan Center for
Economic Research
Tokyo

SHIJURO OGATA   Tokyo

SYLVIA OSTRY
Chairman and Senior Research
Fellow
Center for International Studies
University of Toronto
Toronto

WOLFGANG STREECK
Professor, Max Planck Institute für
Gesellschaftsforschung
Cologne

FRANK K. UPHAM
Professor of Law
New York University School of Law
New York, New York

PAUL STREETEN
Professor Emeritus
Boston University
Boston, Massachusetts

ROBERT WADE
Professor of Political Economy
Sussex University
Brighton, Sussex
and Brown University
Providence, Rhode Island

STEPHEN WOOLCOCK
Professor of Economics
London School of Economics
London

376

Index

Competition policies (*cont.*)
Europe, 216–17; dual thrust in Europe, 228; harmonization of, 333, 337, 338, 340; and Maastricht Treaty, 237
Competitive disinflation, 98, 100, 103
Competitive elitist democracy, 31
Confederation of British Industry, 191, 194; City Industry set up by, 188
Conseil d'Etat, 292
Consorci de la Vila Olimpica, 230
Construction Ministry (Japan), 266, 314
Continental Bank of Illinois, 78
Continental Can, 233
Contractual governance: in Japan, 120–24, 134, 136; versus corporate governance, 243–44
Convergence, 1, 182; "apparent" in Europe, 222–24; arguments against, 19; case for, 12–14; of competition policies in Europe, 216–17; and divergence, 39–41, 59; through external pressures and domestic pull, 16–18; Fordist era of economic, 44–46; of France on Germany, 89–92, 98–100; and globalization, 4–7; of governance models, 345; imposed from without in Europe, 228–36; of institutional forms after World War II, 41–44; in Japanese retail industry, 263; by jurisprudence, 235–36; and lean production in German automobile industry, 138–39, 168–70; mechanisms to best practice, 46–51; national differences in systems of, 109–17; paradoxes in theory of, 57–59; political pressures for, 14–16; politics of, 23–25; potential of Japanese and Anglo-American systems, 132–37; of productivity after World War II, 35–39; real convergence in Europe, 224–28; Structural Impediments Initiative and process of, 291–92; and technological trajectory of industrial societies, 2–4; theory revisited, 46–57; three definitions of, 30–34; toward which or whose model?, 18–19; with Treaty of Maastricht, 236–38; vertical, 229; in whose interest?, 366. *See also* Divergence; Globalization
Corporate governance, 13; American patterns of, 108, 123; and Anglo-American contracting, 109–10; best practice in, 108, 123–26; British version of Anglo-Saxon, 180, 181, 183, 185, 186, 192, 195, 196; changes in U.S. patterns of, 129–31; and compe-

tition in European Community, 179; differences between Anglo-American and Japanese systems of, 109–18; differences in different forms of, 181, 195, 196; French model of, 184; and horizontal rivalry, 124, 125, 126; and information asymmetries, 112; and investor activism, 116–17; and Japanese contracting, 110–12; Japanese patterns of, 13, 108, 123, 344; potential for convergence of Japanese and Anglo-American, 132–37; Rhineland (or Alpine) form of, 180, 181, 183, 186, 195, 196; short-comings of Japanese, 126–29; vs. contractual governance, 243–44
Corporate Partners, Inc., 135
Costa Rica, 39
Council of Ministers, 229
Cross-shareholding, 172, 178, 185

Dahrendorf, Ralf, 312
Daimler Benz: merger with Messerschmitt-Bölkow-Blohm, 224
Dango, 267
Datafin, 193
Decentralization of responsibility, in lean production, 140
de Gasperi, Alcide, 231
De Gaulle, Charles, 91
De Havilland, 233
Democracy: and markets: convergence in development, 31–32
Department Store Act (Japan), 126
Department Store Law (Japan), 269–70, 272, 278, 288
Depression cartel, 207
Deregulation, and banks in Europe, 187
Derivatives: global spread of, 176; lack of regulation for, 64–65
Diet (Japan), 273, 269–70, 283
Direction Générale des Télécommunications, 53
Divergence, 8, 339; and convergence, 39–41, 59; of economic policies in France and Germany, 10; institutional, 365; partial, 33; technological, 82
Diversification, 178
"Diversified quality production," 160
Domar, Evsey, 34
Domestic differences: mutual recognition and, 321; strategies for dealing with, 326–32; trade and, 298
Dore, Ronald, 3, 4, 12, 355, 363, 365
Drastic revisions during structural crises, 54

France, 180; antitrust legislation in, 221,
222; capital market size in, 184; cartels in, 216; convergence with Germany?, 89–92, 98–100; enters Common Market, 92; from first oil shock
to "competitive disinflation," 96–100;
form of corporate governance in, 195;
and international competitiveness in,
91; multinational corporations in, 63;
National Assembly, 24; "national
champions" policy, 224; planned
economy in, 217; publicly listed companies in, 185; regulation of monopolies in, 226; retail regulation in, 292,
295; takeovers in, 193; from Treaty of
Rome to first oil shock, 92–96
Free trade: and externalities of consumption and acquired tastes, 355–
57; and intrafirm trade, 360–62;
maintenance of diversity, 365n; and
managed trade, 353–54; and a quiet
life, 357–59; in services?, 362–63
Freiburg group, 219
Frieden, Jeffry A., 7, 9
FTC. *See* Fair Trade Commission
Fuji Heavy Industries, 117, 125

Gaiatsu, 250, 314
Gaitskell, H., 219
Garrett, Geoffrey, 9, 10
GATT. *See* General Agreement on Tariffs and Trade
Gebroeders Beentjes B. V. v. Netherlands
(1990), 230
General Account Budget, 172
General Agreement on Tariffs and
Trade (GATT), 47, 251, 301, 312,
324, 339, 371, 372, 373; anti-dumping
rules defined by, 215; attacks on, 299;
and domestic differences, 302–5; environment and trade, 320; and mutual
recognition, 340; and overall reciprocity, 349; post-Uruguay negotiations,
339, 341; principle of national treatment of, 306; and rule of law rhetoric, 293; Tokyo Round of, 302, 312;
Uruguay Round of, 16, 24, 256, 293,
306, 340
General Motors Corporation, 79
Gensaki transactions, 173
Germany: antitrust legislation in, 217,
220, 222; "battle of cartels," in, 219–
20; capital market size in, 184; cartels
in, 216, 217; codetermination system
in, 94; contractual governance in, 134;
creation of Federal Republic of, 218;
effect of first oil shock, 97; and em-

ployee representation in, 192; external labor market in, 165; France converged on?, 89–92, 98–100; industrial
relations in, 151–52; interest rates in,
78; international competitiveness of,
91; lack of information disclosure in,
189; lean production and automobile
industry in, 138–39; low takeovers in,
193; multinational corporations in, 63;
publicly listed companies in, 185; relationship banking in, 186; Rhine capitalism of, 183; skill adjustment and
work reorganiztion in, 156–61; social
context of skills and work compared
with Japan, 144–56; social integration
of firms in, 154–56; social market
economy in, 217
Gilson, Ronald J., 119
Giscard d'Estaing, Valéry, 91, 96
Glass-Steagall Act of 1933, 115, 130,
240, 244
Globalization, 6; of competition, 179;
convergence and, 4–7, 333; and cross-
national "sensitivity," 76–78; and finance capital, 73–76; and foreign
direct investment, 70–92, 333; of international economic exchanges, 14;
and its limits, 60; and national systems, 85–88; nation-states in era of,
29–30; of production and finance: evidence in favor, 62–66; qualifications
about, 66–68; and system friction,
333–337; of technology production?,
82–84; and trade, 66–70. *See also*
Maastricht Treaty; Trade
Gourevitch, Peter A., 22, 23, 366, 369
Governmental financial institutions, 172
Gramm-Rudman-Hollings deficit reduction legislation, 316
Great Depression, 216, 217
Greece, 39
Gresham's law, 102
Grossman, Gene M., 319
Guildlike trade associations in Japan,
198, 200

Hamiltonianism, 256
Harmonization, 308, 330, 331, 332, 349;
and competition policy, 333, 337, 338;
of disclosure requirements, 189; within European Community, 15, 24, 33,
181, 196, 329; of financial practices,
176; and NAFTA: labor standards
and the environment, 317–21; of national institutions, 198; of policies,
300; procedures of Japan, 214–15;
symmetric and asymmetric bargaining,

Unilateralism, 338
United Kingdom, 45; antitrust regulation enacted in, 226; cartels in, 216; and foreign direct investment, 70; multinational corporations in, 63; postwar trade reconstruction in, 220; takeover codes in, 243
United Nations Conference on Trade and Development, 72
United States: antitrust legislation in, 45, 132, 134, 137, 197, 217, 218, 246; automobile firms in, 143; changes in corporate governance in, 129–31; corporate ownership structure in, 113–15; exports and GDP in, 66; flexible manufacturing in, 3; foreign direct investment flows into, 70, 72–73; harmonization through leverage in, 312–13; and Japan trade frictions and deregulation, 210–15; lean production plants in, 160; market interpenetration in, 64; mergers and acquisitions in, 344; multinational corporations in, 64; 1987 collapse of share prices in, 78; patents granted in, 65; public disclosure of financial information in, 112; relative decline of, 337; Republican congressional victories (1994) in, 257; steel industries in, 125; takeovers and acquisitions in, 180
Universality, 354
Unmodified transfer, 164–67
Upham, Frank K., 15, 17, 18
Uruguay Round, 16; free trade in services, 362; of GATT negotiations, 16, 24, 256, 293, 302, 306, 338, 340
U.S.-Canada Free Trade Agreement, 317
U.S. Council on Competitiveness, 245
U.S. Department of Justice, 107, 227
U.S. Supreme Court, 246, 294
UTA, 224

Verspagen, Bart, 39
"Vision of the Distribution System in 1990s" (MITI), 281
Voluntary export restraints (VERs), 326, 329, 340, 371
Voluntary Import Expansion (VIEs), 211, 324, 326
Voluntary Restraint Agreement, 289

Wade, Robert, 9, 20, 374
Waelbroeck, M., 232
Wagner Act, 240
Wal-Mart, 288, 295–96
Watanabe, Koji, 18
Watanabe, Shigeru, 129
Williamson, Oliver, 119, 120, 121
Wissen und Können, 157
Womack, James P., lean production interpreted by, 139–44, 149, 150, 154, 156, 163, 164
Woolcock, Stephen, 11, 14, 16, 22, 23
World Bank, 67
World Trade Organization, 299, 303, 330, 332
World War I, 60, 86
World War II, 86; evolution of industrialized countries after, 47; GATT after, 301; growth patterns after, 58; Japan defeated in, 201, 241; Japanese industrial organization up to, 198; trade integration after, 66; U.S. mass production after, 46; U.S. occupation of Japan after, 197, 198, 201, 241
WTO. *See* World Trade Organization

Yamamoto, Isao, 129
Yawata Steel, 199

Zaibatsu, 132, 198, 199, 200, 201, 206, 241
Zero-buffer, in Japanese lean production, 153, 167

Cornell Studies in Political Economy

EDITED BY PETER J. KATZENSTEIN